WHAT THE BIBLE TEACHES

Contributor
FRED STALLAN

Publishers note:
Fred Stallan was converted in the early 1940's in the city of Glasgow, from which time he diligently gave himself to the study of the Scriptures. He was self-taught in Greek, but Spirit taught in the Word, thus fitting him to engage in a very necessary sphere of service for his Lord and over the years he became widely appreciated and respected by many of the Lord's people for his clear presentation of scripture. This afforded to him the privilege of preaching and teaching at many assembly gatherings, both large and small, throughout the British Isles and further afield.

The commentary on Romans was written during a period of increasing weakness and discomfort. He had willingly undertaken the task just a short time before his illness was diagnosed in the spring of 1996, and the publishers are grateful to the Lord for enabling him to complete it just a few months before calling him Home on the 1st January 1998.

The editors willingly took up Mr Stallan's first draft and have completed their work without access to what, under normal circumstances, would have been the patient and helpful cooperation of the author. This was no easy task for them as they endeavoured to ensure that the completed work accurately reflected the teaching of the author, and the publishers are greatly indebted to them for working on the manuscript so carefully. This volume brings to a fitting conclusion the helpful New Testament Series of *What The Bible Teaches* and the publishers wish to place on record their deep appreciation of the editors' valuable contribution over the years to this work, and trust that it will continue to be used for the Lord's glory and for the instruction of His people.

OCTOBER 1998

WHAT THE BIBLE TEACHES

with
Authorised Version
of
The Bible

IN ELEVEN VOLUMES
COVERING THE NEW TESTAMENT

VOLUME 11

JOHN RITCHIE LTD
KILMARNOCK, SCOTLAND

ISBN 0 946351 79 1

WHAT THE BIBLE TEACHES
Copyright © 1998 by John Ritchie Ltd.
40 Beansburn, Kilmarnock, Scotland

All rights reserved. No part of the publication may be reproduced, stored in a retrieval system, or transmitted in any form or by any other means–electronic, mechanical, photocopy, recording or otherwise–without the prior permission of the copyright owner.

Typeset at John Ritchie Ltd., 40 Beansburn, Kilmarnock.
Printed at The Bath Press, Avon.

CONTENTS

Page

PREFACE		
INTRODUCTION		3
CHAPTER	1	11
CHAPTER	2	29
CHAPTER	3	52
CHAPTER	4	79
CHAPTER	5	99
CHAPTER	6	121
CHAPTER	7	145
CHAPTER	8	172
CHAPTER	9	209
CHAPTER	10	237
CHAPTER	11	257
CHAPTER	12	285
CHAPTER	13	304
CHAPTER	14	317
CHAPTER	15	330
CHAPTER	16	353

ABBREVIATIONS

AV	Authorised Version of King James Version 1611
JND	New Translation by J.N. Darby 1939
LXX	Septuagint Version of Old Testament
Mft	New Translation by James Moffat 1922
NASB	New American Standard Bible 1960
NEB	New English Bible 1961
Nestle	Nestle (ed.) Novum Testamentum Graece
NIV	New International Version 1973
NT	New Testament
OT	Old Testament
Phps	New Testament in Modern English by J.B. Philips 1962
RSV	Revised Standard Version 1952
RV	Revised Version 1881
TR	Textus Receptus or Received Text
Wey	New Testament in Modern Speech by R.E. Weymouth 1929

PREFACE

They follow the noblest example who seek to open the Scriptures to others, for our Lord Himself did so for those two dejected disciples of Emmaus (Luke 24:32). Whether it is the evangelist "opening and alleging that Christ must needs have suffered and risen from the dead" (Acts 17:3) or the pastor-teacher "expounding ... in all the scriptures the things concerning himself" (Luke 24:27) or stimulating our hope "through the patience and comfort of the scriptures" (Rom 15:4), he serves well in thus giving attendance to the reading of the Scriptures (1 Tim 4:13).

It is of course of equal moment to recognise in the exercise of able men, the continued faithfulness of the risen Head in giving gifts to the Church, in spite of her unfaithfulness. How good to recognise that "the perfecting of the saints ... the work of the ministry...the edifying of the body of Christ" need not be neglected. Every provision has been made to ensure the well-being of the people of God. And every opportunity should be taken by the minister of Christ and those to whom he ministers to ensure that the saints "grow up into him in all things which is the head, even Christ" (Eph 4:15).

At various times in the post-apostolic period, certain teachers have come to prominence, sometimes because they succumbed to error, sometimes because in faithfulness they paid the ultimate price for the truth they had bought and would not sell. Some generations had Calvin and Luther, others Darby and Kelly, but in every generation God's voice is heard. It is important that we hear His voice today and recognise that He does speak through His servants. The contributors to this series of commentaries are all highly-respected expositors among the churches of God. They labour in the Word in the English-speaking world and have been of blessing to many throughout their years of service.

The doctrinal standpoint of the commentaries is based upon the acceptance of the verbal and plenary inspiration of the Scriptures so that their inerrant and infallible teachings are the only rule of conscience. The impeccability of Christ, His virgin birth, vicarious death and bodily resurrection are indeed precious truths worthy of the Christian's defence, and throughout the volumes of this series will be defended. Equally the Rapture will be presented as the hope of the Church. Before the great Tribulation she will be raptured and God's prophetic programme will continue with Jacob's trouble, the public manifestation of Christ and the Millennium of blessing to a restored Israel and the innumerable Gentile multitude in a creation released from the bondage of corruption.

May the sound teaching of these commentaries be used by our God to the blessing of His people. May the searching of the Scriptures characterise all who read them.

The diligence of Mr. J.W. Ferguson and the late Professor J. Heading in proof-reading is gratefully acknowledged. Without such co-operation, the production of this commentary would not have been expedited so readily.

T. WILSON
K. STAPLEY

ROMANS

ROMANS
Introduction

1. Introductory Remarks
2. Authorship
3. Date and Reason for Writing
4. The Church at Rome
5. The Scope of the Epistle
6. The Integrity of the Epistle
7. Analysis
8. Bibliography

1. Introductory Remarks

The epistle to the Romans must rank amongst the world's greatest literary works. Although all Scripture is given by inspiration of God (2 Tim 3:16) and its penmen were borne along by the Holy Spirit, the writer of this epistle displays a logic in his unfolding of christian doctrine which is unanswerable. The great themes of the christian faith are stated in clear terms. The righteousness of God, justification, sanctification, the ruin of man, the mercy of God, the casting aside of the Jew and much more besides, are all handled with consummate skill. There are no apologies in this treatise. There are no palpable omissions or incomplete conclusions. The gospel, which must surely be the main theme of the epistle, is unfolded in all its many facets. There are no weak links in the writer's arguments. Altogether it is a compendium of christian doctrine, a formal and systematic unfolding of the fundamentals of the faith. Its outlook embraces Jew and Gentile, showing that in God's dealings with both He is absolutely righteous. Any hope for preferential treatment is not countenanced. The writer makes it clear "that there is no difference, for all have sinned and come short of the glory of God" (3:22,23).

Against the total depravity of man, so cogently described in the early chapters, the righteousness of God is portrayed. Nevertheless, the mercy extended in the gospel is seen to be entirely consistent with His holiness. Such is the wonder of God's plan of salvation, nothing of His character is sacrificed in His offer of mercy. His manifested grace is not at the expense of His righteousness. All is in total conformity with His own divine standards.

2. Authorship

The epistle opens with stating the writer's name, and towards the end it closes with the name of the amanuensis (16:22). Paul dictated it and Tertius wrote what he received from the author. The logic of the arguments bears out the word that Ananias received from the Lord that the man he was being sent to help was a special vessel (Acts 9:15). The author knew this within himself, and made clear in the opening verse that he was "separated unto the gospel of God". The epistle has all the marks of Pauline thought. There is an orderly progression but there are places where his arguments are deep, even involved. As to the identity of the author, however, there are no serious claimants other than the man whose name appears as the opening word.

3. Date and Reason for Writing

It is highly unlikely that Paul dictated the epistle to the Romans as he travelled from one place to another during his third missionary journey. The details of the arguments he desired to express would require considered thought before committing them to his amanuensis. This would obviously require time and an undisturbed base. The three months in Greece (Acts 20:1-5) would meet these requirements and if this were to be accepted, the time of writing could be settled with a fair degree of probability. Considering the movements of his fellow-labourers and the aims which he expresses in Romans, all of which shed light on dates, it does seem likely that the epistle was written about AD 57, probably just after he wrote his epistles to the Corinthians.

Before Ananias set out for Damascus to lay hands on Saul of Tarsus, the Lord told him that the man would be a chosen vessel to bear His name before the Gentiles. Later, as Paul the apostle, he declared to the Romans that he saw himself as the apostle of the Gentiles (Rom 11:13). Since Rome was the centre of the Gentile world of Paul's day it was like a magnet to him. He wanted to go to Rome and preach there. When he was in Ephesus, Luke records, "Paul purposed in his spirit...to go to Jerusalem, saying, I must see Rome" (Acts 19:21). Again, after the uproar in Jerusalem, described in Acts 23, the Lord stood by Paul, saying, "so must thou bear witness also at Rome" (v.11). There is little doubt therefore that Paul was destined to go to Rome. His own desire is reflected in one of the reasons he gives for writing: "I long to see you, that I may impart unto you some spiritual gift, to the end ye may be established" (1:11). To this he adds, "So, as much as in me is, I am ready to preach the gospel to you that are at Rome also" (v.15). From that point he launches into an unfolding of the gospel, the terms of which he would preach if the way opened up for him to come to the great metropolis.

4. The Church at Rome

It is not possible to ascertain if the church at Rome was established by one of the apostles. There is no mention in the Acts or in the epistles regarding involvement by Peter or Paul or any of the others. The arrival of the message in the metropolis, however, can be accounted for in several ways. There were people from many nations in Jerusalem on the day of Pentecost who heard Peter preach. Amongst them were "strangers of Rome, Jews and proselytes" (Acts 2:10). It is reasonable to suggest that some of these would carry the news back with them. As the Romans excelled in building roads, communications between countries were good and traders moved freely. As time passed, christian traders in pursuit of their commercial interests carried the gospel with them and Rome would certainly be one of the markets for their wares. It was not long therefore until every stratum of society had been infiltrated by the gospel message. Even christian slaves, prisoners and soldiers played their part in evangelising, as Paul notes in his epistle to the Philippians, taking the message into Caesar's palace. It is not unreasonable therefore to conclude that the beginnings of the church at Rome was the work of the Holy Spirit, using the men and women who were being saved and who were communicating the gospel as they went about their daily occupations.

5. The Scope of the Epistle

The scope is all-embracive. Jew and Gentile are brought in and their relative positions before God are made clear. The church at Rome is recognised as well as the existence of other churches of the Gentiles (16:4). Paul still desired to preach in Rome and would have the Romans know of this desire, Paul now wrote in his epistle what he would have preached, if the Romans were not to have an apostle's personal presence and observe the power invested in him.

Apart from his apostolic office, the human side of the apostle comes out noticeably in ch.15 where he makes known his desire to go to Spain and on the way there to visit the saints at Rome. As much as they needed him, he needed them and their part was to bring him on by prayer or any other means (15:24). Before coming to Rome in the fulness of the blessing of the gospel of Christ (15:29), he would first go to Jerusalem with gifts for the poor saints there. The hazards of such a journey and the opposition he would face from the Jews warranted prayer support and he therefore makes his appeal to the Romans to remember him in this respect.

The commendations and greetings of the final chapter add a warm and fitting ending to what is otherwise a solid and sober compendium of christian doctrine. Although the scope of the epistle is set out in three divisions, doctrinal (chs.1-8), dispensational (chs.9-11), and practical (chs.12-16), what Paul writes in the last five chapters must not be considered to be of less importance than the teaching of the first two divisions. What he records is on par with the rest. The charges made, the advice given and the greetings sent are peerless in their own way and altogether display the breadth of the apostle's thinking.

6. The Integrity of the Epistle

In most commentaries considerable space is given to considerations of the integrity of the epistle to the Romans. A few have suggested that it was really a circular letter which was sent to various destinations, but with different endings. This view leads to a further suggestion that ch.16 did not apply to believers at Rome but most likely applied to saints at Ephesus. In addition, some manuscripts insert the doxology of 16:25-27 at 14:3, causing quite a few to believe that chs.15, 16 are not part of the original autograph. There are other manuscripts where this doxology is found in both chs.14,16, and yet others from which it is omitted altogether.

Since the subject is discussed at length by Denney in *The Expositor's Greek Testament*, the reader is referred to that work. It is acknowledged, however, that other commentaries also discuss this most fascinating problem and a wide range of comments should be examined before coming to any conclusion that the text at any point is suspect. The view expressed by Wm Barclay in the introduction to his commentary on Romans gives a most reasonable explanation. He suggests that the epistle Paul wrote to the Romans had all sixteen chapters, but chs.15,16 referred only to circumstances that obtained in Rome. When this fundamental epistle began to circulate among all the churches, the last two chapters were omitted and only the doxology was retained, being placed at the end of ch.14. Apart from the arguments which have circulated and still circulate about the integrity of the text, the canon of Scripture as acknowledged by scholars down the centuries and accepted by Christians as the infallible word of God includes the epistle to the Romans. The text of the AV is taken therefore as the support for the present commentary and where necessary, reference is made to other versions of the Scripture.

7. Analysis

I. *Introduction* 1:1-17
    1. Salutation 1:1-7
    2. Reason for Writing 1:8-15
    3. Establishment of the Theme 1:16,17

II. *The Righteousness of God* 1:18-3:20

	Pronouncing judgment on sin	
	1. The Gentiles – Guilty	1:18-1:32
	2. The Jews – Guilty	2:1-3:8
	3. The World – Guilty	3:9-3:20
III.	*The Gospel of God*	3:21-5:21
	Proclaiming justification of the sinner	
	1. Principle of Justification – by faith alone	3:21-3:31
	2. Illustration of Justification – from OT Scriptures	4:1-4:25
	3. Blessings of Justification – for those who believe	5:1-5:11
	4. Basis of Justification – the work of Christ	5:12-5:21
IV.	*The Provision of God*	6:1-8:39
	Providing assurance of salvation	
	1. Sanctified and Free from Bondage to Sin	6:1-6:23
	2. Sanctified and Free from Bondage to Law	7:1-7:25
	3. Sanctified and Assured of Eternal Blessing	8:1-8:39
V.	*The Justification of God*	9:1-11:36
	Persuading of the mercy of God	
	1. Seen in God's Sovereign Choice	9:1-9:29
	2. Seen in Israel's Past Disobedience	9:30-10:21
	3. Seen in Israel's Present Remnant of Grace	11:1-11:10
	4. Seen in Israel's Future Restoration	11:11-11:36
VI.	*The Righteousness of God Displayed*	12:1-15:13
	Proving the reality of life in Christ	
	The christian attitude:	
	1. Towards God, the Church and the Brethren	12:1-12:21
	2. Towards the State and the World	13:1-13:14
	3. Towards Neighbours and the Weak in Faith	14:1-15:15
VII.	*Conclusion*	15:16-16:27
	1. The purpose in writing – Paul's reasons	15:14-15:21
	2. The request for prayer – Paul's plans	15:22-15:33
	3. The cause for prayer – Paul's greetings	16:1-16:27

8. Bibliography

Barclay, William. *The Letter to the Romans*. The Saint Andrews Press, Edinburgh, 1955.
Candlish, Robert S. *Studies in Romans 12*. Kregel Publications 1989. First

published by Adam and Charles Clark, Edinburgh, 1867.
Darby, J.N. *Synopsis of the Books of the Bible*. Stow Hill Bible and Tract Depot, Kingston-on-Thames, 1943.
Davies, J.M. *An Exposition of the Epistle to the Romans*. John Ritchie Ltd. Kilmarnock, 1968.
Denney, James. *Paul's Epistle to the Romans. (EGT)*. Wm B Eerdmans, Grand Rapids, 1961.
Grant, F.W. *Romans – Numerical Bible*. Loizeaux Bros, New York, 1932.
Haldane, Robert. *Commentary on Romans*, Kregel Publications, Grand Rapids, 1988. Originally published by R Carter & Brothers, New York, 1853.
Kelly, William. *Notes to the Romans*. G Morrish, London.
Kroll, Woodrow M. *Romans (Parallel Bible Commentary)*. Thomas Nelson, Nashville, 1994.
Laurin, Roy L. *Romans – Where Life Begins*. Kregel Publications, 1988.
Lee, Robert. *Outline Studies in Romans*. Kregel Publications.
MacDonald, William. *Believer's Bible Commentary*. Thomas Nelson, Nashville, 1990.
Moo, Douglas J. *Romans (New Bible Commentary)*. Inter Varsity Press, Leicester, 1994.
Newell, William R. *Romans Verse-by-Verse*. Kregel, 1994. First published by Grace Publications, Chicago, 1945.
Plummer, William S. *Commentary on the Romans*. Kregel Publications, 1993. Formerly published by Anson DF Randolph & Co, New York, 1870.
Robertson, A.T. *Word Pictures in the New Testament.* (vol. 4). Boardman Press, Nashville, Tennessee, 1931.
Stallan, F.E. *Things Written Aforetime*. John Ritchie Ltd, Kilmarnock, 1990.
Stallan, F.E. *Written For Our Learning*. John Ritchie Ltd, Kilmarnock, 1994.
Stanley, Charles. *The Epistle to the Romans*. G Morrish, London, 1885.
Stuart, C.E. *An Outline of St Paul's Epistle to the Romans*. E Marlborough & Co, London, 1900.
Vincent, M.R. *Word Studies in the New Testament*. McDonald Publishing Company, Florida, U.S.A.
Vine, W.E. *The Epistle to the Romans*, Pickering & Inglis, Glasgow, 1935.

Text and Exposition

I. Introduction (1:1-17)

1. *The Salutation*
1:1-7

> v.1 "Paul, a servant of Jesus Christ, called to be an apostle, separated unto the gospel of God,
> v.2 (Which he had promised afore by his prophets in the holy scriptures,)
> v.3 Concerning his Son Jesus Christ our Lord, which was made of the seed of David according to the flesh;
> v.4 And declared to be the Son of God with power, according to the spirit of holiness, by the resurrection from the dead:
> v.5 By whom we have received grace and apostleship, for obedience to the faith among all nations, for his name:
> v.6 Among whom are ye also the called of Jesus Christ:
> v.7 To all that be in Rome, beloved of God, called to be saints: Grace to you and peace from God our Father, and the Lord Jesus Christ."

1 Since Paul was not involved in the establishment of the church at Rome, he obviously judged it necessary to set out his credentials. His pedigree and attainments under Judaism are not mentioned. It was sufficient that he was a servant of Jesus Christ, an apostle, and that he was separated unto the gospel of God. These were the main features of the validation of, all that was necessary to give credence to, the epistle.

Paul was firstly a servant (*doulos*, "a slave"). In this description of his relationship with Jesus Christ, he acknowledges that he was entirely at His disposal. Slaves had no rights. They were owned by a master and were in a permanent relation of servitude to him. Paul was not the only apostle who begins his epistle in this fashion. Peter, James and Jude also commence their letters by declaring that they were slaves. This state of affairs was not irksome. These servants of Jesus Christ had the unique position of being slaves and yet also saints of God, an honour which is true of all who own Jesus Christ as Lord.

Four of Paul's epistles have no reference to his apostleship: 1 Thessalonians, 2 Thessalonians, Philippians and Philemon. The author of Hebrews is unknown, but in any case there is no reference to apostleship by way of introduction. It is thought that the title was omitted in the epistles to the Thessalonians because they were such an endearing company and a reference to an official position would have been out of place. Similarly, since the Philippian epistle deals with christian living, quoting apostleship would not have fitted in with the teaching, especially since Paul was an exponent of what he preached. In addition, the example of Christ who made Himself of no reputation makes any claim for recognition above other believers incongruous. Nevertheless, Paul was an apostle and it was necessary to stress this fact to the Romans. An apostle was "one sent". The word *apostolos* conveys the idea of an individual sending someone off from himself with a commission and credentials to act on his behalf to accomplish a certain mission.

Paul's credentials included the fact that he had been separated. The word he used, *aphorizō*, occurs again in Gal 1:15, where Paul states that he had been separated from his mother's womb. Quite independent of any action the apostle had taken, God in His purposes had marked him off as a special vessel for a special purpose even before he was born. As a Pharisee he was a separated person by his conviction and way of life. Now he was separated to the gospel of God, a different outlook altogether.

2 This verse is parenthetical, coming between the mention of the gospel of God and the fact that it concerned God's Son. It was necessary in the nature of the case to show that the gospel message was not an emergency measure, an overthrowing of all that had been written before and accepted as the word of God. There are close on sixty quotations in the epistle from the OT. In addition approximately forty allusions to the OT have been identified, showing the relevance of the writings of the past to the message of the gospel. In 15:4, the apostle claims that the things that were written aforetime were written for our learning. This is an amazing statement. It implies that the inspired writers were not only writing for their own generations, but, in the wisdom of God and under the guidance of the Holy Spirit, were writing for future generations also. So the message was not an emergency measure or even an afterthought to deal with a crisis which had arisen. It was planned in the distant past of eternity and foretold in the Scriptures.

3 The gospel to which Paul was separated concerned God's Son, Jesus Christ our Lord. In this statement there is a defence of the deity of Christ. If Jesus Christ is the Son of God, then He is a divine Person, co-equal and co-existent with God the Father. This is fundamental to the gospel which is presented to mankind. To confess Jesus Christ as Lord is, in effect, to acknowledge that He is indeed the Son of God. The learned writers of the Septuagint, the Greek version of the OT, were in no doubt about what word would serve as a translation of Jehovah or Adonai, they used the word *kurios* ("Lord").

Having asserted the deity of Christ, Paul follows that by confirming His humanity. Later, to the Philippians he will write that He was "found in fashion as a man" (Phil 2:8); here he declares that He "was made of the seed of David according to the flesh". The AV's translation of *genomenou* ("was made") is unfortunate. There is no thought of having been created. Most other versions render the word differently. The RV has "was born of the seed of David"; JND gives "(come of David's seed…)"; Kenneth Wuest in his expanded translation adopts a slightly different stance and renders it, "Who came from the ancestral line of David so far as His humanity is concerned".

The great fact that Paul wants to establish is that Christ came; and not only does the word cover His coming into the world, the wider inference brings in where He came from and the purpose of His coming. There seems to be no need of argument that He came of the seed of David according to the flesh. With Paul it was a fact. Christ was of the lineage of David. He came in the royal line, and He came according to the flesh. The central figure of the gospel was none other than the Son of God, found in fashion as a man. Nathan's prophetic words to David, "Thine house and thy kingdom shall be established for ever" (2 Sam 7:16) had come to pass. The fulness of time had arrived and Paul's concern for the Romans was that they should know who was concerned. It was not an angel or any other; it was, as he declares, "Jesus Christ our Lord", and He was the Son of God.

4 Having established that the subject of the gospel to which he was separated was in the world "according to the flesh", the apostle moves on to consideration of His deity. Obviously Paul is not simply contrasting these two aspects of the mystery of Christ's person, true as both are, but is going on to reveal new glories which the Lord acquired. He was "declared to be the Son of God with power". The use of *horizō* here is different from Luke's use of the word in Acts 10:42 where it carries the sense "to appoint"; it has rather the sense of Acts 2:23, "Him, being delivered by the *determinate* counsel and foreknowledge of God". The sign by which He was marked out was unmistakeable. He was marked out "to be the Son of God with power". He was the eternal Son before He came into the world in fashion as a man, but through resurrection, a raising from the dead in power, He demonstrated a new glory. He had made known in His public ministry that He would rise again on the third day, and that promise was fulfilled.

The apostle's declaration regarding the subject of the gospel has another facet which has equal force. The Son of God was marked out according to the spirit of holiness. That holiness characterised Him during His life. It bore testimony to His sinlessness. He was impeccable. In every aspect of His life He was in complete harmony with the Spirit of God. His own challenge to His foes, "Which of you convinceth me of sin?" (John 8:46) was never taken up, because there was none who could make an accusation and sustain it. The One who was marked out so clearly and unequivocally in holiness and power will use that power on behalf of His own. It is the guarantee of the mighty harvest which will follow in God's good time.

The RV follows some manuscripts by deleting the words "Jesus Christ our

Lord" from v.3 and inserting them at the end of v.4. The view is expressed that this gives greater emphasis to what Paul has to say in v.5 concerning grace and apostleship.

5 Although Paul is advising the saints at Rome that he received grace and apostleship, he is not necessarily excluding others from having received similar blessing, hence perhaps the use of the plural "we". However, in this epistle more than any other, Paul puts his apostleship on a formal footing. He could not appeal to the believers as one who had worked amongst them; he had never been there. He was nevertheless the apostle to the Gentiles, and as Gentiles in Rome, they were in his allotted sphere of service. He had a similar word for the Ephesians. To them he wrote, "Unto me, who am less than the least of all saints, is this grace given, that I should preach among the Gentiles the unsearchable riches of Christ" (Eph 3:8). His ministry was to call men and women through the gospel unto the obedience of faith; not only initial faith in believing, but faith in the practical sense which will yield obedience to the truth of God as it is revealed in the Scriptures. This apostolic ministry was worldwide as far as Paul was concerned. He had a roving commission to carry the gospel among all nations and he would do it "for his name", or, "for His name's sake" (RV). Ananias had some doubts about Paul but his misgivings were cleared away when the Lord said to him, "Go thy way: for he is a chosen vessel unto me, to bear my name before Gentiles, and kings, and the children of Israel" (Acts 9:15). The gospel was a witness to the Lord Jesus Christ. Since His glory and honour were at stake, the message had to be declared in its fulness so that the Lord was magnified and sinners soundly saved. A faulty gospel would detract from the glory of Christ and have far-reaching detrimental consequences for mankind.

6 In v.1 Paul claims to be a "called apostle": he was an apostle by the calling of God. In this verse he addresses the saints at Rome as "the called of Jesus Christ". They were saints by calling, not saints by birth. There was a dignity conferred upon them. As holy ones they belonged to Christ; they were His possession. The apostle obviously wanted the Romans to know that just as he had been called, so they had been called also, albeit, not to apostleship. The inclusion of "also" in the verse necessarily links the believers with those who in the previous verse are said to have shown obedience of faith. They had obeyed the call of God in the gospel.

7 Although Paul had never been in Rome, it did not hinder him from sending greetings in the most endearing terms. The believers there were *agapētois theou*, "beloved of God". They were the objects of God's love. They were worthy of His love, not because of any merit in themselves, but on account of the value of the sacrifice of Christ and their obedience of faith. In addition, they were "called saints", or, "called to be saints". This does not mean they were named, or styled saints, true as that might be, but they were saints by calling. The order is important. It is not a matter of obtaining a certain level of holiness of life, after which the title or position is earned. It is rather the reverse; the call of God and the sanctifying power of the Holy Spirit effects the change and after that holiness of life is demonstrated.

The greeting, "Grace to you and peace" is a form of salutation used by Paul in most of his epistles. It is a combination of Greek and Hebrew forms and it embraces believers from both ethnic cultures or backgrounds. In a sense, it forms a bridge and conveys to both an expression of goodwill "from God our Father and the Lord Jesus Christ". The deity of the Lord is confirmed in His being one with the Father; both are here seen to be behind the grace and peace brought to them in the epistle from the apostle to the Gentiles.

The salutation with its personal explanations ends here. It has been one long sentence. In 1 Pet 1 the writer covers vv. 3-17 in one long sentence also, the parts of which are joined together by relative pronouns. He moves from one aspect of salvation to another without making a break. Here in Rom 1, Paul follows a similar pattern. There is no break in the first seven verses. The gospel of God which he sets out to declare has many facets and in his introduction the apostle obviously has no wish to introduce any interruption to his flow of thought.

Notes

3 In the phrase "according to the flesh," *sarx* denotes the humanity of Christ. Similarly in John 1:14, "And the word of God was made flesh and dwelt among us". Throughout the NT the meaning of *sarx* is determined by the context in which it is used: of the human body – "the life which I now live in the flesh" (Gal 2:20); of the weakness of human nature – "the law...was weak through the flesh" (8:3); of unregenerate men – "they that are in the flesh cannot please God" (8:8); of the seat of sin in man – "For I know that in me (that is, in my flesh,) dwelleth no good thing" (7:18).

4 The Lordship of Christ, signifying His absolute authority, is stressed also. The death and resurrection of Christ and the establishment of His Lordship, authority, and possession of His people will be brought up again by the apostle (see 14:8,9).

5 The use of the plural here in "we have received" for the singular is not an inclusion of others at this point. The context concerns Paul's apostleship and the grace bestowed upon him.

The RV has "unto obedience of faith". The AV renders, "for obedience to the faith". Robertson in his *Word Pictures in the New Testament* opts for "the obedience which springs from faith (the act of assent or surrender)" (vol.4, p.324).

Haldane comments, "Some understand this of the obedience which faith produces, but the usual import of the expression as well as the connection in this place, determines it to apply to the belief of the gospel".

2. Reason for Writing
1:8-15

> v.8 "First, I thank my God through Jesus Christ for you all, that your faith is spoken of throughout the whole world.
> v.9 For God is my witness, whom I serve with my spirit in the gospel of his Son, that without ceasing I make mention of you always in my prayers;
> v.10 Making request, if by any means now at length I might have a prosperous journey by the will of God to come unto you.
> v.11 For I long to see you, that I may impart unto you some spiritual gift, to the end ye may be established;
> v.12 That is, that I may be comforted together with you by the mutual faith both of you and me.
> v.13 Now I would not have you ignorant, brethren, that oftentimes I purposed to come unto you, (but was let hitherto,) that I might have some fruit among you also, even as among other Gentiles.
> v.14 I am debtor both to the Greeks, and to the Barbarians; both to the wise, and to the unwise.
> v.15 So, as much as in me is, I am ready to preach the gospel to you that are at Rome also."

8 Here Paul begins by expressing what he obviously feels to be an obligation, thanks to God for the faith of these saints. This is not an unusual situation. To the Thessalonians on more than one occasion he wrote that he was bound, indebted (*opheilō*), to thank God for their spiritual progress. The reference to "my God" underlines Paul's personal faith. He would let the saints at Rome know how he saw his personal relationship with his God. This was not necessarily exclusive possession. It was open to the saints at Rome to claim and enjoy the same close relationship made known by the apostle. The Lord is not excluded. The thanksgiving is rendered through Him and its subject is the faith of all to whom Paul wrote. Their faithfulness to God was being proclaimed throughout the whole world. This is not exaggeration. The report of the steadfastness of the believers at Rome was spreading throughout the world of apostolic times. This must have been a great encouragement to Paul as the apostle to the Gentiles. Already he had acknowledged that the faith of the Thessalonians had spread so widely that the good news of the gospel was running ahead of him in his missionary travels (1 Thess 1:8). Now he could acknowledge that there were others who were not the fruit of his labours but whose manner of life proclaimed the reality of their faith in God.

9 In calling upon God to be his witness, the apostle is here assuring the believers at Rome that his prayers for them were not mere formal utterances, occasionally rendered and lacking in substance. They were "without ceasing" (*adialeiptōs*), always being presented to God as the saints and their needs came before his mind. Luke records the same idea of recurring action in connection with the woman who came into the house of Simon the Pharisee and ministered to the Lord. Said He to his host, "...this woman, since the time I came in hath not ceased (*ou dieleipen*) to kiss my feet" (Luke 7:45). She made the most of the opportunity, aware that she might never have another.

The pattern of Paul's prayer life can be judged from his epistles. His remembrance of the saints is not something he boasts about, but is an evidence of the anxious care that was constantly with him. To the Ephesians he wrote, "I cease not to give thanks for you, making mention of you in my prayers" (1:16). He noted their spiritual progress and thanked God for it; likewise to Timothy, "without ceasing I have remembrance of thee in my prayers night and day" (2 Tim 1:3). He so valued his young brother's service he rendered constantly-recurring prayers.

The service to God which Paul mentions here is not bondservice, but rather a priestly one. The sense is caught by the writer to the Hebrews in his use of the word *latreia*. He states, "We have an altar, whereof they have no right to eat which serve (*latreuō*) the tabernacle" (13:10). Paul's exercise was one which was marked by worship. Before God he was always in an attitude of adoration, not only for the grace shown to him but in recognition of the glories of the God he served. That he did it in his spirit must surely mean that it was from the very depth of his soul. Never was it to him a light thing to serve the living and true God.

10 At this verse the prayers of the apostle are specific. His desires to come to the saints at Rome are part of the petitions which he makes at every opportunity. These are not simply mentions of a fact, but beseechings that the way will open up for him to visit the city. He uses the word *deēsis* to describe his petitioning. It is the first of the four words he penned to Timothy when he exhorted him "that supplications, prayers, intercessions and giving of thanks be made for all men" (1 Tim 2:1). These were not different kinds of prayer, but prayer from four different viewpoints, covering every aspect of public prayer. In his epistle to the saints at Rome he wanted to let them know of his earnestness before God about his desire to visit them. It was not something he would consider apart from the will of God. The gracious design of God for his life was what he wanted, hoping that it would open up a way for him to have a prosperous journey, free from difficulties. Nevertheless he would have to wait until the will of God was known. In patience he was prepared to do that, but while he waited, he would supplicate God continually.

11 Paul's earnest desire to see the Romans calls to mind the yearning which Epaphroditus had for the Philippians. That fellow-worker's longing was mixed with heaviness because the Philippians had heard he was sick (Phil 2:26). The same word (*epipotheō*) is used by the apostle to describe the intensity of his desire to visit Rome and meet the saints. It was not merely the satisfaction of meeting them he had in mind; it was that he might impart to them some spiritual gift. The thought associated with the expression *metadō charisma* is more of sharing than imparting. What Paul had received from the Lord he was ready to share with others. Just before the Lord departed from this scene He intimated that the Comforter would come and that He would teach all things (John 14:26). The Holy Spirit had found in Paul a willing depository for the truth of God and it was from this vast store that he wanted to give. He had an abundance of spiritual wealth to share with the saints. The object of the sharing he had in mind was their establishment (*stērizō*, "to prop up"). They would be propped up in the faith by his ministry. From his earliest labours for the Lord, this was Paul's practice. On the return leg of his first missionary journey he visited again the places he had preached the gospel and confirmed (*epistērizō*) the souls of the saints (Acts 14:22). He strengthened them, causing them to stand firm in their faith.

12 The modesty of the apostle shines through in this verse. He was not above admitting that even the most simple amongst the believers could impart something of comfort to him. The compound word for "comforted", found only here in the NT, stresses a sharing in mutual comfort. If the results of Paul's sharing with them was their establishment this would be a comfort to them for what they had received. There is no suggestion that the faith of the believers at Rome was weaker than Paul's. The firmness of his grip on eternal things was not in question, any more than the quality of their trust in God. It was mutual faith, their link with God and their common belief in Him that would be the source and ground of comfort.

13 The expression "I would not have you ignorant" was one Paul used often. The Corinthians and the Thessalonians were addressed in that fashion (1 Cor 10:1; 1 Thess 4:13). It stressed the need to consider carefully what he was saying. It was always on his mind that believers should be fully conversant with what he desired for them. The emphasis here is on the fact that he had often purposed to come to them and wanted them to be in no doubt about it. He had, however, been hindered (*kōluō*, "to prevent"). What had prevented him from coming is not stated, nor was it necessary that they should know. The comment was merely made to remove any possible speculation which might arise regarding his non-appearance. What had been in his mind for a considerable time was a season of spiritual profit at Rome. Both in the preaching of the gospel and in the teaching of the saints, the city appealed to him as a fruitful field. He had reaped great blessings in other countries amongst the Gentiles and he envisaged another great harvest, if only the way would open up for him to get there. Plummer makes an interesting observation on this verse. He states, "Insatiable is the holy desire of a right-minded man to do good and lead souls to Christ".

14 In Paul's epistles he represents himself as a debtor (*opheiletēs*) for different reasons. To the Thessalonians he wrote that he and Silas and Timothy were bound (*opheilomen*) to thank God always for them because their faith grew exceedingly

(II Thess 1:3); and to the same company, that he and his fellow-workers were bound to give thanks always to God for them because God had from the beginning chosen them to salvation (2 Thess 2:13). To the flesh, however, he owed nothing. Neither he nor the saints at Rome were debtors to it to live according to its dictates (8:12). Paul was a man who did not live for himself. As the events of life unfolded before him, they placed him under an obligation either to thank God or to do something about them. Here, he saw the Greeks and the barbarians, the wise and the foolish without Christ, and since he had been entrusted with the gospel, he was their debtor. The only way he could discharge his debt was to preach the gospel to them. In the previous verse the apostle viewed the nations as Gentiles. In this verse he divides them up to let the Romans see that all classes needed the gospel. He was a debtor to the civilised and to the uncivilised, to the learned and to the unlearned. Wherever man was found and in whatever condition, Paul saw himself as being under a binding obligation to preach the gospel of God.

15 The only limitation Paul envisaged was the limitation of his ability, as he notes, "as much as in me is". Rome represented a vast harvest field. His readiness to go there and preach the gospel was never in doubt. Had this been only a case of fulfilling a duty it might then be something which could be done, but done unwillingly. It was not so with Paul. The prospect of evangelising in the great metropolis filled him with a willing and ready anticipation. He was waiting for the will of God to be known (v.10). He was filled with a longing (v.11). In the meantime as he contemplated the situation, he interceded with God that the way would open up for him.

3. *Establishment of the Theme*
1:16-17

> v.16 "For I am not ashamed of the gospel of Christ: for it is the power of God unto salvation to every one that believeth; to the Jew first, and also to the Greek.
> v.17 For therein is the righteousness of God revealed from faith to faith: as it is written, The just shall live by faith."

16 The apostle comes to the conclusion of his introduction by setting out the subject matter of the epistle. The main theme is the gospel. Although the message is one of glad tidings, it will nevertheless tell out how far short mankind had fallen from the standard of God's righteousness. This Paul will proceed to show before he reveals that the gospel has hope and that God has found a way to be just and yet be the justifier of the sinner. The opening words describe Paul's position, "For I am not ashamed of the gospel". Whatever criticism might be directed against him and at the message he bore, he was proud to be associated with it. It was no secret that the Gentiles heaped scorn upon the message. To them the preaching of the cross was foolishness. As for the Jews, it was an occasion of stumbling. It was an offence to their national pride. In the face of these attitudes, Paul wrote to the Corinthians, "For I determined not to know anything among you, save Jesus Christ, and him crucified" (1 Cor 2:2). Therein lay his safety and the secret of his success. Not only was Paul unashamed, but he called upon Timothy not to be ashamed of the testimony of our Lord (2 Tim 1:8), and he commended Onesiphorus for not being ashamed of his chain (2 Tim 1:16). Paul had been shown great grace and he was the custodian of great things. To be ashamed therefore never entered his mind for a moment.

In the opening verse the apostle stated that he was separated unto the gospel of God. That gospel concerned Jesus Christ, declared to be the Son of God with power. That power is now seen to be the means in the gospel of bringing sinners to salvation. This salvation is the possession of every one that believes. In the Scriptures salvation has many shades of meaning, involving deliverance from manifold trials to deliverance from the penalty of sin and eventually from sin's power and presence. In this verse, the aspect of salvation being declared is deliverance from sin's penalty. The announcement is an indication of the great news for mankind which will be outlined as the wonders of God's grace are set out in the epistle. The power (*dunamis*) is an expression of the ability of God to save. Despite the strength of sin and the power of Satan, the power of God in the gospel transcends them all.

The Jews had special privileges. The Lord came to the nation and to His own things and He presented Himself to the people for acceptance. Despite rejection of the Messiah by the Jews, His disciples were sent to them first after His resurrection and ascension. They still held that priority as far as Paul was concerned. To the Jews he would appeal, as if reflecting the reluctance of God to give up His earthly people. Their obstinacy and the fact that the message was universal opened up wider horizons to the apostle and so to the Gentiles the message also went forth in power.

17 In writing of the gospel and its power, Paul makes it absolutely clear that there is no possibility of salvation being obtained by man on any principle other than that of faith. It is faith that accepts the word of God. It is faith that recognises and accepts the merit of the person and the work of Christ. Man, having lost his own righteousness and having fallen into condemnation because of sin, has no merit to plead; he has to turn to the gospel if he will escape the righteous wrath of God. In the gospel, not only is the power of God manifested but the righteousness of God is declared as a fundamental fact of the message. It must be faced and acknowledged, something that Paul will stress as he progresses through the epistle.

Here Paul mentions the righteousness of God. Later he will go into greater detail about it, but at this point, the fact that it has been revealed and that it can be received would seem to be what was uppermost on his mind. Nevertheless, the righteousness of God cannot be glossed over wherever it is mentioned. God can make no compromise with sin. He must judge sinners and punish eternally the impenitent. Happily, God has found a way of justifying the ungodly, a way consistent with His nature, a way in which no aspect of His righteousness is sacrificed in His bestowal of blessing on the unworthy.

The righteousness then is revealed, not in the sciences or philosophies of this world, but by faith and unto faith. Angels were not embraced in this; they were merely onlookers. To mankind has the wondrous blessing been addressed and that on the principle of faith. Believers on the Lord Jesus Christ are those who come into the blessing of justification by faith.

The prophet Habakkuk is called in to show that the principle of acceptance by faith was not a new one; it had operated in his day. Habakkuk's vision was given at a time when his countrymen were about to be invaded by an oppressor. The Chaldeans were ungodly and puffed up, and no better than the Israelites, but God allowed them to chastise the highly-favoured people who had rejected His righteousness by setting about to establish one of their own. Habakkuk's word in that day was, "the just shall live by his faith".

Notes

6 The emphasis of the latter clause is on possession, although it is also true that the call of God was made, and heard and obeyed. Vine asserts that a comma is necessary after "also"; to make the first clause read, "among whom are ye also," i.e. "you are of those who among the nations have obeyed the gospel" (v.5).

11 "For I long to see you" (In current idiom, "I am homesick for you"). *Parallel Bible Commentary*.

13 On "I would not have you ignorant, brethren". Denney comments, "Some emphasis is laid by it on the idea that his desire or purpose to visit them was no passing whim. It was grounded on his vocation as apostle of the Gentiles".

17 Laurin notes, "This righteousness is first revealed and then received. It is not a human discovery. It did not come after centuries of slow search and gradual climb out of darkness. But instead, it was a burst of light. It was a sudden display of the right. It is a gospel effect and not an educational and scientific or historical effect".

II. The Righteousness of God (1:18-3:20)

1. *The Gentiles – Guilty*
1:18-32

> v.18 "For the wrath of God is revealed from heaven against all ungodliness and unrighteousness of men, who hold the truth in unrighteousness;
> v.19 Because that which may be known of God is manifest in them; for God hath shewed it unto them.
> v.20 For the invisible things of him from the creation of the world are clearly seen, being understood by the things that are made, even his eternal power and Godhead; so that they are without excuse:
> v.21 Because that, when they knew God, they glorified him not as God, neither were thankful; but became vain in their imaginations, and their foolish heart was darkened.
> v.22 Professing themselves to be wise, they became fools,
> v.23 And changed the glory of the uncorruptible God into an image made like to corruptible man, and to birds, and fourfooted beasts, and creeping things.
> v.24 Wherefore God also gave them up to uncleanness through the lusts of their own hearts, to dishonour their own bodies between themselves:
> v.25 Who changed the truth of God into a lie, and worshipped and served the creature more than the Creator, who is blessed for ever. Amen.
> v.26 For this cause God gave them up unto vile affections: for even their women did change the natural use into that which is against nature:
> v.27 And likewise also the men, leaving the natural use of the woman, burned in their lust one toward another; men with men working that which is unseemly, and receiving in themselves that recompence of their error which was meet.
> v.28 And even as they did not like to retain God in their knowledge, God gave them over to a reprobate mind, to do those things which are not convenient;
> v.29 Being filled with all unrighteousness, fornication, wickedness, covetousness, maliciousness; full of envy, murder, debate, deceit, malignity; whisperers,
> v.30 Backbiters, haters of God, despiteful, proud, boasters, inventors of evil things, disobedient to parents,
> v.31 Without understanding, covenantbreakers, without natural affection, implacable, unmerciful:
> v.32 Who knowing the judgment of God, that they which commit such things are worthy of death, not only do the same, but have pleasure in them that do them."

18 Having completed the introduction to the epistle, the apostle at this verse commences to deal with the doctrinal matters which he earnestly desired to bring before the saints at Rome. The closing words of v.17, "The just shall live by faith" are irrefutable. The opening statement of v.18, "The wrath of God is revealed from heaven against all ungodliness and unrighteousness of men" makes it clear that there are no exceptions to the principle stated. God's character cannot change. He is altogether righteous, and if there is to be any hope for mankind it must be on the principle of faith and in strict accordance with the holiness and righteousness of God.

From the fall of Adam, the wrath of God has been revealed from heaven against ungodliness and unrighteousness. Every generation since the fall has experienced the wrath of God in some way or another. In national catastrophes and personal tragedies, men have brought upon themselves the results of their ungodly deeds, and although the source is not always recognised, it is clear from this verse that God has not been an uninterested spectator or a silent witness to the impiety of mankind. "Wrath" (*orgē*) as it is linked with God, is not a turbulent emotion; that would be suggested in the synonym *thumos*. Of the two, *orgē* is less sudden in its rise but more lasting in its duration. *Orgē,* in relation to God reflects the settled purpose of wrath, which Paul makes known here is constantly being revealed from heaven on all ungodliness and unrighteousness. There are no exceptions. Jew and Gentile are embraced. Both are classed as impious and unrighteous. The truth of God, whether understood from revelation as with the Jew, or from creation as with the Gentile, is suppressed. The voice of conscience is ignored. What is constantly being brought to the attention of man from these sources concerning the character of God is treated with impiety and scorn, and evil deeds are freely practised. Altogether, the opening words of the doctrinal section of the epistle register a sad indictment of the human race.

19 Any thought of pleading an inability to get to know God by some means or another is dismissed in this verse. The truth of God is still being demonstrated amongst men in a variety of ways. It may even be said that the knowledge of God is manifest in men, because of the God-consciousness that is there. Man has faculties which the brute beast does not possess. He can appreciate that there is a higher hand in nature than mere chance. Even the internal monitor of conscience put there by God is a constant reminder that God exists and that He will not stand back and allow His creatures to act as they like. God is not uninterested. What happens in the world concerns Him. The inhabitants of the world are responsible to acknowledge this fact and to act according to the light they possess. Man is not without the knowledge of God. Paul makes this absolutely clear.

20 Long before Paul made known the wondrous truth of v.20, the psalmist had penned similar thoughts. Wrote he, "The heavens declare the glory of God and the firmament sheweth his handiwork. Day unto day uttereth speech, and night unto night sheweth knowledge" (Ps 19:1,2). Creation is not dumb. The voice of the natural world is loud and clear. Behind creation there is an all-powerful Creator. The things of God that are unseen by natural sight are stated here to be clearly seen in other ways. The things that are made are evidence of God's eternal power and proof of His eternal Godhead. Man's intellect is perfectly capable of taking cognizance of these. At no time in man's history has there been an absence of testimony from creation, as Paul notes here, "For the invisible things of him from the creation of the world are clearly seen". They are understood, perceived (*nōeō*) by the things made. The handiwork of God in creation is not beyond the comprehension of man, even the most primitive.

The power of God is eternal (*aidios*, "always existing"; only here and Jude 6). The apostle is obviously emphasising the fact that God is unchanging. Before the foundation of the world He was there. He is the omnipotent God and by His power He brought the world into being. These things that are made bring the divine attributes of God within the range of man's comprehension and so he is without excuse. Man may not be expected to know the essential nature of the Godhead from creation – that is declared by revelation. He is expected, however, to acknowledge that there is a power outside of himself on a far higher plane, before whom he must bow. If God-consciousness results in his contrition, that would not be unexpected. The awareness of inward sin and the remorse which follows sinful practices would simply be evidence of man's need. To ignore or deny the clear testimony of the eternal God in creation leaves man without excuse and confirms his guilt.

21 The proof that mankind is without excuse is now developed. Although the general belief is that the human race is climbing upward and emerging from the darkness of superstition, the apostle here contends for an opposite view. Man's history proves that he is on a downward course. When men knew God, they glorified Him not as God. The aspect of knowledge that Paul refers to here is what is perceived through the senses, that which comes by observation and experience. If man's history is considered from the flood when eight souls had a new beginning, it is clear that there was a knowledge of God. Creation provided the evidence that behind its wonders there was a Creator's power. But, as Paul asserts and history confirms, man refused to give God the glory for His wondrous works. The obligation which he was under to give thanks for creature blessings was ignored. Gratitude for the breath of life was withheld and what was God's rightful due was never rendered.

The result of refusing to acknowledge God and the claims of God upon His creatures was the development of a way of reasoning which Paul describes, "They became vain in their imaginations". The two words "vain" and "imaginations" are most descriptive. They describe what man fell into by deliberate choice. Both words are in the aorist tense, signifying that it was not a gradual process but an attitude which was adopted and openly flaunted. The verb *mataioō* and its cognate words all point to useless vanity and perversion which man has wittingly practised. The Scripture has many examples of the folly associated with those whose vanity is described so cogently. The word rendered "imaginations" (*dialogismos*) has many shades of meaning, amongst them – reasoning, cogitation, contention. As used here by Paul it describes the various notions arrived at by men to dismiss God from their reckoning. Because of indulging in the foolish process of eliminating God from their thinking the heart of man was darkened. The human race as described in this sad indictment has fallen into darkness from which it cannot deliver itself. Only in the gospel of God is there hope, and that the apostle will bring out after he has rested his case concerning the depravity of man.

22 A further stage in the downward spiral is identified as a profession to be wise. It is more than mere profession, it is assertion. In his account to Agrippa of Paul's appeal to Caesar, Festus observed that the Jews had accused him of having affirmed (or asserted; *phaskō*, "to assert") that Jesus was alive (Acts 25:19). Here men assert, they claim, that they are wise. They persuade themselves that their way of life is a demonstration of their wisdom, but in fact the more they assert it, the more foolish they become. The verb *mōrainomai* suggests "to play the fool" and in doing so to incur the character of folly. The cognate noun is *mōros* from which the word "moron" comes. This aptly describes the attitude of mankind, that human wisdom without God is an ever-upward trend, whereas in fact it is a demonstration of utter foolishness. Having rejected light, the consequence is less light and a darkened heart.

23 The folly is here seen to be perversion at its worst. The substitution of any creature for God, whether bird or beast, is a sin of the most heinous kind. It is the glory, the honour and majesty of God which is demeaned. Such is the level of depravity, even the lowest forms of creation are put in the place of the Creator of the universe. The incorruptible God is exchanged for what is corruptible, known and seen to be corruptible, and the worship due to God is withheld. The corruptible is made into an image, a likeness (*homoiōma*, "a form, shape, resemblance") of what in the perverted mind of man represents God. The idolatry is inexcusable. Gentiles had not the same privileges as the Jews, not having had a revelation from God, but they had creation and conscience and they chose to ignore their witness, preferring rather to follow out their own sinful thoughts and ways.

24 As a result of the perverted thinking and practices of men, God gave them up. Three times the apostle notes what they exchanged and three times he declares that God gave them up. They exchanged the incorruptible for the corruptible and God gave them up (v.24). They exchanged the truth of God for a lie and God gave them up (vv.25-27). They refused to have God in their knowledge and God gave them up (v.28). In this verse God is declared to have given men up to uncleanness. If men by their sinful ways put themselves beyond the providential care of God they will suffer the consequences. There are natural laws which are there to be observed. To flaunt them is to invite trouble. To run riot is to incur retribution of the severest kind. If God hands men over to the outcome of their own lusts they will suffer severely in body. Disease knows no national or social barriers. It is passed from one to another and despite scientific advances the unalterable fact remains, "Whatsoever a man soweth, that shall he also reap" (Gal 6:7). Those who ignore God's laws in creation do so at their own peril.

25 The force of the opening expression of this verse is that man knowingly exchanged what he knew about the true God for something which he was aware was false. The lie he chose was idolatry and all that was behind it. Man may even consider himself to be a mere puppet, but there is no denying who manipulates the strings. Worship and service were not rendered to God although these were His due. They were demeaned and made to apply to the lowest form of creation. Instead of holding the eternal God in reverential awe and allowing honour and respect to flow out to Him, the Creator was exchanged for the creature and God was denied His rights.

It is worthy of note that the mention of the Creator in the context of Paul's argument drew from him a short doxology. The apostle could not let the opportunity pass. At least he could give God the glory and so he stopped his train of thought momentarily to give honour and glory to the Creator "who is blessed for ever, Amen". Another three doxologies will come from the apostle in this epistle. Where they occur is most significant. (See comments at 9:5, 11:36, 16:27.)

26 Once again Paul makes known that mankind has been given up by God. This is not a sentence which has been suspended in the present to be executed in the future. He handed them over to their vile affections to allow them to burn out their lusts among themselves and thereby suffer the consequences. There was no desire for His providential care. God was excluded from man's way of thinking. The idolatry which he embraced brought in its train excesses of the vilest nature, which, as the apostle notes here, included women. They also chose to change what nature taught for practices which were totally unnatural.

27 This verse continues to describe the headlong plunge of mankind into practices of total depravity. It makes sad reading. What could have been fair for God in a world free from blemish was quickly marred by sin and man fell. Despite a new beginning after the flood, the bitter root of sin soon brought forth its fruit and the downward path has continued, gathering speed in every generation. At this point the apostle is constrained to make the outcome clear; men and women are receiving back in full for their error and their perverse wickedness.

28 The deliberate choice of men to disapprove of having God in their knowledge is given here as being the reason why God gave them up. This is the third time within the scope of a few verses that it is noted that God gave them up. Already seen to be given over to uncleanness and vile affections, the third action is a handing over to a reprobate mind; a mind that has failed every test.

The way man thinks has determined the way he lives and that is seen to be one of total depravity. How different from the exhortation of the apostle in his epistle to the Philippians, "Let this mind be in you, which was also in Christ Jesus" (Phil 2:5). To think the way He thought will stand up to the closest scrutiny and pass any test applied from the divine standpoint. Paul's argument here asserts that puny man put God to the test and according to the standards of the reprobate mind, God did not meet the requirements. The darkness of the depraved mind and the conscience which no longer acted as a monitor of good and evil failed to make room for God; He was not retained in man's knowledge. Once more the result of man's rebellion is stated. The barriers which in the providential ways of God were there to restrain evil were removed and everything which was unbecoming according to divine standards was freely embraced and practised.

29 The sinful practices of the ungodly which Paul begins to describe in detail are an indication of how far men and women will sink when sin has taken control of their lives. Although the apostle is depicting the characteristics of men and women in every age, the proof of it was to be seen in the godless society of his day. He lived in a permissive age. In Corinth, from where possibly he was writing, what he depicts was taking place all around him. Nothing was tempered by virtue. Men and women were "filled" with all unrighteousness; they were "full" of envy, murder and much more besides. They were in the full flight of uncontrolled evil passions. There is not a glimmer of light in the verse. Every word portrays an aspect of moral depravity that cried out to heaven for God's intervention.

Of the ten words in the verse ("fornication" is not in the best MSS), the first four, unrighteousness, wickedness, covetousness and maliciousness, are general descriptions of evil. The next five words, envy, murder, debate, deceit and malignity, are more specific, indicating what evil will do. These portray the outworking of the bitter root of sin. By these, sin is recognised for what it is, evidences of the first two words in the verse, "all unrighteousness". The last word, "whisperers" describes a base trait of character and leads on to others of a similar nature which are set out in the next verse.

30 As the apostle continues with his description of unregenerate man, he concentrates on another aspect of evil associated with man. Taking the references to "whisperers" from the previous verse and leading on from it to "backbiters", secretive slander is identified. Not content with personal gratification from sinful practices, harm of others by false statements and foul calumny is seen to be a common trait in man's character. To this the apostle adds, "haters of God" (or "God-haters", only here in the NT). The RV translates the word, "hateful of God" and there are good grounds for accepting that. Either way, the word fits men and women who are astray from God and in total opposition to Him and His laws.

The next three words complete the picture: insolent (AV "despiteful"), proud and boastful; words full of meaning and each describing a facet of human life which, when seen in its entirety, is far removed from the original intention of God for man as part of His fair creation. To these Paul adds "disobedient to parents" and carries his train of thought on to consider further characteristics of man's fallen nature.

31 If the word for "disobedient" is classed with the four words of this verse they are all seen to be negatives. Each one has a prefix. Man is seen to be devoid of certain virtues. Discernment, natural affection and mercy form no part of his make-up. Parental influence is scorned. If covenants are entered into, they are there to be broken, and if an argument is called for, implacable intransigence dismisses any possibility of consenting. At this point the apostle brings his list to a close. What remains now in his indictment of the Gentiles is the solemn conclusion of his guilt before God.

32 Although the voice of God in creation and the dictates of conscience are ignored, fallen man still retains at the back of his mind that there is divine retribution to be faced. He has no argument against the fact that vile practices render the doers of them worthy of death. This may mean more than physical death. Annihilation is held by many as an escape from having to face a righteous and holy God after death. Perhaps Paul had final judgment in mind as well as the cessation of life on earth as he brought this part of his argument to a conclusion.

Notes

16 Denney makes an interesting note against this verse regarding the power of the gospel, "It is demonstrated, not by argument, but what it does, and looking to what it can do. Paul is proud to preach it anywhere".
20 Did Paul have Ps 19 in mind when he dictated this verse? He quotes Ps 19:4 at 10:18. See comments in the author's work, *Written for our Learning*, page 305.
24 "God gave them up" does not mean that God exerted any positive influence in inducing them to sin, but simply that He ceased to restrain them.
28 Wuest, in his *Expanded Translation of the New Testament* makes a point concerning "like" (*dokimazō*). He translates the verse, "And even after putting God to the test for the purpose of approving Him should He meet their specifications, and finding that He did not, they disapproved of holding Him in their full and precise knowledge, God gave them up to a mind that would not meet the test for that which a mind was meant, to practise those things which were not becoming".
29-31 Most of the words listed in these verses are fully explained by Wm Barclay in his exposition of this epistle.

2. *The Jews – Guilty*
2:1-3:8

(a) *Inexcusable and impenitent (vv.1-11)*

> v.1 "Therefore thou art inexcusable, O man, whosoever thou art that judgest: for wherein thou judgest another, thou condemnest thyself; for thou that judgest

> doest the same things.
>
> v.2 But we are sure that the judgment of God is according to truth against them which commit such things.
>
> v.3 And thinkest thou this, O man, that judgest them which do such things, and doest the same, that thou shalt escape the judgment of God?
>
> v.4 Or despisest thou the riches of his goodness and forbearance and longsuffering; not knowing that the goodness of God leadeth thee to repentance?
>
> v.5 But after thy hardness and impenitent heart treasurest up unto thyself wrath against the day of wrath and revelation of the righteous judgment of God;
>
> v.6 Who will render to every man according to his deeds:
>
> v.7 To them who by patient continuance in well doing seek for glory and honour and immortality, eternal life:
>
> v.8 But unto them that are contentious, and do not obey the truth, but obey unrighteousness, indignation and wrath,
>
> v.9 Tribulation and anguish, upon every soul of man that doeth evil, of the Jew first, and also of the Gentile;
>
> v.10 But glory, honour, and peace, to every man that worketh good, to the Jew first, and also to the Gentile:
>
> v.11 For there is no respect of persons with God."

1 Having dealt with the guilt of the Gentiles in the latter half of ch.1, the apostle now turns his attention to the Jews. The opening verses of ch.2 are embracive in their character. The Jews practised "the same things" for which the Gentiles were condemned and it follows therefore that they are also included in the judgment of God. It was grossly wrong for the Jews to condemn the Gentiles for sinning against the knowledge of God they had from creation, since they themselves sinned likewise, despite having revelation; they were privileged to a far greater degree. Indeed it was hypocritical in the extreme for any man to judge another, since all were in the same category: they practised sin. To pronounce judgment on another was an automatic condemnation of the one who passed judgment.

The apostle is not saying that the terms of the judgment passed are wrong although they may be harsh and adverse. That is obviously not the point of his reasoning. What is envisaged by Paul is the stance taken by the moralist who recognises evil in others according to the standards he holds and passes judgment on the evil-doers. The profanity of this is that the moralist himself practises sinful deeds, although not necessarily the same ones. It would have weakened Paul's argument if he had inferred that the sins of the Jews were identical to the sins of the Gentiles. The point made by the apostle is that whether Jews or Gentiles, both sinned *against the light they had* and both were guilty, hence the opening statement of v.1, "Therefore thou art inexcusable, O man, whosoever thou art that judgest".

2 The fact that Paul includes himself in the statement, "we are sure", (or, better, "we know", RV), is proof that all men know intuitively that they cannot sin and escape the consequences of their evil deeds. God's judgment is righteous and it takes into account what men have practised. It is according to truth. Men judge and their judgment might be quite wrong. This is not possible with God, He cannot deny Himself. His standards are in keeping with His own nature and they are altogether righteous. This judgment is against those whose way of life is the pursuit of evil. Paul is not thinking of a situation where someone stumbles and falls into sin. He is not considering isolated cases; he is asserting that man, having dismissed God from his reckoning, follows a course of action which is sinful in its character and wicked in its expression.

The judgment which Paul refers to here and which he and all others know about is not based on hearsay or generalities. It is according to truth: the facts are all recorded in the annals of heaven. When the sentence is passed it will be settled on factual evidence and there will be no appeal against the character of the Judge or against His assessment of guilt. On this account, it is essential that God make clear to all men what He will do and where their way of life will lead them if they pursue it to the end of life on earth.

The conclusion in the previous verse, "Therefore thou art inexcusable, O man" and the question in the next verse, "And thinkest thou...that thou shalt escape the judgment of God?" prove that Paul considered the argument he had put forward was unanswerable. He had vindicated God and had impeached man. Regarding the establishment of man's guilt, he was drawing near to the point where he could rest his case.

3 The apostle's challenge here is perfectly clear. It is an appeal to man's reasoning, as if to say, "Do you really consider that you will escape the judgment of God?" He emphasises what he declared in v.1 regarding the moralist and his hypocritical stance. The Jew was the one who had the greater light and yet had the more-ready tendency to condemn others. There was self-deception in the thinking. He assumed that God would take into account his stance and that he would not be exposed to judgment. This could not be; it would compromise the nature of God to excuse the guilty.

The attitude of the Jew to the charges was not that he would escape the judgment of God, but that he had no case to answer. If indeed he was called to account, in his estimation he would be acquitted. With all his privileges, the Jew should have known better, but instead, he took the ground of the moralist. He considered that his birth as a Jew gave him a guaranteed place in the kingdom and therefore he was above being called in question for his actions or for his judgment of the Gentiles. The little expression, "and doest the same" should be enough to silence any argument against the righteousness of the judgment of God.

4 In the original the word translated, "despisest" (*kataphroneō*, "to think disparagingly"), occurs in the middle of the sentence, coming after "longsuffering". This makes it emphatic, stressing the contrast with God's goodness, forbearance and longsuffering. The despising is an attitude of contempt. Mankind in general and the Jews in particular wilfully ignored the mercy of God, adopting the stance that God would never take action against sin. Instead of recognising that the goodness of God was leading them to repentance, they took the opposite view, that God had no right to interfere in what they considered to be man's world.

The portrayal of the character of God here by the apostle is peerless in its choice of words. Much has been written about the different shades of meaning attached to goodness, forbearance and longsuffering. Each word could stand effectively on its own, but here Paul prefixes the three by a declaration of their wealth, emphasising the riches of their display of the character of God. In Paul's epistles many things are prefixed by "riches" when God is involved in them. Indeed, in his letter to the Ephesians he uses a superlative to describe the kindness of God through Christ Jesus, and he calls it "the exceeding riches of his grace" (Eph 2:7). Such was Paul's appreciation, but here in his epistle to the Romans he notes that the grace of God is not recognised as leading to repentance, or if it is, it is wilfully ignored. The extent of God's appeal to mankind by His Spirit, pointing the way to repentance will never be fully known, but it is there, going on all the time. The desire of God is that men will have a change of mind, a turning from evil to good. The word used here is not putting stress on regret at the consequences of one's actions, but suggests a change of mind regarding the evil of the past, leading to an entirely different and better way of life. Despite the many ways employed by God to point and lead men to repentance, the general response is one of disparagement. Scorn is poured on the suggestion that there is any need for a change. Man likes to think he is a free agent and therefore any attempt to direct him into a path which is not of his own choosing is resisted. Nevertheless, the longsuffering of God gives ample scope for change, but if His appeals are constantly rejected, righteous judgment must follow; it cannot be averted.

5 It is significant that wrath is introduced after the mention of the goodness of God. God by various means leads to repentance but sinful man, despising that, treasures up for himself wrath against the day of wrath. Man is seen to be incorrigible. In his sheer abandon, he amasses a dreadful catalogue of sins, all of which he must face when he appears at the bar of God. According to the insensibility of his impenitent heart he stores up for himself wrath. There is no way that this can be ameliorated. What is done in the body in time must be faced when in eternity. God's goodness cannot be faulted. It is an expression of His character and if its appeal to men fails to lead them to repentance it is because they chose to have it that way.

The writer to the Hebrews wrote, "It is appointed unto men once to die, but after this the judgment" (9:27). Not a few will assert that the sentence in the first part of the verse exhausts any wrath due to them for their sinful manner of life. They maintain that they will die and that is the end of the matter. The Scriptures, however, confirm over and over again that the latter half of the verse is an unalterable fact, "but after this the judgment". Here to the Romans Paul makes plain that this judgment will be revealed in the day of wrath when man's day of probation is over. That judgment will be righteous. It will not be a display of vindictiveness on God's part because His goodness was despised and rejected.

It is not a sudden outburst of anger. It is the revelation of God's righteousness, bringing to bear upon man all the wrath that he treasured up against himself during his rebellious term on earth. He was not created for that. He was given the necessary faculties and resources to represent God in the world, but he fell. Despite the many overtures of God to bring him back he has gone his own way and not even the greatest plan of all, the gospel of the grace of God, has succeeded in turning the tide of departure. The downward spiral continues and inexcusable man moves relentlessly towards the day of reckoning. The judgment that is coming offers no mercy. At that assize there is no room for repentance. As far as man is concerned, the die is cast. His hardness is an obdurate contempt of the goodness of God, an expression of his obstinate impenitent heart.

6 This verse relates to the first five verses of the chapter and introduces the theme of the five verses which follow. It states a timeless truth, one which the Jews knew well from OT Scriptures. The psalmist stated it (Ps 62:12) and Solomon incorporated it in his wise sayings (Prov 24:12). In the psalm, David considers the loving-kindness and mercy of the Lord; He would reward every man according to his works. Solomon in his observations on life in Prov 24 acknowledges the rewards of the next life for some, but remorse for others. In the ministry of the Lord regarding the challenge of discipleship, He referred to the fact that He would render to every man according to his work. Any sacrifice made to take up the cross would be rewarded by Him when He comes as the Son of man in the glory of the Father (Matt 16:27). In this Scripture the deity of the Lord is incidentally attested; He is on equality with the Father; it is He who rewards.

After stating that the impenitent treasure up wrath against themselves, which will have to be faced in the day of wrath, Paul introduces the thought that the deeds (or works, RV) will meet with a response from God exactly corresponding to the character of the deeds accumulated throughout life. There is no escaping this fact. The apostle makes no attempt to soften its implications. It is inevitable. At one session or another in the future, there will be a rendering to every man according to his deeds. This intimation casts its influence forward to the next five verses in which the apostle deliberates on further aspects of the responsibilities of Jews and Gentiles to respond to the goodness of God which leads to repentance.

In this verse, however, the reference to "every man" intimates that there will be no exceptions. There will be no regard of social or religious standing. The privileged and the under-privileged are all embraced and will appear before God to answer for their unrighteous deeds.

7 Difficulties have been experienced by many when considering vv.7-11 of this chapter. The apostle, however, is not asserting that eternal life is obtained by good works or by any means other than what is stated in 1:17 and elsewhere in Holy Scripture, that is, on the principle of faith, "the just shall live by faith". Here, in keeping with what has been asserted about the guilt of mankind, Paul is stating that continuance in well-doing is what God expects of man in every age. He is not discussing in these verses how a person might achieve that end; he is setting forth what God is looking for from all men, whether they be Jew or Gentile and the blessing that would ensue. It would be quite contrary to what is revealed in Scripture if it were concluded from what is written here that eternal blessing resulted from what is generally perceived as doing good.

In this verse Paul continues the thought of appearing before the bar of God. He anticipates a contention that to meet the requirements of God, patient continuance in well-doing may be pleaded as evidence of following after what is good and acceptable to God. The word even allows that the continuance is in the face of adversity and opposition. In addition, there may be a diligent seeking after glory, honour and immortality, all most commendable desires. Nevertheless, however admirable these yearnings may be, man's best efforts do not take him even up to what God expects from mankind, far less beyond into the realm of merit.

It is significant that Paul's argument does not make mention of motive. The hidden force which draws men on is not brought out. The incident of the rich young ruler's interview with the Lord illustrates the point. He asked the question, "What shall I do that I may inherit eternal life?" After the Lord had quoted the second half of the decalogue to him, he replied, "Master, all these have I observed from my youth" (Mark 10:20). He was not challenged by the two commandments on which hang all the law and the prophets, "Thou shalt love the Lord thy God with all thine heart, and with all thy soul" (Deut 6:5), and, "thou shalt love thy neighbour as thyself" (Lev 19:18). The high standards of his life were not subjected to those tests. His great possessions kept him from passing even the lesser test. The force of Paul's argument at this point in the epistle is not an evaluation of the virtuous thoughts and deeds listed, but a dismissal of any works of the flesh, however good, as having any claim on God for eternal life. Later, he will expound in detail how eternal life can be obtained, and will show that the only power for patient continuance is faith. Although patient continuance in well-doing is not the means of obtaining eternal life, it has characterised those in all ages who, through faith, bore the stamp of God's approval. It was what God looked for in His saints and there were those who manifested it, despite the difficulties of the days in which they lived.

The writer to the Hebrews has listed examples of men and women who lived their lives in patient well-doing. Starting with Abel, he highlights what marked him out: by faith he "offered unto God a more excellent sacrifice than Cain, by which he obtained witness that he was righteous, God testifying of his gifts". Another antediluvian follows in the divine record, "By faith Enoch was translated…and was not found, because God had translated him: for before his translation he had this testimony, that he pleased God". And so the writer, guided by the Spirit, lists the worthies of the past, noting against each what may be described as "well-doing", concluding with a divine assessment, "of whom the world was not worthy".

Those who have been faithful to their calling down the years, who by faith sought for "glory and honour and immortality" and who continued patiently in well-doing, will have as their reward eternal life. They may not have realised their hopes in life but they laboured "that they might obtain a better resurrection" (Heb 11:35).

8 By way of contrast with what is outlined in v.7, the base things of man are declared in this verse. There is no difficulty in accepting that men who have thrown off all restraint can descend to these levels of wickedness. They are said to be "contentious" ("factious", RV), that is, they rebel against anything which savours of restriction from the divine side. They have a quarrel with God and therefore reject the truth as it is revealed to them in different ways. In the world there is no lack of appeals to conscience but the desire to obey unrighteousness takes precedence. Sin has become habitual and its power drives men on to do what is knowingly wrong.

The terms "indignation and wrath" are indications of how the righteous God is affected by evil. Although many hope that a merciful God will excuse them in the end, these two words show how He is moved. It is a slight upon the character of God to suggest the He is oblivious to what is going on in the world which He created for His own pleasure and glory. His laws are violated and His character maligned. His dignity and majesty are of no account. It is no surprise therefore to read of His indignation and His wrath. It has found expression in manifestations of His displeasure in all ages, but the awesome fact is that its final display has yet to take place.

There are many examples in the Scriptures of "them that are contentious". As man's history opens, Abel is commended for his faith, an example of patient well-doing. Cain, however, leaves his mark in another way. Of him, and others like him, Jude records, "Woe unto them! for they have gone in the way of Cain". He it was who heard the words of the Lord, "Why art thou wroth? and why is thy countenance fallen? If thou doest well, shalt thou not be accepted? and if thou doest not well, sin lieth at the door" (Gen 4:6-7). But envy of his brother's well-doing overtook him and Abel's murder resulted. In answer to the Lord's question, "Where is Abel thy brother?" he replied, "Am I my brother's keeper?" thereby showing his contentiousness. He was a rebel, one who obeyed not the truth, but obeyed unrighteousness. All those who have gone in the way of Cain will have their just deserts when they appear at the bar of God.

Whether in antediluvian days, patriarchal days, the years of the wanderings of the children of Israel, the times of the kings or in the apostolic era, the pattern has been the same. Cain, Nimrod, Esau, Korah, Ahab, Alexander the coppersmith and many more have shown themselves to be rebels against the authority of

God. They are classed by Paul as "contentious", those who have resisted the will and the ways of God, who have not obeyed the truth.

9 The universality of the punishment of evil-doers is settled in the expression, "upon every soul of man". Any hope that the Jew had of favoured treatment is dismissed. Paul states, "of the Jew first and also of the Gentiles". It is not possible that anyone will escape the tribulation and the anguish. The choice of words to describe this has great force. "Tribulation" (*thlipsis*, "pressure", "compression") signifies the intensity of the suffering. "Anguish" (*stenochōria*, "a narrow place", by metonymy "distress", "straits", "anguish") denotes a condition from which it is impossible to escape. This, states Paul, is the lot of every soul of man that does evil, that practises sin habitually.

The Jew may consider that he has not offended the majesty of God and may feel that he can denounce the Gentiles as the real offenders. This, however, will not stand. The sentence is that the Jew is first. He is the greater offender. He is the one who has the law, the privileges and the greater light and it is he therefore who will receive the greater condemnation. His privileges aggravate his culpability since he has treated what he received from God with disdain. If he should protest against the severity of the charges, the question must then be asked, why was he never broken by the kindness and goodness of God and why was he never humbled by the mercy extended to him? The answer must lie mainly in the sin of pride which considers that God is under some kind of obligation to the Jew and being of that race is an automatic title to His favour. The hereditary advantages which the Jew claimed to have are dismissed in Paul's reasoning. Sins committed by the Jews are no less odious than those committed by Gentiles.

10 The apostle now introduces a contrast to what he has stated in the preceding verse. If it were possible for mankind to meet the standards of God by working that which is good, the joyous conditions listed here would apply. No one has been found throughout man's history who has come up to God's requirements. If even one had, then the plan of God for man's redemption would have been unnecessary. The sentence of Scripture, however, silences all speculation by a clear statement, "…there is none that doeth good, no, not one" (3:12).

The thrust of Paul's argument considers the situation (it may be hypothetical) where working that which is good, be it by Jew or Gentile, brings in its train a blessed reward. The "glory" which he mentions looks forward to a state of blessedness. Where God dwells and where sin never enters is a sphere of bliss beyond the dreams of man who has known only conditions on earth where sin and its consequences are ever present. Likewise "honour" suggests what is associated with God and what is His due, but what He will share with those who will inherit the kingdom. "Peace" is the climax, a condition of joy and tranquillity where no aggravation of any kind exists. Once again Paul remarks that all of this is to the Jew first and then to the Gentiles. If the Jew was first in condemnation because of his privileges, he is now seen to be first in reward if he walked according to the light he had. Sadly, not even the Jew has attained to it, as the Scripture states, "…we have proved both Jews and Gentiles, that they are all under sin" (3:9).

The situation need not be understood as hypothetical if it be allowed that those who persist in the patient continuance of well-doing, who seek for glory and honour, do so by faith; they indeed will receive glory and honour and peace. Since there is a well-established history of the Jews in Holy Scripture, the faithful acts of many in past dispensations are fully documented. The faithful who are not ashamed are included in the embracive statement of Heb 11:33-39 and they will receive their reward. The history of the Gentiles, however, is not covered in the same way. Their righteous acts and deeds of well-doing are known to God. It is encouraging therefore to note that Paul did not forget them. Rewards will be to every man that worketh good, to the Jew first and also to the Gentile.

11 Having made an allusion to the OT at v.6, that God will render to every man according to his deeds, Paul makes another one in this verse to show that there is no partiality with God. If in the future there will be righteous judgment upon all, although not necessarily dispensed at the same time, there is an indisputable feature about it, "there is no respect of persons with God".

The allusion here is undoubtedly to Deut 10:17, supported probably by 2 Chron 19:7. This is not the only occasion that Paul will cull this principle from the OT. He will do it again in his epistles to the Ephesians and Colossians in connection with what is expected from masters and servants. All need to be reminded that there is no partiality with God. Men in high estate do not command a more privileged position before God than others who are lower on the social scale. To be true to His character God must act righteously and judge everyone according to the same rule.

Here in Rom 2 Paul proves that Jew and Gentile fell far short of what law, or conscience without law, showed was right according to God's standards. Jew and Gentile were without excuse. Even if the Jew argued that according to Exod 15:26 "diligent hearkening" was more important than "doing", such sophistry was dismissed in the sweeping statement, "For not the hearers of the law are just before God, but the doers of the law shall be justified" (v.13). There was no escape from the inevitable, the day of wrath was coming and at the assizes there would be no partiality shown. There would be no respect of persons in that solemn time of judgment.

When Moses revealed to the children of Israel that God "regardeth not persons, nor taketh rewards", he was reminding them that they should not consider themselves to be the sole objects of God's care. The law clearly stated that God loved the stranger and that provision was to be made for all such. In this context Moses made it clear that God was not bound to one nation, that there was no respect of persons with Him. Similarly, Jehoshaphat's advice to the judges of

Israel at a later date intimated the same warning. God did not accept bribes; He could not be bought. There was no respect of persons with Him. In Paul's argument the same principle applied. Jews could not look for special favours just because they were Jews. There were no sides with God.

Notes

3 *Logizē* ("reckonest thou") is emphatic. Paul seems to question man's powers of reasoning, by asking, "Do you really consider that you will escape?" or, as v.4 begins, "despisest thou?". These are the two points of issue.

4 "Goodness" *(chrēstotēs)* is active beneficence in spite of ingratitude. Trench says that this is a grace which is not on the countenance only but pervades and penetrates the whole nature, mellowing there all that would have been harsh and austere.

Barclay maintains that "forbearance" *(anochē)* is the Greek word for a truce, a chance to be grasped at a given time, a cessation of hostility that has a time limit.

"Longsuffering" *(makrothumia)* expresses patience in respect of persons. The synonym *hupomonē* is more patience in respect of things or events. While both of these graces are ascribed to the saints, only *makrothumia* is an attribute of God. There may be a resistance to God in men but there can no resistance to God from things.

6 In connection with the universality of judgment and the Lord's involvement in it, see Ps 110:5,6.

7 "Immortality" *(aphtharsin)* is rendered by JND as "incorruptibility". Since it refers to the believer's body in the future, this is the preferred reading.

The "seeking" in this verse is in contrast to the "treasuring up" of v.5.

"Eternal life" here not only denotes endless existence, but suggests quality of life also.

"Patient endurance *(hupomonē)*. *Hupomonē* is one of the great words of the NT. Often referred to as conquering patience, the ability to deal triumphantly with anything that life can bring.

8,9 "Contentious" *(eritheias)* the RV renders this "factious". It implies a captious, disobedient disposition. The thought of strife is also in it.

"Do not obey" *(apeitheo)* means, to be uncompliant, to refuse belief and obedience, to refuse to be persuaded. Wuest renders, "those who out of a factious spirit are both also non-persuasible with respect to the truth and persuasible with respect to unrighteousness, wrath and anger".

11 It would certainly amount to respect of persons if God showed favour to the Jews, particularly in the light of the argument that there is no difference, "for all have sinned and come short of the glory of God" (3:23).

In this section, Newell makes interesting comments on the judgment of God. He suggests that Paul's view is that the judgment will be according to seven principles. These Newell notes as follows:

1. God's judgment is according to truth (v.2)
2. According to guilt (v.5)
3. According to works (v.6)
4. Without respect of persons (v.11)
5. According to performance, not knowledge (v.13)
6. God's judgment reaches the secrets of the heart (v.16)
7. According to reality, not religious profession (vv.17-29)

(b) *The impartiality of the Judge and His judgment (vv.12-24)*

v.12 "For as many as have sinned without law shall also perish without law: and as many as have sinned in the law shall be judged by the law;
v.13 (For not the hearers of the law are just before God, but the doers of the law shall be justified.
v.14 For when the Gentiles, which have not the law, do by nature the things contained in the law, these, having not the law, are a law unto themselves:
v.15 Which shew the work of the law written in their hearts, their conscience also bearing witness, and their thoughts the mean while accusing or else excusing one another;)
v.16 In the day when God shall judge the secrets of men by Jesus Christ according to my gospel.
v.17 Behold, thou art called a Jew, and restest in the law, and makest thy boast of God,
v.18 And knowest his will, and approvest the things that are more excellent, being instructed out of the law;
v.19 And art confident that thou thyself art a guide of the blind, a light of them which are in darkness,
v.20 An instructor of the foolish, a teacher of babes, which hast the form of knowledge and of the truth in the law.
v.21 Thou therefore which teachest another, teachest thou not thyself? thou that preachest a man should not steal, dost thou steal?
v.22 Thou that sayest a man should not commit adultery, dost thou commit adultery? thou that abhorrest idols, dost thou commit sacrilege?
v.23 Thou that makest thy boast of the law, through breaking the law dishonourest thou God?
v.24 For the name of God is blasphemed among the Gentiles through you, as it is written."

12 Having stated categorically that there is no respect of persons with God, the apostle moves on to apply this to the judgment which Jew and Gentile must face. It will be totally impartial; there will be no argument against it. No allegations will be sustained that either Jew or Gentile has been treated unfairly or that one or the other has been placed at a disadvantage, the one because of lack of light, or the other because of having too great a burden to bear in striving with the law.

The Gentiles are considered under the expression, "For as many as have sinned without law". They did have a law, however, the law of conscience. In every person there is a monitor, an awareness of right and wrong, a voice which speaks in the inner man and either commends or condemns actions performed. Conscience is a legacy from the fall of man in the garden of Eden. It was after Adam sinned that conscience came into play. From that time until the flood, a dispensation or age of conscience prevailed and this was the monitor that spoke to man. It did not control him, however, as it was an age of violence and corruption which came to an end in the great deluge in Noah's day.

Here Paul establishes that all who have sinned who did not have some revelation from God, such as the law of Moses, will still perish. They had the witness of creation and the voice of conscience; one testified of the existence of the Creator and the other constantly commended or condemned. The sentence is that those who are found guilty at the bar of God will perish (*apollumi*, "to bring to nought", "to render void"). It is not annihilation, it is the loss of well-being. Extinction is not contemplated in the word of God.

The second class considered are those who have sinned in the law, or, under law (RV). Here Paul refers to the Jew to whom was given the law at Sinai. The Jew was placed under an obligation to keep the law, which the people promised to observe, saying, "All that the Lord has spoken we will do" (Exod 19:8). But as history proved, they chose sin. The sentence therefore is that those who have sinned in law shall be judged by law. The greater the privilege the more severe will be the condemnation. As for the Judge He will be totally impartial.

13 The AV introduces a parenthesis from v.13 to v.15, suggesting that the teaching of v.12 is taken up at v.16. Although it makes good sense to link v.16 with the end of v.12, there is no despite done to the passage if the flow is continued through the three verses. It is acknowledged, however, that many hold to the parenthesis; some even suggest that it begins at v.11, but as this would create a parenthesis within a parenthesis, it is very doubtful whether the apostle intended the passage to be understood that way.

The situation relating to future judgment is clearly set out in v.12. The latter half of the verse states that as many as have sinned in law shall be judged by law. To this the Jews would object. Since God chose them as His people and gave them the law, they must hold a special place in His favour. Against such a claim the apostle lays down a principle which applies to all laws, "for not the hearers of the law are just before God, but the doers of the law shall be justified". The law was not given to be contemplated or discussed; it was given to be obeyed. The children of Israel understood this when it was given, saying, "All that the Lord hath spoken we will do" (Exod 19:8). Since the Jews did not fulfil this promise they are condemned. They have demeaned the One who gave the law by hearing it, but refusing to practise what it stated. The Jewish mind considered that hearkening to the law was more important than doing it, basing this idea on Exod 15:26. Such a view is firmly repudiated by the apostle in this verse; only the doers of the law shall be justified.

This is the first mention of the word "justified" in this epistle. It is one of the key words, and it should be noted that it occurs in various forms: "just", "justified", "justification", "righteous", "righteousness" are all from the same root and the exact meaning in each case is determined by the context. Here the meaning of "justified" is that the law of God can bring no charge against the individual. Mere hearers of the law will never be justified before God in this legal sense; only doers of the law will be declared righteous. At this point the apostle is not explaining how it is possible for sinners to be justified before God; he will come to that. As the context makes plain, he is stating that it is essential, if justification under the law is to be found, that those who are under law meet all its demands. The principle is made clear in Lev 18:5, "…which if a man *do*, he shall live in them, I am the Lord".

14 The Gentiles are now considered. In v.12 the principle was set out, "For as many as have sinned without law, shall also perish without law". With this statement the Jew could have no complaint: Gentiles would have no advantage. Although Gentiles had no revelation from God they were still responsible to act righteously according to their inward sense of moral duty. The fact that they have not done this is sufficient to establish the guilt of the Gentiles and the righteousness of God in bringing them to justice. The apostle reasons that when the Gentiles, who do not have divine precepts, follow the principles of their moral conscience and do the things which the law requires, these principles become a law to themselves and to each other. The fact that they do things that are right is a proof that there is within them, in some measure, an intuitive sense of the difference between right and wrong which dictates to them. If the Jew considered this with an unbiased mind, he would be bound to see that the Gentile with no written law, doing what the law required, was less culpable than the Jew who had the written law in his possession yet did not comply with its demands.

The principle is correct which states that where there is no law there is no transgression. It is not true, however, to maintain that where no law exists there is no sin. If the Gentiles, by following their moral conscience, do the things that the law requires, the converse is also true: when they act contrary to the voice of nature within they sin. There is a moral element in the constitution of man.

That many Gentiles "do by nature the things contained in the law" cannot be denied. In every age there have been those who did not commit adultery; who did not kill, and who did not bear false witness against their neighbours. Indeed, in many nations, some even the most pagan, honour for father and mother is sacrosanct. To claim, however, that this has been true of Gentiles of every nation is too general. That would be an overstatement of the case and it would contradict the teaching of the apostle in ch.1. Again, it must be acknowledged that of those who did, few if any maintained these standards out of any respect for God, indeed it is doubtful if God featured in their thinking. Nor is it taught here by the apostle that when they did what was right it was acceptable to God in the sense that it was credited to them for righteousness. It merely proved that there was a law written in their hearts which accused them when they did things contrary to what they knew instinctively was right and proper.

15 This verse does not say that the *letter* of the law is written in the hearts of the Gentiles. That would not be true since the law as such was not yet given to them. What the apostle asserts is that when the Gentiles do by nature the things contained in the law, they demonstrate that the *work* of the law is written in their hearts, that is, what the law expected of them by way of conduct. It may also include the sense of guilt which results when conscience is violated, and a dread of some kind of retribution.

The expression "written in their hearts" is possibly an allusion to the fact that the law was written on tables of stone by the finger of God. It demonstrates that before the law was given to the children of Israel, the Creator had already written indelibly in the hearts of men what He expected from them as moral beings. To this the apostle adds another factor, "their conscience also bearing witness", which, although another monitor, is not the same as "written in their hearts". Conscience is the knowledge of good and evil. If what is done is right, conscience commends it. If what is done is wrong, conscience condemns it. It bears witness either to accuse or to excuse. Conscience, however, is not a directing influence which will always remain static. Paul wrote to Timothy and warned him about those whose consciences were seared through as with a hot iron. Their consciences had become hardened through constant violations and they were therefore past feeling. Here the apostle extends the accusing and the excusing to apply to one another. Amongst themselves men recognise what is wrong in the conduct of their fellows and pass judgment. In the same way, but possibly to a lesser degree, they also recognise what is commendable in others and so the response of conscience is to excuse.

It is significant that the apostle notes that the accusing and the excusing is in their thoughts (*logismos*, "a computation", "act of computing", "reasoning"; only here; 2 Cor 10:5 in NT). The idea seems to be that the actions of others are the subject of reasonings before judgment is passed, one way or another – it is not done lightly.

16 If the parenthesis marked out in the AV is accepted then the reference to judgment day of this verse follows the closing words of v.12. This would read that those who have sinned in the law will be judged by the law in the day when God shall judge the secrets of men by Jesus Christ. If, however, the parenthesis is ignored then the conscience will be the rule by which God shall judge the secrets of men. This view seems to put the Jew into the background since the apostle's argument in vv.13-15 concentrates on the Gentile. Taking the passage with the interruption, there is little doubt that Jew and Gentile will appear before the bar of God when sinners have to face Him in judgment.

In the law courts of the world those who are in the dock are tried on the basis of the evidence led against them. The secrets of the accused are beyond the judge. What is in the heart or mind and what is not brought out in evidence is hidden from the court. This will not be the case in the judgment stated here. The secrets of men will be revealed. God will not only take into account what is external but He will deal with what has been concealed. It is essential, however, that God's judgment should be exact, and to be that, what is open and what is concealed must come under review for sentence.

The judgment will be by Jesus Christ. The One who was rejected by men when He was here in grace will take on the role of judge, since all judgment has been committed into His hands. This was intimated by Paul when he preached at Athens, "God hath appointed a day, in the which he will judge the world in righteousness by that man whom he hath ordained" (Acts 17:31). The message the apostle preached on that occasion is an example of what he states here: that Jesus Christ will judge according to his gospel. Although the gospel announced salvation, it also intimated the fate of those who reject the Saviour, the One who is the central theme of its message.

He does not elaborate on the time when this judgment will take place. It is obvious from the context that he is not thinking of believers, although he taught the Corinthians that believers will have a session when their secrets will be manifested (1 Cor 4:5). This will be at the judgment seat of Christ. In this verse the apostle is referring to the particular time when unbelievers will have their secrets judged. The judgment of sinners will take place at the end of the millennium and at the great white throne. The description of this most solemn assize is given in Rev 20:11-15, and is referred to by the apostle Peter as "the day of judgment and perdition of ungodly men" (2 Pet 3:7).

Paul states that God will judge the secrets of men by Jesus Christ. The judgment will fit the crime and there will be no right of appeal. The books will be opened and the dead, small and great, will be judged out of the books according to their works. Another book, which is the Lamb's book of life, will also be opened. This will merely confirm that the names of those who appear at the great white throne are not written therein. It is a most solemn scene. As those who appear there are consigned to an eternal doom, called in Scripture "the second death", they will have no excuse and therefore no thought of appeal for mercy. The sad fact is that there is no need for any to appear at the great white throne. Man is well aware that there are two destinies, heaven or hell. He can have no complaint therefore, if by choosing to ignore or reject the overtures of God in mercy, he finds himself separated from God for all eternity.

17 The opening words of the verse are given in the RV, "But if thou bearest the name of a Jew". There is good manuscript authority for "But if", instead of "Behold" as in the AV. The change alters the emphasis and increases the sense of responsibility of a bearer of that name. Although the name "Jew" does not appear in the LXX, it is mentioned in 2 Kings 16, Jer 32 and some of the later books. It seems that it was attached to the captives from Judea while they were in Babylon and gradually it became a general name for Hebrews thereafter. Paul was not ashamed of the name, claiming on one occasion that he was a Jew of Tarsus (Acts 21:39). When it suited his purpose, however, he could claim to be a Hebrew of the Hebrews (Phil 3:5), and on another occasion, "an Israelite of the seed of Abraham" (Rom 11:1). The Jews did not seem to object to being named as such; it marked them out from the Gentiles as being different and this suited their national pride.

Here Paul states that the Jews rested in the law. No other nation had a law such as was given to them. Moses declared that it would be the envy of others. He exhorted the children of Israel, "Behold I have taught you statutes and judgments...keep therefore and do them; for this is your wisdom and your understanding in the sight of the nations, which shall surely hear these statutes, and say, Surely this great nation is a wise and understanding people" (Deut 4:5,6). The Jews were well aware that they were the custodians of statutes and judgments from God and that they did not need to borrow or compile another code of practice from the philosophies of the Gentile nations. They were proud of what they had and they could afford to rest in it. Therein lay the danger. Their resting in the possession of the law did not automatically mean that they obeyed its precepts.

That they made their boast of God is an evidence of their relationship with Him. Moses had said, "What nation is there so great, who hath God so nigh unto them?" (Deut 4:7). The Jews had the true God, the Gentiles had the false gods. The Jews boasted of God, but the danger was in thinking that God was beholden to them. He was under no obligation to respond to them to the exclusion of all others.

18 It seems clear that the apostle here means that the Jews knew from their knowledge of the Scriptures what God expected from them. He is not asserting that the Jews knew what the will of God was in a practical sense as something in the light of which they walked day by day. In addition, in his approval of things which differ (or, more excellent, AV), the Jew revelled in the fact that he had a better economy, better priestly services, better temple worship, better religious feasts and much more, all of which was superior to anything the Gentiles possessed. The problem with the Jew was that he must have known also that God disapproved of his abuse of the things which were more excellent. The many privileges of the Jewish people should have resulted in pointing the nations to the God who had so richly blessed them, but despite their boasting and their revelling in what they had, their manner of life did not draw the Gentiles to the true God.

That the Jews were instructed out of the law was not in doubt. Indeed the scribes and the Pharisees had so finely honed the teaching of the law to suit themselves that they came under the censure of the Lord during His public ministry. They championed different schools of religious learning, holding to teachers whose views on certain parts of the law were substantially at variance. They pressed insignificant details at the expense of the weightier matters which affected the lives of the ordinary people. They could argue about the letter of the law but the spirit of it was missing. They failed to grasp the mind of the Lord in the daily issues of life and as a result their application of the law to themselves and others was seriously flawed.

19 The outcome of the Jew's boasting about who he was by birth, what he possessed in the law and other privileges, was a persuasion of absolute superiority. He had persuaded himself that the nations round about were so inferior in every respect that they needed to be taught. In itself this was not something which was foreign to the mind of God. In millennial times the law shall go forth "out of Zion" and all nations shall "flow unto" the mountain of the Lord's house (Isa 2:3). What was incongruous about the Jew's confidence was that for all his knowledge he was as guilty before God as the Gentiles. To set himself up as an instructor, a leader of the blind was utter presumption. After the Lord had branded scribes and Pharisees as hypocrites on one occasion, He told His disciples "They be blind leaders of the blind. And if the blind lead the blind, both shall fall into the ditch" (Matt 15:14). As far as being an influence for good was concerned in a world of spiritual and moral darkness, the Jew was a total failure. Although conversant with the will of God, he disqualified himself from teaching others by reason of his wilful disregard of what was expected from him.

Isaiah prophesied in his day that the time was coming when those who walked in darkness would see a great light (Isa 9:2). Matthew records that after John Baptist was cast into prison, the Lord left Nazareth and dwelt in Capernaum that it might be fulfilled which was spoken by Esaias the prophet, "The people which sat in darkness saw a great light" (Matt 4:14,16). And so it turned out to be; many who sat and walked in darkness during the short period of the Lord's public ministry saw the great light and were delivered from the power of darkness by His grace and power. The Jew should have been engaged in this ministry. He persuaded himself that he was a light to them that were in darkness, but the true position was that he was no more in the light than those he wanted to lead.

20 The persuasion of the Jew did not restrict itself to being a guide of the blind; this verse asserts that he also considered himself to be "an instructor of the foolish, a teacher of babes". The RV translates "instructor" (*paideutēs*) as "corrector". The only other occurrence of the word in this form is Heb 12:9 where the AV renders, "Furthermore we have had fathers of our flesh which *corrected* us". The young need those who will train them, hence the many amongst the Jews who performed that task. Here Paul is not considering the Jewish boys but those who were lacking in knowledge, those who were immature when compared with the attainments of the Jew in the law. The Jewish view according to Paul's argument here was that any who were not Jews need to be corrected and the Jew saw himself as ideally suited to be the corrector.

The "babes" mentioned are obviously proselytes. This was the way the Jews considered those who came to the Jewish faith, they were babes, newly-born ones. When the proselyte was baptised the part of his life before baptism was wiped out. What Paul is considering here is that the Jew relied on his knowledge of the law and even boasted in it. His way of life proved that it was at best a form of things. Although he attached great importance to his attainments and persuaded himself that he was capable of leading and teaching others, the truth was that his condition belied his claims. He was no better than those he wanted to correct. Before God he was as guilty as the Gentiles, and therefore in no position to correct those who were religiously unenlightened or to teach those who had any thoughts of establishing links with the Jewish faith.

21 In v.17 the RV introduced a change from "Behold" (AV) to "But if". This verse follows on from that with, "Thou therefore", signifying that those who were proud to bear the name of a Jew were being challenged to respond to what was expected of one who was named or styled in this way. The apostle here is unmasking the Jew, who was hiding behind a facade of practical holiness, while the real position was one of hypocrisy. During the public ministry of the Lord He branded scribes and Pharisees as hypocrites on several occasions, and in the sermon on the mount He cautioned His hearers on three occasions against the dangers of hypocrisy (Matt 6:2,5,16). Here the solemn charge is levelled as an interrogation. The Jews proudly took the position of being teachers of others, but they did not apply the teaching to themselves. It was in effect, another way of stating the well-known saying; "Do as I say, but do not do as I do". There is also the possibility, however, that they did not teach themselves and therefore, being untaught, were ignorant of what the law contained.

The charge against another that he should not steal would certainly lose its force if the person making the accusation was guilty of the same crime. Paul seemed to know that thieving in his day was prevalent. It is not a general charge against the nation collectively but against individuals among whom thieving was rife. It is unlikely that the apostle would have implied such a gross evil if he had not been in a position to prove that it existed regardless of status in the nation. Their accusation against others was not something done in a corner, it was preached (*kērussō*, "to announce openly", "to proclaim as a herald"). The word also implies that the one who announced openly that a person should not steal was acting on higher authority, that is, he had a message from God in this respect. The fact that the preacher was also guilty of stealing condemned him before God and before others who were aware of the hypocrisy of the situation.

22 As Paul continues his denouncement of the Jew he introduces another of the ten commandments. Having posed the question "Dost thou steal?" he now makes another interrogatory charge, "Dost thou commit adultery?" Perhaps he raised these two serious breaches of the law because they were prevalent amongst the Jews. If this had not been the case, his denouncement would have been rejected and his case against the Jew seriously flawed. Adultery was a capital crime according to the law of Moses. It stated, "the adulterer and the adulteress shall surely be put to death" (Lev 20:10). The Jew was not ignorant of this, and indeed as posed by the apostle, he was ready to condemn others for committing such a grievous sin. While there may be some who would dismiss the charge as hypothetical, the probability of wide-spread guilt cannot be dismissed lightly. Paul must have been sure of his ground before making such a serious allegation against his fellow-countrymen.

Idolatry was always a great temptation as far as the Jew was concerned. Such was the danger of becoming occupied with idols, prohibition was introduced at the beginning of the commandments. "And God spake all these words, saying...Thou shalt have no other gods before me. Thou shalt not make unto thee any graven image...Thou shalt not bow down thyself to them, nor serve them: for I the Lord thy God am a jealous God" (Exod 20:1,3-5). Here, however, Paul is not denouncing the Jew for being an idol-worshipper; he acknowledges that idols were abhorred (*bdelussomai*, "to detest", "to loathe"). The apostle's accusation concerned sacrilege (*hierosuleō*, "to despoil temples"). What was on Paul's mind in this connection is not clear. Some consider that he was referring to making the temple a house of merchandise (see John 2:16); others to robbing God (see Mal 3:8), and yet others to despoiling heathen temples when occasion arose to do so. The law forbade making any gain from the spoiling of heathen temples. Graven images, and even the gold and silver which was on them, had to be burned lest the people were ensnared (Deut 7:25). It may be that Paul knew that the appropriation of things from heathen temples was common practice and it was to this he was referring. The thrust of the accusation of this verse would seem to be an acknowledgment of a loathing of idols but a readiness to profit from trading in their sale, a practice roundly condemned by Moses. The end result was much the same as physically despoiling the heathen temples.

23 The Jews had several distinctive features which distinguished them from the Gentiles. The main one was the possession of the law and in this they gloried. Over generations they had added to it and without doubt had been guilty of breaking it. Nevertheless, regardless of knowingly breaching the law's requirements, they maintained their boasting that they were custodians of a code of practice given to the nation by God.

The charge made against the Jew by Paul was that through the transgression of the law God was dishonoured. This was not only because of overstepping the mark before God, but by bringing reproach on His name. The failure of the Jew to conform his life to the requirements of the law caused the Gentiles to blaspheme. They not only blamed the Jew for his unscrupulous and sinful ways, but they directed their reproach at God whom the Jew maintained favoured the Jewish nation above all else. The sad situation described here is that the blame for the Jew's shortcomings was levelled at God. In the mind of the Gentile the Jew and his God were inseparably linked. An example of this is seen in the proclamation of Cyrus, "Who is there among you of all his people? his god be with him, and let him go up to Jerusalem, which is in Judah, and build the house of the Lord God of Israel, (he is the God)" (Ezra 1:3). Unfortunately other Gentiles did not see the situation in the same way as Cyrus saw it, and they made the God of the Jews the object of their scorn.

24 This verse leads on from the charge raised in v.23, "Through breaking the law dishonourest thou God?" The expression "as it is written" undoubtedly refers to a situation in the OT where the name of God had been blasphemed among the Gentiles because of the ungodly behaviour of the Jew, as the Scriptures are called upon to bear witness to the veracity of Paul's accusation. There are two passages in the OT which were probably on the apostle's mind. The words of v.24 are the same as recorded in Isa 52:5 LXX, but the thought is more like the context of Ezek 36. Isaiah's ministry was directed against the Babylonians who oppressed the people and who blasphemed the name of God continually every day. Ezekiel, however, preached that the land had been left desolate in his day because of the profanity of the people. Their manner of life had caused the nations to blaspheme the name of God. They were a shame to the God who had chosen them out from amongst the nations and had given them every blessing.

Here Paul's condemnation of the Jews was not based on the distant past. The situation had not changed and in Paul's travels he could not have failed to observe that the name of God was still being blasphemed amongst the Gentiles because of the practices of the Jews. They had traded on God's goodness and they considered that they were above reproach. They were Jews by birth, but Paul's argument in the passage to meet this attitude was that it was not a matter of race but one of character. The Jews were no better than the Gentiles, despite the fact that they were the most privileged and highly-favoured people on the earth. Their knowledge of the law had not made the differences to their manner of living which would have obliged God to make them the head of the nations as He had planned. The fact that they were the tail and not the head was their own fault. They had not given evidence that they were fit to take the lead amongst the nations of the world.

Notes

12 In "for as many as without law sinned", since the aorist tense (*hēmarton*) is used, there is the suggestion of a looking back to the years of life when the sins were committed. Burton calls it a "collective historical aorist" (Denney).

15 "Which show" (*hoitines endeiknuntai*) may be equivalent to "inasmuch as they show".

The expression "written in their hearts", when contrasted with "written on tables of stone" is equal to "unwritten" (Denney).

20 The form (*tēn morphōsin*) Lightfoot calls "the rough sketch", the outline or framework; Robertson "the outline without the substance".

22 The verb "abhorrest" (*bdelussomenos*) had the meaning originally, "to turn away from a thing on account of the stench". See "abomination" (Matt 24:15).

"Dost thou rob temples?" (*hierosuleis*, from *hieron*, "temple:; *sulaō*, "to rob"). The town clerk (Acts 19:37) said that the Jews (Paul and his companions) were "not robbers of temples", proof that the charge was sometimes made against the Jews (Robertson).

23 Trench remarks upon "the mournfully numerous group of words" which express the different aspects of sin. It is according to Vincent *hamartia*, "the missing of the mark"; *parabasis*, "the overpassing of a line"; *parakoē,* "the disobedience to a voice"; *paraptōma,* "a falling when one should have stood"; *agnoēma,* "ignorance of what one should know"; *hēttēma,* "a diminishing of what should be rendered in full measure"; *anomia,* or, *paranomia,* "non-observance of law"; *plēmmeleia,* "discord". – Vincent.

(c) *Dependent on outward forms but devoid of inward reality (vv.25-29)*

v.25 "For circumcision verily profiteth, if thou keep the law: but if thou be a breaker of the law, thy circumcision is made uncircumcision.
v.26 Therefore if the uncircumcision keep the righteousness of the law, shall not his uncircumcision be counted for circumcision?
v.27 And shall not uncircumcision which is by nature, if it fulfil the law, judge thee, who by the letter and circumcision dost transgress the law?
v.28 For he is not a Jew, which is one outwardly; neither is that circumcision, which is outward in the flesh:
v.29 But he is a Jew, which is one inwardly; and circumcision is that of the heart, in the spirit, and not in the letter; whose praise is not of men, but of God."

25 The sign of circumcision was another mark by which the Jew differed from the Gentile. It was introduced as a sign of the covenant God made with Abraham (Gen 17:10-12), and confirmed in the law later with Moses (Lev 12:3). It was required of every Jewish male to be circumcised in the eighth day of life. The rite of circumcision was practised by the Jews as a distinguishing sign of the Jewish nation. It was not long, however, until circumcision became a mere formality, causing Moses to write, "Circumcise therefore the foreskin of your heart and be no more stiffnecked" (Deut 10:16). As the years passed, succeeding generations proved themselves to be no better, causing Jeremiah to write, "Circumcise yourselves to the Lord and take away the foreskins of your hearts, ye men of Judah and inhabitants of Jerusalem" (Jer 4:4). In apostolic times, while Jews held rigidly to the rite, they were no better than their forefathers, which is obviously the reason why Paul is so scathing in his denouncement here.

The Jew was proud to carry the name nationally. He took his stand on having privileges which were not in the possession of the Gentiles. One of these was the law given by God to the children of Israel. Although they had pledged themselves to honour it and obey it (Exod 24:3), in practice they transgressed its commandments. In truth, the standards of morality amongst the Jews were no higher, and indeed in some ways much lower than what were demonstrated by the pagans around them. Perhaps Paul is introducing a note of irony here when he states that circumcision became uncircumcision if practised by those who were breakers of the law. It does not go as far as saying that a Jew became to all intents and purposes a Gentile when the law was ignored, but the inference is that the Jew was no better than the Gentile and the outward sign of circumcision was a rite which meant nothing.

26 The apostle continues on the subject of circumcision. To the Jew the rite was another reason for his pride and complacency. The Gentile was referred to disparagingly as uncircumcised. The scorn with which the Jews viewed the Gentiles in this relation is seen in many passages of the Scriptures. The parents of Samson chided with him over his desire for the woman of Timnath, saying, "Is there never a woman among the daughters of thy brethren, or among all thy people, that thou goest to take a wife of the uncircumcised Philistines?" (Judges 14:3). This attitude was a common one. The danger, however, was that the sign became the main issue and not the fact that those who were marked by it were expected to be characterised by the same believing faith as Abraham, with whom the covenant was made originally.

Paul is not saying here that the uncircumcised Gentiles fulfil the righteousness of the law. His line of reasoning is hypothetical. He supposes that if a Gentile could meet the law's requirements then his uncircumcision would be counted as circumcision. The Gentile, although not marked out by the rite in which the Jew prided himself, would be on the same level of acceptance as the Jew. The apostle's argument is that whether a person is privileged or unprivileged, advantaged or disadvantaged, circumcised or uncircumcised, the crux of the whole matter is whether there was observance or violation of the law. For the Jew to pour scorn on the Gentile and refer to him scurrilously as uncircumcised, was a travesty if he failed to respond to what was required from him as one who was under an obligation to observe and to keep the commandments. At the bar of God the distinction between Jew and Gentile would not come into consideration if both failed to meet what was expected of them. As far as the views expressed in this section by Paul, the unbiased Jew was bound to see that the apostle's reasoning on uncircumcision being reckoned as circumcision was perfectly sustainable if the Gentiles did what the Jew failed to do.

27 Paul's argument in this verse contrasts circumcision and uncircumcision as representing the two classes of people on the earth. He envisages the uncircumcision, the Gentiles, those who do not bear in their flesh the mark of circumcision, fulfilling the righteous requirements of the law, being a condemnation of the circumcised Jew who had the written law but did not fulfil it. Indeed "by the letter and circumcision" they transgressed its precepts. In other words, by the use they made of the terms of the covenant and the rite which was its seal, they violated its most sacred meaning, and invalidated their claims to the blessing it promised to the devoted heart. The Jew who had the privileges and the greater light would be condemned by the Gentile who had none of the benefits conferred upon the Jew. In the public ministry of the Lord He taught that the men of Nineveh would rise in judgment on the generation of His day and condemn them because the Ninevites repented at the preaching of Jonah, and a greater than Jonah was there in grace. In the same way the queen of Sheba would rise up in judgment on the same generation because she came from the uttermost parts of the earth to hear the wisdom of Solomon and a greater than Solomon was there in their midst (Matt 12:41,42).

Although Paul's argument is hypothetical, there are many examples in the Scriptures of those, such as the Ninevites and the queen of Sheba, who, without the knowledge of the law, acted in a way that put to shame those who had its letter in their possession. In NT times, the case of Cornelius is another example of the uncircumcised manifesting features which were a condemnation of the ways of the circumcised. Of him it was stated that he was a devout man who feared God with all his house, gave much alms to the people and prayed to God alway (Acts 10:2). This did not go unnoticed in heaven. Although he came under the conclusion of Rom 3:21, "All have sinned and come short of the glory of God", in the mercy of God the gospel was preached to him and he believed its message. Without controversy therefore, the saying is true, "God will be no man's debtor".

28 This verse introduces a conclusion. The apostle is not using hypothetical examples here to establish his case against the Jews. The statement, "For he is not a Jew who is one outwardly" must be taken as proven. A Jew who prided himself in the name and who considered that being born a Jew gave him favour with heaven was grossly mistaken. Externals, such as circumcision, are meaningless unless accompanied by conformity to the law. The titles and signs which the Jew judged would avail with God, would prove to be valueless in the day of reckoning that was bound to come. If all that he could produce in that day was a sign or a name in support of his claim for acceptance, he would find himself rejected. As Paul makes clear, he is not a Jew whose only plea is externals. If that was all he had, he would be no better than the Gentile.

In Paul's list of personal credentials which he sets out in his epistle to the Philippians, the first one he mentions is that he was circumcised on the eighth day. He was, as some state it, "an eighth-day child". This, and his other attainments in Judaism, even that he was blameless touching the righteousness of the law, he counted loss for Christ (Phil 3:5-7). When therefore he denounced the Jews, he was condemning them for a position of strength. No one could accuse him of making assertions without having a full background knowledge and experience in Judaism. He had been in the very centre of the religious hierarchy. Indeed, before king Agrippa, he claimed that the Jews would testify "that after the most straitest sect of our religion I lived a Pharisee" (Acts 26:5). Clearly then, the case he had built up was to break the confidence the Jew had in his external signs and observances in order to prepare him for the gospel which was man's only hope for acceptance with God.

29 The conclusion of the apostle's argument is that he is not a Jew who is one outwardly, neither is circumcision of any value which is outward in the flesh. The true Jew, as far as God's standards are concerned, is one who is a Jew inwardly and not one who depended on the signs which were external. It was circumcision of the heart that mattered, not a legal claim that had as its basis the observance of a prescribed rite.

This assertion should not have been strange to the Jew. Moses made it perfectly clear to the children of Israel that God looked for something more than mere outward conformity. After he had given the people a rehearsal of God's way with them, he charged them saying, "Circumcise therefore the foreskin of your hearts, and be no more stiffnecked" (Deut 10:16). Later when he made known what God would do for Israel when they were brought into the land of promise he told them, "And the Lord thy God will circumcise thine heart and the heart of thy seed, to love the Lord thy God with all thy heart and with all thy soul, that thou mayest live" (Deut 30:6). Later still in the history of the nation, Jeremiah charged the people, "Circumcise yourselves to the Lord, and take away the foreskins of your heart, ye men of Judah and inhabitants of Jerusalem" (Jer 4:4). In Paul's day the position was just the same, a true Jew was one who was circumcised in heart and spirit and not in the letter, which here means the commandments which directed the Jews in the rite of circumcision.

The reference to the spirit signifies the inward depths from which would come the evidence of reality. It is a work on the soul which the Spirit of God would accomplish, and this would not manifest itself in mere external rites but in devotion for and consecration to the Lord (see Deut 30:6). The externals could be seen, reminders of the Lord's condemnation of the scribes and Pharisees, "They make broad their phylacteries, and enlarge the borders of their garments, and love the uppermost rooms at feasts, and the chief seats in the synagogues" (Matt 23:5,6). They sought the praise of men, but the true Jew was not influenced by that, his praise was of God and in that he rejoiced.

Notes

29 Heart circumcision expresses the contrast to circumcision in the flesh. This is what Paul seems to be expressing when he adds, "in the spirit and not in the letter".

Heart circumcision is not obtained without the work of the Spirit of God; the law in itself cannot effect it.

(d) *The objector – let God be true but every man a liar (3:1-8)*

> v.1 "What advantage then hath the Jew? or what profit is there of circumcision?
> v.2 Much every way: chiefly, because that unto them were committed the oracles of God.
> v.3 For what if some did not believe? shall their unbelief make the faith of God without effect?
> v.4 God forbid: yea, let God be true, but every man a liar; as it is written, That thou mightest be justified in thy sayings, and mightest overcome when thou art judged.
> v.5 But if our unrighteousness commend the righteousness of God, what shall we

v.6 say? Is God unrighteous who taketh vengeance? (I speak as a man)
v.6 God forbid: for then how shall God judge the world?
v.7 For if the truth of God hath more abounded through my lie unto his glory; why yet am I also judged as a sinner?
v.8 And not rather, (as we be slanderously reported, and as some affirm that we say,) Let us do evil, that good may come? whose damnation is just."

1 From a consideration of Paul's indictment of the Jew and the severity of his condemnation, it may well be thought that he has overstated his case. The Jews had the law, a code of practice given to them by God. No other nation was so highly privileged. That, however, was not an automatic exemption for divine judgment if they failed to keep it. The rite of circumcision, an outward seal of the covenant with Abraham and his descendants through Isaac, was only of value if it represented an inward conformity. Circumcision of the heart was the real test, not the mere sign in the flesh.

The opening words of the verse, *ti oun*, rendered by some, "What therefore", seem to imply an opportunity for any objectors to answer the apostle's charges. The imaginary objector is made to ask in v.1, "What advantage then hath the Jew? or what profit is there in circumcision?" The questions are very pertinent. If the apostle's indictment of the Jews in ch.2 is incontrovertible, it may well be asked, "What profit is there in being one of a chosen race?" If there is no advantage over and above the Gentiles, why be governed by law, or indeed, why be subjected to circumcision if the outward seal of the covenant does not give some advantage over the uncircumcised?

It seems clear from the questions which the apostle anticipates will surely be asked by a Jew, that the severity of his denouncements would need to be defended. To bring his fellow-countrymen down to the level of all other nations, even pagans and idolaters, placed Paul under an obligation to prove beyond any doubt that the position was exactly as he had portrayed. In fact, his argument had insisted that the Jew was more culpable. The privileges served only to increase the Jew's condemnation.

In addition, since Paul had already stated that he was ready to preach the gospel at Rome (1:15), it was essential that nothing should be raised that would be a stumbling-block to any who might hear the message. His reasoning must therefore be sound. He had to ensure that there were no flaws in his argument. The unbiased Jew must be made to face the facts as he had outlined them. This he proceeds to do.

2 The apostle now proceeds to answer the first question he has raised. If any should suggest that there is no advantage in being a Jew, he refuses to consider it. The hypothetical objection had no substance. His opening words of defence, "much every way", imply that there were many advantages. These he will list later on in the epistle (9:4,5), but at this juncture he judges that one will suffice to prove the point he has made.

Following his claim, "much every way", he states, "Chiefly (or, primarily), because that unto them were committed the oracles of God". It is possible that Paul was thinking of the well-known words of Moses, "And what nation is there so great, that hath statutes and judgments so righteous as all this law, which I set before you this day?" (Deut 4:8). Even in the time of Moses the challenge to the nation was clear; the children of Israel were highly-privileged in having the oracles of God committed to them. Here, however, the apostle is not saying that of all the advantages which the Jew had, this was the first in order of importance. What he is implying is that it was basic, and that having the oracles of God entrusted to them, the Jews had a code of conduct and a revelation from God about what He wanted men and women to know about Himself and about what brought pleasure, honour and glory to Him. The oracles of God were the communications of God. They were in fact the very words that He spoke and having that uniqueness they could be accepted in their entirety. The Jews were therefore the custodians of the communications of heaven. In a similar way Paul looked upon himself and his fellow-labourers as custodians of the gospel, it was entrusted to them (1 Thess 2:4), a privilege which he highly esteemed.

The oracles not only embraced the Jews collectively and as individuals, they also set out God's plans for the future. From the beginning of man's history, the coming of the Messiah was intimated. The prophetic word of the oracles of God revealed what God had in store for the world and also for the world to come. To the Jews this treasure was entrusted: it was indeed a distinct advantage to be a Jew and to be the custodian of the oracles of God.

3 The opening words of this verse, *ti gar*, rendered variously, "For what?"; "For how?"; "What then?"; seem to offer the objector another chance to reply. The expanded translation of Kenneth Wuest conveys this sense, "Well then – if as is the case, certain ones did not exercise faith? Their unbelief will not render the faithfulness of God ineffectual, will it?"

Following the interrogative opening, "What then?", it may be that the apostle meant the following words to be considered more as a categorical statement, "for what if some did not believe?" Of that there is no doubt. How many are included or excluded in the word "some" is not stated. It is sufficient for the purpose of the argument to leave it in a way that an unbiased Jew would accept the validity of the charge. The thrust of Paul's answer to the question of v.1 should not be lost by interpreting the committal of the oracles of God to the Jews as being fulfilled in the sense that they were custodians only. What is contained in these living oracles (as Stephen styled them, Acts 7:38), concerning the Messiah is the crux of the matter. The events of the OT, diverse as they were over many generations, were leading up to that moment intimated by Paul, "But when the fulness of the time was come, God sent forth his Son, made of a woman, made under the law, to redeem them that were under the law" (Gal 4:4,5).

Another aspect of the question is raised. It follows on naturally from the preceding point. How many were involved in the unbelief does not alter the validity of what is stated. The Messiah had come and had been rejected. According to the Jews, He had not come up to their requirements. The question to be faced then is whether their unbelief rendered the plans of God ineffectual. The inference that the many prophecies and the carefully-preserved genealogies and the faithfulness of God were made of no effect could not stand for a moment. God had kept His word. There were no flaws in His character; no shortcomings in His dealings with the nation. The want of faith in man will never alter the faithfulness of God. Any thought of such a possibility is met by the apostle in the opening words of the next verse, "God forbid".

4 Although the expression, "God forbid" is termed archaic and is better rendered, "Let it not be", the old English conveys something of Paul's indignation which the more literal translation misses. The suggestion that God could be less than true is certainly an affront. That His character should be maligned by doubting His faithfulness would be impiety of the worst kind. God cannot lie. The Jew was perfectly well aware of that. It was enshrined in the revelation given to him. Nevertheless, to make the truthfulness of God depend on what fickle man might say was totally unacceptable, and it is little wonder that there is such an uncompromising outburst from the apostle, "Let God be true, but every man a liar". To this, there are no exceptions, every man is embraced in the sweeping statement.

To reinforce his point and to vindicate the character of God, the apostle introduces a quotation from Ps 51:4 LXX, "That thou mightest be justified in thy sayings and mightest overcome when thou art judged". The psalm from which he quotes is a confession of sin by one who had enjoyed the favour of God. The particular transgression which gives rise to the psalm causes the writer to pour out before God his acknowledgement of guilt, "Against thee, thee only, have I sinned, and done this evil in thy sight". The confession is made because of the outrage to the holiness of the character of God. If one as highly-favoured as David had fallen from grace and had deserved the punishment which sin had brought upon him, there was no possibility that the Jew, however privileged, would escape the judgment of God. The quotation was a very telling one in support of the argument the apostle had advanced in his hypothetical objection.

David's confession justified the sentence of God upon him. He acknowledged that he had no defence when God came into judgment against him. To his credit he vindicated the character of God by accepting the righteousness of His dealings with him. The Jews therefore could not expect leniency when one so highly revered among them as David unreservedly and with deep contrition had accepted that the sentence of God passed on him for his sin was rightly deserved. By citing David's experience, the apostle in his argument had demonstrated that what he had advanced was entirely consistent with OT teaching.

5 In the first objection raised by the apostle, he focused attention on the unbelief of the Jew. Now, he raises another imaginary situation but he changes his stance and concentrates on unrighteousness. The scope of his argument widens. If the subject matter is unrighteousness, then all are embraced, including himself. When he states, "I speak as a man", he not only includes himself but he removes any objection that he was standing aloof from the situation he was introducing. Not only so, by inserting the comment after the hypothetical protest, he demonstrates that he can reason as any man will reason when challenging the righteousness of God in His dealings with men. The Jews were very prone to argue in this fashion.

In his comment in ch.1 about the gospel, Paul had shown how God was righteous in His gracious overtures to those who exercised faith (1:17). In the following verses the unrighteousness of man was seen to warrant the exercise of the wrath of God. The argument now turns on a supposed proposal that if a righteous God can offer salvation to men who have no merit of their own and still remain righteous, then the unrighteousness of man must enhance the righteousness of God. If this were so, then God would be unjust in punishing men for their sin.

The very suggestion that our unrighteousness might in some sense magnify the righteousness of God causes Paul to express himself in a short question, "What shall we say?" He seems to be asking, "What conclusion can we come to, or what inference can we draw from what has been advanced?" The further question leaves the objector to supply the answer, "Is God unrighteous who taketh vengeance?" If God brings wrath to bear upon the ungodly, which includes Jew and Gentile, privileged and unprivileged, is He unrighteous in doing so? The answer must be a resounding "No", and in the next verse the apostle proves that it could not be otherwise. Although the comment, "I speak as a man" applies to what he has just advanced and admits to putting forward reasoning as any man would reason, it does not mean that what he is saying is merely a personal remark which has less force than the rest of his submission. It demonstrates that he can change his stance to bring out a human point of view, but it does not alter the thrust of his argument that there is no unrighteousness with God.

6   That God will judge the world is a maxim which is evident to all who will read the Scriptures. To the Jew it was a recognised truth. As far as Paul was concerned, his background in Judaism and his enlightenment in the christian faith confirmed the inevitability of divine judgment. In his address at Athens, he made it clear to the Athenians that God had appointed a day in which He would judge the world in righteousness (Acts 17:31). There would be no exceptions. Any view which conflicted with Paul's stance on this point must be rejected in its entirety. Another maxim which was self-evident to Paul was that God must be just; if He were not just, He could never judge. The corollary is also self-evident, since He is the judge He cannot be unjust.

Any Jewish claim that God would be unrighteous if He judged the favoured nation, did not put due emphasis on their sinful history. In the song of Moses, the disobedient ways of the Israelites are clearly stated and their judgment is foretold, "For the Lord shall judge his people" (Deut 32:36). Their attitude was that since God bore with the nation despite their sin, He would be unrighteous in the end to take vengeance. The reasoning of Jew or Gentile which postures that unrighteousness in man has the effect of demonstrating the righteousness of God is so seriously flawed, it cannot stand. If it had even an element of truth in it, then the question raised in this verse would have to be faced, "then how shall God judge the world?" Since, however, the Scripture testifies time and again that God will undoubtedly judge the world and do it righteously in every case, it must follow that the objection raised is dismissed; it is entirely wrong.

7 A third question is now raised. It follows on from the previous question which asks, "Is God unrighteous who taketh vengeance?" – a proposition refuted in v.6. The phrase, "the truth of God" may simply mean that God is true and truthful in all His ways, as stated in v.4. Perhaps, however, the apostle intended the expression to mean God's revelation made in clear and unmistakeable terms concerning man's culpability and His own righteousness.

In the objector's question raised by Paul, he postulates that if the truth of God, either about His character or His predictions, is enhanced by anyone telling a wilful lie, why should the liar be punished for causing the glory of God to be displayed? The objector's reasoning is preposterous. The very sins which were being defended at the expense of the character of God, were still evil and could never be anything less than heinous in the sight of God. All the objections put forward to condemn Paul and the gospel he preached were puerile. They cast aspersions on the character of God but they did nothing to change the character of sin, or ease the conscience of the sinner.

The personal terms in which the question is put intimate that indirectly Paul was turning the perversity of the Jewish objectors upon themselves. This was the argument they were advancing in their own support. The falsehood which they were attributing to Paul concerned the gospel, the terms of which declare that a sinner can be forgiven and God will still remain righteous. If therefore Paul was being judged by the Jews as a sinner, they had to take their argument through to its logical conclusion and answer Paul's question, that if his falsehood enhanced the glory of God, why were they judging him as a sinner? This put the Jews in a dilemma. They could not advance an argument which supported their own warped view and refuse to acknowledge that the same principle applied to the man and to the message they were condemning.

8 In seeking to escape from the condemnation into which his own sin had brought him, the Jew was obliged to say that the apostle and those of the christian faith were advocating, "Let us do evil, that good may come". The delusion of being above judgment caused the Jew to turn to antinomianism in an endeavour to excuse himself, but yet charge the Christians with declaring what was false by any reasonable standards. The hopelessness of the Jew's case was that he was practising what he accused Paul and his fellow-believers of doing.

Slanderous reports were in circulation. Those who slandered alleged that Paul and his fellows were rejecting any obligation to observe any reasonable standard of thought or behaviour which existed amongst the nations. Their accusations inferred that moral law was brushed aside and some went as far as to assert that the Christians said, "Let us do evil, that good may come". This preposterous statement is not taken up by Paul. He dismisses it with a curt reference to the future judgment of the slanderers and all who were associated with them, "whose damnation (or, condemnation) is just".

Paul's preaching of justification by faith conflicted with the Jewish view that justification was by works. This did not mean that the Christians could completely ignore the precepts of the law and practise loose-living. If this had been the case then Paul would have been obliged to apply the closing words of v.8 to those who had embraced the christian faith. They would be the ones who were condemned. This, as is plain, was not the situation. The Jews were sinners and in their endeavours to divert attention from their own culpability, they accused all and sundry of sinful practices. Despite their protestations, their guilt before God was clear – they were without excuse.

Notes

1 "Advantage" (*perissos*) carries the meaning, "over and above", as in Matt 5:37, "Whatsoever is more than (over and above) these cometh of evil".
2 "Much every way" is Paul's swift answer to re-assure the Jew that what God had promised was true and not under threat by what he had stated.
3 For "shall make without effect" (*katargēsei*), see note against v.31 about *katargeō* where the apostle uses the same argument about making the law void.
4 *En tois logois* ("in thy sayings") is a translation of Hebrew words which mean "when thou speakest", i.e., apparently, "when thou pronouncest sentence upon man". Here the sense must be "that thou mayest be pronounced just in respect of what thou hast spoken", i.e. the oracles or promises entrusted to Israel (EGT).
5 "God...who taketh vengeance?" is literally "God, the one inflicting wrath?" That there is a day appointed when God will at last judge the world is stated by Paul at this stage as an indisputable fact, one which the Jew would scarcely deny. That the Jew would be exposed to this wrath is what Paul had to prove.

3. The World – Guilty
3:9-20

v.9 "What then? are we better than they? No, in no wise: for we have before proved both Jews and Gentiles, that they are all under sin;
v.10 As it is written, There is none righteous, no, not one:
v.11 There is none that understandeth, there is none that seeketh after God.

v.12 They are all gone out of the way, they are together become unprofitable; there is none that doeth good, no, not one.
v.13 Their throat is an open sepulchre; with their tongues they have used deceit; the poison of asps is under their lips:
v.14 Whose mouth is full of cursing and bitterness:
v.15 Their feet are swift to shed blood:
v.16 Destruction and misery are in their ways:
v.17 And the way of peace have they not known:
v.18 There is no fear of God before their eyes.
v.19 Now we know that what things soever the law saith, it saith to them who are under the law: that every mouth may be stopped, and all the world may become guilty before God.
v.20 Therefore by the deeds of the law there shall no flesh be justified in his sight: for by the law is the knowledge of sin."

9 Following the condemnation of the Jew in vv. 1-8, the apostle asks the question, "What then?" meaning, most probably, "What conclusion can we come to now?" This is followed by another question which has drawn various suggestions from commentators. The AV renders the word *proechometha*, "are we better than they?" The RV gives, "are we in worse case?" and in the margin, "Do we excel ourselves?" Nestle's text gives "Do we excel?", a rendering favoured by Thayer, but not supported by any outside evidence.

Since this is the only occurrence of the word in the NT, there are no other examples of its use for comparison. If the AV is followed, then the question "Are we better?" is met with an emphatic "No". Jew and Gentile have both been found guilty before God and the privileges of the Jew have not served to portray him in a better light. If the RV is followed, the question "are we in worse case?" is also met with a resounding "No". Since Paul links himself with his fellow-countrymen here, "are we in worse case (or, better)?" he seems to be saying that we who are Jews are neither inferior nor superior to the Gentiles. He has already proved that both Jews and Gentiles are all under sin. What he will now lead on to is not a separate condemnation of each, but a general denouncement of the whole world.

That all are "under sin" should not be taken as anything less than being in a condition where all are found guilty before God. The apostle identified the same situation when he wrote to the Galatians, "But the Scripture hath concluded (entirely enclosed) all under sin" (3:22). To be "under sin" is the opposite of being "under grace". The latter expression covers all who have confessed Christ as Saviour and have therefore been delivered from the bondage of sin. All who are not "under grace" are "under sin" and there are no exceptions. While that embraces the thought of being under sin's dominion, it does not modify the sentence, that judicially, all under sin are guilty before God.

10 In pursuance of his answers to Jewish objections, Paul now introduces a chain of quotations from the LXX, some of which are exact and some free renderings. The listing of a chain, or catena, of scriptural references was a rabbinical practice, and obviously a custom the apostle was in the habit of using.

He will do it again at ch.9, where he introduces a long chain of scriptural references to reinforce his argument at that point. To have a chain of quotations from the Scriptures used against them to prove their sinfulness was a heavy blow to the Jews. The portions selected by the apostle left no scope for them to claim that they were different from the Gentiles and therefore due special consideration as a nation favoured by God.

The questions raised and answered by Paul demonstrate that God is entirely righteous in His dealings with Jew and Gentile. Every act of God in punishing men and women for sin is just and there is no partiality with Him. The view that sin actually demonstrates the glory of God because it gives Him opportunities to show forth His mercy, is shown to be a perverted attempt to escape from being under condemnation. The conclusion which must be faced is supported from the inspired writings of the past, "As it is written, There is none righteous, no, not one".

The first reference in the chain of quotations is to Ps 14. It seems that the apostle had the depravity of man on his mind, as he quotes again from the psalm in the next verse. The psalmist introduces the universality of sin by stating in the opening words, "The fool hath said in his heart, There is no God". In the third verse he records his judgment of the human race, "They are all gone aside, they are all together become filthy, there is none that doeth good, no, not one". This epithet used by Paul exposes the utter folly of any, whether Jew or Gentile, to think that there can be any evasion of the inevitable judgment which must fall on all as a result of sin. This was not merely the apostle's opinion that he was expressing. It is covered by the words, "It is written", a point which could not be argued against, especially by the Jews, to whom, as the writer noted earlier, were committed the oracles of God.

11 In this verse the apostle continues to prove from the OT that the whole world is guilty before God. The statement in the previous verse that there is none righteous is augmented by another quotation from Ps 14 that there is none that understandeth and there is none that seeketh after God. At first sight this sweeping statement appears to conflict with individual cases noted throughout the Scriptures that there were pious men and women who in their day lived uprightly. What must be taken into account is the searching of God to find one who answered to His requirements in every aspect, but He found none, until His Son came into the world and lived a perfect life. In Him God found His delight. Every thought, word and action in His life brought the Father pleasure.

Here again, the Jews could have no objection to the apostle's statement. It was from the Scriptures and could not be restricted by applying it to the Gentiles only. The psalmist in Ps 14 makes it clear that God looked down from heaven upon the children of men, and this included the Jews. The purpose of His search was to find if there were any who understood and who sought after God. His conclusion was that there was none. All had become filthy and there was "none that doeth good, no not one". Against this the privileged Jews had no argument. It was another extract from the Scriptures they pledged to uphold and obey. It did not suit their pride to be told they were all together become filthy. They were quite happy to associate that with the Gentiles, but they had laws of ceremonial cleansing which they claimed to observe, and they did not consider that they should be included in such a general condemnation. The truth was that they professed by lip but in heart and life they were no better than the Gentiles they despised.

The categorical statement that there is none that understandeth asserts that there is no one, either Jew or Gentile, that perceives or comprehends the true position of accountability for sin. Despite worldly wisdom, the absence of understanding in the crucial matter of getting right with God is seen to be a universal failure in the human race. Even the enlightened Jew with the oracles of God in his possession, did not grasp the significance of the damage sin had done. All were far away from God in sin and all were under condemnation. That this was the position in the psalmist's day is a confirmation that it was not a new development, it was there from the fall in Eden's garden. Further on in the epistle Paul refers again to a lack of understanding. At 15:21 he makes known that the Gentiles were in darkness and without understanding until he brought the gospel to them as the apostle of the Gentiles. Here, however, the lack of understanding is another feature of the alienation of man from God, brought about by Adam's sin and passed on to each succeeding generation to work out in sinful practices.

12 This verse continues the quotation from Ps 14. The apostle reiterates what the psalmist stated in his day, that all have turned aside, they have gone out of the way. What is inferred is that all have deviated from the path which they knew was the right one. The Gentiles knew it to be so instinctively and the Jews were aware of it by revelation. Already the apostle had declared that the Gentiles had the work of the law written in their hearts, their consciences also bearing witness. They did by nature the things contained in the law, which pointed them in the way of righteousness. As for the Jews, they had the oracles of God committed to them and they also knew what God expected from them. Both therefore were without excuse. They were far astray from God, having deviated from the path of righteousness by their own choice. David in his day was aware of it and stated the situation clearly in Ps 14. Paul was also aware of the way that mankind had deviated from what was right, and his quotation from the Scriptures gave the divine assessment of the direction in which the human race was travelling – it was one of departure from God!

The verdict of the psalmist in Ps 14:3 is that mankind had become filthy, or as Paul states, "they are together become unprofitable". The word rendered "unprofitable" is interesting. It describes things in the world which have turned bad or sour, such as fruit or milk when they lose their freshness. The Hebrew scholars who worked on the LXX inserted the word in their translation to describe

David's assessment of the human race. Paul included the same word in his epistle to the Romans to emphasise that what was pronounced good at creation had become sour and in fact was good for nothing. Paul's verdict therefore confirms what David had already recorded, all together had become unprofitable. It is then on that account, a sad indictment of the human race, to have it recorded in the Scriptures, that "there is none that doeth good, no, not one".

13 In continuing his chain of OT quotations, Paul takes a part of Ps 5 and joins it to a part of Ps 140. He follows the practice he had obviously learned under Judaism of running portions of the Scripture together to establish the point he wished to make. Here it is clear from the passages he selected that he had in mind the various organs of the body which, when used to communicate, made known the depravity which was in man. He associates the tongue with deceit and the poison of asps with the lips. From one of the psalms which he quotes, he adds that the throat is an open sepulchre. In his denouncement of mankind he makes no apology for using the strongest terms and pictures to establish the true position of the human race in its alienation from God. If all the world is guilty before God, no hope is given that can possibly be interpreted as a means of escape from the righteous judgment of God.

The apostle notes that the poison of asps is under their lips. This is what the psalmist had already stated in Ps 140:3. It is a fitting picture of the evil propensities of man astray from God. The asp, being an adder whose poison can be fatal, holds its venom in a small sac at the root of the tongue. It is concealed until the hollow fang shoots out and pierces the skin of its victim. It is a very fitting illustration of the evil which man can perpetrate and it is little wonder that Paul stresses the fact that there is no good in him.

In Ps 5:9 which the apostle quotes here, the psalmist refers to the throat being an open sepulchre. This is a graphic picture of vileness. An open sepulchre is an unsealed grave, an offence to the senses. It is something from which a man instinctively withdraws because of the corruption within. Paul takes up the illustration in his epistle to the Romans thereby affirming what was already written, that the same corruption proceeds from the mouth of man. These quotations from the word of God could not be rejected by the Jews as applying only to the Gentiles. The universality of the statements was apparent from the writings of David who was held in high esteem. It was therefore a very strong condemnation of the privileged Jews, one which included them in the pronouncement of the guilt of the whole world. The verdict is, "There is none righteous, no, not one".

14 In the preceding verse, the throat, the tongue and the lips have been taken up by the apostle to illustrate various aspects of evil in man. In this verse he takes up the mouth which he states is full of bitterness and cursing. The descriptive language suggests that the mouth is fully loaded with foul speech to the extent that there is no room for anything else. It is clear that the verse is a quotation from Ps 10:7. The teaching of the psalm is a call to God to come in and judge the wicked. The insolence of evil men considered by the psalmist knows no bounds. In his scorn he says, "I shall not be moved: for I shall never be in adversity". He acts as if there is no possibility that he will ever be called to give an account in a day of reckoning. In his portrayal of evil man, the psalmist records, "His mouth is full of cursing and deceit and fraud: under his tongue is mischief and vanity" (10:7). It is a sorrowful picture of mankind as the psalmist saw it in his day. As far as Paul was concerned, the situation had not changed. He also saw mankind as deserving the judgment of God and he made no allowances for the privileged Jew; he was also embraced in the universal condemnation.

The figurative language of the OT, brought together by Paul in his chain of quotations, has a severity about it which some might consider to be grossly inaccurate. It could be argued that not every man is characterised by a filthy tongue, deceit, outrageous cursing and bitterness. It has to be remembered, however, that the apostle is considering the character of man astray from God. In this condition there is no limit to his evil propensities, and although the flesh can manifest a degree of refinement, it is still flesh and it is antagonistic to God. Refined flesh is no nearer to acceptance with God than vulgar flesh. God can be reproached and His Christ can be rejected without an outward demonstration of outrageous malediction. Those who consider that they are not marked by the traits set out by Paul in these verses are either not aware of the heinousness of sin or they are not willing to acknowledge it. People who think that way have no knowledge of the holiness of the character of God, neither have they any appreciation of what it cost the Lord Jesus Christ to settle the sin question at Calvary.

15 In this verse Paul continues to quote portions of the word of God in support of his denouncement of mankind. The readiness of man to shed blood is not an overstatement. It is a graphic reminder that from the time of Abel, man's history has borne witness to the swiftness of man to turn to violence. Man has never accepted that life is precious and that it is not his prerogative to take it. God may delegate the taking of life to the "powers that be" on the principle of a life for a life, but the decision to take life is God's and He has never given up that right to man.

There are two portions of the word of God from which Paul could have taken the words of v.15. The wise man's advice in the book of Proverbs is good counsel, "My son, if sinners entice thee consent thou not. If they say, Come with us, let us lay wait for blood...My son walk not thou in the way with them, refrain thy foot from their path: For their feet run to evil, and make haste to shed blood" (Prov 1:11,15,16). The prophet Isaiah's message addresses the same evil but from a different standpoint. The prophet gives the reason in ch.59 why God did not answer prayer; it was because of sin in Israel. Although His hand was not shortened that it could not save, the iniquities of the people had caused a separation, their hands were defiled by blood.

There is a consummate skill in the way that Paul runs the various portions of

Scripture together to give such a graphic picture of man as he is before God. Although the apostle was guided by the Holy Spirit, it is obvious that his knowledge of the word of God was such that he could bring out the very passage that applied to the situation he was describing. This verse gives the opening words of Isa 59:7, "Their feet run to evil and they make haste to shed innocent blood". The Jews could not argue with what Paul stated. They were well aware of the wise man's words of wisdom and the prophet's message. They could not dismiss their verdicts. They were addressed to their forefathers and the Lord made it plain in His ministry that the Jews in His day were no better than they were. What Paul stated was further evidence of the hopeless position of Jew and Gentile.

16 This verse is a continuation of the quotation from Isa 59:7. The phrase which precedes "Destruction and misery are in their ways" is not taken up by the apostle. This is given in Isa 59:7 AV, "...their thoughts are thoughts of iniquity", and rendered in the LXX as, "...their thoughts are thoughts of murder". It is not apparent why Paul should pass over the reference, unless he considered that the quotation, "Their feet are swift to shed blood" covered thoughts of murder which found a place in the human mind.

Destruction and misery describe what is brought about by man's inhumanity to man, which, as one national poet says, "makes countless thousands mourn". Throughout man's history, destruction and misery have abounded as nations have warred with each other. In it all there was no thought of God as to how He viewed the distress which resulted from violence at every level of man's way of life. In His sovereignty, God might allow one nation to chastise another, but there was nothing in the affairs of men to bring Him pleasure. They brought upon each other desolation and distress, but although misery was their lot, it did not cause them to change their ways.

17 The statement, "And the way of peace they have not known" completes the quotation from Isa 59:8. If there is a swiftness to shed blood and a readiness to cause destruction and misery, it follows that the way of peace is not known. Sin brings in its trail ruin and corruption. All the attempts of men to bring about a lasting peace in the world have failed because the sin question has never been addressed. Since strife abounds at all levels of society, the way of peace is foreign to mankind. Isaiah prophesied that it would prove to be elusive to the Jews. Paul also knew it to be so and his endorsement of what the prophet stated condemns the Jews as well as the Gentiles. No unbiased person would argue with what Isaiah and Paul stated. The way of peace was outwith the range of man's knowledge and he was therefore incapable of securing it.

18 This is the last quotation from the OT in the apostle's list. It is taken from Ps 36. The evils which the psalmist details in Ps 36:1-4 resemble in many ways what

Paul sets out in Rom 3. Whereas he terminates his list by quoting, "There is no fear of God before their eyes", the psalmist commences with the statement and then declares what proceeds from it. It is evident that the Gentiles did not read God in creation and the Jews did not heed God in revelation. There was therefore no fear of God in either as they pursued their own ways of perversity and depravity.

From Paul's argument it is obvious that man is not measured by comparing man with man. He is measured by the standards laid down by God. For the Jews therefore to consider that they were to be preferred over the Gentiles was without foundation and at the best a vain hope. Their inflated ideas of their own importance blinded them to their true position. By lip they acknowledged God and the law, but their ways were a denial of any claims to be God's peculiar people. As for the Gentiles, they acted as if there was nothing sacred and that all things were common. The inward monitor should have had the effect of mellowing their lives to some extent, but history proved that there was no fear of God with them. The lack of reverential awe for the Creator demonstrated that man had dismissed Him out of his reckoning.

19 Having used the Scriptures to great effect to prove that his denouncement of Jew and Gentile was not merely a personal opinion, Paul now anticipates another objection from the Jew. He is obviously under no misapprehension about strong protests coming from that source. His condemnation has been scathing. He has passed censure on Jew and Gentile without giving either a glimmer of hope. Because of their privileged past, it is to be expected that the Jew will be more ready to respond. To be cast in the same mould as the heathen and be under the same condemnation was, to the Jew, totally unacceptable. To meet the objections which he knows will come from that source, Paul gives his final assessment of the situation.

The reference to the law in this verse stands for the OT Scriptures. Although he writes, "Now we know that what things soever the law saith, it saith to them who are under the law", it is apparent that he means that the Jew had the oracles of God (2:2). They were under an obligation to abide by every detail. The apostle had just used quotations from the psalms and the prophets against them and they could not deny the accusations of the voices from the past. They were as guilty as the Gentiles. It was pointless to try and shift the blame and apply it to the heathen while they persuaded themselves that they had no charges to answer.

The testimony of Scripture is undeniable. It states that every mouth will be stopped. There will be no defence from any at the bar of God. The Jew will not plead his birth or his favour. The moralist will not put forward his good works as a defence. The foul-mouthed and evil workers will stand in silence. An unbiased Judge will pronounce sentence and all the world will be declared guilty before God. It is a solemn consideration. No voice of appeal will be heard. No cries for mercy will be made. The final judgment in the last great assize will leave none with anything but remorse for not having listened in time to the overtures of God in grace.

20 The RV changes "Therefore" to "Because". The omission of the definite article before "deeds" and before "law" in the original makes the verse read, "Because by deeds of law there shall no flesh be justified in his sight". This indicates that the conclusion the apostle has come to is wide enough to include any accredited law by which man is governed. The Jews had the Mosaic law. The Gentiles had "the work of the law written in their hearts, their conscience also bearing witness" (2:15). There was no escaping the implications of Paul's summation. There were no works of law in existence amongst men which would justify them in the sight of God.

At 2:13 Paul has already stated that doers of the law shall be justified, that is, declared righteous. This statement, however, is qualified by other references in Scripture. In his epistle to the Galatians, Paul wrote, "Cursed is everyone that continueth not in all things which are written in the book of the law to do them. But that no man is justified by the law in the sight of God, it is evident" (3:10,11). James in his epistle declared, "For whosoever shall keep the whole law, and yet offend in one point, he is guilty of all" (2:10). Since all have sinned and come short of the glory of God, it is apparent that no one has been found amongst men who is sinless. Paul's conclusion is therefore unassailable, "By the deeds of the law there shall no flesh be justified in his sight". It may be that the apostle had Ps 143:2 in mind when he made this concluding statement. Some commentators think that he did, but since the psalmist makes no reference to deeds or works of law, Paul's reference to it may only be in principle.

Although the conscience is a monitor which accuses or excuses it falls short of being an infallible guide. The law, however, is not affected by man's opinions, its commands are clear and unequivocal. Its prohibitions could not be ignored although they could be disobeyed. If the law's commands were transgressed, the transgressor knew about it and with that breach came the knowledge of sin. Whether the Mosaic law or the law of nature, the conclusion was the same, "by the law is the knowledge of sin".

Notes

9 By "we have before proved" (*proētiasametha*); "we previously accused" (*proaitiaomai*, "to charge beforehand"), possibly Paul means here the charges he has made from the beginning of the epistle, although charges drawn from the Scriptures cannot be ruled out.

The preposition *hupo* in "all under sin" (*hupo hamartian*) carries the meaning here that all are under the power of sin. Sin is in command and men are under its authority.

Although the apostle has dealt with many facets of sin, this is the first mention of the word in the epistle.

A similar expression occurs at Gal 3:22 where the apostle states that the Scripture has shut up all things under sin. Hogg and Vine make the interesting comment against the expression "hath shut up", stating, "*sunkleiō*, to shut up with, as fish are enclosed in a net (Luke 5:6) i.e., completely, and without possibility of escape" – *The Epistle to the Galatians*, page 158.

10-18 Newell suggests that from the divine standpoint, God speaks, first as a Judge (vv.10-12), next as a Physician (vv.13-15), and finally as a divine Historian (v.16-18).

Barclay notes, "In Rabbinic preaching, stringing texts together was called *charaz*, which means 'stringing pearls' ".

12 "Unprofitable" (*achreioō*, "worthless") is literally "to render useless".

19 "What things the law saith" is obviously intended to be confined to the law of Moses. "Them that are under the law" are Jews. The preposition here rendered "under" is *en* ("in"), not *hupo*, as at v.9. The thought is more being tied up to it rather than being under bondage to it.

20 If it were possible to attain to the perfect state where the demands of the law were met in every respect, the failures on the way to perfection would condemn. By the law is the knowledge of sin. Transgression is conflict with the law and failure to obey is therefore recognised as sin. The law was not given to cure man of sin; it was given to show up sin. It shows where man goes wrong but it does not supply the means of correction. There is no mercy in the law, it can only condemn. By law-works, therefore, there is no possibility of being justified before God.

III. The Gospel of God (3:21-5:21)

1. *The Principle of Justification – by faith alone*
3:21-31

> v.21 "But now the righteousness of God without the law is manifested, being witnessed by the law and the prophets;
> v.22 Even the righteousness of God which is by faith of Jesus Christ unto all and upon all them that believe: for there is no difference:
> v.23 For all have sinned, and come short of the glory of God;
> v.24 Being justified freely by his grace through the redemption that is in Christ Jesus:
> v.25 Whom God hath set forth to be a propitiation through faith in his blood, to declare his righteousness for the remission of sins that are past, through the forbearance of God;
> v.26 To declare, I say, at this time his righteousness: that he might be just, and the justifier of him which believeth in Jesus.
> v.27 Where is boasting then? It is excluded. By what law? of works? Nay: but by the law of faith.
> v.28 Therefore we conclude that a man is justified by faith without the deeds of the law.
> v.29 Is he the God of the Jews only? is he not also of the Gentiles? Yes, of the Gentiles also:
> v.30 Seeing it is one God, which shall justify the circumcision by faith, and uncircumcision through faith.
> v.31 Do we then make void the law through faith? God forbid: yea, we establish the law."

21 Before he dealt with man's great need, Paul stated that he was not ashamed of the gospel: for it was the power of God unto salvation to every one that believed. In it the righteousness of God was revealed (vv.16,17). It was essential that every claim that man thought he had for acceptance with God should be dismissed. And so in great detail the apostle argued to prove that the whole world was guilty before God and that there was no possibility of escaping the wrath of God which must inevitably fall on all mankind. From this point, however, he proceeds to bring in the gospel which he has already mentioned briefly in ch.1. This gospel will not be confined to one nation. It will have a universal appeal. No law will be required to put it within the sinner's reach; it will be based on the principle of faith, as Paul had already stated (1:17). Nevertheless, while the gospel will be within the range of man's capabilities of acceptance, the infinite cost to provide salvation will also be given the utmost stress.

Having stated his case about the guilt of the whole world, the apostle introduces a new train of thought, "But now, apart from law", meaning, that no law, Mosaic or otherwise, had anything to do with what he was about to declare. He is swift to add, however, that the righteousness of God, about which he will speak, is witnessed (or, attested) by the law and the prophets. What was written aforetime in the inspired writings was not in conflict with the message for the present; indeed the law and the prophets were totally compatible with the gospel of God which he was now declaring.

Here the righteousness of God is said to have been manifested. In addition, as the apostle proceeds, he will show how righteousness can be credited to the believer. The law is not relaxed or set aside, but is seen to be fulfilled in the strictest judicial sense, all its claims having been satisfied in respect of those who are justified by faith. At this point, however, the purpose of the apostle is to show that under the law, God did show grace towards sinners. Through Moses, He set out the law of the offerings whereby sinners could draw near to Him. Through the prophets He showed grace and by their ministry He appealed repeatedly and in a variety of ways to an erring people. All of His dealings in the past were in accordance with His righteousness and now that righteousness, attested by law and prophets, was being declared in the gospel, the terms of which Paul was commissioned to make known to all mankind.

22 There are two words which will appear frequently in following chapters. These are "righteousness" and "justify". They are very similar in meaning, and indeed, as found in the Scriptures, are from the same Greek root (*dikaios*, "just, or righteous", so, *ho dikaios*, "the Just One", one of the titles of the Messiah; *dikaioō*, "to make, or render right", "to justify"). Having therefore stated that the righteousness of God is manifested (in the cross of Christ), the apostle now proceeds to show how the benefits of this can be appropriated. He will make known how believers on the Lord Jesus Christ can be pronounced and treated as righteous and considered by a righteous God as if they had never sinned.

The first great announcement is that the righteousness of God (mentioned four times in this context) is now being proffered to mankind. It is not obtained through faith in God, but through faith in Jesus Christ (not "faith of Jesus Christ", as in AV). God's plan of salvation involves the cross. There is no hope apart from the cross. The righteousness of God (not the righteousness "from God", as in NIV) is inextricably linked with the work of Christ at Calvary. It was there that God "made him to be sin for us, who knew no sin; that we might be made the righteousness of God in him" (2 Cor 5:21). It was at the cross that Christ met every demand of the law, enabling it to be said of believers, "But of him are ye in Christ Jesus, who of God is made unto us wisdom, and righteousness, and sanctification, and redemption" (1 Cor 1:30).

The offer is universal; it is unto all them that believe ("and upon all" is omitted in the RV but not by JND). The Lord's command to His disciples was, "Go ye into all the world and preach the gospel" and this worldwide commission is confirmed in what Paul states here. It is preached to faith and is in what Paul states here. No nation is marked out for special favour. If there is no difference so far as sinnership is concerned, there is no difference so far as the offer of salvation is concerned. Those who carry the gospel take it to all mankind in every corner of the world and they have the assurance that those who exercise faith in the One who is central to the message will be credited with the righteousness of God.

23 This verse is a continuation of the theme of v.22. Since it was first penned it has been at the core of gospel preaching. Apart from the recognition and acceptance of the fact that all have sinned, salvation cannot be offered. The individual must face the fact. It is not dismissed as general sin, neither does it imply the identification of a single sin; it involves an acknowledgment that sin is in the nature and it has worked out in practice. Neither Jew nor Gentile can claim exemption, for there is no difference. Different degrees of culpability are not considered, for all come (or, "fall", RV) short of the glory of God.

The reference here to the glory of God may indicate the perfections of His character, involving the standards which are associated with His person. These are seen in the OT in the various displays of His worth down the years. It may be, however, that Paul meant it to be understood by considering the person of the Lord Jesus Christ. The apostle was moving into a new phase of the plans of God. The age of grace had dawned. The Son of God had come. The glory of God was seen in Him, as Paul made known to the Corinthians, "For God who commanded the light to shine out of darkness, hath shined in our hearts, to give the light of the knowledge of the glory of God in the face of Jesus Christ" (2 Cor 4:6). However it is understood, it stresses the fact that the glory of God is an indication of the standard to which man, or any created intelligence, can never attain. The distance is infinite.

24 There is a considerable difference of opinion regarding the connection between the opening words, "being justified" and what has gone before. If they do not connect with v.23, then v.23 is obviously an interruption to the apostle's flow of thought to prove that there is none that has a claim on God to be justified apart from faith in Jesus Christ. It would seem to suit the context better to link "being justified" with "all them that believe" of v.22. This reaffirms that justification is on the faith principle and only those who exercise faith come into the benefit of this great pronouncement from God. Taking v.23 into account, however, it certainly shows where the whole world stands in guilt before the declaration of God's grace is made in v.24.

Here the apostle states that justification is by grace. At v.28 he makes known that a man is justified by faith. At 5:9 he declares, "Much more then, being now justified by his blood, we shall be saved from wrath through him". The three words used in this epistle to qualify justification view the subject from different aspects. Justification *by grace*, intimates that it springs from the vast reservoir of God's free favour; it can never be earned; it is entirely gratuitous. To be justified *by blood* makes known the cost of making it available to man. Nothing less than the blood of Christ shed at Calvary will open up the way to enable God to come out in grace to the guilty. As to appropriation of the blessing, this is on the principle *of faith*, through personal belief on Jesus Christ, and the confession of Him as personal Saviour.

To be justified before God is a concept which is set in a legal frame. In Paul's argument in the first three chapters of the epistle he has laboured to bring in the whole world guilty before God. He has made it clear that there is none righteous (3:10). If any are going to be justified (declared righteous) it will have to be in God's way, as man has no righteousness of his own. Man, however, will never become righteous or holy. The Bible is clear on that point. What is conveyed in being justified is that a person is accounted or reckoned just through the exercise of faith in Jesus Christ. The relationship before God is changed from being a condemned sinner to being a redeemed saint. The pronouncement from God's side does not imply that the justified has never sinned; it declares that God in grace can look on the sinner as if that person had never sinned. The sinner is *reckoned* righteous, not, as is often erroneously taught, *made* righteous.

Justification is stated to be according to the grace of God. It is a free gift. It is characteristic of God that from His infinite resources of love and free favour He can come out in blessing where it was never earned. The thought of merit or work can never come into the situation where the grace (*charis*) of God is concerned. If work had any part in it, grace would cease to be a free gift, it would be reckoned as a debt. This principle will be considered by the apostle later in the epistle (see 4:4-6).

The means by which justification is made available is stated to be according to the redemption that is in Christ Jesus. The word used by Paul here for "redemption" (*apolutrōsis*) stresses deliverance. A different word is used where the emphasis is placed on the cost of redemption. Since the setting of the verse is in a legal frame, the point the apostle is making is that the guilty can be justified and set free, but that is only made possible by the work of Christ. That His sacrifice is inferred in the word cannot be overlooked, and that aspect will be developed in the following verses. Here the basis of deliverance from the penalty of sins is the work of Christ Jesus.

25 Having stated that justification was brought about through the redemption that is in Christ Jesus, the apostle now proceeds to show that God has set Him forth to be a propitiation, or, a mercy seat (JND). The word for "propitiation" (*hilastērion*) is found once more in the NT and that is in Heb 9:5 where it is translated "mercy seat". It has cognate words, however, and these are found in the Gospels and in 1 John. The mercy seat was part of the furnishings of the tabernacle and it is likely that Paul had the ritual associated with it in his mind when he wrote to the Romans. Some hold that since *hilastērion* is given is Heb 9:5 to describe the piece of furniture known as the mercy seat, it settles the meaning of the same Greek word in Rom 3:25.

It is open to question whether Paul intended that his use of *hilastērion* was met fully in the thought of the mercy seat as part of the ritual associated with the Jewish system. Certainly his knowledge of the tabernacle details as set out in Exodus, and the law of the offerings given in Leviticus would suggest that he meant *hilastērion* to be understood against the OT background. This assumes, however, that the readers of the epistle were also conversant with the tabernacle furnishings, which no doubt the Jews were to some extent. It does not follow that at Rome and elsewhere the Gentiles were equally knowledgeable, although they might have been conversant with the sacrificial connotations associated with the word. It is questionable if Paul meant here that propitiation (*hilastē rion*) should be limited to the mercy seat and what it represented as part of the tabernacle furnishings.

It is clear from the various lines of thought put forward as interpretations of Rom 3:25 that there is difficulty in understanding how much was intended to be taken from the phrase, "whom God set forth to be a propitiation". That the verse is central to the teaching of the epistle can hardly be overlooked, and although it is beyond any to plumb the depth of the statement, there are certain aspects about it which are reasonably clear. Who it was who was set forth presents no problem, as vv.24,25 state that it was Christ Jesus. Why God set Him forth, firstly before Himself and then by public manifestation, is also clear – it was that He might show His righteousness in passing over sins of the past, as one has noted, sins which were BC and not AD. They do not refer to two periods in a believer's life. As to when He was set forth must surely be first of all at the cross in His expiatory sacrifice, followed by His resurrection in power, and after that as the mercy seat where God and the sinner can meet. Here it should be remarked that from man's side, there is no question of approaching God on the ground of human merit; it must be, as the verse implies, through the blood and on the principle of faith.

Regarding the evident symbolism used by Paul, it must be remembered that in the ceremonial procedures of the OT, the mercy seat was not the place where atonement was made. It was the place where the blood was sprinkled, where it was left as a witness that a sacrifice had been made and that the divine claims had been met. God could therefore accept the people and deal with them righteously in grace. This procedure, however, had to be repeated year after year. It was, nevertheless, anticipatory of the true expiatory sacrifice which would be made once for all in the fulness of time.

The benefits of the sacrifice of Christ as the propitiation are made good through faith in Him. The expression, "by his blood" stands here for the sacrificial death of Christ. The life is in the blood (Lev 17:11) and the shedding of it therefore is the evidence that a life has been given up. If the blood had not been shed and the life had not been given up, there would have been no hope for mankind, as the writer to the Hebrews makes clear, "without shedding of blood there is no remission" (Heb 9:22).

Once again Paul brings in the righteousness of God. In this context he wants to make known that God was righteous in passing over the sins of the past. The worthies of OT times were sinners, and therefore exposed to judgment on that account. In view of the sacrifice to come and in virtue of the blood that would be shed, God passed over the sins. He was righteous in doing so. The value of the expiatory sacrifice at Calvary reached back to the beginning of man's history and its efficacy will reach forward to the end of it. God exercised forbearance in the past. He demonstrated the righteousness of His forbearance in the propitiatory sacrifice of Christ, setting forth in Him that there was mercy for those who were characterised by faith.

There is a striking difference between the mercy seat and Christ as the propitiation. Although the mercy seat was before the face of God, it was not seen by the people. It was approached once a year by the high priest that blood might be sprinkled on it. By contrast, God has set forth Christ to be a propitiation (or, mercy seat). He is an open declaration that the sacrifice has been made, the blood has been shed and He is now the mediator between God and man, in mercy giving man access to the Father. His propitiation enables God to deal mercifully with all who exercise faith in Christ.

26 The opening words of this verse are not merely a repetition of the declaration of v.25. There is a distinct contrast between the declaration of His righteousness aforetime (RV) and the declaration of His righteousness at this present season (RV). God was righteous in passing over the sins of the past in view of Calvary. Now the apostle is making known that God continues to show forth His righteousness and that is done by justifying those who exercise faith by believing in Jesus. These are the ones whose sins are remitted. Before the sacrifice of Christ sins were not remitted, they were passed over.

In justifying the ones who believe in Jesus, God declares that He is just. His action becomes His character. He always acts in accordance with His own righteousness. Since Christ has died there is now no need for God to act in forbearance as far as sins are concerned. He no longer requires to continue His patient toleration. He can now justify the sinner since Christ has effectively dealt with the sin question at Calvary.

From Adam to Christ, God had "passed over" sins. He was perfectly entitled to bring down His wrath on individuals but in forbearance he held back. In this there could be no question of connivance with sin. The sin question was not forgotten. God was not ignoring that it was there. He would have ceased to be righteous if He had allowed sin to be unaccounted for, either in judgment or dealt with by sacrifice. In His grace He passed over the sins of the past but in His righteousness He took up the matter of sin at the cross. It was there that He "made him to be sin for us, who knew no sin; that we might be made the righteousness of God in him". (2 Cor 5:21).

Here the apostle announces that it is God who justifies. There is not another who can do so in righteousness. None other has the fitness to act in this way. If

God had to delegate the great work of justification to another, who himself needed it, God would deny Himself, and such a thought is unthinkable. If there is a carping by the unrepentant that the severity of God is unrighteous, they have only themselves to blame. If in unbelief there is a refusal to bend to God's method of justifying sinners, there can be no complaint. It is declared that God can justify those who believe in Jesus.

27 From the Jewish standpoint, prior to the gospel being brought in, there were grounds for glorying. The Jews could boast of their special position; no other nation had such close relationship with God. They could glory in their privileges, not the least being that they were entrusted with the oracles of God (3:2). When, however, the gospel of God came, the ground of glorying ceased. The work of Christ brought to an end the unique place enjoyed amongst the nations. There was nothing left to support boasting, leading Paul to pose the question, "Where is boasting then?" Why boast when there is nothing left to boast about? The boasting here is the act of boasting, not the ground of it. As far as the occasion for it is concerned, that was excluded, shut out finally at the cross. Jewish glorying therefore had no support; it was of no consequence; it was empty.

This leads the apostle to pose another question. If all boasting is excluded, "By what law? of works?" In this he anticipates a question from an objector. Someone will surely ask, "If the ground of boasting is removed and all glorying is therefore empty and futile, what is the principle that shuts it out?" "By what law? of works?" The futility of holding on to works of merit of any kind is made clear in the apostle's answer, "Nay, but by the law of faith". Since there is no definite article before "law", the phrase would be better rendered, "a law of faith", here meaning the gospel which has faith and not merit as the principle on which it operates.

The reference to a law of works here must include all works. It is not simply what might be termed "religious works", but any kind of works, whether they be religious, moral or social. Anything that man may be tempted to plead for recognition as merit for acceptance with God is shut out. Boasting is excluded. The law or principle or plan which now has divine authority is that of faith, inseparably bound up in the terms of the gospel. The righteousness of God is declared in its message. It intimates that those who believe in Jesus will be justified. It is universal in its scope. All men everywhere, regardless of nationality, can come into its blessings, but only on the principle of what Paul terms here, "the law of faith".

28 The RV gives the opening words of this verse, "We reckon therefore". This is a more accurate rendering than the AV, "Therefore we conclude". The apostle's calculated opinion, arising from what he has just stated, confirms that a man is justified by faith without the deeds of the law. What he states is not the conclusion of an argument, or the final word of a submission; it is his own confirmed view that he is expressing. He reckons that what he has just said leads him to confirm that there is no possibility of a man being justified apart from faith. By using *anthrōpos* ("a man"), and not *anēr* ("a male"), he is virtually saying "a person", that is, male or female. In addition, the general word used means he is referring to any man, as distinct from Jew or Gentile.

There is no ambiguity about what the apostle now declares. Justification is by faith, apart from the works of the law. To be cleared from every charge that could be raised is a blessing far beyond anything that human thought could devise. At Antioch in Pisidia he preached, "By him all that believe are justified from all things, from which they could not be justified by the law of Moses" (Acts 13:39). The law by its charges impeached all who were under it. There was no escape from the condemnation it announced. It only served to highlight the fact that sin reigned. How God could clear the sinner without righteousness losing anything of its character is indeed an amazing situation. To do this apart from any deeds of merit, is an additional cause for wonder. The chosen way may find no support in human reasoning but it was God's way, and this was what Paul preached.

29 If a person can be justified, as made known in v.28, the only way that this could be withheld from all, is that God would be the God of the Jews only. In that case He would be under an obligation to bless the people to whom He was committed. This would certainly suit the Jews, and if Paul had restricted his question to, "Is he the God of the Jews only?" they would have given a resounding "yes" as the answer. The apostle, however, follows by asking another question, "Is he not also of the Gentiles?" This is undeniable. That He is the God of the Gentiles also is axiomatic. Paul takes it for granted that no one would be so foolish as to suggest that there was more than one God.

It is obvious that the apostle introduced the thought to counteract the limited view of Jewish thinking. He had been brought up to think as the Jews thought. He knew that they had chosen to forget that God was not limited to one nation. It suited their pride but it was far from being the true position. God was the God of the Gentiles also. This basic fact had to be stated for several reasons. If justification were by law, then God would be the God of the Jews, because the Gentiles were not under law. The corollary has also some merit in such an argument. If He were the God of the Jews only then justification would be on the principle of law. Such reasoning was unthinkable. God was the God of the Gentiles also and justification was on the principle of faith.

In addition, Paul has been leading up gradually in his overall argument to the declaration of the universal concept of the gospel. This he will develop further, but it was essential that he should establish the point as he went along that God was not tied to the Jewish nation exclusively. To have allowed that would have nullified the gospel message, a main theme of which was that it was worldwide in its scope. Paul in his preaching made it abundantly clear to the Athenians that the God of his message had made the world and all things therein and had made of one blood all nations of men to dwell on the face of the earth. If men sought the Lord they would find Him, and He was not far away from any of them (Acts 17:24,26,27). God was not the God of the Jews only, He was also the God of the Gentiles.

30 Paul's train of thought continues. Since there is one God and not a God for the Jews and a God for the Gentiles, the Jews are reminded that their concept of the situation is completely false. God was not committed to them only. It would be natural for an objection to arise in the Jewish mind against what Paul was stating. The possibility of pagan people being the object of God's concern to the extent of being justified by faith alone was to them unthinkable. To such an objection, the apostle's answer would be a categorical assertion, "Yes, He is the God of the Gentiles also". Amongst the Gentiles there would be many gods, but this is not what Paul is counteracting. He is not stating a case for monotheism. The Jews would have had no fault with the view that there is one God. This basic fact was enshrined in the oracles which had been committed to their trust. What they would not accept readily was that the one God they professed to serve was the same God who would accept Gentiles and justify them on an equal footing with themselves.

Regarding the Gentiles, their position was no less serious than that of the Jews. Because of their lack of knowledge and appreciation of the nature and character of the true God, they might have considered that what Paul had stated was relatively unimportant. Since there were many gods amongst them, the thought of a God of the Jews and a God of the Gentiles would not have the same degree of offensiveness in it as it would have for the Jews. Nevertheless, there were not two sets of standards. Already both Jew and Gentile had come under the condemnation of v.23, "All have sinned and come short of the glory of God". To have any hope of salvation from the burden of sin, both would have to deal with the same God and on His terms.

In this verse then, the position is stated clearly. Using language which suits his references to the law, the apostle now affirms that God will justify the circumcision, but He will do it by faith. As already declared, it will be to those who believe on Jesus. This is unalterable. The God of the Jew and the Gentile will make no difference. He will justify both, but it will be on the same principle. The blessing will be within reach of every man. Faith will be the way to obtain it, a stumbling block no doubt to some and foolishness to others, but this is God's method and He will not change it to accommodate anyone.

31 The question which is raised in this verse is a natural response to what has gone before. The thrust of Paul's reasoning has been that God justifies on the principle of faith. Any thought of justification by law has been rejected at every stage. It may well be asked then if the law is superfluous. Is it rendered useless?

This, Paul will not allow. He answers, "God forbid, yea, we establish the law". The apostle had to be careful that his emphasis on the principle of faith did not cause some to overreact. Some might have considered that the law was rendered null and void. That of course was never on the apostle's mind. As he states, here, he establishes the law, he upholds it. Indeed, later in the epistle he emphasises this point, noting, "that the righteousness of the law might be fulfilled in us who walk not after the flesh, but after the Spirit" (8:4).

Regarding the demands of the law, the Jew lowered its standards to suit his practices. He knew he could not keep it, but in order to live with it, its requirements were modified. The proper attitude to the requirements of the law would have been to uphold it in every respect and cast himself on the Lord's compassion for his failure to keep it. He would then have found that there is mercy with the Lord. When the apostle wrote, "Yea, we establish the law", he did not mean that its standards were lowered. He meant that the law was upheld by conforming to its requirements, even although that meant carrying out its sentence to the letter. In this, however, the severity of the law's demands was not a subject for negotiation, it was unalterable.

There was only one way that the law could be established and that was by carrying out its precepts. Justification by faith alone does not nullify the law, rather it makes it meaningful. Its demands were fully met once and for all at the cross. It was there that its penalty was fully exacted. It was in the sacrifice of Christ that its requirements were exhausted. It was on account of that work therefore that God could in righteousness justify all who believed in Jesus.

Notes

21 "Without the law", "apart from the law" (RV), has emphasis. It denotes that righteousness is made available altogether apart from (*chōris*), "on a distinct footing from", "irrespective of" law (any law).

The law bore witness to an outward righteousness provided by God, but the law could provide nothing. From the standpoint of the offerer, every offering brought to the altar as a sacrifice for sin, was in itself a witness that the offerer had no righteousness of his own; through his offering he was cast upon God for it.

22 Some manuscripts omit the words "and upon all". Many commentators, however, argue for their retention. Wm Kelly states, "But I agree with the judgment of those who retain the received text in this". He also states, "God's righteousness addresses itself 'unto all' men without exception; but the benefits depend on faith in Jesus Christ, and hence only reaches and takes effect 'upon all that believe'".

24 "Freely" (*dōrean*), signifies "for nothing". Justification we are told here costs the sinner nothing. In Gal 2:21 we are told that if it comes through the law, Christ died "for nothing". "We contribute nothing, the whole charge is freely supplied by God" (EGT).

25 On the word "propitiation", Dr G Thomas says, "Propitiation always means something that causes or enables someone to act mercifully or forgivingly. God requires the propitiation by reason of His justice and He provides it by reason of His mercy" (J.M. Davies).

26 Trench says that *kairos* is time contemplated simply as such, the succession of moments. The synonym *chronos* embraces all possible *kairoi*. Here, *kairō* stresses that the declaration is in the present season. The length of the season is not the point.

Of "That he might be just and the justifier" Robertson notes: "Nowhere else has Paul put the problem of God more acutely or profoundly. To pronounce the unrighteous righteous is unjust by itself (Rom 4:5. God's mercy would not allow Him to leave man to his fate. God's justice demanded some punishment for sin. The only possible way to save some was the propitiatory offering of Christ and the call for faith on man's part".

27 Of "excluded" (*exekleisthe*), Vincent comments, "A peculiarly vivid use of the aorist tense. Boasting *was* excluded by the coming in of the revelation of righteousness by faith".

"By what law"? – By what principle or procedure was boasting excluded?

28 "We conclude" (*logizometha*) – Better, "We reckon" (*logizomai*, to count, to calculate, to consider).

"Justified by faith without (apart from) the deeds of the law" – Faith and law-works are mutually exclusive as far as a basis for justification is concerned (see Gal 2:16).

30 The change of preposition, "By faith...through faith" may be significant. Several views have been expressed. It is clear that "through (*dia*) faith", as applied to the Gentiles is "by means of faith" – by that principle! "By faith" or "out of (*ek*) faith" as applied to the Jews, may be in contrast to "out of works of law" (v.20). Or, "out of faith" may be personal faith, whereas "by *the* faith" may emphasise the Person and message believed. Or, the definite article may endorse that a Gentile is justified by the self same faith out of which a Jew is justified.

31 "Make void" (*katargoumen*) occurs twenty-five times in Paul's writings. *Katargeō* implies making something inefficient, rather than making it altogether useless. Regarding the fig tree (Luke 13:7), "Why *cumbereth* it the ground", that is, why permit it to debar the ground from being put to better use? There was nothing wrong with the ground!

2. Illustrations of Justification – from the OT
4:1-25

(a) *Two accredited witnesses from the past (vv.1-8)*

v.1 "What shall we say then that Abraham our father, as pertaining to the flesh, hath found?
v.2 For if Abraham were justified by works, he hath whereof to glory; but not before God.
v.3 For what saith the scripture? Abraham believed God, and it was counted unto him for righteousness.
v.4 Now to him that worketh is the reward not reckoned of grace, but of debt.
v.5 But to him that worketh not, but believeth on him that justifieth the ungodly, his faith is counted for righteousness.
v.6 Even as David also describeth the blessedness of the man, unto whom God imputeth righteousness without works,
v.7 Saying, Blessed are they whose iniquities are forgiven, and whose sins are covered.
v.8 Blessed is the man to whom the Lord will not impute sin."

1 As Paul's argument enters a new phase, he commences with an expression which is characteristic of this epistle, "What shall we say then?" It seems to imply an invitation to pass judgment on what has gone before. If any thought that the doctrinal outline of 3:21-31 was flawed, what did they think of the case of Abraham? The apostle had made it clear that justification was by faith alone; that was the principle on which the blessing could be received, not the principle of works. To illustrate that he now turns to the Scriptures to find cases which exemplify what he has stated. The examples are those of the OT worthies, Abraham and David, both held in reverential awe as fathers of the Jewish nation, the greatest patriarch and the greatest king.

Regarding his first witness from the OT, the apostle poses the question, "What shall we say then that Abraham our father, as pertaining to the flesh, hath found?" Here Paul identifies himself with the Jewish people. He refers to Abraham as "our father". Being a Jew he had the same respect for the forefather of the nation. He was a true descendant and that could not be denied. From that standpoint therefore he raises the question. Regarding the word *eurēkenai*, rendered "hath found", some manuscripts omit it and some textual critics consign it to the margin. It is retained, however, by the RV and others. On the basis of its acceptance, Paul seems to ask, "In the experience of Abraham, did he find righteousness by working for it or did he do any exploits that earned it for him?" Having posed the question, he proceeds to answer it and prove that merit in no way entered into the situation as far as Abraham was concerned.

Regarding the expression "according to the flesh" various views are in circulation concerning its precise meaning. Some hold that the apostle was referring to circumcision, suggesting that circumcision contained all the promises that God had made to Abraham (Haldane). Some think that "flesh" is synonymous with "works" as argued in ch.3, and referred to in 4:2 (Plummer, quoting Hammond). Others see in it a question, "Was Abraham justified in anything which pertained to the flesh?" (Vincent). The most uncomplicated meaning, however, is that the apostle is stressing the ancestral link, that he and the Jews were of the lineage of their forefather, Abraham. This then stands in contrast with the spiritual relationship brought out in v.11, where he states "that he might be the father of all them that believe though they be not circumcised".

2 The Jews believed that Abraham was justified by works. Doubtless there were meritorious acts in the patriarch's life. His response to the call of God, his gracious dealings with his nephew Lot, his readiness to battle with Chedorlaomer, his refusal to comply with the king of Sodom's requests and many more are faithfully recorded, but not one of them was the basis on which he was reckoned righteous. Despite the evidences of spirituality of a high order in Abraham, the apostle's statement remains true; if he had cause for boasting, it was not before God. Even if all his accomplishments were taken together they would not add up to a claim to be accounted righteous.

Scripture is clear in its pronouncement that there is none righteous, no not one, there is none that doeth good.

If indeed Abraham had something to boast about then Paul's argument in ch.2 was invalid. He had asserted that birth, ceremonial observances, custody of law and national privileges were of no value. If it could now be proved that God had accepted any act of Abraham which could be counted for righteousness, then all that Paul had advanced in support of the gospel had no substance. In this verse, however, the apostle repels any suggestion that Abraham had anything to boast about; if he had, it was only before man, not before God.

The question raised in v.1 regarding what Abraham found, must be answered unequivocally: he found nothing to glory in before God. It is not suggested of course that Abraham did boast in his works. It would be an injustice to the patriarch to portray him as one who laid claim to righteousness on the basis of what he did. Paul's reply to a Jewish objection to his assertion that justification is by faith alone is that not even Abraham, the forefather of the nation, had a claim on God through his works. He was entirely dependent on the mercy of God.

3 By asking the question, "For what saith the scripture?" the matter is taken out of the realm of supposition or personal opinion. The appeal to the Holy Scriptures implies that what is recorded therein is the divine mind on the subject. This then is the final word. About it, the Jews could have no objection. As already stated, they were custodians of the oracles of God, the infallible Word, and there was no way of avoiding the implications of that. Here Paul personifies the Scripture and makes it speak. What does it say? It says, "Abraham believed God and it was counted unto him for righteousness". No Jew needed to be told whereabouts in the Scripture this momentous statement was made. He could turn to the book of Genesis and put his finger on it, but did he accept it personally?

It has been said that there were nine successive manifestations of God to Abraham and that the appearance in Gen 15 is the fifth, or central one. Certainly the principle which is established in 15:6 is pivotal; it is the basis for all God's dealings with mankind, even in the present age of grace. There in the history of Abraham is embedded the central theme of the gospel, "Abraham believed God". It is of interest to note that in Gen 15, a most remarkable chapter, there are several words which appear for the first time. These are "righteousness", "counted", "believed", "fear not" and even a phrase, "the word of the Lord came". These are all voices from the past, which in their day were encouragements to Abraham, but are pledges of greater things to come, although their fulfilment lay thousands of years further on in the purposes of God in Christ.

It has to be acknowledged that prior to Gen 15:6, righteousness was not reckoned to Abraham. The state of being "right" with God was not one that Abraham had arrived at prior to believing the word of God that his seed would be as the stars of heaven for number. Undoubtedly Abraham had faith before the experience of Gen 15, but his response to the seemingly impossible promise was such an emphatic trust in God that it was reckoned to him for righteousness. God Himself was the object of his faith, the word of God was the ground of it and the crediting of righteousness was the result.

There are two other occasions in the NT where Gen 15:6 is quoted. In each of the three passages the context is different. The background in Rom 4 portrays Abraham as a man who staggered not at the promise of God through unbelief; but was strong in faith, giving glory to God. He considered not the deadness of his own body or that of Sarah's womb but believed the word of God when He said, "...so shall thy seed be" and as a result, Isaac was born.

In Gal 3, Paul upbraids the Galatians for yielding to Judaisers. They were in danger of returning to law-works. He had to remind them that their beginning in Christianity was by faith: the works of the law were not involved. If they supposed that they had secured the favour of God by works then they had to consider Abraham whom they revered. His beginning was on the basis of faith and he was reckoned righteous on that ground, but those who claimed to be his descendants did not act according to the same principle. Paul found it necessary therefore to bring to the attention of the Galatians the verse which contained the basic principle of the gospel, "Even as Abraham believed God, and it was accounted to him for righteousness" (v.6).

James in his epistle considers the scene on mount Moriah where Isaac was offered up on the altar. Even if there had been no intervention to hold back the knife, Abraham would still have believed God, the God of resurrection. He had promised Abraham that in his seed all the nations of the earth would be blessed and Abraham believed that, even though his successor was on the altar. James, whose practical ministry called for works of faith, saw in the act of Abraham the fulfilment of Gen 15:6, and so he recorded, "And the Scripture was fulfilled which saith, Abraham believed God, and it was imputed unto him for righteousness: and he was called, the friend of God" (2:23).

As a result of Abraham's implicit acceptance of God's word, Paul states that his belief was counted unto him for righteousness. The verb rendered "counted" is *logizō*, "to reckon". It is exactly the same as Gen 15:6 LXX and is the word rendered "imputed" at 4:22. Plummer devotes much space in his commentary in an attempt to prove that "imputed" gives the correct sense of what God did for Abraham. In this connection, however, Vine makes a valid point. He asserts that "reckoned" gives the proper sense, since whatever is reckoned to a person cannot have been his originally and naturally. The preferred reading of Rom 4:3 is therefore, "Abraham believed God, and it was reckoned unto him for righteousness".

4 This verse declares a general principle. If a person works he is due remuneration, what is owed to him is a debt; his remuneration could never be considered as being according to grace. As it is found here, the primary application is obviously to Abraham. He was justified apart from works, but the principle involved in his justification has far-reaching implications.

The person who cannot see beyond working for salvation must recognise that what is received in return is in the nature of payment for work done. The solemn fact, however, is that the person who works is the one who estimates the amount of work that requires to be done because there is no guidance in Scripture in support of that view. The question must then be faced, What remuneration is due in return for the work done? Who calculates that? Again, the Scripture is silent. A moment's reflection on the holiness of God should be enough to reject any thought of obtaining salvation by working for it. And yet, many millions in every generation labour to obtain life. In the economy of God, obtaining life comes before labour. In the estimation of men, labour comes before obtaining life and therein lies man's miscalculation.

If it were true that an abundance of good works earns life, then only a few would be saved. Those who failed to reach it, by however small a margin, would be lost and their labours, performed with the best of intentions, would be in vain. This is exactly how matters would turn out in practice as far as many religions and their adherents are concerned. How far astray it is from the ways of God! Free grace is declared in the gospel, but yet how few there are who are prepared to believe the message and take God as His word, just as Abraham did and as a result was reckoned righteous.

5 Abraham is a classical example of the opening words of this verse, "But to him that worketh not". He did not do any works of merit which might have resulted in his being accounted righteous. There was nothing in him or about him to boast about before God. He simply took the Lord at His word and believed it. As for his seed becoming as numerous as the stars, that was beyond his powers to initiate, but he believed that the Lord could do it and that put him in the class which comprises, "him that worketh not, but believeth on him that justifieth the ungodly".

There can be no argument that men are ungodly. Many Scriptures prove this to be so. In Jude's short epistle the term is used five times to describe the ungodliness of men. It would be expected therefore that a holy God could do no less than pronounce judgment upon them. He would be perfectly righteous in dealing with man according to his deserts. The marvel of it is that He has found a way whereby the ungodly can be justified. Apart from the gospel these two words "ungodly" and "justified" are mutually exclusive, and indeed, apart from the gospel, it is paradoxical to say that the ungodly are justified.

How God can justify the ungodly is the miracle. He not only pardons the sinner who believes His word, but He reckons him righteous. He does not make him godly and He does not make him righteous, but He declares him to be righteous on the ground of the sacrifice of Christ on the cross and His resurrection in power and glory. The ungodly who confess their total unworthiness and cast themselves unreservedly on the mercy of God, these are the ones whose "faith is counted for righteousness".

To the Jew, what Paul was asserting was totally unacceptable. As far as he was concerned, the ungodly were the impious Gentiles. He believed his good works would see him through. He thought his God-given system of religious observances was bound to have merit with God. In view, however, of what Paul taught here, a radical change of mind was necessary. The Jew was as ungodly as any other man, and only repentance (a total change of heart and life) and faith in the Lord Jesus Christ for salvation would suffice. All else was valueless.

6 But is it valid to infer from the case of Abraham that God justifies "the ungodly"? To the history of David the apostle now turns for his second illustration from the OT Scriptures. He will draw attention to a precedent already established in the word of God, in which God had forgiven a sinner and justified the ungodly. Admittedly the blessings of which David spoke looked forward to the cross, whereas what Paul was making known was based on the finished work of Christ. In anticipation of the cross of Christ, God could show grace in OT times and there is perhaps no clearer example than in His dealings with David. There was precedent therefore for what Paul was declaring and no Jew could deny that the Scriptures which he professed to uphold bore testimony to the truth that the apostle was making known.

If the Jews found fault with Paul's teaching about forgiveness of sins, justification by faith and the justification of the ungodly, the objections would carry no weight; the precedent for what Paul was advancing was already established. From the lives of two worthies of the past, Abraham and David, revered so highly by the Jews, the lessons were clear and could not be denied. God had reckoned righteousness on the principle of faith. Paul was not asserting that there was righteousness in faith; he was stating that the faith that is reckoned for righteousness is that which acknowledges personal sinnership and relies entirely on God for mercy.

From the ways of God with two of His servants of the past, Paul had made known that the principle on which God was working was the principle of faith. It was only on that basis that David knew, and so could describe, the blessedness of the man to whom God reckoned righteousness. True, the quotation which follows in the next verse makes no mention of the words "without works", but it is obvious that there was no possibility of David being justified by works, and so what Paul adds at the end of the verse is a confirmation of what he has already stated so strongly. This blessedness which David described did not come by human effort. Even the Jew would have to admit that the penitential psalm from which the quotation was taken would not admit of any suggestion of works of any kind. If blessedness was experienced it was inextricably linked with the mercy of God. It was joy freely bestowed by God in His compassion.

7 The quotation from Ps 32 is an excellent example of how a Jew, schooled in the OT Scriptures, could lift the appropriate statement from the word of God and apply it to whatever circumstance was under consideration. Ps 32 is one of David's seven penitential psalms. It is also one of the thirteen *maschil* or teaching psalms. After David was confronted by Nathan the prophet in connection with his dreadful sin, he was brought low in contrition and promised he would teach transgressors God's ways. In this *maschil* psalm therefore, David sets out his experiences, and burdened down with a sense of guilt, he seeks to warn others.

It is not all gloom and despair, however, as the psalm begins with a beatitude and ends with a shout of joy. This blessedness is not only the joy of having transgressions forgiven and sins covered; the suggestion is there that the sinner is aware of the compassion of God. Happy is the man who knows what God has done with his transgressions. The penitent may never forgive himself, but God has put them away for ever, never to be recalled. His sins are covered, buried out of sight, just as Pharaoh and his hosts were covered by the Red Sea. It is little wonder therefore that David could pronounce the blessedness of the man, since he was blessed, not because of his works of merit, but in spite of his evil deeds.

The two men introduced by Paul as illustrations of the ways of God in the past were the most illustrious of the Jewish forebears. The Jews could not cavil at the apostle because the gospel intimated justification by faith; the precedent was there already in the Scriptures in the experience of Abraham. Neither could they protest about the declaration that God justified the ungodly; the case of David was there to prove it. The gospel message therefore was not novel. What Paul was intimating was perfectly in keeping with the Scriptures. Neither justification by faith nor justifying the ungodly were new procedures, and it was clear that God could do so and still remain righteous.

8 Paul continues to speak of the blessedness of the man who found mercy from the Lord. The quotation in the previous verse is taken from Ps 32 LXX in which the Hebrew text is changed from "Blessed is *he* whose transgression is forgiven, whose sin is covered", to "Blessed are *they* whose transgressions are forgiven, and whose sins are covered". David wrote about one man, but Paul, following the LXX, wrote about many. Possibly he was thinking of all who would come into the benefit of the work of Christ by responding to the call of the gospel.

This verse carries on with the quotation from Ps 32 but stops short of the final clause of v.2 which goes on to say, "in whose spirit ('mouth', LXX) there is no guile". Here is another example of the Spirit guiding His penman to quote what was necessary and no more. Paul's argument was dealing with transgressions being forgiven and sins covered. Anything more than that was not relevant at this point and so he stopped. What concerns him is the happiness of the man to whom the Lord will not impute sin, which is a negative way of re-stating the words of v.6 concerning the blessedness of the man unto whom God imputeth, or reckons, righteousness.

The word rendered "impute" *(logizomai)* occurs eleven times in this chapter;

it means to occupy oneself with reckonings or calculations, to reckon or count; to reckon anything to a person, to put it to account, either in his favour or what he must be answerable for. Some maintain that it is an accounting expression, meaning that the debt is not reckoned. This of course is a source of joy to the sinner. Here then, Paul emphasises the happiness of the man whose debt of sin is not charged to him. God has taken care of it and in doing so remains righteous. Apart from the work of Christ on the cross He could never have done that.

Notes

1 "Father" (*propatora*) is better rendered "forefather".

The meaning of "flesh" (*sarka*) in the Scriptures is determined by the context, e.g. 1 Cor 15:39, what the body is made of, its substance; Gal 2:20, the human body, "And the life which I now live in the flesh"; John 1:14,, concerning the body of the Lord Jesus, all that was true of His manhood, "And the word was made flesh and dwelt among us"; Rom 8:9, unregenerate man, "they that are in the flesh cannot please God".

3 Thus far in the epistle "righteousness" has been mentioned only as an attribute of God (1:17, 3:5,21,22,25,26). Now for the first time it is spoken of as that which is reckoned to one that believes. Righteousness is the character or the quality of being right or just (Vine).

6 "Describeth" (*legō*, "to lay", or "lay before", "to relate") the RV translates as "pronounceth", suggesting that David was making a declaration of the blessing which had come to the man.

7 "Iniquities" (*anomia*) is the violation of law, whether unknown or wilfully violated.

"Forgiven" (*aphiēmi*, "to send away", "to dismiss") infers that the person is dealt with as if he were innocent.

"Sins" (*hamartia*, "failure", "a missing of the mark") are here in the plural, the many occasions of sinning being in view.

"Covered" (*epikaluptō*, "to cover up", "to cover over") occurs only here in the NT.

(b) *The spiritual fatherhood of Abraham (vv.9-25)*

v.9 "Cometh this blessedness then upon the circumcision only, or upon the uncircumcision also? for we say that faith was reckoned to Abraham for righteousness.
v.10 How was it then reckoned? when he was in circumcision, or in uncircumcision? Not in circumcision, but in uncircumcision.
v.11 And he received the sign of circumcision, a seal of the righteousness of the faith which he had yet being uncircumcised: that he might be the father of all them that believe, though they be not circumcised; that righteousness might be imputed unto them also:
v.12 And the father of circumcision to them who are not of the circumcision only, but who also walk in the steps of that faith of our father Abraham, which he had being yet uncircumcised.
v.13 For the promise, that he should be the heir of the world, was not to Abraham, or to his seed, through the law, but through the righteousness of faith.
v.14 For if they which are of the law be heirs, faith is made void, and the promise made of none effect:
v.15 Because the law worketh wrath: for where no law is, there is no transgression.

v.16 Therefore it is of faith, that it might be by grace; to the end the promise might be sure to all the seed; not to that only which is of the law, but to that also which is of the faith of Abraham; who is the father of us all,

v.17 (As it is written, I have made thee a father of many nations,) before him whom he believed, even God, who quickeneth the dead, and calleth those things which be not as though they were.

v.18 Who against hope believed in hope, that he might become the father of many nations, according to that which was spoken, So shall thy seed be.

v.19 And being not weak in faith, he considered not his own body now dead, when he was about an hundred years old, neither yet the deadness of Sara's womb:

v.20 He staggered not at the promise of God through unbelief; but was strong in faith, giving glory to God;

v.21 And being fully persuaded that, what he had promised, he was able also to perform.

v.22 And therefore it was imputed to him for righteousness.

v.23 Now it was not written for his sake alone, that it was imputed to him;

v.24 But for us also, to whom it shall be imputed, if we believe on him that raised up Jesus our Lord from the dead;

v.25 Who was delivered for our offences, and was raised again for our justification."

9 Having dealt with two illustrations from the Scriptures in the persons of Abraham and David, and having described the blessedness of those who have been justified apart from works, Paul now turns to the scope of justification and the subject of circumcision. He begins by posing a question, "Cometh this blessedness then upon the circumcision only, or upon the uncircumcision also?" Here the circumcision are the Jews and the uncircumcision are the Gentiles. The blessing therefore that David announced (v.6), is it pronounced upon the Jews or upon Gentiles also? The fact that David was under the law and was circumcised does not weaken Paul's argument. Indeed, when it is considered alongside Abraham's experience, it merely serves to prove the universality of the blessing, for Abraham was blessed before circumcision was introduced and before the law was given.

Regarding justification by faith which Paul has been propounding, the objection he anticipates from the Jews is obviously that Abraham and David were both circumcised. Since circumcision was an outward sign of the covenant between God and Abraham, the question may well be asked, "Is not circumcision valid as the ground of justification?" The apostle's answer to this is that it was because of his faith that Abraham was reckoned righteous. This statement implies that circumcision was not involved in the patriarch's justification. Moreover, Scripture is clear that circumcision was introduced some fourteen years after God had reckoned Abraham righteous. The Jews therefore were placing too much reliance on the observance of the rite and were missing entirely the first basic requirement, that faith was the principle governing a relationship with God.

The little expression, "for we say", could mean that Paul and his fellow-believers affirmed that Abraham's acceptance was by faith and was quite apart from circumcision. Or it could be an appeal to his fellow-countrymen to admit that the evidence of Scripture supported the views he had propounded. Taken either way, and both views have some merit, the following verses will prove that the rite of circumcision was not involved when God reckoned Abraham righteous.

10 Another question is posed. It makes an appeal to the inspired history of the Scriptures. The unfolding drama of the life of Abraham, called by James "the friend of God", records the outstanding expression of his faith in Gen 15, and his circumcision, about fourteen years later, in Gen 17. These are the facts recorded by Moses, the revered law-giver, and with this the Jew could not argue. The apostle then answers his own question. He anticipates that the Jew will give the same answer. Abraham's justification came before his circumcision. There is no way of escaping the implications of the fact that Abraham was justified while in uncircumcision.

There is no doubt that God entered into covenant relationship with Abraham and that the promises given to him were unconditional. The covenant promised land, which in its extent embraced most of the Middle East, although Abraham never possessed any more than ground for a grave in Canaan. Nevertheless, that promise will be fulfilled in the millennial age which has still to come. The covenant also included Abraham's "seed". His natural seed, the Hebrew people, were given the covenant sign, circumcision. The line of descent was through Isaac and through Jacob, not through Ishmael or Esau. This narrowed down the Messianic line, as the Messiah was also Abraham's "seed". In addition to that, in its widest sense, Abraham was "father of all them that believe": a spiritual people, those who became spiritual heirs by exercising the same trusting faith in God as Abraham showed in Gen 15. When therefore Paul raises the subject of circumcision at this point in the epistle, the Jew is obliged to re-think his position. Has he allowed the outward sign to displace what was the real issue, a faith like that of his father Abraham?

11 Although the rite of circumcision contributed nothing to Abraham's justification, this does not mean that circumcision was empty and futile. Paul here asserts that it was a sign. It bore testimony in Abraham's case that justification had been reckoned. The Scripture states that it was a token of the covenant between God and Abraham (Gen 17:11). When it was given to Abraham, the sign had meaning. It was outward in the flesh but it bore witness to the uprightness of the man who was marked by it and who was in a right relationship with God. Later in the history of the nation, Moses and the prophets had to remonstrate with the people of Israel and remind them that circumcision of heart was what was needed, since the outward sign had lost its meaning.

Circumcision was also a seal. It ratified the covenant. It had no value in itself, but it bore witness to the importance of the transaction which had taken place. It was also a seal of the righteousness of the faith that was Abraham's before he was circumcised. This, states the apostle, was that he might become the father of all them that believe, though they be in uncircumcision. Abraham would be at the head of a long line of spiritual men and women. Jews and Gentiles could therefore be blessed entirely independently of circumcision, but if righteousness was going to be reckoned to others of succeeding generations it would be in the same way as Abraham received the blessing.

Circumcision, however, was not futile. God desired a nation which would be separated from other nations and would be in covenant relationship with Him. The people would be marked by the sign and it would be a seal of their special position before God. Great things would be expected of them, but, as their conduct proved, in practice they did not respond to the high privileges which God had bestowed upon them. The Jews were swift to claim that they were Abraham's children and that they had Abraham's seal, but they did not follow in Abraham's steps.

12 If Abraham was to be the father of all who believe, it was essential that the divine method of justification should be inaugurated before he was circumcised. In the plans and ways of God, Abraham was to be the pattern of all who would be justified by faith. He was to be the head of a spiritual race of people, taken out from the nations of men by the call of God.

The Jews held fast to their claim that Abraham was the father of their race. To them, circumcision was the outward sign and seal that proved it. Paul, however, sweeps aside such reasoning by stating that Abraham was the father of the circumcision to those Jews who walked in the steps of the faith that Abraham had before he was circumcised. No doubt this would be a shock to the pride of the Jews. That Abraham was father only to those who were in step with his faith was a blow to their self-esteem. In addition, the fact that the Gentiles could also claim him as their father, since he was the father of all that believe, was quite contrary to all that they held sacred.

From the apostle's reasoning therefore it is clear that the Jews who depended so much on their natural descent from Abraham and who prided themselves in it, would not come into the good of it by natural relationship only. They would have to set aside prejudice and come in the same way as the believing Gentiles. Only on the ground of faith as exhibited by Abraham before he was circumcised would they find acceptance with God.

13 The promise to which Paul alludes in this verse is stated in Gen 17. It was not given to Abraham because of his works. This is made clear in vv.2,3 of this chapter. Neither did the patriarch receive the promise through the law, because the law of Sinai was not in vogue when the promise was given to him. On what basis then did Abraham receive the promise that he would be the father of many nations? It was on the principle of the righteousness of faith. Abraham took God at His word and as a result he was reckoned to be right or just. Clearly what he did had no merit in it as something to boast about, as the apostle has already made known; it was simply that he believed God implicitly and it was reckoned to him for righteousness (v.3).

In this verse Paul declares that Abraham was given the promise that he would be the heir of the world. This statement was not the subject of a fresh revelation given to the apostle, it was based on the record of Gen 17, and even earlier (Gen 12:3). In the biblical sense, it was not necessary for the heir to enter the possession to be credited with it. It was sufficient that it had been assigned to him. So in this verse, alluding to the Genesis account, Canaan was promised to Abraham and his seed. It was to be an everlasting possession. Its wider implications are embraced in the promise, "thou shalt be a father of many nations" (Gen 17:4). In addition, if taken in a spiritual sense, the implications are even wider, "that he might be the father of all them that believe" (v.11).

The promise was not only to Abraham, but to his seed. In some NT references, Abraham's "seed" refers to Christ (Gal 3:16), but here, obviously the word is used in a general sense to take in all Abraham's descendants. The apostle's line of reasoning was intended to prove that any blessing derived from being Abraham's seed was not necessarily gained by being born a Jew. The Jews were quick to claim in the presence of the Lord, "We be Abraham's seed" (John 8:33). This was refuted by the Lord, "If ye were Abraham's children, ye would do the works of Abraham" (John 8:39). The Jews claimed exclusive rights to being Abraham's seed, but theirs was not a valid claim.

14 The apostle continues to reason hypothetically. He asserts, "For if they which are of the law be heirs, faith is made void, and the promise made of none effect". If by obeying the law men and women become heirs, then faith is an empty thing. As a principle it has no force. In addition, the promise which Paul has spoken about in the previous verse is rendered inefficient. (See note on *katargeō* at 3:3,31. The implication is that the promise has lost its substance; it carries no weight.) If the Jews were heirs as a result of their association with the law, then faith did not enter into the matter, and the promise given to Abraham was of no consequence.

In the apostle's argument here, faith and the promise stand together. If the law is considered to be the principle whereby blessing can be obtained, then all that Paul has argued for from the beginning of the epistle in relation to justification is nullified. This assertion, of course, cannot stand. Not only was the promise about Abraham's seed given before the law was introduced, it antedates the basic faith-principle of Gen 15:6. Shortly after Abraham left Ur of the Chaldees and stepped out in obedience to the call of God, the promise was given, "Unto thy seed will I give this land" (Gen 12:7). Instead therefore of the law taking precedence over faith and promise, the apostle will now show that it cannot provide a title to being an heir to the blessings of God.

The covenant with Abraham promised a land. In its extent it covered much of the Middle East, from the Nile to the Euphrates. Abraham's seed, his natural descendants, have never possessed any more than a small portion of what God promised to the patriarch. The fact, however, that the Hebrew people have never taken over all the inheritance does not alter what God promised; the land will still be theirs, but not until the Lord takes up the reins of government in the millennial age. In that day God will fulfil the promise He made to Abraham, thousands of years before. As far as the Jewish nation is concerned, the inheritance will not be theirs because of their association with the law, it will only be on the ground of promise.

15 The law, the fulfilment of which was impossible because of the sinfulness of man, was still upheld by the Jews as the standard by which the great matters of life were decided. It was given to Israel. No other nation possessed such a revelation from God. By reason of this the Israelites were marked out as special. But the law could not give life. In effect, all that it did was to work wrath, because failure to keep its commandments brought condemnation. The Jew knew that this was the case. The law which he guarded so jealously and professed to uphold had no power over the flesh, it could not deliver from sin. Indeed, Paul will note that it stimulated sin because the flesh responded to its prohibitions by sinning all the more.

The existence of law brings forth transgressions. If law did not exist then there would be no precepts to break. Although men are sinners by nature and by practice, where no law is in force the precise nature of sin is not brought home to the conscience. Although sin exists and men are aware that they are sinners, the absence of law means that they have no clear guidance about what is right and what is wrong. When law is brought in, the position is changed. The precepts can then be observed, but because of the sinful nature which man possesses, these turn out to be broken commandments which work out for the sinner the wrath of God.

As far as heirship is concerned, it is evident from Paul's reasoning that to be possessors of a clear title to the promised inheritance would necessitate showing the same quality of faith which Abraham demonstrated. If law is brought in, the promise is excluded. Law has the witness in itself. If its commandments are broken, wrath is the only outcome. To plead adherence to the law, which they could not keep, only exposed the Jews to wrath, and did nothing for them as far as providing them with a title to the inheritance promised to Abraham.

16 Having argued that the law could do nothing but bring condemnation, Paul asserts again that the promise could not be made good to the Jews by the law. The promise in itself had no conditions attached to it. The apostle used the word "promise" (*epaggelia*), which suggests goodness, extended unconditionally. The promise therefore was of faith that it might be of grace. From man's side, faith is the pre-requisite. On God's part it is grace, free unmerited favour. If faith had anything meritorious about it, then grace would be ruled out. Since, however, law and works of merit are excluded, and grace is introduced alongside faith and promise, the picture is complete. Paul can now go on to consider in some detail the nature of Abraham's justification.

The promise therefore is by faith that it might be by grace. The fulfilment of the promise to Abraham and his seed is not based on obedience to the law but on the free favour of God. In His sovereignty God determined to act according to His own grace. No protest from man can be countenanced. If He so decrees, that is the end of the matter. God will have the promise made sure to all the seed. The word used for "sure" (*bebaios*), is sometimes used as a legal guarantee. Peter uses it in that sense, "strive diligently to make your calling and election sure" (2 Pet 1:10) – provide the guarantee in a godly life that God did not make a mistake in His choice or in His call in the gospel. Here the grace of God is the guarantee that the promise will be made good to Abraham's seed.

The promise is not to Abraham's natural seed only, but to all of his spiritual seed also. Only those, however, who exercise the same faith as he did are included in this statement. Whether Jew or Gentile, a right relationship with God can be obtained only through faith. When faith is exercised then the link with Abraham is forged. It is then that he becomes to the faithful, "the father of us all".

17 Although the Jews looked upon Abraham as the father of the nation, Paul calls in the witness of the OT to prove that Abraham had a wider heritage. He refers to Gen 17:5, the occasion when the name Abram ("exalted father") was changed to Abraham ("father of a multitude"), "for a father of many nations have I made thee". If the fatherhood of Abraham had any meaningful relationship with any, it was only as "the father of us all". The universal fatherhood of Abraham is declared by Paul to be in accordance with the Scriptures, "as it is written, I have made thee a father of many nations". The seed of Abraham is not restricted to the descendants of Isaac, the child of promise, or to Ishmael, the product of the flesh, but includes all down the ages who will have exercised implicit faith in the word of God. Abraham's belief not only settled his standing before God personally, it had far-reaching effects for millions who would seek to be justified on the same basis.

Abraham's only son was Ishmael when Abraham then stood in the presence of God and was made the father of a great posterity, the natural and the spiritual. Nevertheless, he had no doubt that God was able to perform all that He had promised. The God in whom Abraham trusted was the quickener of the dead. This expression is capable of having more than one interpretation. It is possible that Abraham believed in the ability of God to raise the dead. This is evidenced in the mount Moriah experience when Isaac was placed on the altar. Even if there had been no intervention, Abraham believed that God would give him back his son from the dead. This is made clear by the writer to the Hebrews, "Accounting that God was able to raise him up, even from the dead, from whence also he received him in a figure" (Heb 11:19). Since, however, the apostle refers in v.19 to Abraham's body as being now dead, and to the deadness of Sarah's womb, it is more in keeping with the context to link the quickening power of God to Abraham and his wife.

In the sight of God, Abraham was the father of many nations. Naturally and spiritually he was the fountain-head. As he and Sarah were beyond the age of producing children when the promise was made, the power of God had to come into their lives and quicken their dead bodies. The patriarch could never have been the father of us all (v.16), if the power which quickeneth the dead had not operated in the bodies of Abraham and Sarah. This is also confirmed by the writer to the Hebrews, "Through faith also Sarah herself received strength to conceive seed, and was delivered of a child when she was past age, because she judged him faithful who had promised. Therefore sprang there even from one, and him as good as dead, so many as the stars of the sky in multitude, and as the sand is by the sea shore innumerable" (Heb 11:11,12).

The expression, "calleth these things which are not" is also capable of more than one interpretation. It may be understood to mean God's creative call whereby He can even call worlds into being. Out of nothing He can bring forth what He determines. It may mean, however, that He can speak of the future, even the far-distant future, and about things which do not yet exist, and address them with the certainty of present existence. As Paul is considering the seed of Abraham and his being the father of many nations, the latter view is probably what the apostle had in mind.

18 A literal translation of the opening words of this verse in the original reads, "who beyond hope on hope believed". What was promised to Abraham had all the appearances of impossibility. He had nothing which the natural eye could identify as the foundation for what was promised, "so shall thy seed be". Nevertheless, faced with the absence of substance for all human hope, he believed with all confidence. His hope was not a blind irrational response. It was an attitude of mind and heart that acknowledged that the One who had made the promise would bring all to pass according to His word. How He would do it was not in question. It was quite beyond Abraham's capabilities to work that out. What faced him was that there was no hope in the natural course of things, but with a joyful hope he believed implicitly what the Lord promised.

The quotation is from Gen 15:5. The phrase, "according to that which was spoken" expresses the divine view. It removes any thought that Abraham had any involvement in the matter, except to believe implicitly what God had promised. The background in Gen 15 is an interlude where Abraham has veered off the path and God had dealings with him. The concern of the patriarch that he had no child is clearly evident. It was he who raised the subject of seed and implied that God had withheld an heir from him. Nevertheless, a look at the stars which were beyond numbering and the promise, "so shall thy seed be" settled the matter: "he believed in the Lord; and he counted to him for righteousness". God did not withhold an heir from Abraham, He merely delayed giving him one in order that he might see that His plans would not come to pass through the strength of the flesh.

19 Although Paul stated that Abraham was not weak in faith, the Genesis account to which he alludes in this verse would seem to indicate a measure of unbelief. When God intimated to His servant that he would father a son in his old age, Abraham laughed. If the laughter, however, had been born of unbelief Paul would not have been able to state that he was not weak in faith, which is another way of saying that he was strong in it. It must therefore mean that Abraham heard news that was beyond acceptance by natural standards, and that while giving vent to the laughter of amazement, it called forth the response of faith and action on his part.

When the Lord appeared to Abraham in the plains of Mamre and referred to the subject of the child that would be born to him and his wife, Sarah heard and she laughed within herself . She had then to learn two lessons. The first one concerned the almighty power of God, put to Abraham in the form of a question, "Is anything too hard for the Lord?" The second lesson concerned God's knowledge of the thoughts of the heart. Sarah laughed within herself, but God knew what she was thinking and He knew there was within her the laughter of unbelief.

The reference to the book of Genesis does not take into account the laughter of Abraham or the laughter of Sarah. Paul does not mention it, neither does he say anything about the impassioned plea that Abraham made on behalf of Ishmael. The child of Hagar was Abraham's son and it was natural that he should plead for him. What Abraham did not take into account was the fact that at best Ishmael would have been only a substitute. God had no intention of building on the strength of the flesh. He would build on the child of promise who would come forth from a body as good as dead and from a womb, the deadness of which was beyond question.

The point being made by Paul is that Abraham, contrary to what others would have believed, or would have done, on the basis of his hope on God, did what God required. The weakness of the body did not weaken his faith. He considered his body and he acknowledged that it was dead (see RV, JND notes). He considered also that God was able to do what He had promised. Although he pleaded for Ishmael, which would have been only a second-best arrangement, even if God had agreed, he nevertheless believed that God would fulfil His promise in His own way. To a man who was about a hundred years old and to a woman who was about ninety years old, the intimation given to them called for the utmost faith.

20 The literal translation of this verse in the original is more expressive. It reads, "but against the promise of God he did not decide by unbelief, but was empowered by faith, giving glory to God". The opening words are emphatic by reason of their position. The stress is put on Abraham's decision. Against the promise of God he did not waver. He knew what he was doing and he did not doubt for a moment. There was not even a momentary hesitation through unbelief, just a ready demonstration of the strength of his faith. The phrase, "was strong in faith" is rendered in the RV, "but waxed strong through faith", although the literal translation seems to express the sense better, "but was empowered by faith". His absolute confidence in God empowered him to believe the promise and to go forward in the good of it.

The closing comment of the verse, "giving glory to God" is what accompanied his stance in faith. By taking God at His word he acknowledged what was true of God, His omnipotence and His many attributes. The reference is not to the expression of worship, but to what emanated from his conduct. His wholehearted belief brought glory to God. There was by his action, as it were, a rendering of the honour and praise that is always due to the God of glory, but which is so seldom rendered, either by word or deed, by those who have benefited from His grace.

21 If the great problems of life are looked at from a human point of view only, pessimism is bound to be present. In connection with Abraham, there is never even a hint of pessimism in his dealings with God as recorded in Gen 15. Indeed, the very opposite seems to have been the case, as is apparent from the word used by Paul in this verse. The patriarch was fully assured within himself, not from any outside pressures, that what was promised would come to pass. The consideration of the stars for number was not a factor which gave him the assurance mentioned here; it was his trust in God who was able to multiply his seed just as He had brought myriads of stars into being by His creatorial power.

The full assurance stated here is a summing up of all that Paul has recorded about Abraham. Here was a man who against hope believed in hope, who was not weak in faith and staggered not at the promise of God through unbelief. His mind was never divided by pessimistic thoughts about himself or doubts about the ability of God. He was, as Paul stated so clearly, strong in faith, giving glory to God. It is understandable therefore that Paul should conclude his reasoning on the nature of Abraham's justification by stating that this notable servant of God was fully persuaded that God was able to perform all that He had promised.

22 Here Paul repeats what he has already stated at v.3. The allusion is to Gen 15:6, a key verse of Holy Scripture. It is used again to answer any who thought it was possible to be justified by the deeds of the law. It is another reminder that the father of the nation was reckoned righteous on the principle of faith. He did not strive to earn the blessing. Although what God promised militated against the hope that he had, he never lost his assurance that God was able to perform.

In Gal 3:6, Paul quotes Gen 15:6 to counteract the inroads of Judaism. If the Jews considered they had gained the favour of God through law-works, they should consider how the one they claimed to be their father was reckoned righteous – it was through faith! The Galatians were in serious danger of supplanting Christ by Judaising teaching that belief in Christ was not sufficient.

Christ would then be supplemented by works of law. Paul's argument is that when the gospel was preached to the Galatians, Christ and Him crucified was graphically portrayed to them and they were totally convinced. The beginnings of the Galatians were therefore by faith and they had to consider that Abraham's beginning was on the same basis.

The argument in Romans is noticeably different. Paul is not considering Judaising teaching; he is setting out the underlying principles of the gospel, the only message that addresses the need of sinners. As he does so, he deals with the relative positions of Gentiles and Jews and makes clear to both that faith is the only principle on which God reckons righteousness.

23 The argument which Paul has centred on the life of Abraham was not merely a setting out of historical facts. He has stressed that the Genesis account of how Abraham was reckoned righteous gave no scope for believing in a mixture of works of merit and a weak faith. The patriarch waxed strong in faith and works of merit were not involved in any way. The respect which Paul shows to the Scriptures may be in part the result of having been brought up to regard them as the oracles of God. Apart from that it is clear from the series of quotations that he made earlier (3:10-18), that he, like the Pharisees and scribes, could run portions of the Scripture together and make them into a cohesive and telling case in an argument or submission on most subjects.

Here the apostle makes known that what was written in the Genesis account was not for Abraham only, "but for us also". It was written that others in succeeding generations would recognise that the principle of faith was the one which God took into account. The relevance of the OT Scriptures in the daily lives of Christians is brought out later in the epistle, where the apostle states that the things that were written aforetime were written for our learning (15:4). This is a remarkable statement. It implies that the inspired writers of the past were not only writing for their own generations but in the wisdom of God and under the guidance of the Holy Spirit were writing for future generations also. Not only so but it infers that in every age, following the completion and circulation of the sacred writings, the recipients of them were responsible to read them, consider them and apply them to daily living.

In this verse, the apostle states that what was written about Abraham's righteousness and how it was reckoned was not for Abraham's sake only. The next verse develops the point, but here some important principles are established. Paul's reference to what was written emphasises his support for the inspiration of the Scriptures. They were divinely arranged to deal with the time then present and also to apply to other generations as well. In addition, since what Paul was writing was under the guidance of the Holy Spirit the union of both Testaments is confirmed as being the inspired word of God.

24 The particular issue of what was written is the reckoning of righteousness to Abraham and the principle on which it was done. If God could reckon righteousness to Abraham, Paul's argument is that God can do it again, provided the kind of faith the patriarch demonstrated is the ground of it. The case of Abraham was a representative one. It was designed to be an example of how God could enter into dealings with mankind. Paul stood on the threshold of the gospel age, and as he made known the gospel message he was aware that the central core of the message was faith. Just as it was with Abraham, so it was with the gospel, "For by grace are ye saved through faith; and that not of yourselves: it is the gift of God: Not of works, lest any man should boast" (Eph 2:8,9). These verses from the epistle to the Ephesians are very nearly a summary of what Paul has set out in the early chapters of this epistle.

So Paul states that the things that were written were "for us also", or as the RV has it, "but for our sake also", putting the stress on the NT aspect of the subject. Nevertheless, while that is so, the phrase is not merely one with a future application, it covers all God's dealings with believers in every age. The promise of the children of Israel to do everything that God said was soon proved to be incapable of fulfilment. Their history confirmed that law-works and works of merit were unavailing. Righteousness was reckoned on the principle of faith.

Faith is seen to rest upon God. He it is who raised the Lord Jesus from the dead. The mighty power which had worked in Abraham and Sarah, bringing life out of bodies which were dead as far as producing children were concerned, had been in operation again. It had raised "Jesus our Lord" from the dead. Here the apostle stresses the resurrection as the basic fact of the gospel of God and in addition he emphasises the Lordship of Christ. The faith that believes is now centred on Jesus and it acknowledges Him as Lord.

25 In the apostle's argument there are two great facts before him at this point. Christ was delivered up to the death of the cross and this was on account of our offences. Paul also states that Christ was raised again for our justification. The work that was undertaken at the cross was complete. As a result of that finished work, justification is secured for all who believe. Although the blessing is received on believing, the work which made it possible was finished by the Lord on the cross to the glory of God and on account of that God raised Him from the dead.

This verse seems to be an allusion to Isa 53. The first part of the verse appears to be a reference to Isa 53:5, "He was wounded for our transgressions, He was bruised for our iniquities". The word here for "delivered" (*paradidōmi*), is used in the latter half of Isa 53:6 LXX, "And the Lord gave (*paradidōmi*) him up for our sins". Or it may be that Paul had Isa 53:12 LXX before him, "And he bore the sins of many and was delivered (*paradidōmi*) because of their iniquities". Whatever verse the apostle had in mind, it seems clear that the sufferings of Christ as portrayed so graphically by Isaiah influenced him in his choice of words.

The reason why he was delivered up was because of our offences, our trespasses (*paraptōma*; see note at 2:23). Mankind has transgressed. The only hope for eternity was in the work of Christ. His death on the cross was where God settled the sin question.

At this point Paul is stressing what was secured by the death and resurrection of Christ. The argument does not dwell on the blessings obtained when the sinner believes. That will be developed later. Here he makes known that what was necessary to enable God to justify sinners was made good at the cross. As a result, Christ was raised from the dead. There was no argument against this fact. Apart from having been seen by so many witnesses, the resurrection was a confirmation that God had accepted the sacrifice of Christ as meeting all the demands of His holiness.

Notes

9 Paul's argument here makes clear that Gentiles do not defer to Jews to take upon themselves circumcision; it is the Jews who have to come in the same way as Abraham before cicumcision was introduced. In that, they are no different from Gentiles.

11 The Rabbis spoke of circumcision as being the seal of Abraham. If Abraham had not been circumcised he would have been the father of uncircumcised believers. By being circumcised after his justification, he became the father of the circumcised also. He is therefore the father of all them that believe.

12 "To them" instead of "of them" indicates the advantages of the relationship as well as the relationship itself (Vine).

The usual word for "walk" (*peripateō*), indicates activities apart from relation to others. The word used here, *stoicheō*, indicates the general conduct of a person in relation to others, so may be rendered "to keep step with others".

"In the steps of that faith" possibly refers to the period of Abraham's life from his call from Ur of the Chaldees until he was circumcised.

13 "Heir of the world" is not an OT expression, although the idea is in the promises (Gen 12:3 etc). Paul is perhaps thinking that the principle of faith demonstrated in Abraham will be the only worldwide principle affecting all mankind. In that sense, all who believe are part of the inheritance.

14 This verse indicates that the Jews cannot claim what is assigned to Abraham. If as individuals they abandon law-works and exercise faith, they and Gentile believers will then be fellow-heirs with the one who received the promises. As a nation, God has a future for Israel, but that is not the point here.

17 Alford considers "those things which be not" to mean the nations which should spring physically or spiritually from Abraham. They were not in existence when God spoke, nevertheless He spoke of them as being in existence, and this word, Abraham believed. It is certainly true that it is as easy for the Almighty to look forward as to look back. Of God's foreknowledge Paul will speak later in the epistle (8:29).

"Quicken", a compound word, would be better rendered "make alive".

21 In "fully persuaded" (*plērophorētheis*), "fully assured", as "things which are most surely believed among us" (Luke 1:1), the primary idea is being filled with a thought or conviction (Vincent).

3. *Blessings of Justification – for those who believe*
5:1-11

> v.1 "Therefore being justified by faith, we have peace with God through our Lord Jesus Christ:
> v.2 By whom also we have access by faith into this grace wherein we stand, and rejoice in hope of the glory of God.
> v.3 And not only so, but we glory in tribulations also: knowing that tribulation worketh patience;
> v.4 And patience, experience; and experience, hope:
> v.5 And hope maketh not ashamed; because the love of God is shed abroad in our hearts by the Holy Ghost which is given unto us.
> v.6 For when we were yet without strength, in due time Christ died for the ungodly.
> v.7 For scarcely for a righteous man will one die: yet peradventure for a good man some would even dare to die.
> v.8 But God commendeth his love toward us, in that, while we were yet sinners, Christ died for us.
> v.9 Much more then, being now justified by his blood, we shall be saved from wrath through him.
> v.10 For if, when we were enemies, we were reconciled to God by the death of his Son, much more, being reconciled, we shall be saved by his life.
> v.11 And not only so, but we also joy in God through our Lord Jesus Christ, by whom we have now received the atonement."

1 Although the word "Therefore" links v.1 with what has gone before, the apostle at this point in the epistle introduces a new theme. The effects of the faith which has been so much the subject of his argument are now going to be declared. Having therefore set out God's method of justifying sinners, Paul begins to deal with the blessings which come to those who have been justified by exercising faith in Christ. The whole matter hinges on the wonderful truth of the closing verse of ch.4, "Who was delivered for our offences, and raised again for our justification". In the immediate context, this is the basic fact which is linked to the new theme by the word "Therefore".

The verb translated "being justified" is in the aorist tense. It is a participle in the passive voice, indicating an event in the past when the person justified received the blessing. It is therefore better rendered, "having been justified by faith". It is of interest to note that from this point there will be a change of emphasis. It seems clear that having established the principle on which God justifies sinners, the great truths of the gospel will now be developed.

The AV states that the result of justification is peace with God through our Lord Jesus Christ. Because of considerable manuscript authority in support of *echōmen*, ("let us have"), as against *echomen* ("we have"), commentators are divided in their understanding of this phrase. The point at issue is whether Paul had broken with exposition and turned to exhortation. The RV has adopted the subjunctive mood and has rendered the passage, "let us have peace with God", thereby favouring exhortation. In accepting this reading, some insist that it simply means entering into the conscious enjoyment of justification. Many, however, prefer the AV reading as suiting Paul's unfolding of the truth. They hold that having been justified, the believer has peace with God. This is one of the blessings resulting from justification and it seems preferable to follow this line, despite the considerable weight of manuscript authority against it.

The word peace (*eirēnē*) occurs 88 times in the NT and is found in every book. Peace is one of the completely new relationships which have been brought about by the work of Christ. Indeed the Lord Himself, just before His departure from this scene, said to His disciples, "Peace I leave with you, my peace I give unto you, not as the world giveth" (John 14:27). Some passages, however, stress that peace should be diligently pursued (see 1 Pet 3:11; 2 Pet 3:14).

The idea behind peace is the absence of war or strife, and sometimes to obtain it, a person has to be involved in strife, or to be isolated from society, or insulated from outside influences to the point of being a recluse. Peace, according to Scripture is not like the worldly idea. It really sums up everything that makes for a person's highest good. It stresses right relationships between God and man and between man and man. It is not a negative word, speaking of the temporary absence of things which disturb the tranquillity of living, but a word which describes security, serenity, welfare and right relationships. The NT makes it clear that it comes from God (Rom 15:33; Phil 4:7). It also comes from the risen Lord (John 14:27). It comes through believing, as Rom 15:13 makes clear, "joy and peace through believing". When it is in exhortation, there are many spheres in life where it is called for, as in the home (1 Cor 7:15), or in the church (Col 3:15). Peace in the heart and life should rule out personal ambitions, prestige and bitterness. In this opening verse peace is introduced by Paul as the first of the blessings resulting from justification, and whether the phrase is looked at as an exhortation or as exposition, it suggests much of a practical nature.

2 Having established that peace with God is a blessing which belongs to the justified, the apostle now introduces the thought of access into "this grace wherein we stand". This blessing comes also through Jesus Christ. The RV stresses that it is the perfect tense which is used, "we have had", signifying that when justification took place, access was also involved and it continues into the present. The word given for "access" (*prosagōgē*), is used in Eph 2:18 for access to the Father, "For through him we have both access by one Spirit unto the Father". Here, however, the thought is more the entrance into the grace of justification, as stated at 3:24, "Being justified freely by his grace through the redemption that is in Christ Jesus", although it may also mean the limitless grace of God that is extended to those who are justified. Clearly, however, since the access is through the Lord Jesus Christ, there is also an introduction to the free favour of God which is an abiding condition.

Again the apostle stresses that this was not earned; the access was by faith. Some manuscripts omit "faith", but since the subject matter links with "justified by faith" of v.1, the principle is firmly established. The unmerited favour of God is a permanent position. Those who are justified are secure and there is no possibility of being separated from the blessing. If Christ was delivered up for our offences and raised again for our justification, our standing before God is inviolable. Nothing can possibly separate the believer from what has been won through the work of Christ.

The "rejoicing" here can be understood in two ways. It is either "let us rejoice" (RV) or "we rejoice" (AV). The word in the original is capable of being understood in either sense. It is again a question of exhortation "let us rejoice", or exposition, "we rejoice". Either way it is in hope of the glory of God. The hope here is the full assurance of enjoyment of the future display of the essential attributes and character of God.

3 Having made known that the future is sure and certain, the apostle turns to a consideration of the present. The sacrifice of Christ has guaranteed the future. The question now arises as to whether it has any influence in the present for the justified. Tribulation in the world is inevitable. It was the experience of the Lord when He was here in the flesh and it was the common lot of the apostles who represented Him after He had ascended to the right hand of God. Here Paul, who at the time of writing had suffered for testimony's sake, admits to rejoicing in tribulation. It is the same word as is used in the previous verse, "rejoice in hope". The AV rendering gives "we rejoice". The RV, however, follows its earlier preference for exhortation and reads "let us rejoice". Either way, the sense is much the same.

At first sight, glorying seems to be an odd response to the distressing circumstances which arise in daily living. The pressures which Paul had in mind were not solely the weight of adverse circumstances as they affect the body. Coping with these is bad enough, despite the apostle's ministry about glorying in them. There are pressures also which come upon the mind and upon the soul. They are not necessarily sent by God, but doubtless in his wisdom, He allows them. Nevertheless, whether they come singly or in greater numbers, the way to deal with them is clear, and that is "patient in tribulation" (Rom 12:12). There is no doubt that tribulations make deep impressions and often leave scars which never heal, but they are part of the lessons in the school of God, as Paul notes here, "tribulation worketh patience".

It is not the divine intention that His saints should succumb to tribulations. The word used here for "patience" speaks of conquering fortitude, a triumphant upward path to glory. It is the spirit which no circumstance of life can ever defeat. It is the ability to deal triumphantly with anything life can do. It is conquering patience. To lie down in despair and let the trials of life flood over the soul is not the response God expects. He wants from His saints the fortitude that will turn adversity into triumph. The circumstances of life which seem so adverse are not sent or allowed for the purpose of crushing out spiritual life, but are experiences which should lead to a deeper and greater appreciation of the love of God.

Paul states that tribulation worketh patience. The word "worketh" (*katergazomai*) has the idea of bringing out as a result, to realise in practice, to "bring to the goal" (Bengel). The word looks at the final result, bringing something to a conclusion, a full and complete accomplishment. Paul uses the word in his epistle to the Philippians where he encourages the saints to "work out their own salvation". There he means that the work begun by God in a believer must be worked at in the christian life until life is finished, until God's work is wrought out in the believer. To stop halfway or to lose impetus is contrary to the idea in the word. So here, tribulation worketh patience; it brings its trials through towards the goal, and on the way through it works out patient endurance. In its turn, patient endurance will work out its own result and this will be considered in the next verse.

4 While exhibiting fortitude under pressure, two other aspects of triumphant christian living are brought out. Patience worketh experience. Paul did not mean that patience was carried through to a conclusion and then a new circumstance was brought in which in turn was taken through to the goal. Obviously what was before his mind and what he was conveying was that while patiently coping with tribulations the one in the trials was proving that he had the approval of God.

The word rendered "experience" (*dokimē*), has rather the sense of proof by trial, the state or disposition of that which has been tried and approved. The saint who is undergoing tribulation and who exhibits fortitude in the trial, brings glory to God. That faith in Him which never wavers, despite the adverse circumstances, is most precious to God. Dealing with life's problems as God would wish is what earns divine approval.

In all these tribulations there is hope. Not only is the present taken care of, but the future does not lose its impact. Hope is one of the key words in the epistle to the Romans. Its message of encouragement permeates the whole. In this verse it is intended to bring comfort and give a sure anchorage to the soul. In some people tribulation works disappointment, even despair, so that instead of testing the mettle of the soul and tempering it in the process, misery is produced. This is because hope is wrongly placed – the expectation is not heavenly, but earthly.

5 Hope in the NT is not mere expectancy; it carries with it the assurance of faith. Later in this epistle, Paul will refer to the God of hope (15:13), the only reference in the NT to this title. In this, God is seen to be the author of hope, the source of it. But He is also characterised by hope – He never despairs because He is over all and all power is with Him. He never fails and He never gives up His saints as hopeless. Men and women may give up others as hopeless but God never has to admit that anyone is beyond His power to save or to help. With mankind, hope can be the expression of the uncertain, whereas the language of the NT indicates something which is quite different, "the full assurance of hope unto the end" (Heb 6:11). The Christian's hope is based on the living God who is utterly reliable and whose purposes, however long their fulfilment may tarry, can never be frustrated.

In this verse Paul's statement, "hope maketh not ashamed" seems to have more in it than just a comment about his confidence in God for the future. It appears rather to be a stance taken in the present, the outcome of a firm belief in what has been won for the believer by the work of Christ on the cross. Indeed, "hope maketh not ashamed" may be taken as a general principle. As far as Christians are concerned, they will not be put to shame by the world if they have grasped spiritual things with a firm grip. If hope is strong there is more likelihood of an open avowal of things believed. Hope cannot be worked up by self-effort – it is by the operation of the Holy Spirit of God.

It is thought that Paul had Ps 25 in his mind when he wrote that "hope maketh not ashamed". In that psalm, the psalmist cries, "O keep my soul and deliver me: let me not be ashamed; for I have put my trust in thee" (v.20). In the third verse of the psalm he expressed his desire, "yea, let none that wait on thee be ashamed; let them be ashamed that transgress without cause". The psalmist was jealous for the honour of God. Many were watching him to see if he would be ashamed of his testimony to the faithfulness of God. How pleased they would be if he went back on his trust, having found his hopes on God dashed. He was under scrutiny by his enemies to see if the God in whom he trusted would sustain him in all of life's trials.

The psalm would be well-known to the apostle, since it was the second of the seven penitential psalms and the third of nine acrostic ones. He would be aware of its contents and especially of the fears of the writer. The psalmist's desire was that his hope and trust in God would be free of shame. He was expressing in fact, a general principle, just as applicable when it was penned as it was in Paul's day and in every succeeding one. According to Paul, if "hope maketh not ashamed", it is because the love of God is shed abroad in our hearts by the Holy Spirit which is given to us. The love of God is said to be "poured out", or better, "it gushes out" by the Holy Spirit. That love is not a demonstration of human affection or emotion, it is divine love, dwelling in and flowing from the believer. There is no substitute for it and it cannot be imitated. Although this is so, the believer can experience it and this is seen in the fact that hope is not put to shame. The hope is real. It is centred on Christ and because it is firmly fixed on Him it engenders a trust which will never be ashamed.

As far as the believer's own personal experience is concerned, hope in God does not bring in shame. If there is patience in tribulation there will be no despair to rob the believer of joy. His hope set on God will enable him to face anything that he will meet and he will not be ashamed of God or of his relationship with Him. God's love, having been shed abroad in his heart, will remain with him and carry him through.

6 As proof that the love of God has been shed abroad in our hearts, the apostle brings in the death of Christ. Without having to say so, the difference between God's love and human love is apparent. This he will develop in vv.7,8. Here it is indicated in the phrase, "Christ died for the ungodly". It was when "we were without strength", helpless and powerless to deliver ourselves from the bondage of sin, and unable to obtain justification by any merit of our own. It was a hopeless situation, and it was as true of the religious Jew as it was of the irreligious Gentile. All are ungodly (v.6), sinners (v.8), enemies (v.10), but yet, all are included in the commendation of God's love, expressed in the sacrifice of Christ.

The phrase "in due season" emphasises that when Christ died for the ungodly, it was not an emergency measure. It was at a divinely-appointed time, one to which the ages of the past were all heading. The cross of Calvary is the central point of God's dealings with the human race. He was righteous in passing over the sins of the past because Calvary and all it entailed was coming. He is righteous in forgiving sins on the other side of the cross because the death of Christ is an accomplished fact. He has met all the claims of God against sin. As far as the place in the calendar of God is concerned, Paul's word to the Galatians is clear, "But when the fulness of time was come, God sent forth his Son" (4:4). Here in Rom 5 a different word for "time" is used, which emphasises more the conditions which applied when Christ died.

The due season of the purposes of God, involved the death of Christ and that for ungodly men and women. There is no thought here that some were godly and therefore outwith the necessity of having a Saviour who would need to die for them. The absence of the definite article before "ungodly" in the original, emphasises the kind of people for whom Christ suffered the penal consequences of sin: they were ungodly.

7 The theme introduced in v.5 concerning the love of God is continued in this verse by way of contrast. Human love, which at the best is very limited, is seen here to fall far short of taking a righteous man's place in death, even if that were called for or demanded. The righteous man spoken of here is one who is upright by human standards. It is the general conduct of the person Paul introduces, not someone who has been reckoned righteous by God, as has been the subject of the earlier chapters of the epistle. Although the thought is hypothetical in character, the truth of it is real. There are few, if any, who would enter into a death situation for another, unless there was at least a small chance of escaping the ultimate sacrifice before the final moment.

Paul, however, presses on with his submission. He supposes another case. This time he introduces a good man. Not so much a man who is marked out as intrinsically good. That would be similar in many respects to the upright man in his first illustration. If he had meant that, he would have used *kalos* to describe the person. The word he uses, *agathos*, describes someone who is useful, one who is occupied with things which would be beneficial. Such a person would appeal to the affections of another, possibly by reason of having been helped by practical kindness. Even here there is hesitancy: for such a person, one would even dare to die. There is but the possibility of the sacrifice being made. It has more chance of being put into practice than dying for a righteous person, but it is still far short of being an act likely to happen. The contrast is the great point. The love of God has no unlikely element about it. It is His own love; it is unique; there is nothing comparable in the human realm. The next verse will show what class of person is embraced by the love of God and how far His love is prepared to go on behalf of those who have no claim upon Him for mercy.

8 The contrast is now put into proper perspective. Human love at its best may make a sacrifice for the good man. That possibility is surpassed by the certainty of what God has done. He commends His love, presents it in its true character. It is a demonstration of undeserved devotion. Of His own goodness, not induced in any way by the object of His love, He bestows divine compassion without conditions. Here the objects of His love are not described as good, but identified for what they are – they are sinners. The word used is the most general and embracive word for sinners. There is no possibility of anyone slipping through the net. All men, everywhere, in every age, come under the condemnation, as already stated, "For all have sinned, and come short of the glory of God" (3:23).

The love of God does not require an improvement in moral standards before it acts. The wonder of it is that it was while we were yet sinners that it was demonstrated. The most unlikely evidence of His love is declared in a few words, "Christ died for us". In due time Christ died for the ungodly. Now it is made more personal, Christ died for us. There are no exceptions. All are embraced. Those who are looked upon as bright or good have to be classed with all others. In general terms all are ungodly and all need to be saved. On a more personal note, however, there is no escaping the fact, "Christ died for us". The apostle includes himself and those who laboured with him, making it clear to all who would read his epistle that there were no exceptions. The need was universal, but the remedy did not fall short, for "God so loved the world, that he gave his only begotten Son". Paul was not in possession of John's Gospel, but he was certainly aware of the scope of the love of God for mankind, and in his unfolding of the truth of the gospel, he made it known wherever he found opportunity to declare it.

9 This verse begins with the expression, "Much more then". It will arise again in vv.10,15,17. Its force here is that it introduces the outcome of the two great facts of v.8, God's love and Christ's death. The love of God cannot be in doubt if it expressed itself in such a sacrificial way to sinners as the death of Christ makes known. It follows therefore that any blessing which is offered to sinful men and women cannot fail to be realised, because the greatest demonstration of the love of God has taken place. As a result, the certainty of present and future blessing for the justified cannot be gainsaid. If God has made provision at such a cost whereby sinners can come into fellowship with Him, all else by way of blessing for the redeemed must follow unchallenged.

In the earlier part of the epistle justification is said to have been by faith. That was God's method and that was the principle on which He operated and by which the blessing was appropriated. The apostle also stated that justification was by grace (3:24). From the great reservoir of the free, unmerited favour of God, He moved out to those who had no merit of their own to plead. Now, in this verse, the great means by which justification is reckoned is noted as the blood. The shedding of the blood is the evidence firstly of a life given up, and secondly of a sacrificial offering have been made. In the OT offerings the sacrifice of the victim was for the expiation of sins. However, as the Scripture states clearly, the sacrifices under the law "can never take away sins, But this man (Jesus Christ), after he had offered one sacrifice for sins for ever, sat down on the right hand of God" (Heb 10:11,12). Where Christ is now is not in Paul's mind when he refers to the death of Christ, but rather what God is intimating through the gospel as a result of it.

Having made known the great truth of justification by blood, another grand note is struck by the apostle, "we shall be saved from wrath through him". Already in this epistle Paul has written about the wrath of God. He intimated that the wrath of God is revealed from heaven against all unrighteousness (1:18). He declared again that hard and impenitent sinners were treasuring up to themselves wrath against the day of wrath and revelation of the righteous judgment of God (2:5). Eternal punishment was the only outcome for those who will appear at the great white throne to face the wrath of God.

Here, however, it is not only the final day of wrath which is before the apostle's mind, but the time of judgment on earth which is to be marked by the pouring out of the vials of the wrath of God. There are many facets of salvation, each one determined by the context in which it is found. One aspect is the promised deliverance of the church from the wrath to come (1 Thess 1:10). It is when men shall say, "Peace and safety, then sudden destruction cometh upon them" (1 Thess 5:3). To the same church, however, Paul intimates, "For God hath not appointed us to wrath, but to obtain salvation by our Lord Jesus Christ" (1 Thess 5:9). Here in v.9, whether Paul meant wrath in the immediate or distant future, the outcome was the same, those who are justified by blood will not be overtaken by it. God will ensure that the objects of His love will be delivered from wrath in all its manifestations. This, Paul will declare in a great announcement later in the epistle, "There is therefore now no condemnation to them which are in Christ Jesus" (8:1).

10 The crux of Paul's argument in this verse is the second mention of "much more". Once again the apostle proves from the establishment of the leading theme that the secondary theme must follow. The opening words "For if" do not suggest a doubt. Without controversy we were enemies, and without controversy, when we were in that hostile situation, we were reconciled by the death of His Son; it follows, without any doubt, that now we are reconciled we shall be saved by His life. Without present reconciliation by the death of Christ, future salvation by His life would not be inevitable. Our eternal security depends entirely on the fact that He lives.

The main thrust of the apostle's argument is still the commendation of the love of God. It was while we were yet sinners that God demonstrated His love in the death of Christ. On that basis, if sinners were justified by His blood, without doubt they will be saved from the wrath to come. Parallel with this thought, the love of God is further demonstrated in wondrous grace – enemies are reconciled. Since that is the case, it follows that nothing can hinder their future salvation by His life. It is remarkable that God did not seek a change in man's hostile state before He acted. It was while we were yet sinners and when we were enemies that Christ died for us. Sinnership by nature and by practice put us in a helpless and hopeless position. Rebellious wickedness made us His enemies. Despite the immensity of the guilt, God commends His love. He did it at Calvary and He has done it ever since. Sinners and enemies are not outwith its scope.

Amongst the great words employed by the Holy Spirit in the NT to describe what has been brought about by the sacrificial work of Christ, reconciliation ranks high. Apart from vv.9,10 there are two other passages in the NT which deal with the subject in depth: 2 Cor 5:19,20; Col 1:20,21. There is also a brief reference at Eph 2:16. Because mankind had been alienated from God by wicked works and was without hope of ever being accepted if left to his own efforts, God acted in grace. It was He who took the initiative and through the death of Christ laid the basis of reconciliation. It was man who needed to be reconciled, not God. It was not man who did the reconciling, it was God and He did it through the Lord Jesus Christ.

When reconciliation is in question, it is man's enmity that comes into view. Hence here in v.10 the apostle states that it was while we were enemies we were reconciled to God by the death of His Son. The thought behind reconciliation is that of change. It is a divine work and it brings about a change from a state of enmity to one of acceptance and friendship. It implies that those who are reconciled will not be exposed to the wrath of God which was their due, but are restored to His favour. In Col 1:20,21, Paul reveals that reconciliation has a much wider scope than blessing for mankind. There he makes known that through the blood of His cross God can reconcile all things to Himself, whether they be things on earth or things in heaven. In v.10, the apostle is stressing the commendation of the love of God, and as he pursues that theme, the great work of reconciliation is brought in to show the extent of God's labour, reaching out to those who were enemies in a state of alienation.

The reference to being saved by the life of Christ takes Paul's argument beyond the cross. Since the work at Calvary was finished to the glory of God, there is no need for further sacrifice or suffering. In the context, Paul refers repeatedly to the death of Christ; it was the demonstration of the love of God. For those who believe, it is the guarantee of forgiveness, justification and reconciliation. The fact that Christ now lives, is a declaration that present and future deliverance is assured through Him. Because He lives, having been raised from the dead and having ascended to God's right hand, the pledge of life removes all thought of doubt and links the believer with the living Saviour.

11 To be saved from wrath through Him and to be saved by His life are great blessings. Paul seems to exhibit no little pride in being associated with the love of God and the work of Christ. His opening words in this verse, "And not only so", suggest that he has not finished his declaration of all that is contained in the commendation of the love of God, there is more to follow. This he makes known as joy in God through our Lord Jesus Christ. Clearly it was never God's intention that those who exercised faith and came into the benefits of the work of Christ should remain in a state of remorse. There was joy in God. The justified and the reconciled could exult in Him. Obviously it was a triumphant conclusion to all that the apostle had set forth. If those who benefited gloried in God through the Lord Jesus Christ it would bring honour and joy to God who made it all possible.

The mention of the Lord Jesus Christ through whom rejoicing was occasioned, leads Paul to return again to the subject of reconciliation. The word rendered "atonement" in the AV is better rendered "reconciliation". In v.10 the verb form (*katalassō*) is given; in this verse it is the noun (*katallagē*). The work of atonement is the offering of Christ on the cross as a sacrifice. This could not be received by mankind. What has been received is the reconciliation, the change of state from being enemies to being "accepted in the beloved" (Eph 1:6). Reconciliation is the effect of atonement. It is one of the many blessings into which believers enter as a result of the atoning work of Christ. Although contemplation of His atoning work should lead to rejoicing, this is not what Paul means here. It is rejoicing in the blessings which have accrued from the atonement, particularly reconciliation which is the subject of the immediate context. The source, however, is the love of God which is declared in the death of Christ. When Christ died for us it was not when we were morally upright, but while we were yet sinners.

Notes

1 "Our Lord Jesus Christ" is His full title, claimed by many to be a key phrase in this chapter (see vv.11,21). Paul often uses the title, "Christ Jesus" signifying that the One who was with the Father became incarnate. The title "Jesus Christ" speaks of the One who humbled Himself, endured the death of the cross and was exalted.

2 The first two verses of the chapter stress four great christian blessings: justification, peace with God, present standing in grace, boasting in the hope of glory.

The present standing in grace means that there is perfect present favour, every cloud that could hide God's face removed, notes JN Darby.

3 "Tribulations" (*thlipsis*) include afflictions, trials, distressing circumstances.

For "patience" (*hupomonē*) see note at 2:4.

5 When used in the passive voice, as here, "shed abroad" (*ekcheō*, "to pour out") has the meaning, "to gush out". See Acts 1:18.

6 There is considerable manuscript authority to support the reading for the opening words, "Indeed", or "Since then", or "So surely as" (see EGT note). It is beyond doubt that we were devoid of strength and helpless, but at the time determined by God, Christ died for the ungodly.

7 In "Peradventure" (*tacha*, "perhaps", "possibly"). there is no supposition of certainty. To Philemon Paul writes of Onesiphorus, "For perhaps he therefore departed for a season" (v.15).

8 "Commendeth" (*sunistēmi*) dispels any uncertainty. It is used to describe one of the glories of Christ in Col 1:17: "And by him all things consist" or, "held together in virtue of him".

"Sinners" (*hamartōlos*, "depraved") describes those who miss the mark, deviate from the path of virtue.

10 Since "we were reconciled", we are the objects of reconciliation, not the subjects of it. It is God who reconciles. The work is His.

11 "We also joy in God", or, "also boasting in God". There is no conflict with 3:27, "where is boasting then? It is excluded". To make one's boasting in God is the ultimate response for all that He has done.

4. *Basis of Justification – the work of Christ*
5:12-21

> v.12 "Wherefore, as by one man sin entered into the world, and death by sin; and so death passed upon all men, for that all have sinned:
> v.13 (For until the law sin was in the world: but sin is not imputed when there is no law.
> v.14 Nevertheless death reigned from Adam to Moses, even over them that had not sinned after the similitude of Adam's transgression, who is the figure of him that was to come.
> v.15 But not as the offence, so also is the free gift. For if through the offence of one many be dead, much more the grace of God, and the gift by grace, which is by one man, Jesus Christ, hath abounded unto many.
> v.16 And not as it was by one that sinned, so is the gift: for the judgment was by one to condemnation, but the free gift is of many offences unto justification.
> v.17 For if by one man's offence death reigned by one; much more they which receive abundance of grace and of the gift of righteousness shall reign in life by one, Jesus Christ.)
> v.18 Therefore as by the offence of one judgment came upon all men to condemnation; even so by the righteousness of one the free gift came upon all men unto justification of life.
> v.19 For as by one man's disobedience many were made sinners, so by the obedience of one shall many be made righteous.
> v.20 Moreover the law entered, that the offence might abound. But where sin abounded, grace did much more abound:
> v.21 That as sin hath reigned unto death, even so might grace reign through righteousness unto eternal life by Jesus Christ our Lord."

12 The apostle's treatise enters a new phase at this verse. In a sense he has been dealing with the work of Christ in connection with the matter of sins, but from this point to the end of ch.8 he deals with the question of sin as a root. It is not so much what we have done but what we are by nature. After experiencing the forgiveness of sins and being assured of many other blessings, many are perplexed to find the bitter root of sin still with them. Many have fled to monasteries and lives of seclusion to try to flee from the root of sin, but all to no avail. Sin is universal. There are no exclusions. All have inherited Adam's fallen nature.

If it were possible to trace one's genealogy back over the years, all would arrive at Adam. He is the head of the human race. Regarding Adam, Paul asserts, "By one man, sin entered into the world". The Genesis account is perfectly clear on this point. The result of this man's sin is stated, death enters, "and so death passed upon all men". The Genesis account again bears witness to the veracity of this assertion. The three words, "And he died", are repeated after each name given as the history of man unfolds. The concluding proof of the apostle's assertions that death passed upon all men is then given, "for that all have sinned". The whole human race is covered by the statement. Regardless of race or standing, "all have sinned".

When Adam was created in innocency he was free from death. Death came in as a result of his disobedience. The command of God was unequivocal, "But the tree of the knowledge of good and evil, thou shalt not eat of it, for in the day that thou eatest thereof thou shalt surely die" (Gen 2:17). Physical death and spiritual death became his lot because he disobeyed the warning. In his own admission of guilt, he confessed, "The woman thou gavest to be with me, she gave me of the tree, and I did eat" (Gen 3:12). Adam then became the possessor of a fallen nature. He was a sinner and his descendants after him partook of his fallen nature. It was not possible for the head to propagate sinless seed when he himself had sinned and was therefore a sinner. He could beget only sinners and the human race therefore was affected; all were born in sin.

It is significant that there is no mention of Eve in Paul's argument. Since she is noted in Scripture as the mother of all living (Gen 3:20), it might have been thought that she too would have been considered a progenitor of the race. The apostle does not say, however, "as by one woman sin entered into the world", although in a sense that was true as he notes elsewhere, "And Adam was not deceived, but the woman being deceived was in the transgression" (1 Tim 2:14). If Adam had not sinned, Eve would have borne the punishment alone. Although she was deceived, it was when Adam transgressed the commandment God had given him that sin entered and he plunged his posterity into ruin. The commandment forbidding the eating of the fruit of the tree of life was not given to Eve, it was given to Adam as the representative man on earth.

Adam was the head of the race that was to follow and he was therefore responsible to God for what he did as being the first man. The Scripture confirms his leading position, "Adam was first formed, and then Eve" (1 Tim 2:13). For a brief period Adam was still innocent and Eve was not; he was the head, Eve was not, although they were "one flesh". He was the representative man, hence the reason Paul makes eight references in Rom 5 to his offence. In addition, although it is stated "as by one man sin entered into the world", Adam was a type of Christ as head of a race; Eve could never have taken this position and so the whole argument centres on Adam.

Regarding the expression in 1 Tim 2:14, "was not deceived", Vincent remarks, "Interpreters have tried many ways of explaining this expression, either by supplying *prōtos* (first), or by saying (as Bengel) that the woman did not deceive the man, but persuaded him; or by supplying 'by the serpent' ". He goes on to say that the AV misses the force of "was in the transgression" and opts for "hath fallen into transgression". It is clear, however, that Eve, having been deceived, brought in transgression. Adam was guilty of disobeying God.

A parenthesis to meet possible objections before proceeding (vv.13-17)
Sin was in the world

13 In the period between Adam and Moses there was no divine revelation, either spoken or written, which men could breach, so sin as a transgression was not put to man's account. If there was no law then that which did not exist could not be transgressed, nevertheless men died just the same; death reigned from Adam to Moses, as the next verse asserts.

It is clear that vv.13-17 are a parenthesis. Having alluded to the OT Scriptures to show that man participated in the sin of the head of the race, and this was the reason for death becoming the lot of every man, Paul then interrupts his argument to deal with possible objections. The universality of sin and the result that all are sinners is not readily accepted by all. There are still many in every walk of life who cling to the belief that God will recognise works of merit and look upon them favourably. However, the proof of being under the headship of Adam is that all die, for all sinned in Adam. A similar argument is outlined in Heb 7:9,10 where it is set forth that Levi although he was yet unborn paid tithes in Abraham. He was, as the writer to the Hebrews states, "in the loins of his father" and, therefore, what Abraham did Levi did. Accordingly Paul seeks to prove that death was not principally the result of the personal sins of mankind, but rather the outcome of being descended from a fallen head. Death was inevitable because all partook of Adam's sin and the proof of it was evident, all died as a result.

Although Adam's posterity until the time of Moses did not sin after the likeness of Adam's transgression, the depravity of the human race should not be overlooked. The murder of Abel by his brother, the ungodliness against which Enoch testified, the tower of Babel and all that was associated with it, and the immorality of the Sodomites, are all evidences of the depths of sin into which the human race descended. It would be entirely wrong to consider the time from Adam to Moses as being less heinous in its character because there was no law and therefore no transgression. The sin and wickedness of mankind came up before God and He repented He had made man. As this verse states so plainly, "sin was in the world".

14 The argument of v.14 is that Adam overstepped a direct prohibition of God and he was therefore a transgressor; the many after him were not transgressors as they broke no direct commandment. Nevertheless they were descendants of Adam, they fell in him; the proofs of it were that they practised sin and they died; death passed through to all.

The apostle states that death "reigned" from Adam until Moses; death exercised universal dominion over the entire race, not one was exempt. By making this statement he anticipated any objections that there was no law from Adam to Moses and therefore those who lived before and after the flood were not transgressors. This Paul freely admits, but presses the fact that men were nevertheless sinners; they had inherited Adam's fallen nature, and as a result of that they died. Although they had not sinned after the similitude, or likeness, of Adam's transgression, the end result was the same as if they had: death passed through to them without exception.

Paul now states that Adam was a figure, a type (*tupos*) of Him that was to come. He was a type of Christ, but in one respect only: he was the head of a race. His one act left its imprint on the whole race. However, since it was a fallen race, the conclusion is that all suffer because of the head. As a result of the offence of one, the members of the race died. The statement that Adam was a type of "him that was to come" proclaims that a new head was coming. He would not be the head of a fallen race but the head of a new race. The head of this new race is Christ, the last Adam, not the second Adam, which would leave room for a third Adam. There will be no third race and therefore no third Adam. Finality is stamped on the new race and Christ, the last Adam, is its head. Those who are members of the new race are those who have acted on the principle of faith and have taken Christ as their Saviour.

15 The apostle now introduces an important contrast. It is between the one offence of Adam and the lavish, unstinted, bounteous free gift of God. Because the offence came in by Adam that does not mean to say that the free gift came in by Adam also. On the contrary, all that Adam brought in was sin and death – the many coming after him died. By coming into the world, Christ, the last Adam, enabled grace to abound unto the many, and so the race was given hope. The clear lesson in the apostle's argument is that the action of the head affects the race. Adam sinned and fell (the word "offence" includes the act and its consequence), and so death passed through to all. Condemnation came as a result of one trespass. Despite the many trespasses, accumulated through the ages of time, the grace of God and the free gift superabounded unto the many, through one man, Jesus Christ.

The apostle had brought in an important contrast. He now brings in an important change. The offence of the first Adam had an appalling effect on the race and the many died. The last Adam's coming into the world introduced a complete change. As head of the new race He brought in hope for all who were prepared to range themselves under His headship by faith. Because of Adam's one offence death came in to reign, as the previous verse states. There is no doubt that death is a monarch to which all must bow until the Lord comes for His own. Although the last enemy that shall be destroyed is death (1 Cor 15:26), the day is coming when death shall be swallowed up in victory (1 Cor 15:54). It has been conquered and its sting has been taken away; Christ has triumphed over it.

In addition to setting out an important contrast and making known an important change, the apostle has also established an important principle: the race is affected by what the head does. Adam sinned, but there was not a new beginning for all with a second Adam. The new beginning God planned was entirely different from the one which began in Eden's garden. Adam's descendants partook of his fallen nature and so death passed through to the many, here meaning through to all. This is an undeniable fact. Regarding the new race, by one Man, Jesus Christ, a contrast to the first man, the gift of grace superabounded unto "the many". It was extended to the many affected by Adam's fall, but only those who believe come into the good of it.

16 In v.15 there was a contrast between the actions of the first man, Adam, and the second, Christ. One brought in the trespass, the other the free gift of grace. Another contrast is made in v.16. The apostle introduces the thought again of the gift and makes it clear that it did not come in through the one that sinned. What he brought in was exposure to judgment and condemnation. The gift from God in grace, brought in by Jesus Christ, indicates that the blessings God had in His heart and which He determined to make available to mankind in His grace, were given through Jesus Christ. He was the channel through whom God would dispense His grace. But Christ was also the means whereby the gift could be made available to mankind on a righteous basis. It was His work on the cross which laid the foundation for the gift in grace. All the blessings intimated in the gospel depended on that. Since that sacrifice was unassailable in every respect, the gift falls into the same category. It takes its character from the work of Christ. It cannot be questioned.

The judgment came in "by one". This can be either masculine or neuter gender. If "one" is neuter then Paul is contrasting the offence with the free gift. This seems to be what he has in mind in view of the closing words of the verse, "but the free gift is of many offences unto justification". If, however, the masculine gender is adopted "the one" means Adam, and the link is then with the opening words of the verse, emphasising that the one that sinned did not bring in the gift, what he brought in was judgment. Two words are used by Paul in this connection. The judgment (*krima*) which befell the human race by reason of Adam's offence was condemnation (*katakrima*), signifying the sentence that had been passed. Apart from the provision of God by His grace, there was no hope. Sin called for judgment and as a result mankind was condemned.

The many trespasses did not overwhelm the free gift. God was not defeated by reason of the abounding of sin. Despite the many offences, justification came by the free gift. The contrast here considers that the one offence of Adam resulted in condemnation, but the many trespasses of the human race did not outdo the free gift. God's grace, demonstrated in the work of Christ resulted in justification. God's plan for the world paved the way for the damage done by Adam's sin to be rectified through the work of His Son.

17 This verse ends the parenthesis which began at v.13. It introduces another contrast. Once again attention is drawn to one man's offence. From these oft-recurring references to Adam's sin, it is clear that the gospel Paul presents leaves no room for works of merit, or even hope for mankind apart from what God has done in grace through the work of Christ. The language used by Paul is strong, "death reigned by one". The offence of one introduced a tyrant and it has exercised its tyrannical rule over the human race through all the ages. Death is such a certainty that it is looked upon as the last enemy to be faced. It is the result of being under the headship of Adam.

It must not be thought that what has been won for the new race by the action of its head is lacking in certainty. If all the members of Adam's race can count upon is death, that is a miserable outlook compared with the certainty of what has been won by Christ. This is confirmed by the use of the expression, "much more", the fourth time Paul has used it to advance his argument in this chapter. It comes between two facts. The leading fact is a certainty, but it is superseded by a second fact, which has a much greater degree of certainty. The contrast is between "death reigned by one" and "they...shall reign in life". The obvious contrast would be that life reigns where once death reigned, but that is not what Paul stated. The contrast is much stronger than that. Those who receive the grace shall actively reign in life with Christ in His coming kingdom.

There is a clear distinction between the two subjects of this verse. Those who will reign in life as members of the new race are seen to be those who receive the grace and the gift of righteousness. Reigning in life belongs only to believers. They gladly received by faith the blessings which superabounded to them. If death reigned as a tyrant, with a claim upon every member of Adam's race, the activity of the grace of God was not of a lesser nature. Its superabounding power was a far greater force. The final triumph is not a bowing to death but the fact that many who were once under its mastery have been liberated by a transforming power and they will reign in life. They will have a role in the kingdom. They will not have a mere passive existence throughout eternity, but will actively reign in life with Christ. The whole verse vibrates with exuberance as the apostle attempts to convey the wonder of this divinely-given grace.

The Return to the Teaching of v.12 (vv.18-21)

18 This verse commences with the word "Therefore". The original has two words which the RV translates "So then". The words could also read "Wherefore then", referring to what has gone before and the results which stem from that. The parenthesis was completed at the end of v.17, so the verse returns to what the apostle set out in v.12. The leading theme in this verse concerns two actions and their results. Regarding the first action the AV reads, "as by the offence of one", making "one" refer to Adam. The RV renders this, "So then through one trespass", making the "one" refer to the offence. Regarding the second action the AV reads, "by the righteousness of one" making the "one" refer to Christ. The RV gives, "through one act of righteousness" causing the "one" to be understood as the act of righteousness. Both of these standpoints are equally true, but most are agreed, taking the context and the thrust of the apostle's argument into account, that the RV renderings are to be preferred.

The first action involved Adam and it was as a result of his one offence that judgment came upon all men to condemnation. The whole human race was condemned. The sentence of death which was passed on all was not only physical in its extent, but spiritual also. It was not only temporal, it was eternal. As a result of that one offence the whole human race was plunged into ruin. The AV and the RV follow through from there with the words, "even so" which bring in the second action from God's side. By one act of righteousness the free gift came upon (*eis*, "unto") all men unto justification of life. By that one act of righteousness on the cross, the remedy for the ruin of man was established. Whereas the one offence resulted in judgment and condemnation, the righteous act of Christ provided for those who believe the justifying which results in life.

The words "free gift" are in italics, but they are rightly included. Merit and good works do not enter into the situation. Neither is there any suggestion that the free gift means an automatic pardon for all. God's free gift is offered "unto" all, but only those who respond in faith come into blessing. They are the ones who are justified; they are the ones who have life. This thought is stated again in the next verse, but the sad fact is not altered that those who remain in sin by choice or by neglect, wilful or otherwise, face judgment and condemnation.

Regarding condemnation, first mentioned at v.16, the consequences associated with it are most serious and solemn. While judgment intimates the sentence passed on sinners by reason of the conscious choice of remaining sinners and therefore despising God's grace, condemnation intimates the abiding state of alienation to which sinners are consigned. Although judgment is passed on sinners and they are overtaken in death, it is only after they appear at the great white throne that they are consigned in final condemnation to eternal punishment. There is no escape from condemnation. Once the boundary line of death is passed, the judgment cannot be reversed, condemnation is inevitable. There is no indication in Scripture that a further opportunity will be given after a soul passes unsaved into eternity.

There are several examples in Scripture of situations where condemnation resulted from sin and depravity. The Genesis account of the overthrow of Sodom and Gomorrha is the most notable. The evil citizens of these two cities were consumed with fire and brimstone and as a result are now awaiting final punishment. Both Jude 7 and 2 Pet 2:6 refer to Sodom and Gomorrha. Both state that the record of what happened to these two cities was set forth as an example, to which Peter adds, "unto those that after should live ungodly". The awesome feature about Sodom and Gomorrha is that, apart from Lot, there was none righteous there. It is little wonder that Peter records that God turned both cities into ashes and condemned them with an overthrow. To this Jude adds the solemn note that they will suffer the vengeance of eternal fire.

The introduction of the thought of condemnation by Paul suggests that the readers of his epistle would know what was involved. He gives no examples, but the Jews at least were familiar with the Genesis account of the destruction of the cities of the plain. This is confirmed by clear references given by Matthew and Luke in their Gospels and by Peter and Jude in their epistles. Happily, as Paul will state later, "There is therefore now no condemnation to them which are in Christ Jesus" (8:1).

19 As Paul follows through with his argument, he introduces two families. The first were made sinners through the disobedience of the head, Adam. The second family shall be made righteous through the obedience of one, Jesus Christ. These two families are contrasted in this verse. They take their relative positions from their heads. Disobedience marked Adam, obedience marked Jesus Christ. Sin is universal and the expression "the many" used so often in the apostle's argument, covers all of Adam's race: all are sinners. Although the same expression "the many" is used in this verse to describe those who will be made righteous, only those who exercise faith and believe in the Lord Jesus Christ will come into blessing.

The words "were made" are the aorist indicative of *kathistēmi* ("to render", or, "to make"). What is signified is that Adam's one act of disobedience in the past settled the matter for his posterity. All that followed in subsequent generations were affected by that one act of disobedience, they were constituted sinners. The words, "shall many be made", the future indicative of *kathistēmi*, show that through the obedience of one, Jesus Christ, a righteous title to life is freely given now to all who believe and they will enter into the good of it in heaven. That life is theirs for all eternity. Nothing will affect it now or in the future. It is the inviolable possession of those who are under the headship of Jesus Christ.

There is also in this verse a contrast between two characters. The effect of the one's disobedience is seen in the conduct of those who are his descendants. They were constituted sinners by his one act of disobedience, and they demonstrate it in that they practise sin. Those who are under the headship of Christ and are blessed through His one act of obedience, walk in newness of life and their conduct brings pleasure to God. The obedience of Christ is not a reference to what marked Him in life, although that is perfectly true; it is a reference to the culmination of His life, His one act of righteousness. His obedience took Him to the cross, but it is the final voluntary sacrifice that the apostle sets forth by way of contrast to Adam's one act of disobedience.

It is possible that Paul had Isa 53:11 in mind when he made known to the Romans that many shall be made righteous. Considering his knowledge of the OT and the way he alludes to appropriate passages throughout his writings, it would not be surprising if the prophet Isaiah's words came before his mind. The prophet wrote of the righteous servant of God, "by his knowledge shall my righteous servant justify many, for he shall bear their iniquities" (Isa 53:11). Being righteous in Himself, the servant considered by Isaiah can justify many and absolve them from the penalty of their guilt, since "He shall bear the sins of many". He had the power to do it and the right to do it. Since, however, it is God who is the speaker in the verse, it is He who declares that His servant will justify many. Considering the many prophecies in the OT about the Messiah and that they were all fulfilled by the Lord Jesus, there is justification for an element of fulfilment of Isaiah's prophetic statement here in v.19.

20 Amongst the many reasons why the law of Moses was brought in, the one which is given in this verse is most significant. Paul makes known here that it came in that the true character of sin might be displayed. If in the world, and in particular that aspect of it which is religious, there had been any merit, the law of Moses would have been welcomed as a standard to which mankind could be conformed. In the case of Israel in particular it was not so, nor is it so today worldwide, as Paul will reveal later in principle: the carnal mind is not subject to the law, neither can it be (8:7). The prohibitions of the law only cause the flesh to fall further short of God's requirements.

The apostle makes the point here that the law "entered", it came in alongside sin, or in addition to sin. In v.12 it is stated that sin entered and so did death as a result of the offence of one man. Now it is made known that in addition to sin and death the law entered. The purpose of its entrance was twofold: firstly that the true nature of sin might be made manifest, and then to show the answer to the degree of sin in the abounding grace of God. It did not minimise sin, indeed it magnified it. The question may then be asked, "Did it minimise grace?" It is clear that it did not do that either, for "where sin abounded grace did much more abound". God in His mercy had the remedy. Sin was rampant, but God in grace has gone beyond the abounding of sin, and, as the next verse shows, it was that grace might reign through righteousness unto eternal life by Jesus Christ our Lord.

The entrance of the law did not solve the problem of sin; it only aggravated it. Sin was not obliterated, indeed it proliferated under law. The standard against which man was measured only showed how far short he fell. The law's prohibitions stirred up within him the desire to break its commandments. By the law, man recognised the sinfulness of his actions, but instead of altering his ways of life, he transgressed further by flouting the law's precepts. The restrictions which the law imposed for his good were an irritant that drove him to cast aside restraint, and so sin abounded. By going against what he knew to be right and just he caused the trespass to abound.

However, if sin abounded, grace did much more abound; it super-abounded. Under the law there was no salvation. The sad lesson of Israel's failure under trial for over two thousand years, was there for all to behold. The law could not save, it could only condemn if its precepts were broken. There was neither grace nor forgiveness for those who were under it. God, however, saw the plight of the human race. He had the remedy and here again it is introduced. It is made known as super-abounding grace. Regardless of the abounding of sin, grace completely outstrips it. No matter how far sin can go, grace can go further. There is no situation where the grace of God is found to fall short as being unable to meet the challenge brought about by the abounding of sin. The adversary will never be able to boast that sin has been taken beyond the point where the grace of God could go no further. The sacrifice of Christ, not only satisfied the demands of God's holiness, it provided a basis for God's grace to abound in such measure that it is capable of meeting every need.

21 The closing verse of the chapter tells us that grace was displayed because sin reigned. The human race under its head, Adam, left to itself had only one end before it – death! Sin reigned as a monarch. There was none that did not come under its rule, and its end was inescapable. Sin's pleasures were short-lived. Behind them the dictator was in control and its power over mankind led to death. This chapter of the epistle has introduced a new head. The next chapter will introduce a new master. The old master, sin, will be seen to have lost its power when the new master brings in the remedy.

Here, however, Paul states that grace comes in to reign. It has a power which tells out the character of the God who exercises it. As it reaches out to sinners it does so in full conformity to righteousness. There was no righteousness in the reign of sin; it only led to death. How different is the reign of grace, it leads to eternal life. There is a view that death is what keeps sin on the throne. So long as death is the portion of mankind, sin is enthroned. Grace, however, reigns and eternal life, both here as a possession, and in eternity in fulness, is made available in righteousness. How it is done is in full accord with God's righteous character, not at the expense of it. No charge of unrighteous dealings can be made against Him because of His grace to mankind.

The promise of eternal life which comes in with the grace of God is through Jesus Christ our Lord. The chapter opens with the great statement that being justified by faith, we have peace with God through our Lord Jesus Christ. In v.11 we learn that through our Lord Jesus Christ we have received the reconciliation. In the last verse the apostle intimates that eternal life is offered by the grace of God and it is through our Lord Jesus Christ. So, apart from our Lord and Saviour and His sacrifice on the cross, the favour and the grace of God could never have been extended to those who had no claim upon God for mercy. The apostle does not interrupt his train of thought to insert a doxology at this point, although one would have been expected. He has more good news to tell out and upon the unfolding of this he concentrates his attention.

Notes

12 Death as an experience was not known in Eden's early days. The intimation of it, "for in the day that thou eatest thereof thou shalt surely die" (Gen 2:17), was nevertheless understood and Eve understood its meaning also (Gen 3:4). For mankind since Adam's fall, death is a divine appointment, "It is appointed unto men once to die, but after this the judgment" (Heb 9:27).

13 "...is (not) imputed" (*ellogeō*, "to put to one's account") occurs only here and at Philem 18, "put that on mine account". The word Paul has been using is *logizomai*, "to reckon"; see 4:6.

17 "Abundance" (*perisseia*) is better "a super-abundance". The measure of the abundance is seen in the use of the word in John 6:13, "the fragments which remained *over and above* unto them which had eaten".

In the writings of Paul, righteousness (*dikaiosunē*) has a peculiar meaning, opposed to the views of Jews and Judaizers. The Jews as a people (and many Judaisers) supposed that they secured the favour of God by works conformed to the requirements of the Mosaic law, as though by way of merit they would attain to eternal salvation. But the law demands perfect obedience in all its precepts. Obedience of this kind no one has ever rendered (Rom 3:10), neither Jews nor Gentiles (Rom 1:24-2:1), for with Gentiles the natural law of right written on their souls takes the place of the Mosaic law (Rom 2:14).

Paul teaches that it is through faith that men embrace the grace of God, revealed and pledged in Christ, and this faith is reckoned to men as *dikaiosunē*. That is to say, *dikaiosunē* denotes the state acceptable to God which becomes a sinner's possession through that faith by which he embraces the grace of God offered in the expiatory death of Christ.

Dikaiosunē, righteousness, is said to be the virtue or quality or state of one who is righteous. It contains the idea of virtue, integrity, purity of life, uprightness. It is the condition which is acceptable to God. Thayer suggests that when the word is used of God, it refers to His holiness. When used of Christ, it denotes His perfect moral purity, sinlessness.

18 Note *henos paraptōmatos*, "one offence"; *henos dikaiōmatos*, "one righteous act".

20 Note *hamartia eisēlthen,* "sin entered" (v.12); *nomos pareisēlthen,* "law entered (alongside)"; *hamartia epleonasen*, "sin abounded"; *charis hupereperisseusen*, "grace super-abounded".

IV. The Provision of God (6:1-8:39)

The main theme of the apostle's message at the commencement of this epistle is "condemnation". The doctrine of sin is clearly and fully set out. The universal guilt of mankind is pronounced. There are no exceptions. Gentiles (1:18-32), Jews (2:1-3:8), and the world (3:9-20) are all embraced. It follows that since universal guilt is established, there is a universal need. The plight of the whole human race is such that apart from divine intervention there is no hope for it; all are hopelessly lost with nothing to look forward to but judgment.

In the grace and mercy of God provision was made to meet the universal need of mankind in the sacrificial work of Christ. Sinners, under the bondage of sin could be set free; the guilty could be justified and those under the sentence of death could find life. This wonderful message is declared from 3:21 to 5:21. The intimation that men and women can be justified freely by His grace is one of the pillars of the gospel message. This blessing is shown to be outwith human merit or law-works; it is obtained solely on the principle of faith. The first main division of the epistle ends with the announcement that where sin abounded, grace has super-abounded, and where sin reigned unto death, grace reigns through righteousness unto eternal life through Christ Jesus.

A new outlook entirely commences at ch.6 and runs on to the end of ch.8. The apostle considers the provision of God so that the christian life can be lived triumphantly. Sin no longer reigns as a monarch. The justified have no obligation to it, having changed masters. Sin is no longer the master of those who have been freed. They have a new master and in His service, righteousness and holiness are the characteristic features. If, however, the solid base of chs.1-5 had not been laid, there would have been no support on which to build the superstructure of chs.6-8. The ministry of sanctification, seen in its various aspects in these three chapters would have been inapplicable. The christian life could not have begun, apart from belief in the message of the gospel. With, however, a new head, and a new master, the justified can go on through chs.6 and 7 to experience the new power which is dealt with in ch.8.

1. *Sanctified and Free from Bondage to Sin*
   6:1-23

Under the old head, Adam, there was no hope for humanity. Under the new head, Christ, there is righteousness, grace, life and assurance of deliverance from the wrath to come. Those who ranged themselves under the headship of Christ were justified by grace and by blood. They were delivered from the penalty of sin by one act of righteousness on the part of Jesus Christ at the cross, and their standing before God is unassailable.

In the lives of Christians, however, sin is still a power to be faced. It threatens the tranquillity which should be the justified believer's way of life. It was the old master, under whose power all were held. Suitably described as binding, blinding and grinding sin, it held all in bondage. It was the taskmaster which held all in a vice-like grip. Left to their own resources, all were undone, heading for certain death and condemnation.

With the problem of the presence of sin to be faced, Paul turns his attention in this chapter to life under a new master. Under the old master, sin, and under the headship of Adam, there was nothing but bondage, but under the new master there was freedom. The justified were also the sanctified. God had not only provided salvation but He had also sanctified those He had reckoned righteous. He had acted again for the benefit of those on whom He had set His love, by giving them the power and the incentive to live triumphantly for Him.

In Rom 6 Paul shows that continuing in sin after being justified by the grace of God is at variance with life in Christ. The two concepts are totally incompatible. Being under a new master, the Lord Jesus Christ, life is lived "unto God" – a characteristic expression in this chapter. In a series of contrasts, Paul sets out his argument to demonstrate why it is that those who are liberated from sin's power should live righteously for the pleasure of God.

(a) *The principle of deliverance from sin (vv.1-7)*

v.1 "What shall we say then? Shall we continue in sin, that grace may abound?
v.2 God forbid. How shall we, that are dead to sin, live any longer therein?
v.3 Know ye not, that so many of us as were baptized into Jesus Christ were baptized into his death?
v.4 Therefore we are buried with him by baptism into death: that like as Christ was raised up from the dead by the glory of the Father, even so we also should walk in newness of life.
v.5 For if we have been planted together in the likeness of his death, we shall be also in the likeness of his resurrection:
v.6 Knowing this, that our old man is crucified with him, that the body of sin might be destroyed, that henceforth we should not serve sin.
v.7 For he that is dead is freed from sin."

1 Paul commences with the characteristic question which he uses frequently in this epistle, "What shall we say then?" In view of abounding sin and super-abounding grace (5:20), he seems to invite comment on the situation. Since the penalty of sin has been dealt with and there is no fear of having to face wrath to come, in time or in eternity, the question is, Why struggle to combat sin's presence? If all is well with God and eternal bliss is the believer's portion, why not let sin have free course in the life, since there is abounding grace to cover it?

The question raised by Paul does not merely ask, "shall we continue in sin?" but "shall we continue in sin that grace may abound?" Antinomianism propounds that since there is a super-abounding of grace to cover sin, continuing in sin will produce more grace. Sinning therefore would merely serve to display more of the grace of God, and since His grace will always outstrip sin, indulgence in sinful practices is the logical conclusion. If this loathsome error should be taken up and acted upon by the unconverted, their condemnation would be all the more severe when they appear before the great white throne. If a believer should act on the absurd and slanderous suggestion that there is licence from God to sin, one would be entitled to question if a link existed between the Saviour and the one who had professed to be saved.

For a Christian to adopt the view that he cannot sin is a deceiving of self. Sinless perfection is not taught in Scripture and every one's experience, if an honest admission, proves that sin is still present. The ability to sin is still there after conversion. However, there is no longer any reason why one should give in to sin's demands, because of deliverance from sin's penalty. To say that sin's presence compels one to commit sinful acts is totally wrong. The scriptural position is clear, "if any man be in Christ, he is a new creature, old things have passed away; behold all things have become new" (2 Cor 5:17). Continuing in sin is an assault on the basic doctrines of Christianity and it is this preposterous view that Paul addresses in Rom 6 to show that it is a contradiction of new life in Christ.

2 Having posed the question, Paul now answers it. Continuing in sin to draw out from God more and more grace to cover it is perverse. To the apostle the idea is preposterous. His reply demonstrates his abhorrence of the very thought of it. "By no means", or "Let it not be", or "Far be the thought" is his mind on such a suggestion. And so he follows that with another question, the answer to which will surely settle the matter finally.

The pronoun "we" in the question makes it clear that believers, the justified of the previous chapter, are addressed and that Paul includes himself in what he poses, "How shall we, that are dead to sin, live any longer therein?" The verb in the question is in the aorist tense and should be rendered, "How shall we, who died to sin, live any longer therein?" It points backwards. If it be asked, "When did believers die to sin?" the answer is not, "When they experienced the new birth". Certainly at that moment they were changed; they passed from death to life; they became new creatures in Christ Jesus (2 Cor 5:17). But as being "in him" they died with Him when He died to sin at the cross. He is finished with the sin question, having "appeared to put away sin by the sacrifice of himself" (Heb 9:26). When He returns, He shall "appear the second time, without (apart from) sin unto salvation" (Heb 9:28). The believer's union with Christ is such that being "in Christ" means that when He died, the believer died. The sin question ends there. Paul therefore asks, "How shall we that are dead (who died) to sin, live any longer therein?"

Paul is not saying here, as some represent him to say, "We ought to die to sin". Although the thought is commendable, it is not what the apostle taught. It must not be construed to mean escape to some monastery or environment where temptation (at least outwardly) does not make its presence felt. Those who have retreated from society have not escaped from the power of sin although they have persuaded themselves that they have escaped from its presence by shutting the world out of their lives. Sin in this chapter is the root, not the fruit. The root cannot be excised by human effort. It has been inherited from Adam and apart from the radical change called for in the gospel of God, it will continue to torment those who have not surrendered their lives to Christ. The next verse will show how the problem of sin should be faced.

3 The opening words are a challenge. The original *ē agnoeite* signifies, "or are ye ignorant?" The apostle is alleging something much stronger than just a lack of knowledge. The phrase introducing the question which forms the verse, directs attention to what he has just stated, "How shall we, that are dead to sin, live any longer therein?" It highlights how incongruous is the thought of continuing in sin that grace may abound. It presupposes that all who were baptised were aware of the inconsistency of such a consideration. From the beginning of the chapter the apostle has followed the rabbinical practice of debating by question and answer, no doubt the result of his early training. Here, his skill and logic in argument are clearly demonstrated as he deals with a situation which history has proved, would have far-reaching implications.

The RV gives "all we who were baptised" for the AV rendering, "so many of us as were baptised". This removes any suggestion that some were not baptised. Paul includes himself in the statement, "we were baptised", the record of Luke in Acts 9 confirming that he submitted to the ordinance shortly after he was converted.

Although baptism as a rite was practised by the Jews, what the apostle is referring to here is christian baptism by water. It involves immersion and its basic message is burial. Burial is a testimony to the fact that death has taken place. In Paul's teaching, he has declared that believers have died to sin. Christians are not asked or commanded to die to sin. It is not anything that is done by way of self-sacrifice as a demonstration of holier or higher living. It is true of every genuine believer in the Lord Jesus Christ.

Complying with the call to be baptised is not an option; it is mandatory. The NT does not envisage unbaptised believers. The pattern in the Scriptures is "hearing, believed and were baptised" (Acts 18:8). It is associated with the preaching of the gospel. Although it is not part of the gospel message which must be obeyed before salvation is secured, nevertheless it is expected from all who believe the message of the gospel and trust Christ as Saviour.

The AV renders, "baptised into Jesus Christ". A more accurate rendering would be, "baptised unto Jesus Christ". AT Robertson comments, "The translation 'into' makes Paul say that the union with Christ was brought to pass by means of baptism, which is not his idea, for Paul was not a sacramentarian. Baptism is the public proclamation of one's inward spiritual relation to Christ attained before baptism". By rendering the preposition as "unto", it expresses that to which the believer is baptised and the better reading of the phrase is therefore "unto Christ Jesus".

There is no support from Scripture for being baptised in secret and then keeping the matter a secret thereafter. Christian profession is involved. Obedience to the rite is a proclamation that those who have submitted to baptism have died to sin. Such is the reality of union with Christ at the time of conversion, believers died with Him through being in Him. Baptism therefore proclaims that death has taken place and that burial followed.

Death for Christ was physical death. Although it is not physical death for the believer, the link is nevertheless real in the sight of God. Baptism therefore is a sign, an ordinance willingly entered upon, which acknowledges there was a time past in the believer's experience when there was a passing from death to life through faith in Christ, and death to sin thereby.

4 It is clear from the opening words of this verse that baptism professes burial with Christ, He is the object. It also professes burial unto death – that is the end in view. Commentators are divided about the rendering of the preposition *eis*, as to whether it should be "into" or "unto". The AV and the RV give "into". This is supported by Vine and others. AT Robertson, however, comes out strongly for "unto", stating, "*eis* is at bottom the same word as *en*. Baptism is the public proclamation of one's inward spiritual relation to Christ attained before the baptism. See Gal 3:27 where it is like putting on an outward garment or uniform. So here, unto his death, in relation to his death, which relation Paul proceeds to explain by the symbolism of ordinance". CE Stuart takes a similar view, stating, "…'unto' would be better than 'into', expressing that to which we are baptised. So 1 Cor 10:2, Israel was baptised *unto* Moses, thus taking their place as his disciples".

At this point, complete identification with Christ and His work for the believer is noted. Initially it is the death of Christ and the believer's professed relation to it which is seen. The significance of this comes out in the succeeding verses. Here the scriptural mode of baptism is made plain. The implication of the words, "buried with him by baptism" could never be anything less than immersion. Sprinkling could never answer to the symbol, and all the less so, the sprinkling of infants, who have no active involvement in what is taking place. The passive role in infant sprinkling bears no relation to what is involved in baptism as taught in the Scriptures.

Of the resurrection of Christ there is no doubt. That is clearly taught here. His resurrection is said to have been through the glory of the Father. Since Christ by His death glorified the Father, it follows that the Father's glory was involved in not leaving Christ in death. In this epistle reference has already been made to the resurrection and the power of God in raising the Lord from the dead. Paul wrote by the hand of his penman, "if we believe on him that raised up Jesus our Lord from the dead; who was delivered for our offences, and was raised again for our justification" (4:24,25). The resurrection of Christ is so fundamental to the christian faith, that it is given frequent mention by the writers of the NT. However, it is clear that it is the union between Father and Son which Paul is stressing at this point. The almighty power of God was exercised in raising Christ from the dead and there was displayed in that act the glory of the Father in every respect of His excellence as He responded to the glorious work of the Son. Regarding the phrase, "glory of the Father", this is the only occurrence in this epistle. Elsewhere Paul refers to the glory of God (see 3:23).

There are two distinct views about what Paul intended should be understood from the remainder of this verse. The practical outcome of the resurrection as far as the subject of baptism is concerned is stated in the words, "even so we also should walk in newness of life". One school of thought sees the believer figuratively under the death, burial and resurrection of Christ. This is reflected in the believer's baptism. It professes that he died and was buried and that he rose again to walk in newness of life. When the believer is immersed in baptism, burial is understood to have taken place. When the believer comes up out of the water that person is looked upon in figure as having been raised, just as Christ was raised from the dead. What is understood generally is that a new person has come up out of the water, the "old man" is left buried and all the old habits with him.

The other view, propounded by CE Stuart and others, is that baptism signifies burial; the thought of the resurrection of the believer in figure is not involved as far as the teaching of Romans is concerned. This stance is taken because, in the context, it is the presence of sin that is in view. Deliverance from its power is a result of having died with Christ and having died to sin thereby. The apostle's appeal therefore is "know ye not, that so many of us were baptised into Jesus Christ were baptised into his death? Therefore we are buried with him by baptism into death". Christians, according to Stuart, are not viewed in Romans as risen. They are certainly viewed in Colossians as risen (2:12, 3:1), and in Ephesians (2:6), but resurrection for believers is viewed in Romans as future, "We shall be also in the likeness of his resurrection" (v.5).

The oneness of believers with Christ is now seen. The life which they enjoy is a new kind of life. The expression must not be limited to mean a different way of living. Just as truly as the believer died with Christ when He died, so is the link with Him where He is now. Believers make their way through this world in newness of life which has its source and subsistence in a resurrected Christ in glory. The apostle seems to take for granted that believers know they have life in Christ. It is a new life, new in quality, altogether different from the life derived from the old head, Adam. The old life came to an end at the cross. From then sin had nothing to appeal to and therefore its strength as a taskmaster was nullified as far as believers were concerned. They walk through this world in newness of life, a life which does not respond to sin and over which sin has no influence.

5 Having established that newness of life is what characterises the walk of the believer in the present, Paul now turns to the future. It holds out the promise that if called upon to pass through the article of death or when the Lord comes, there will at last be freedom from the presence of sin. Although the power of Christ's resurrection is working within the saints at present (Col 2:12; 3:1), the actual resurrection in the future is what Paul considers in this verse. The knowledge of this settled state to come is seen in the verses which follow to have a practical effect in the present.

The first half of the verse is a confirmation of complete identity with Christ. It asserts that union with Him in His death means complete union with Him in every other aspect, including the resurrection. The apostle has laboured to show that baptism is a figure of the reality of that union, which is confirmed in the statement, "we have been planted in the likeness of his death". There is no doubt about that. Baptism confirms it, and, as has been seen, the only logical conclusion of baptism is walking in newness of life.

The choice of *sumphutos* (rendered "planted"), seems to infer more than what is suggested in the words "planted together". The word at root has the meaning of growth, springing up. If this is carried through in application, the link with Christ in His death is not only homogeneous, but vitally true in growth. This makes union with Christ a clear-cut situation. There are no shades of grey as far as this union is concerned. The position of the mere professor, in view of the teaching of the Roman epistle, is one which is fraught with peril. The risk involved in not making absolutely sure of one's eternal salvation is a dangerous gamble, and one which could have catastrophic consequences.

The RV reads, "For if we have become united with him by the likeness of his death", stressing that identification with Christ is the point in the passage. Although the construction of the AV text is closer to the original, asserting a uniting with the likeness of His death, the RV seems to be more in keeping with the context of the opening verses of the chapter.

The latter half of the verse "we shall be also *in the likeness* of his resurrection" is variously understood. Stuart leaves out the three italicised words and reads, "we shall be also of his resurrection". From this he asserts that resurrection here is viewed as future. Newell holds that to be united "in the likeness of his resurrection" refers to the "walking in newness of life". Vine expresses the view that although the future is included, the phrase expresses the inevitable consequence, both now and hereafter, of our identification with Christ and His death. This, he states, is confirmed in the next two verses (vv.6,7). He goes on to say that "newness of life" in v.4 is expressed now in the phrase, "the likeness of his resurrection".

Doubtless vv.6-9 follow the train of thought and show that death and resurrection affect the present. As to the resurrection, the certainty of it is a great encouragement. The knowledge of God's provision for the future is also a great comfort. Regarding provision for the present, the reality of union with Christ is a great incentive to be dependent entirely upon Him for victorious living. If we died to sin, the life which we now have and now exhibit is new life in Christ.

6   The apostle does not say how or when those he addressed came to know about "the old man" and what happened to him. Understanding what is meant by "the old man" is vital. Although the title, "the new man" is not used in the context of Rom 6, understanding what it means is also crucial if the christian life has to be lived out in a full and accurate way. There are two other passages in the NT where the two expressions are used. These are Eph 4:22 and Col 3:9. A brief consideration of them may cast some additional light upon what Paul teaches in Rom 6.

It is held by most commentators that "the old man" is the person we were before conversion. This is no doubt correct, although it may be too simplistic to leave the matter there. From Paul's standpoint, he considers it something which can be identified as peculiar to him, and which is also identifiable in every believer. Some equate "the old man" with "the old nature", but neither "the old nature" nor "the new nature" is a scriptural expression, although the idea might be sound enough.

"The old man" is characterised by that evil principle which is in a person as being a child of Adam. Doubtless it is in some ways what the believer was before being "in Christ". If considered as having an identity, "the old man" is recognisable by others when displayed in certain deeds. These deeds are described in some detail in Col 3.

The expression "the old man" which is used only by Paul, was obviously a concept that the apostle brought into being to describe what can be dealt with and indeed was dealt with judicially at the cross. Here in v.6, Paul states, "Knowing this, that our old man is crucified with him". Crucifixion and death are not necessarily synonymous terms. Crucifixion means judicial dealing. Pilate was a Roman governor and he exercised his authority in crucifying the Lord. Crucifixion was normally the sentence pronounced on criminals, but the Lord in suffering crucifixion was dealt with judicially by God as the sin-bearer. Regarding sentence on "the old man", that evil principle was condemned to crucifixion – it came to an end judicially at the cross. Bondage to it therefore should be for the Christian a thing of the past, seeing it was crucified with Christ.

In Col 3 the deeds of "the old man" are listed. The Colossian believers were encouraged to put away all the evil deeds once and for all. Nothing was to be spared (Col 3:8). In the next verse the apostle considers this action to have taken place, stating, "having put off the old man with his deeds". The word "old" (*palaios*) suggests outworn, antiquated, decrepit, useless. In Colossians (and Ephesians) the matter is not left there. The "new man" is considered to have been put on, once-and-for-all. This man is fresh, new altogether, as opposed to "the old man" who is marred and withered by sin. The line of ministry in Rom 6 is different and reference to the "new man" is not required for the subject Paul had before him. There is no contradiction in terms between the teaching of Romans and the other two epistles. In Rom 6 the judicial sentence is passed on that evil man inherited from Adam. The practical outcome of that is seen in the other epistles. The "old man" is stripped off, and cast aside and with him go his evil deeds. The "new man" is put on, and having been put on once-and-for-all, the features of risen life in Christ are displayed. The "putting off" and the "putting on" are not actions which are repeated according to one's whims and state; they are considered as once-for-all transactions.

The purpose behind the crucifixion of "the old man" is stated, "that the body of sin might be destroyed, that henceforth we should not serve sin". To understand the word "body" in the NT, it must be taken in conjunction with the word or words associated with it. Sometimes it is synonymous with the word "flesh", but for most part there is an essential difference between them. The emphasis on "body" is that it is a living vital organism – it is an instrument of natural life. Here the "body of sin" denotes the body as being possessed by sin and ruled by its power. Sin is seen here to be the master to whom the body as a slave belongs, and to whom it is obedient to do its will. In the context of Paul's teaching in Rom 6 the body is looked upon as being under a tyrant's control. But as "the old man" has been crucified with Christ, then the body has been rendered inactive; it is useless for the purpose of sin. Sin can find no response in it. This answers the question raised in v.1, "Shall we continue in sin?" It proves that the believer is no longer under any obligation to obey the promptings of sin. Being under a new master, the believer is free from slavery.

There is no thought in v.6 of the crucifixion of "the old man" being an experience peculiar to some Christians and not to others. It is fundamental to the christian faith that "the old man" was crucified with Christ. It should not be considered as an experience to be sought after. That is not what the passage teaches. It was at the cross the crucifixion took place. On conversion, the believer then comes into the scope of it. There is no question of improvement of "the old man", he came to an end at the cross. When the believer looks back to Calvary and acknowledges "there I died with Christ", what was inherited from Adam, which was incorrigible, is seen to have been nailed to His cross.

7 The conclusion arrived at from what has been stated about crucifixion is that legally sin has no longer any claims on the believer. If "the old man" has come to an end, the question of sinning no longer arises. The apostle states "for he that is dead (or, has died) is freed (justified) from sin". From the believer's point of view, having died with Christ, death has annulled all obligations. A dead person cannot sin and cannot be punished for sin, hence the believer in the reality of knowing himself dead in Christ's death enjoys freedom from sin's power.

In the AV the text reads "is freed", the perfect participle of *dikaioō*, and is better rendered "has been justified". The thought is the legal termination of all claims by reason of death. In the passage it is not physical death, but nevertheless it is just as real in the sight of God. He sees the believer united with Christ, the One who dealt with the sin question at Calvary and endured its penalty. By that act, the legal consequences are annulled; they can no longer be pressed. That being so, the power of sin is rendered inactive and there is no longer any obligation on the believer's part to have anything to do with it.

It should be noted that this verse deals with being justified from sin, not justified from sins, an aspect of justification which has already been dealt with in the epistle. Sin, the root principle, is looked upon in this context as being a tyrant. It is in some ways personified, something which is real, and yet because it has been dealt with judicially at the cross, the believer's former connection with it has ceased. This does not mean that a believer is sinless. Sinless perfection is not taught in Scripture. It means that the obligation to sin no longer exists because of the sentence passed on it and carried out at Calvary. There is power in the new life to live triumphantly, and this will be set out later in the epistle. If ch.6 reveals that there is a new master, ch.8 will show that there is also a new power. It is an unfortunate feature of christendom that many try to rise to higher heights of what they think is acceptable to God in good works, instead of looking to the Scriptures to see what God has done to make men and women acceptable to Him. The cross of Christ is the answer to man's predicament, if only he would cast himself on the mercy of God to open his eyes to see it.

Notes

1 There is good manuscript authority for *epimenōmen* (aorist subjunctive; "are we to continue?").
2 Wuest paraphrases "How shall we, that are dead to sin?" as "How is it possible for us, such persons as we are, who have been separated once for all from the sinful nature, any longer to live in its grip?"
3 Water baptism is in view, not baptism into the body (as in 1 Cor 12:13) as some hold. "Baptised unto his death" precludes the idea of baptism in the Spirit.
4 *Kainotēti* ("newness") as at 7:6, "serve in newness of spirit and not in the oldness of the letter", is from *kainos*, "new in character, species or mode". It describes the quality of life.

Peripateō ("to walk") is used figuratively to describe the character and conduct of christian living, wherein there is the demonstration of the features of newness of life.

Newell makes an interesting note, "Now mark in this verse that it is Christ who is raised from the dead, and the saints are to walk, consequently, in 'newness of life'".
5 *Sumphutoi,* ("planted together") occurs only here in the NT. This word has emphasis in the text, a key fact.

Gegonamen, "we have become", stresses an action having continuing effects, leaving a condition of lasting significance.
6 *Katargēthē* is from *katargeō* ("to annul", "to render useless for a specific purpose"). See note at 3:31.

Douleuein ("serve") is the present infinitive of *douleuō*, "to serve as a slave".

The contrast between "the old man" and "the new man" is noted in Eph 4:22-24; Col 3:9,10. In Eph 4:24 the new man is *kainos anthrōpos*, but in Col 3:10 he is *neos anthrōpos*. *Kainos* is "new", different from that which was formerly, so *kainos anthrōpos* is a new man, one who differs from the former man. He is looked upon as superseding an old one which has grown old and withered through sin. *Neos* is "new", newly made, fresh, new altogether. These two words, *kainos* and *neos* are used interchangeably on occasions, but there is a distinct difference, which is clearly seen in connection with the two views of "the new man".

Although the body is a constituent part of man, the word "body" is used in a variety of ways in the NT. It can mean the body of a man in life, or in death, or in resurrection. Metaphorically it is used in many ways and the context should always be taken into account when determining the meaning.

(b) *Service: the new and old masters – Christ Jesus (vv.8-18)*

v.8 "Now if we be dead with Christ, we believe that we shall also live with him:
v.9 Knowing that Christ being raised from the dead dieth no more; death hath no more dominion over him.
v.10 For in that he died, he died unto sin once: but in that he liveth, he liveth unto God.
v.11 Likewise reckon ye also yourselves to be dead indeed unto sin, but alive unto God through Jesus Christ our Lord.
v.12 Let not sin therefore reign in your mortal body, that ye should obey it in the lusts thereof.
v.13 Neither yield ye your members as instruments of unrighteousness unto sin: but yield yourselves unto God, as those that are alive from the dead, and your members as instruments of righteousness unto God.
v.14 For sin shall not have dominion over you: for ye are not under the law, but under grace.
v.15 What then? shall we sin, because we are not under the law, but under grace? God forbid.
v.16 Know ye not, that to whom ye yield yourselves servants to obey, his servants ye are to whom ye obey; whether of sin unto death, or of obedience unto righteousness?
v.17 But God be thanked, that ye were the servants of sin, but ye have obeyed from the heart that form of doctrine which was delivered you.
v.18 Being then made free from sin, ye became the servants of righteousness."

8 The previous verse is a general statement drawn from everyday life that death terminates all charges; it closes down all claims. Any obligations to sin are therefore annulled. What is undeniable from the inevitable end of life is true of all men, but what follows in v.8 applies only to believers. It is significant that the pronoun "he" is used in v.7, but coming into the next verse Paul reverts to the pronoun "we", taking up his position again with all who are noted as having died "with Christ".

Having dealt with the sin question and the annulment of its claims on believers, Paul now clarifies the Christian's present and future position. The opening words do not suggest a doubt. They could be rendered, "But since we died with Christ".

This is taken as a fact, one which Paul considers he has proved to be the case. He asserts therefore, "we believe that we shall also live with him". He does not separate himself from other believers as if there were different schools of thought on the matter. The opening words, "we believe" are uttered on behalf of all to record the acceptance of a fundamental fact of the faith, which is, "we shall also live with him".

Regarding living with Him, although the future is undoubtedly involved since the future tense is used, the present cannot be ruled out. Indeed, the fact that we died with Christ, demands further comment on the present christian position. Already attention has been drawn to newness of life. In this, the believer is encouraged to walk (v.4). The features of it have to be demonstrated in a world which is hostile to God. Life in Christ, is the blessing which believers possess. They will never lose it. It will continue right into eternity. It does not depend on the efforts of the saints for its maintenance, but on what God has done through the work of His Son and what He continues to do through the work of the Holy Spirit. Nevertheless, active saints, living for God, are the channels through which God is acting for His own glory and the good of mankind.

9 To introduce the subject of "the old man", Paul began by using the present participle of *eido*, "to know". The knowledge implied in this word is that which is gained through a personal acquaintance with a person or object, as in Matt 7:23, "I never knew you" – "I have never had a true and personal connection with you". So while Paul does not say in v.6 how those who were addressed came to know about "the old man", it has to be assumed that it was more than hearsay. They were aware within themselves of the readiness to sin. In addition, since conversion, they had come to know God through the gospel and in the various ways He had chosen to communicate His truth. In various ways they would have acquired knowledge of some of the implications of the death of Christ.

Now in v.9 Paul makes another appeal to knowledge. This time, however, he uses the present participle of *oida* when he states, "knowing that Christ being raised from the dead dieth no more". This word implies that the subject has come within the person's sphere of perception or experience, and may include hearsay. What had come within the scope of knowledge in this verse was that Christ, having been raised from amongst the dead, would never die again. In the Scriptures, there were examples of many who had been raised from the dead, including Lazarus, the daughter of Jairus, the son of the widow of Nain, but they all returned to the grave. They were mortal and death therefore had a claim upon them. Death had no claim upon the Lord Jesus. He was capable of dying, but was not subject to death. He laid down His life voluntarily and He took it up again, as He said He would (John 10:18).

The knowledge of His resurrection, to which the apostle refers, was not an event which was short of publicity. Apart from the many predictions made by the Saviour that He would rise again, the apostles gave witness in no uncertain way in their preaching, as the accounts in the Acts make plain. In addition, the Lord appeared to over five hundred brethren at once (1 Cor 15:6) and it would certainly be naive in the extreme to think that they did not relate the experience over and over again, wherever they went. Paul's reference therefore to knowledge of the resurrection of Christ is in keeping with the obvious facts that were widely spread in apostolic times. Christ had died and He was raised in triumph by the power of God.

Death had no more lordship over Him. Of His own volition He had bowed to it once, but never again would He enter into death. He had defeated it and the day had been appointed when it would be swallowed up in victory (1 Cor 15:54). To the church at Corinth Paul gladly declared, "But now is Christ risen from the dead, and become the firstfruits of them that slept...But every man in his own order: Christ the firstfruits; afterward they that are Christ's at his coming" (1 Cor 15:20,23). The mighty harvest will follow.

10 The RV renders the opening words, "For the death that he died". This rendering emphasises the kind of death that He died. It was one which was full of significance. It was such that only Christ could face. No other was fit to enter into death and deal with the issues which were involved. In this verse therefore the emphasis is on the death of Christ to sin. All that was related to sin, its power, its penalty and even its presence were dealt with in the death of Christ. It will never be repeated. The reference to "once", meaning "once for all" declares the finality of His death. It met all the claims of sin, and so now He is finished with the sin question altogether.

Just as there was emphasis on the kind of death Christ died, so the same construction must be placed on the kind of life that He lives. He lives unto God. His life has no other focus and knows no other horizon. What God has in His plans for the future involves His Son. He it is who will carry out God's purposes as the age draws to a close and the new age follows. In addition, His life at present is on behalf of His saints. His high-priestly ministry and His advocacy on their behalf are involved in His present life. The apostle's statement, "but in that he liveth, he liveth unto God", or as the RV renders, "but the life that he liveth, he liveth unto God" is full of meaning; it directs attention not only to what God derives from the life that He now lives, but to what in a secondary sense is for the benefit of His saints.

11 What has been stated since the beginning of the chapter is applied practically in this verse. The significance of the death and resurrection of Christ and the life that He now lives demands an answer from believers. Physical death on their part may not be actual, but by use of the word "reckon" (eleven times in ch.4 in R.V.) believers are placed under an obligation to live up to the expected response. To reckon themselves dead is what God expects from His saints. Christian living is not passive. Believers are not looked upon as having no active part in dealing with the question of sin. If Christ died unto sin once-for-all, those who believe in

Him and have benefited from His sacrificial work have a duty as debtors to His grace to give the answer which is required from them.

The word "reckon" is imperative. Reckoning oneself to be dead implies a permanent state. Notice the added emphasis in the little word "indeed". The apostle does not contemplate times when there is forgetfulness of the christian position and sin therefore finds inroads into the life. What is obviously implied is that sin's demands find no response because what is dead cannot answer. In this chapter sin is the old master. Those who were slaves to it are seen to have been freed from its bondage and to be under the new master, the Lord Jesus Christ, and His service is not onerous.

The reckoning has another implication. The apostle considers the believers as being alive unto God in Christ Jesus, not "through Jesus Christ", as in the AV. This is the first time in the epistle that the truth of being "in Christ" is mentioned. This position is true of all believers. Although being justified by faith and being under the headship of Christ is a confirmation that all such are "in Christ", the declaration of it here in Scripture removes all doubts. The emphasis therefore is on the believer's complete identification and union with Christ. It is not a blessing which can be lost, the connection can never be severed. As far as duration is concerned, it is eternal. The appeal of the apostle as a result is for the life to be lived towards God in every aspect, on the grounds of what is owed to Him because of His grace and compassion in Christ Jesus.

12 The conjunction "therefore" has considerable significance here. It is a bridge between v.11 and v.12 and it places strong emphasis on the connection between Paul's injunction in v.11 and his appeal in v.12. Failure or refusal to reckon oneself "to be dead indeed unto sin, but alive unto God" will allow sin to come in and reign. It will find a ready response to the unguarded. The appeal then in v.12 to bar sin from having the opportunity to reign will have fallen on deaf ears. Paul's earnest plea depends on obedience to the injunction of v.11. If believers do respond and reckon themselves dead unto sin, they will not obey sin and the lusts associated with it.

The thought of sin reigning is not new in this epistle. In 5:17 it was made known that by one man's offence death reigned. In 5:21 the apostle declared that sin reigned unto death, but grace reigned through righteousness. As to sin reigning as a monarch, it is understandable why Paul was so deeply concerned about not giving it the opportunity to reign in the mortal bodies of the saints. These bodies were the temples of the Holy Ghost and they were bought with a price. It follows therefore that believers have to glorify God in their bodies because they are God's (1 Cor 6:19,20). Nevertheless, sin is not dead. It reigns as a monarch and in the world it has many loyal subjects. Believers, however, are entitled to resist its overtures by assuming the state of death on the grounds that they died with Christ. Sin's appeal therefore, however impassioned, is futile because the dead cannot respond.

Paul's reference to bodies being mortal is difficult to understand in the context of this verse. The most likely explanation seems to be that he meant it as a reminder that resistance to sin saved the body from acting out the proferred temptations and lusts. Although the body was mortal, subject to death, it had still to be preserved for the service of God. The day of redemption had not arrived and until it dawned, the mortal body should be kept from sin's contaminations. Although the body belonged to God, later in the epistle the apostle will call upon believers to exercise the privilege, though they be tenants only, of offering their bodies as living sacrifices, holy and acceptable unto God as their reasonable service (Rom 12:1,2).

13 The AV does not mark the distinction between the two occurrences of the word "yield" in this verse. Regarding these, CE Stuart makes an interesting comment. He remarks, "The reader who can consult the original should notice the use of tenses in the Greek, impossible to mark in English. 'Neither yield': here the verb is in the present, expressive of the continuance of the action, i.e., 'at no time do it'. 'But yield': here it is the aorist, to express that it should be done once for all, and never to be revoked, or to need repetition". In brief, the first occurrence of the word says, "stop doing this"; the second says, "do this now, and do it once and for all".

The word "yield" (*paristēmi*) is given correctly in the RV as "present". It is used at 12:1, "present your bodies, a living sacrifice". It has many shades of meaning, such as, "to devote", "to place beside", "to range beside", but here it is best rendered, "to place at the disposal of". The exhortation then would be "stop placing your members at the disposal of sin, but place them once and for all as instruments of righteousness at the disposal of God".

The change from "mortal body" to "members" is worthy of note. The apostle seems to be emphasising that it is the various members of the body which are active in sinning. The body contains and controls them all, no doubt, but the members are the expressive parts. Through them the body works, either for good or ill. There is undoubtedly a world of difference between members being used as instruments of unrighteousness by sin, and instruments of righteousness by God. The word "instruments" (*hoplon*) denotes a military weapon. To press that meaning would introduce into this context implications which the passage would not support. Experience confirms that the members are instruments through which the body works, and sadly, not always in the right direction.

The expression "as those that are alive from the dead" is capable of being understood in several ways. It may mean that the appeal is to those who were once dead in sins, but having been converted, are now alive to God. Perhaps, however, it was intended by the apostle to be the outcome of v.11, "reckoning oneself dead unto sin, but alive unto God", where the emphasis is more on responsive action than on a change of state. There is also the possibility that in a context where baptism is taught, a plea for an action such as called for in this verse would be appropriate. Taking all these into account, the emphasis in the plea seems to be made to those who were once dead in sins and in the habit of sinning, but are now changed people. As such, a decisive action is called for which will prove that a change has taken place when the members of the body are engaged in right actions. Righteousness here has a practical bearing and infers deeds which are righteous by God's standards.

14 The apostle appears to be saying that if believers present themselves unto God with all that such a once-for-all action implies, then sin will not exercise lordship over them. This of course will only be the result of total commitment. Sin will find no response from believers whose members are wholly engaged in acts of righteousness. Because the future tense is used in the first part of the verse, the words seem to indicate more of the nature of a promise than a fact. Either way, the end result is the same; sin has no place and therefore no power over committed believers.

The conjunction "for" seems, however, to direct attention to a different reason, or at least another reason why sin shall not have dominion. It is because believers are not under law but under grace. Law here must stand for the legal principle and not necessarily, or solely, the law of Moses. Gentiles were not under the Mosaic law, but, as was argued earlier in the epistle, they were nevertheless under law to God. In addition, sin worked through the prohibitions of the law. The law was the strength of sin (1 Cor 15:56). There was no possibility of accomplishing righteous acts for God if legal principles were involved. Any thought of "thou shalt" or "thou shalt not" is totally foreign to the christian position. Israel had already proved that mankind was incapable of fulfilling the legal requirements. Sin exercised dominion over that nation and will do so over all who place themselves under principles of law to seek acceptance with God.

A new form of control is brought in as the result of the sacrificial work of Christ. Those who are justified are governed by a different principle: they are under grace. The unmerited favour of God is extended freely to the undeserving, to people who have no meritorious cause in themselves. They find that they are the objects of unbought love. Ascetic practices and strivings to reach impossible standards are left behind. When the principle of grace is the rule all law-works are set aside. When free of the law's condemning power, the freedom that comes with the grace of God wins from responsive hearts works of righteousness. If the simple, and yet profound statement, "for ye are not under the law, but under grace" had been observed how much heartache would have been saved to those who tried by their strivings to find peace with God, but failed.

15 Paul's interrogative question occurs again. "What then?" he asks. In view of all that has been stated between v.1 and v.14, particularly about being under grace, the characteristic expression is posed to provoke thought. At v.1 the same question was raised to show the total inconsistency of counting upon super-abounding grace to cover abounding sin. Here at v.15 another absurd situation is posed. Since believers are not under law but under grace, is that an excuse to engage in sinful practices? "Away with such a thought" is the apostle's swift reply. The AV gives "God forbid" to express Paul's indignation at such a suggestion, and while the phrase reflects the vigour of the original, it is not an accurate translation.

It is obvious that Paul had a deep concern about the possible abuse of grace. The attitude of being able to count on super-abounding grace to cover abounding sin was reprehensible to him. His outbursts of protest are understandable. From another point of view freedom from constraints and prohibitions of law introduces the same concern. Will advantage be taken of the freedom under grace to practise sin? It is little wonder that Paul calls for a once-for-all presentation as being alive from the dead. It is the only safeguard against the possibility of falling back into sin.

The idea of abusing the grace of God by sinning with impunity was abhorrent to Paul. To sin knowingly and to do it without concern about the certainty of God's intervention in some way or another is the height of folly. To misinterpret the grace of God and consider it as toleration of unrighteousness is far removed from the truth. In addition, to think and act that way is a slight on the sacrifice of Christ and what it cost Him to put away sin. Before God could show grace, the sin question had to be dealt with and that was settled at Calvary in the death of Christ. Grace, with its accompanying mercy and compassion, was not just the expression of God's benevolence. To show unmerited favour had, as it were, to be paid for, and nothing less than the death of Christ could cover it. There was no licence under law to commit sin, and it is certain that being under grace does not change God's character. His standards remain the same in every dispensation of His dealings with mankind.

16 As in the introduction to v.9 where the apostle uses the same word, so again he issues a challenge about something which was surely common knowledge. What he was posing was not a closely-guarded secret. It was not the possession of a few but a well-known fact. Those who present themselves as slaves to another recognise the implications. That person is the master. He is not the master in name only, but he is due obedience. Slaves are the property of their master and they have no rights. They are bound to him and they are entirely at his disposal. Freedom of choice does not enter into the matter. In Paul's day slavery was common, indeed the Roman Empire could hardly have functioned without slaves. It was they who did most of the nation's menial work.

The word rendered "yield" is the same as in v.13 and is better rendered "present". The word "servant" (*doulos*) considers the servant in relation to his master. Nevertheless, a slave who was incapable of working was of no value to the master and would be disposed of without compunction. However, this is not exactly the pattern of things in this verse. The bondservants, for such they are, do not wait to be purchased, but offer themselves as slaves to sin to obey sin's commands. It is when they come under the mastery of sin that they become bondservants.

The principle, nevertheless is clear, bondservice implies obedience. Sin is personified and if sin is the master then sin's demands must be obeyed. The end result of yielding to that master is death. In Paul's arguments here, however, there is an alternative. There is another master. This master is also personified. There is therefore a choice; it is either bondservant of sin or bondservant of obedience. One is unto death and the other is unto righteousness. Righteousness in this verse denotes the manner of life and the right actions which are acceptable to God and which bring Him pleasure. The outcome of serving sin is awesome and yet it is ignored by those who freely offer themselves to sin to be its slaves. If the stark reality of death in all its aspects, present and future, were taken into account there would not be a readiness to cast aside freedom to serve God in acts of righteousness. A moment's consideration of what has been won for sinners by the sacrifice of Christ should be enough to turn the justified away from sin to live for the glory of God.

17   In the previous verse two masters were identified. On the principle established in the beatitudes, "No man can serve two masters" (Matt 6:24), it is either sin or obedience unto righteousness in this context. If sin is obeyed, this is a tacit admission that the other master is rejected. Paul, however, finds himself a debtor to thank God. As he considers the former lives of those to whom he wrote and thinks of the change by grace, he gives the full credit to God. In unconverted days sin reigned. Sin was the despotic monarch and unregenerate men and women were the slaves. But, whereas they were in bondage to sin, the apostle has to acknowledge a complete change in those who obeyed from the heart.

The verb, "obeyed" is in the aorist tense and looks back to a time when the gospel of God was heard and believed. It was not a mere mental assent to the terms that were declared; it was a conscious decision from the heart. The fact that they were servants of sin would indicate the acknowledgment of sinnership and a departure from that condition when they were saved. This is borne out by the apostle's words, "ye have obeyed from the heart that form of doctrine that was delivered you". The tense of the verb also indicates finality. When they obeyed they had no thought of returning to the old habits associated with being bondservants of sin. The break was clean and permanent and this is taken into account by Paul.

The expression, "that form of doctrine", describes what they believed. The word "form" (*tupos*, "a type") indicates the framework of the gospel message preached. Those who believed that message metaphorically placed themselves in that frame. The body of teaching, the terms of the gospel, the truth of God for sinful men and women was what was announced and those Paul is addressing conformed their lives to it. Their belief was from the heart. They recognised that the grace of God was being extended to them and they bowed to that. It was an opportunity to escape from the thraldom of sin and they grasped it willingly. It was indeed a day of good tidings when they heard the good news of the gospel and from the heart they believed it implicitly.

18 This short verse continues the theme of v.17. Having believed the message of the gospel, the result was freedom from sin. This is not quite freedom from sinning; it is rather freedom from the taskmaster's bondage. If therefore delivered from slavery, the obligation to the old master ceases. No longer are those who have obeyed from the heart the subjects of sin's dominion.

Paul continues to press the thought of being slaves. He states, "ye became servants", or more literally, "ye were enslaved". This phrase represents one word, *edoulōthēte*, which is aorist, passive voice. At a time past, the change of masters was made. As the passive voice is used, the change was effected by a power outwith those who believed. They were willing participants, but the power to make the change was of God.

Once again Paul resorts to personifying. In v.16 he personified sin and obedience. Now he personifies righteousness. He does not say that the change of masters was from sin to God, but from sin to righteousness. In v.16 righteousness was the result of coming into the service of obedience. Now the apostle makes righteousness the master under whose sway the believers were brought as bondservants. Again, the principle that no man can serve two masters is inferred. If in the bondservice of righteousness, sin has to relinquish its title to rule those who were once its willing subjects. As in v.13, righteousness means living righteously and doing righteous acts. It describes the kind of conduct in daily living which meets with God's approval.

Notes

8 "If we jointly died with Christ, we believe that we also jointly live with Him" (Rotherham).
On *suzēsomen* "we shall live with", Alford remarks, "The future, 'we shall also live with him', as in v.5, is used because life with Him, though here begun, is not here completed".
9 *Kurieuei* ("hath dominion") is the present indicative of *kurieuō*, "to lord over", as in v.14; 7:1. Death had its day of dominion when the Lord voluntarily submitted to it. Now, as at the right hand of God, He will never bow to it again.
10 The adverb *ephapax* is a strengthened form and indicates "once for all".
With "the death that he died", the kind of death that he died, compare Gal 2:20, "the life which I now live", i.e. "the kind of life which I now live".
11 "Likewise" is translated "Even so" in the RV. The application of the argument set out in the previous verse is now pressed, but with particular emphasis on the close of v.10.
12 EGT comments on the reference to "mortal", "the suggestion of *thnētos* is rather that the frail body should be protected against the tyranny of sin, than that sin leads to the death of the body".
14 For *kurieusei* ("shall have dominion"), see note at v.9. Here, "sin shall not lord over". The

point being pressed is that action should be taken to stop sin lording it over. There is no need to take up a defeatist role and let sin have full sway.

15 In brief, if there is no claim from the legal side and there is freedom under grace, does that give an entitlement to sin with impunity? Paul's outburst of protest answers that question effectively.

16 See comment on *doulos* at 1:1. This word describes one who is in permanent relation of servitude to another, whose will is swallowed up in the will of another. A slave belonged to a master and he was altogether at his master's disposal. Many of the slaves in Roman times were cultured and highly-literate people who had the misfortune of being taken in war. These unfortunates ceased to have a will of their own; their wills were swallowed up in the will of another.

17 "That form of doctrine" is not to be understood as a distinct type of teaching which belonged to Paul and not to other apostles. They all preached the same gospel and taught the same things.

(c) *Service now has a new meaning (vv.19-23)*

> v.19 "I speak after the manner of men because of the infirmity of your flesh: for as ye have yielded your members servants to uncleanness and to iniquity unto iniquity; even so now yield your members servants to righteousness unto holiness.
> v.20 For when ye were the servants of sin, ye were free from righteousness.
> v.21 What fruit had ye then in those things whereof ye are now ashamed? for the end of those things is death.
> v.22 But now being made free from sin, and become servants to God, ye have your fruit unto holiness, and the end everlasting life.
> v.23 For the wages of sin is death; but the gift of God is eternal life through Jesus Christ our Lord."

19 It is not a rare thing for Paul to allude to what men say and how they say it. In his gospel address to the Athenians as recorded in Acts 17, he preached, "as certain also of your own poets have said, For we are also his offspring". So here, he takes into account their limited spiritual perception and speaks in familiar human terms. He does not speak above their heads, but comes down to the level at which men and women communicate with each other in everyday conversation. It suited Paul's purpose to do so. He did not want any to miss the importance of what he wanted to say because they could not understand the way he said it.

Haldane does not agree with this interpretation of the clause, "I speak after the manner of men". He maintains that the apostle was referring "to the illustration of the subject by the customs of men as to slavery". "This", Haldane asserts, "establishes the propriety of teaching divine truth through illustrations taken from all subjects with which those addressed are acquainted". No careful reader of Scripture would deny that the Lord and His apostles used human customs to illustrate divine truth, but regarding this passage most commentators teach that Paul was meaning human language and style.

There was a time when those addressed yielded their members servants to uncleanness, and but for the grace of God they were heading for certain ruin. The reference to the infirmity of the flesh here means their inability to comprehend things which were spiritual. There was no spiritual understanding. If Paul had not resorted to everyday speech, much of what he was bringing to their attention would have been lost on them. There was a weakness of discernment. It was brought about by the corruption and weakness derived from their fallen nature, a state that is true of all the unregenerate.

There is also a reminder in the opening words of the verse of their being under the headship of Adam with all that such a state implies. They were not responsible for being born with a sinful nature, but they were responsible for their sinful acts. They gave themselves over to carry out what sin dictated. They were on a downward slope, going from bad to worse. Each sin committed was an incentive to commit another. They went from uncleanness to iniquity which ended in iniquity of a grosser nature. There is no middle course, indeed no middle course has been suggested throughout Paul's argument. It has been either death or life, sin unto death or obedience unto righteousness, servants to uncleanness and iniquity or servants to righteousness unto holiness.

Haldane does not accept that the phrase "iniquity unto iniquity" means moving from one degree of iniquity to another. He maintains that it is evident that the phrase is to be understood on the principle already mentioned above, namely, that in the first occurrence iniquity is personified, and in the second, it is the conduct produced by obedience to this sovereign. They surrender their members to the slavery of iniquity as to a king, and the result is that iniquity is practised. However, the weight of opinion about the phrase "iniquity unto iniquity" favours the progression of evil. Once embraced and practised it goes on without hindrance to grosser forms.

Just as Paul multiplied epithets to describe the degradation and shame of men and women in their unregenerate state, so equally does he in his description of the contrast he introduces. Righteousness and holiness are personified. Being bondservants to them suggests a totally different course of life. Under sin they had pursued the business of sinning with a will and a total disregard for the consequences. Now as bondservants of righteousness they are to pursue holiness with the same vigour. Righteousness, as in the previous verses, suggests right conduct and acts for God. Holiness describes the godly condition of heart and soul that is maintained when carrying out godly deeds. Although the stress is on the two words, "righteousness" and "holiness", behind them is the God of grace. In reality, the change from being slaves to sin in all its forms to being slaves of the God who made it all possible is a dramatic one. Service has a new meaning when it is entered into with a change of masters.

20 The previous verse ended with a reference to holiness, or perhaps more accurately, sanctification, as in the RV. Basically sanctification implies separation to God. Associated with the word are different shades of meaning, depending on the context. It is viewed in Scripture as past, present and future. It is a work which God does in His saints, just as justification is a work which He does for them. Sometimes sanctification is viewed as being instantaneous; sometimes as progressive. Sometimes it is positional; sometimes it is practical. God the Father, God the Son, and God the Holy Spirit are all involved in different aspects of the work of sanctification. For example, it is God the Father in 1 Thess 5:23; God the Son in Heb 10:10 and God the Holy Spirit in 2 Thess 2:13.

In v.19 the aspect is not so much the setting apart for a purpose, but the conscious yielding as servants to holiness, in contrast to the former state of yielding as servants to uncleanness. The former state was one of filth and dirt, the new state is one of moral suitability to the service of God. Those therefore who have been separated to God enjoy the benefits of a sanctified life, but they are expected to respond and maintain a condition of heart and soul which corresponds with the separated state and which gives character to righteous acts.

In this short verse there is a reminder again from the apostle to those he addresses that they were formerly bondservants of sin. They were entirely subject to the dictates of a tyrannical master. As such they had no link with righteousness. There was nothing that bound them to it. They were free; they had no obligation to it and as being willing servants of sin, they would have no desire to be involved with conduct which was righteous by God's standards. Here Paul does not include holiness when he makes mention of freedom. It is only freedom from righteousness. Possibly what was outward and more readily recognisable was more of a contrast to the lawlessness ("iniquity", AV) mentioned in the previous verse. Certainly righteousness and lawlessness are contrasted in Heb 1:9 (see RV, JND). In v.22, in connection with fruit, he omits righteousness and includes holiness. He does not say, "ye have your fruit unto righteousness, and the end everlasting life". No doubt there is some significance in the omission of the word in v.22, just as there is here where "holiness" is left out.

21 The question which the apostle raises in this verse was obviously intended to be a reminder that serving sin produced nothing of value to anyone. The years spent in sinful practices were wasted. They yielded no fruit. There was, doubtless, self-gratification and lustful pleasure at the time, but no fruit for eternity. Looking back, as Paul suggests, there was nothing but shame for past actions. We recall the words of Saul to David, "...behold I have played the fool, and have erred exceedingly" (1 Sam 26:21). The question therefore demanded an answer, an admission that there was no fruit. Living under sin's domination was useless and empty as far as yielding anything of acceptance for God; there was no benefit to others.

The apostle supplies the conclusion. Those who had been awakened by the grace of God would have no argument with it. The end, the issue of it all, was death. Those who lived in sin but were saved before sin took its toll in physical death were the fortunate ones. Others were no doubt overcome by death while still pursuing evil and they had the consequences still to face at the great white throne. Death does not mean cessation of existence. Annihilation is not taught in Scripture. The scriptural position is clear, "It is appointed unto men once to die, but after this the judgment" (Heb 9:27). That is unalterable for all who die in their sins. There is no possibility of having another chance to put things right with God after the fatal line is crossed.

22 The change from death to life is noted by the apostle here in a manner that suits the context. He remarks, "But now being made free from sin". That implies that the chains are snapped, the bonds of sin are broken. Since there is no middle course there can be only one outcome and Paul records it, they had become "servants to God". If they had not become servants to God, they would still have been slaves to sin, because there is no third master in the reasoning of Paul. Those who think that they can do without God in their lives are sadly mistaken. They are still in bondage to sin and Satan. The degree of sin is not the criterion, but to whom one is a bondservant. Not all of sin's subjects live lives of sinful abandon, but they are in bondage nevertheless. They may see themselves as paragons of virtue, but "their virtues are as polished vices" (Plummer).

While under the dominion of sin there was no fruit; there was nothing of value for anyone. But in the service of God it was a vastly different situation. There was fruit unto holiness, or sanctification, as the RV renders it. It does not say that the fruit was unto righteousness. It is not right conduct but a right condition that is envisaged. The end is not death; that was the issue of the former life. In the service of God the end is everlasting life. The great sheet-anchor for the soul in this connection is what the Lord announced in His earthly ministry, "Verily, verily, I say unto you, He that heareth my word, and believeth on him that sent me, hath everlasting life, and shall not come into condemnation; but is passed from death unto life" (John 5:24).

23 This verse concludes Paul's argument on service. The end of serving sin is death (v.21). The end of serving God is eternal life (v.22). Another set of contrasts is introduced in this verse to emphasise what is due from serving sin and what is not due or earned – the free gift of God! Sin has been noted as a monarch reigning over its subjects. The metaphorical language of the apostle, in terms which are easily understood (v.19), makes it clear that sin will never fall behind in paying its dues. Just as military rulers paid their soldiers wages for placing their lives at risk, so sin will pay wages to all who join in its war against the will of God. There is only one currency, however, when the final settlement is made and that is death. Sin carries its followers to the grave and there it leaves them. At that point the pleasures of sin for a season end. When life ceases sin has no more power to exert. The soul that sins dies and from then there is nothing to look forward to but judgment.

In many ways this is one of the saddest verses in Holy Scripture. Gospel preachers down the years have stressed that the paymaster, sin, will never hold back paying what is its due. Their pleadings in most cases have fallen on deaf ears. Men and women push the thought of a pay day to the back of their minds. Sin is a pleasure, and, as it has been noted in v.19, once it is tasted it becomes a habit until only the grosser forms of evil satisfy. Death here is physical at the end of life. Sin has no power beyond the grave. The solemn fact is, however, that the ruin that results from serving sin is not exhausted at death; there is a reckoning to be faced beyond the grave.

The contrast to the solemn opening words is now introduced. It is this that brings gladness to the gospel preachers. They have no joy in intimating the wages of sin, although in faithfulness to God and man they have to make the situation clear. But the contrast, that the gift of God is eternal life, makes the telling out of the message a joyous experience. It is the free gift (*charisma*) of God which is intimated. It is a gift of free grace, unmerited and unearned. Sin pays wages to those who are its willing subjects. They earned death. Every sin and every day lived in sin adds to the final reckoning, and despite the fact that the terms of payment are announced beforehand, men and women press on in sin to the end.

The free gift of God is quite different. There is no final day of settlement as with the payment of sin's wages. The gift is given freely at the point of believing. Eternal life becomes a present possession, enjoyed on earth and continued uninterruptedly into eternity. Communion with God is entered into in this life and never ceases. It is everlasting in its duration. How such a blessing can be extended to mankind is explained; it is "in Christ Jesus". This is a result of what He has done. He laid down His life to settle the sin question once for all, and now all who believe in Him partake of His risen life. His full title is given: He is Christ Jesus our Lord. Thankful acknowledgement of His Lordship is the glad response of those who reap the blessings resulting from His sacrificial work.

Notes

19 Apart from Haldane, there are others who consider that Paul was only referring to slaves and not generally "after the manner of men". WM Kroll writes, "Paul uses the human analogy of a slave in order that the weakest flesh may understand".

It is said that *akatharsia* ("uncleanness") began in the physical world and ended up in the moral world. Medically it was used of the impure matter gathered round a sore or wound. It is rendered variously in the NT, indicating impurity which awakens disgust. It is the quality of that which is soiled and dirty.

In the LXX *akatharsia* is used about thirty times to denote ceremonial and ritual impurity. Anyone so described could not approach God or share in the worship of the people. To try it would invoke the wrath of God, "Whosoever...that goeth unto the holy things, which the children of Israel hallow unto the Lord, having his uncleanness upon him, that soul shall be cut off from my presence: I am the Lord" (Lev 22:3). (The world of Paul's day was characterised by uncleanness of the most vile nature.)

The word "iniquity" (*anomia*, "lawlessness") is from *anomos*, "lawless", "not subject to law", hence "impious". A lawless society is one which knows no bounds. Lawlessness begets lawlessness, and indeed men's lusts are their own laws. Paul is noting here that as sin is practised, it becomes easier to perform, until it loses its terror and it becomes effortless. As the AV states, "iniquity unto iniquity".

2. Sanctified and Free from Bondage to Law
7:1-25

To understand the teaching of Rom 7, acknowledged to be a most difficult chapter, it is necessary to ascertain whose experience the apostle is describing. Is it the experience of the natural man, or of the Christian, or of an imaginary man, or of Paul himself that is under review? If it is held that the apostle is writing about himself, is he describing what he was before conversion, or the state he found himself in immediately after the Damascus Road experience, or is he describing how he found himself reacting to the law as a mature believer in the service of Jesus Christ his Lord?

Wm Kelly asserts that the source of the difficulty with Rom 7 is ignorance of the christian position or standing, and consequently of his relation to the law. He further avers that if the first six verses of the chapter were understood there would be no obscurity. Regarding Rom 7 he states, "It is impossible to understand the passage if applied either to a natural man or a Christian. There may be, there is, a transitional state constantly to be found in souls when they are born again, but not yet in conscious deliverance, and this is the question here. Paul may have passed through, as most do, this experience more or less during the three days, when without sight, he neither ate nor drank. He was converted then, no longer a natural man, but not yet submitting to the righteousness of God...The state described, however, is in no case I believe final, but transitional, though bad and legal teaching may keep a soul in it till grace acts fully, it may be, on a death bed or its equivalent".

If Wm Kelly's view is understood aright, he seems to be saying that failure to understand on the part of believers the teaching of the first six verses of the chapter, leaves them vulnerable to the pronouncements and prohibitions of the law. Many never become aware that they died with Christ to the law, and consequently never know deliverance from the law all their christian lives. His view that Paul learned this during his three days of blindness may be true, but there is no indication in Scripture that such was the case.

There is such a diversity of opinion on Rom 7, that a degree of hesitancy in expressing a view is understandable. Some are clear in their minds, even dogmatic that their stance is the correct one. Darby, for example, states that the passage is not the condition of any one at all, and goes on to prove it to his own satisfaction. Be that as it may, it is held by many that the extensive use of the present tense throughout is an indication of present experience, and therefore of Paul's after conversion. This view has merit, but using the present tense is a well-known practice in certain submissions to gain emphasis, and it is judged to be inconclusive as far as proving the point here is concerned.

If the passage refers to the natural man, the unregenerate, is Paul describing the struggles of the natural man just as the natural man would experience them; that is, is he doing so as a believer looking on or looking back to a time when in that condition? The upholders of the case for the unregenerate think that the struggles Paul describes cannot be those of a believer since the Christian is called to peace and not to conflict. In addition, since Paul writes of the wretched man crying for deliverance from the body of death, it cannot be that he is describing christian experience. Since also there is no mention of the Lord or of the Holy Spirit, it is held by many that Paul must be describing the natural man who is still in the darkness, alienated from God.

From v.7 onwards, if what is set out by the apostle is his experience prior to conversion, when he was unregenerate, then the view that the natural man is being discussed, if even obliquely, is very valid. In support of that, it is a reasonable assumption that not all that Paul described under the personal pronoun "I" can be attributed to his condition after conversion. However, it seems right to conclude that all his comments, whether of himself, or of an imaginary person, were made to assist believers to come to a better understanding of what was involved in having died with Christ to the law and then being "joined to another". If this were not so, to go into such detail and use such vivid language, if no practical or doctrinal lessons were being taught for the benefit of believers, would be pointless. There is therefore, it is submitted, more than a passing reference to the experience of Christians in Paul's reasoning.

The main topic of the chapter is the law and how it affects people. So much had been said about it in the early part of the epistle, that it became necessary to address some of the problems it created in the lives of those confronted by it. It was not essential that Paul should have experienced every problem the law could create before he tackled the subject. It was enough that he could speak from his experience and spiritual insight and use the personal pronoun so freely to put the law into perspective in the lives of fellow-believers. In this respect then he is speaking from his own experience, for who but one who was such a chosen vessel could address such a complex situation? It is not christian experience he is dealing with in the chapter, but it can hardly be denied that there is much that may be the experience of a Christian. It is also manifest that he is not dealing with the natural man, but there are allusions to the unregenerate state. The reference to being "in the flesh" (v.5), and "I was alive without the law once" (v.9), are examples. He could hardly deal with such an involved subject without alluding in some way to how and where the law applied in times past, even in hs own life as a Pharisee of the Pharisees.

The most reasonable approach to the chapter would seem to be that Paul is writing *from* his experience, not necessarily *of* his experiences. He is addressing believers about the many facets of the law, what it is intrinsically, how if affects Christians, and what stand they should take in relation to it. Sin is also a problem. It is ever present, waiting to take advantage of the pronouncements of the law, or its prohibitions. If every believer realised that they had died to the law through the body of Christ, just as they had died to sin, and they acted accordingly, many of life's struggles, portrayed so dramatically by Paul, would be avoided. That there are struggles cannot be denied. Even if Paul is personating an imaginary person, the struggles he describes are no less real. While believers are in the body, they have to live with the bitter root of sin inherited from Adam, and sin will therefore exert itself at every opportunity. As will be seen in the consideration of the chapter, there is nothing wrong with the law; the culprit is sin which takes every occasion it can to use the law to bring people into bondage and ruin. It is this complex situation which Paul addresses in the chapter. His obvious burden to get the message across accounts for the vivid terms used.

(a) *An illustration from nature, the law and the old husband (vv.1-6)*

v.1 "Know ye not, brethren, (for I speak to them that know the law,) how that the law hath dominion over a man as long as he liveth?
v.2 For the woman which hath an husband is bound by the law to her husband so long as he liveth; but if the husband be dead, she is loosed from the law of her husband.
v.3 So then if, while her husband liveth, she be married to another man, she shall be called an adulteress: but if her husband be dead, she is free from that law; so that she is no adulteress, though she be married to another man.
v.4 Wherefore, my brethren, ye also are become dead to the law by the body of Christ; that ye should be married to another, even to him who is raised from the dead, that we should bring forth fruit unto God.
v.5 For when we were in the flesh, the motions of sins, which were by the law, did work in our members to bring forth fruit unto death.
v.6 But now we are delivered from the law, that being dead wherein we were held; that we should serve in newness of spirit, and not in the oldness of the letter."

1 In the previous chapter, the apostle made the fundamental statement, "ye are not under law, but under grace" (6:14). The opening verse of ch.7 takes up a vital issue in connection with it, and the question is posed, "Know ye not, brethren...that the law has dominion over a man as long as he liveth?" The RV renders the opening words, "Or are ye ignorant, brethren?" In view of the argument put forward in ch.6 and the statement of 6:14 there was a challenge to be faced by those he addresses as brethren. Either they accepted what Paul advanced: that the justified were free of all obligations to the law; or they were ignorant of the principles of law as being under it, or of understanding its implications by any other means.

The short parenthesis "for I speak to them that know the law" is an acknowledgment on Paul's part that not all the brethren were as ignorant of the law as might be inferred from his opening remark. Although there is no definite article in front of "law" which might suggest the principle of law, it seems most likely that the Mosaic law was uppermost in the apostle's mind. There was certainly a substantial body of Roman law, and the laws of other nations, but the knowledge of the Mosaic law was not confined to the Jews. The Romans in particular had more than a superficial acquaintance with it. As the argument of ch.7 develops it becomes more obvious that the Mosaic law is what was intended, although the principles advanced would be true of any legal system.

The underlying motive in the argument which will be developed, centres on how a person stands in relation to law after conversion. Will a desire to be under law in some way or other bring one into life or bondage? The apostle begins to address this in v.1 by the completion of the question he has raised, the law had dominion over a man only as long as he lived. It was beyond dispute, neither sin nor law could lord it over a dead person.

2 The opening verse referred to law in general. In this verse the apostle selects a part of it which concerns the law of marriage, to provide an illustration from a natural occurrence to deal with the believer's freedom from the law's claims. The principle from v.1, "as long as he liveth" gives the lead into the analogy of v.2. The first major point which Paul wishes to establish is that death severs any relationship with the law. There is no argument against the fact that the claims of the law end in death. All obligations to it cease.

The illustration which is applied is one of significant consequence. A married woman is bound to her husband while he lives. The words "which hath a husband" represent one word in the original, *hupandros* ("married"). Although it does not occur again in the NT it does feature in the law of jealousy in Num 5:29 LXX, where it is translated, "married". From this it can be assumed that the relationship between the woman and her husband in the illustration is a stable one supported by the law of marriage. The stability of the union is further indicated by the fact that she is bound (*deō*, "to bind by a legal or moral tie"). So, in Paul's argument, the point is stressed that as long as the husband lived the woman was bound to him.

No matter how stable a relationship may be in life, if one partner dies, that is the end of it. In the case here, it is the husband who dies and the woman is therefore freed from the marriage bond, she is loosed from the law of her husband. The marriage contract is null and void and the surviving partner is released. In the eyes of the law, any prohibition on the woman against remarrying is withdrawn; there is no legal reason why she cannot enter into a marriage contract with another man. The apostle has laboured in his illustration to establish this point. As his argument develops it will be necessary to show that there was in the past a firm obligation to the law, in order to press the significance of release from it so as to be free to be "married to another" (v.4).

3 The illustration is pressed further in this verse. Under the marriage laws, Mosaic, Roman or other, if a married woman "marries" another man while her husband is alive she will be designated an adulteress. Society will brand her for what she is and she will bear the stigma of it. The point, however, is not really a moral one; it is given to strengthen the argument that the possibility of being bound to two men at the same time cannot be introduced, whether the suggested breach in the marriage situation existed or not.

In order to establish a legal entitlement to be "married to another", Paul had to remove all possible objections to his illustration. It would have destroyed the analogy completely if there could have been the possibility of two husbands or two men in an adulteress situation. This would have implied that Christ and the law could have co-existed as competing powers in the believer's life. Such a thought, of course, was anathema to the apostle. Christ had no equals. No other association could be tolerated. He must be supreme and the burden of the apostle in this context is to ensure that the pre-eminence of Christ is not diminished in any way by over-elaboration of the analogy.

The conclusion, however, is in no doubt. The husband dies, the woman is free. If she marries another she is no adulteress. As far as the law of marriage is concerned she is perfectly honourable. The re-marriage in the illustration is essential for Paul's application. She is "discharged" from the first husband by reason of his death and is therefore free to re-marry. In the next three verses the apostle will draw upon the illustration to show where the believer stands in relation to the claims of the law and what results from deliverance from it. Still continuing with the illustration, the effects of having a new husband will be introduced.

4 In this verse Paul's analogy is seen to take an odd turn. In the illustration the husband dies and the woman is free from any legal tie which will bind her to him; she is no longer under his authority. This is a very reasonable illustration, but when the application is made, the logic seems suspect. Taken at face value, if the old husband represents the principle of law, the Mosaic law in particular, then it would have been expected that the law should die and therefore all who were under it should be free from any obligation to it. That, however, is not the case. The law is very much alive and this verse will show that it is those who believe who die to the law in the death of Christ. The end result is the same; the law can extract nothing from those who are dead, but the lead up to this conclusion is not what one would have expected in the analogy used.

A consideration of the situation will show that the apostle's reasoning is not as suspect as might have been thought. From the commencement of ch.6 he has shown that the believer can only live triumphantly for God in this world if the truth of having died with Christ is grasped and acted upon. That is where identification with Christ takes place. The only point where Christ could be identified with men and women who are sinners was at the cross. There was no possibility of union with Christ in life. He was holy and separated from sinners; there is nothing in Scripture to support those who are trying to live for God based on an association with Christ in His humanity. Those who claim to follow Him because they judge that He was a good man, whose example they should follow, are grossly mistaken. It is presumptuous to think that such a link could be forged, apart from the fact that it is derogatory of the true nature and purpose of the death of Christ.

The two words "ye also" link those addressed with the woman in the illustration. Just as she was freed from obligation to her husband, so the believers are free from bondage to the law. This freedom arises from the fact that "ye are become (or, were made) dead to the law by the body of Christ". It is not to be sought as an experience. It is true of all who are in Christ. The apostle stated at 6:14, "ye are not under law but under grace". This condition is common to every believer. Since death has intervened, the law has no further claim. Those who were made dead to the law are outside its domain.

Just as sin found no response from a corpse, so the law is put in the same position. Its demands are annulled, because they cannot be served on the dead.

The apostle states that believers were made dead to the law by the body of Christ. What the Lord in grace partook of, flesh and blood, He took to the cross. It was in the body that He suffered. It was this body that was crucified on the cross, the witness to the reality of the kind of death that He died. It was in death in the body that He satisfied the demands of the law against us and met the righteous requirements of God. It is a comprehensive term, used by Paul to convey the judicial nature of the death of Christ. However the force of "by the body of Christ" is not the propitiation made at Calvary, but that in His death, we died to the law.

The purpose of the break in the first union is noted as freedom to be joined to another. This is really the crux of the matter. Having died with Christ and therefore to the law, the new union is made. The link is now with a risen Christ, recalling the references to the resurrection in 6:4,5,9. This is the answer to any who would maintain that being dead to the law is a title to act without restraint. That cannot be, as the break in union with the first husband leads to "marriage" to another.

The practical outcome of the new union is now stated. It is "that we should bring forth fruit unto God". There was no hope of bringing forth fruit while under law. The Lord made that plain during His earthly ministry. Referring to the Pharisees and scribes, He said, "In vain do they worship me, teaching for doctrines the commandments of men" (Mark 7:7). Religious observances have no saving value. Even with the converted, outward forms are of no value unless accompanied by inward reality, as the Scripture states, "Behold, thou desireth truth in the inward parts" (Ps 51:6). The fruit which meets with God's approval is the fruit of the Spirit. To the Galatians, the apostle made known the great qualities of this fruit. These have the hallmark of God's approval, "Love, joy, peace, longsuffering, gentleness, goodness, faith, meekness, temperance". These marks of the spiritual could never have been produced while under bondage to the law. They could be produced only under the Spirit's influence.

5 There have been several references to "flesh" already in this epistle (1:3, 2:28, 3:20, 4:1), all with meanings consistent with the context in which they are found. In this verse, however, the word refers to a state in which believers were before they were converted. It is the unregenerate state, out of which they were delivered when they believed the message of the gospel. It was while in this condition that they were "married" to the old husband, the law, to use the analogy which Paul has already introduced. Christians are not now "in the flesh" in the sense conveyed by the expression in this verse. The next verse will make this clear by introducing a contrast.

The phrase "the motions of sin" as in the AV is archaic. The RV has "sinful passions" which is preferable. It is the evil desires or affections forbidden by the law to which Paul is referring here. The law by its prohibitions stirred up sinful thoughts, leading to corrupt practices, the working out of passions through the members of the body. It was by (or, through) the law that these passions came into play. It is clear why the apostle emphasises this here. He is reminding the believers that this was the undesirable condition in which they were when they were in bondage to the law and before they were "joined to another". Any thought of holding on to the law in any shape or form was therefore fraught with danger. It brought them nothing but trouble in the past and it is certain that it had not changed its potential for bringing further problems. The only safeguard was to respond to the fact that they had died to it in the death of Christ and that being "joined to another" removed all obligations.

The power of the law is acknowledged here by the apostle. When the believers were "in the flesh", the unregenerate state, the law worked in their members, fretting the self-life into action. It was a force to be reckoned with in daily living. The energy which it generated in the members of the body (see 6:13,19), brought forth fruit, not fruit unto God, as in v.4, but fruit unto death. Writing to the Galatians, the apostle stated, "Now the works of the flesh are these" and he listed the evil practices which characterise the unconverted. It was obviously a burden to him, as he states, "I told you before, as I have told you in time past, that they which do such things shall not inherit the kingdom of God" (Gal 5:19-21). In the context of Rom 7, these works of the flesh are seen to be set in motion by the law.

6 At 6:22 it was noted that the chains of sin were broken. The announcement, "But now being made free from sin" opened up new horizons. No longer was it a case of being slaves of sin to practise the things that would afterwards bring shame, but freedom to serve God and bring forth fruit unto holiness. A similar development is now described. The apostle states that believers have been delivered from the law. The law had no further interest in them because they had died with Christ. The word for "delivered", rendered "discharged" in the RV, has occurred several times in the earlier part of the epistle (see note at 3:31 on *katargeō*). The significance here is that the law has no use for those that are "made dead" to its claims. The conclusion of the analogy is not that the law died but that the believer died to it through the body of Christ. In the unregenerate state, believers were held down by the law, but after conversion they were liberated from its bondage.

It is not a case of being set free to remain in a state of limbo, but that we should serve in newness of spirit. The service Paul refers to is still bondservice. This was the main theme of his argument prior to introducing the analogy of marriage. Now that he has made it clear that the law has no further interest, he returns to the metaphor of bondservice. The thrust therefore of his argument brings in again the idea of a change of masters. Once in slavery to sin and the law, but now (using the same word, but with an implied softer emphasis), it is bondservice to God. There is no harshness in the requirements of the new master. What He looks for is service in newness of spirit.

There is a distinct contrast between "newness of spirit" and "oldness of the letter". It is the contrast between Pentecost and Sinai, between the Spirit's empowering presence and the Law's relentless "thou shalt" devoid of enabling grace. It has no reference to the "letter and spirit" of Holy Scripture. The phrase "newness of spirit" means new in character or species (see note against *kainotēti* at 6:4). The phrase "oldness of the letter" implies something that has grown old and withered (see note against *palaios* at 6:6). Service in newness of spirit describes the freshness of the life, the new life of the delivered believer, perennially fresh, bursting with fruitfulness. While the reference to "spirit" here has the idea of freedom in contrast to the bondage of the law, the influence of the Holy Spirit should not be ruled out. The "letter" stands for the external form, the written demands of the law which are unbending. The contrast is striking. Newness of spirit implies liberty of thought and movement, oldness of letter infers bondage and restriction.

Writing to another company, the apostle stated, "God, who also made us able ministers of the new testament (covenant); not of the letter, but of the spirit: for the letter killeth, but the spirit giveth life" (2 Cor 3:6). Of the outcome of being a minister of the old covenant there is no doubt. By its very nature, form and design the law did not offer life, it only brought in death. The oldness of the letter, as Paul describes it here in Rom 7, has no place in the service of God. What applies now is newness of spirit and newness of life. The reference to "oldness" may infer that the reign of law, Mosaic or other, had been of old, well-tried and made worse by the addition over many years of the traditions of the fathers. The law was not new and fresh. It had exercised its domination over successive generations and it had held them down. They were bound, with no hope of release from its authority until the work of Christ on the cross provided the opportunity to break away from its rule. Happily newness of spirit in the service of God is a totally different life, displacing all the fear and despair of the past and replacing the hopelessness of it all with freshness and new horizons altogether.

Notes

1 "Brethren" are not brethren in the flesh, Jews only, but christian brethren. "…to them that know" is literally "to (ones) knowing". *Ginōskō* signifies knowledge by the process of experience.
2 *Katērgētai* may be rendered "she is loosed (discharged)". See note at 3:31 for the force of *katargeō*.

Newell does not accept that the law is the old husband in this analogy. He maintains that the husband is Adam. Our relation to him was such as nothing but death could break. Others consider that the first husband is the old nature. In this connection, Vine makes a valid point, "This…is hardly consistent with the 6th verse, which says that we have died to that in which we were holden, that is to say, the law".

3 *Chrēmatisei* ("she shall be called"), is the future indicative of *chrēmatizō*, here meaning "to designate", "to style". The word implies more than just giving a name to something. The disciples were called (*chrēmatisai*) Christians first at Antioch (Acts 11:26).

5 The past of *pathēmata* ("passions") and *pathēma* ("emotion", "passion") is *paschō*, "to be affected by a thing whether good or bad". So here the passions and emotions while in the flesh were sinful and they were kindled by the law and its prohibitions.

6 *Kateichometha* ("we were held fast") is the imperfect passive of *katechō* ("to hold down", "to hold downright").

(b) *An important question – Is the law sinful? (vv.7-16)*

> v.7 "What shall we say then? Is the law sin? God forbid. Nay, I had not known sin, but by the law: for I had not known lust, except the law had said, Thou shalt not covet.
> v.8 But sin, taking occasion by the commandment, wrought in me all manner of concupiscence. For without the law sin was dead.
> v.9 For I was alive without the law once: but when the commandment came, sin revived, and I died.
> v.10 And the commandment, which was ordained to life, I found to be unto death.
> v.11 For sin, taking occasion by the commandment, deceived me, and by it slew me.
> v.12 Wherefore the law is holy, and the commandment holy, and just, and good.
> v.13 Was then that which is good made death unto me? God forbid. But sin, that it might appear sin, working death in me by that which is good; that sin by the commandment might become exceeding sinful.
> v.14 For we know that the law is spiritual: but I am carnal, sold under sin.
> v.15 For that which I do I allow not: for what I would, that do I not; but what I hate, that do I.
> v.16 If then I do that which I would not, I consent unto the law that it is good."

7 The apostle now falls back on the expression which he has used several times, "What shall we say then?" In view of what has been set out, what is the opinion, or what conclusion can be arrived at? He answers by asking another question, "Is the law sin?" The question is prompted as a result of what he has just stated, that when those to whom he wrote were in the unregenerate state they gave expression to sinful passions. These were incited by the prohibitions of the law. They worked through the members of the body and they brought forth fruit unto death. It seems reasonable to suggest therefore that the link between sin and the law proved that the law was evil. To this suggestion the apostle quickly answers, "God forbid", "Away with such a thought". He will not tolerate that for a moment.

His defence of the law begins. The AV has "Nay" but this should be as the RV, "Howbeit". He is going to say that although the law provided an occasion to sin, it was not the cause of sin. If a sinner could prove that the law was sinful and that it was the cause of his sin, he had a good case to present in his defence. This, however, is not the case. The law was not sinful. By reason of its very nature, its prohibitions resulted in sin rising in rebellion to do what the law clearly forbade, or it refused to do what the law stated was right and proper. The law's effect was to make sin known, but in itself the law was not evil.

The apostle is clearly speaking at this point of his own experience. This, no doubt, is the best way to get his point across to those he addresses. He states that his present knowledge of sin would not have been so particular if it had not been for the law. This also infers that he is admitting that he would not have been so aware that he was a sinner had it not been for the law. His pedigree as a self-righteous Pharisee, set out in Phil 3, bears witness to the fact that he was one of a class who would have been reluctant to admit that they were sinners, and just as guilty before God as all others. The parable of the Pharisee and the publican at prayer, as told by the Lord, testifies to this pharisaical belief. Prior to his Damascus road experience, Paul was a self-righteous, religious man. He had respect for the law, and indeed strove hard to keep its commandments, but he was not willing to admit, if indeed he was aware, that the law condemned him.

He goes on to say that he had not known lust, it had not come within his experience. The inclination to pursue lustful practices was not a compelling force with him, until the law had said, "Thou shalt not covet". Within himself he had not known coveting until the law in the form of the tenth commandment came to his attention. There was nothing wrong with this part of the decalogue; in fact there was no defect in the law. It merely pointed out to him the sinfulness of sin. The tenth commandment is not any more important than the rest. Clearly, however, by reason of its general nature, "Thou shalt not covet", the principle contained in it is applicable to the others. Apart from the prohibition making known that the desire to have what is forbidden is sinful, he would not have been aware of the sin of covetousness. Because it is one of the ten commandments, lusting after forbidden things was in fact against the will of God, since it was His will that was expressed in them. If, in an attempt to lessen the degree of guilt, it were pleaded that there were desires but that they fell far short of lust, such a defence would not stand. Coveting is not measured by degree as far as the law is concerned. It says distinctly, "Thou shalt not covet". Any breach of that is sin.

8 The culprit is seen in this verse to be sin. The law was not to blame. It had undoubtedly brought sin to life by reason of its restraints. It provided sin with an excuse, a reason to exert itself and cause havoc. Paul says, "it wrought in me all manner of concupiscence" (lust, as at v.7). He had been unaware of the tendency to covet until the law had said, "Thou shalt not covet". Here he enlarges on the thought expressed in the previous verse by declaring that it was "all manner of lust". It was not confined to a single instance. The flood-gates, as it were, were opened. Sin took advantage of all the possibilities which had come to light because of the law's restraints and it brought forth all forms of sinful reactions.

The word the apostle uses to describe the working of sin in him is *katergazomai* (used at 1:27; 2:9; 4:15; 5:3). It carries the meaning of bringing something through to the goal, as at Phil 2:12, "*work out* your own salvation". It therefore describes the thoroughness and energy of sin. The whole effect of sin is to carry through to ruin. Here in v.8, Paul states that it took advantage of the commandment, which indicated merely what was the true character of coveting. Sin, however, took advantage of that and set in motion all manner of lusts, which were lying dormant before the law drew attention to coveting.

Although the real culprit has been identified, Paul makes it clear that apart from the law sin was dead. He personifies sin here in order to place it in proper perspective. The force of the expression means that it was dormant. It was asleep. The state which Paul wants to convey is an absolute one. He does not allow that any form of sin is acceptable. Sin cannot be trifled with in that way. If it has the slightest opportunity it will take occasion to exert itself and as is noted in this verse, the introduction of the commandment, "Thou shalt not covet", was enough to bring it to life. Man's fallen nature is such that to place a prohibition upon him only stirs up rebellion against it. Sin in him awakened all manner of lustful desires and these led on to sinful actions. Although there was nothing wrong with the law, had it not made known right and wrong sin would have been dead to all intents and purposes.

9 This verse raises quite a number of questions. Is Paul personating an imaginary character or is he speaking from his own experience? If he is referring to himself, to what time in his life does he refer when he states, "I was alive without the law once?" Denney comments, "This is ideal biography. There is not really a period of life to which one can look back as the happy time when he had no conscience; the lost paradise in the infancy of men or nations only serves as a foil to the moral conflict and disorder of maturer years, of which we are clearly conscious". AT Robertson remarks, "…a seeming life. Sin revived, it came back to life, waked up, the blissful innocent stage was over, the commandment having come. My seeming life was over for I was conscious of my sin, of violation of law. I was dead before, but I did not know. Now I found out that I was spiritually dead".

Newell takes a different view. He considers that Paul's statement, "I was alive without (apart) from the law once" refers to the first happy stage of the apostle's christian life. He maintains that Paul would not affirm that a man dead in trespasses and sins was "alive". Neither does he consider that the time to which Paul refers covers his persecution days when he was exceedingly zealous for the traditions of the fathers. He asserts that those who would make the struggle of Rom 7 in any sense that of an unregenerate Jew under the law should remember that for a Jew there was no such struggle. An unregenerate Jew was occupied with outward things and rested there. If he were "ceremonially" clean and kept the feasts, new moon and sabbath days there was no struggle in his heart. Rather, Newell considers that Paul "certainly distinguishes here between his early christian life of rejoicing in the new-found Redeemer and that later experience in which God exercises him about indwelling sin and deliverance therefrom".

Kelly has little to say about the verse. Having commented about the law and its inability to save from sin, he merely remarks, "Thus what pointed to life only proved an instrument of death. But if the living man die, law cannot quicken the dead." Vine states, "Thus the condition referred to is that of freedom from a disturbing conscience, a condition of supposed happiness through the absence of a realisation of alienation from, and opposition to, God". He continues, "But when the commandment…presented itself to conscience and broke in upon the fancied state of freedom, imposing its restriction upon the natural tendencies, sin revived, or, sin came to life again and I died. That is to say, 'I became conscious of the sinfulness of sin and realised that I was in a state of separation from God. Separation is the essential feature of death' ".

It is clear that when Paul wrote to the Romans he knew the truth that he had "become dead to the law by the body of Christ" (v.4). He had died with Christ to law and sin. If he had not been in the good of it, he could not have pressed acceptance of that truth on others, neither could he have developed the argument in the rest of the chapter. As to what point in his experience the truth of having died with Christ was revealed to him is not known. Kelly avers that it was during the three days of his blindness. Be that as it may, it is highly unlikely that all that he builds upon it is the product of his imagination. The allegorical approach is restricted to the first four verses. After that, although the terms he uses are dramatic in the extreme, it would be wrong to accuse him of exaggeration. Taking what commentators have said about "ideal biography" and "the seeming life", it would not be right to expect readers of his epistle to conform to his teaching if he himself were engaging in flights of fancy. If he were on the outside, commenting on someone on the inside, then that someone must at one time have been himself and not another.

It is accepted that he is not describing normal christian experience, but it cannot be ruled out that it may be the experience of a Christian. It is also accepted that the struggles he describes were in the past, although his vivid language suggests that the effects of them had lived on with him.

As to v.9, the use of the personal pronoun "I" is a vivid way of illustrating a point which had the widest possible application. The phrase "I was alive" refers to the condition he was in before the force of the law had impinged upon his freedom of thought and life. That he was "apart from the law" cannot refer to his youth or the years before his conversion. In the Jewish nation, the law was taught to boys from their early years and the Jews did not consider themselves to be in bondage to it. He was alive in the sense that the commandment had not pointed to him specifically and made known that he was dead, separated from God.

The coming of the commandment may be a reference to law in general or to a particular aspect of it such as "Thou shalt not covet". Either way, when the force of it came home to him, then sin sprang into life and "I died". He found himself condemned to death, without the moral power to live righteously, and bereft of the self-satisfaction which once he had known. He could not ignore it. His happy days were over. Death came in. The contrast is between "I was alive" and the result when that was no longer the case. There is no middle course. If life goes, death must follow. The teaching is no doubt couched in vivid dramatic terms, but its message is clear concerning the force of the law when its demands are pressed.

10 This verse amplifies what is said about the commandment in v.9. When its force came home to the apostle, sin revived; it sprang into life and death was the result. Prior to that, Paul was either unaware of its thrust or he chose to ignore it, but a critical point in his life came when he could ignore it no longer. The commandment which was "unto life" (RV), or was intended to bring life, was found to be unto death. In the author's book *Written for Our Learning*, this verse, together with v.11, are taken as having two allusions to the OT. The first one is to Lev 18:5 and the second to Gen 3:13.

Paul argues that there was no fault in the law; it was holy, just and good. It promised, "Ye shall keep my statutes, and my judgments: which if a man do, he shall live in them: I am the Lord" (Lev 18:5). The law was a signpost pointing to life, but all its appeals for conformity to its standards were in vain, and in the end, sin revived and slew the deceived. Nevertheless, the law, although powerless to help and with no mercy for the sinner, is faultless. The fault lay with the sinful root in man; it produces sin and in the end it brings in death.

The verse to which Paul alludes, Lev 18:5, is from the law of holiness and chastity, a passage well-known to the Jews. The particular part referred to makes it clear that in order to obtain life, it was necessary to do all that God commanded. The impossibility of finding life on that principle is stated in this verse, "I found to be unto death". Later in the epistle at 10:5, the apostle quotes Lev 18:5 to show again the impossibility of finding life on that principle. Indeed, there would be total despair were it not for the intimation that there was a righteousness that could be obtained on another principle – the principle of faith.

However, it was not the intention of the Law-giver to bring in death through the law. This is made clear in the Lord's reply to the lawyer's question, "What shall I do to inherit eternal life?" The man quoted accurately from the law and it drew from the

Lord the advice, "Thou hast answered right: this do, and thou shalt live" (Luke 10:25-28). But not one attained to life through keeping the law; rather it found out the bitter root of sin in mankind. The word "found" (*heurethē*) is passive, meaning, it *was found* to Paul, it came to him without any search on his part. He was not pursuing the commandments in order to obtain life, but it was brought home to him by them that although they promised life, the bitter root in him could not respond, and instead, the commandments led to death.

11 The opening words return to the teaching of v.8. Sin, lying dormant, took occasion by the coming of the commandment to spring to life. In v.8 it is noted that when it exerted itself it wrought all manner of lust. There seemed to be no containing of it as it wrought havoc. In this verse, where once again the apostle states that sin took occasion through the commandment, the emphasis is not on sin going on the rampage, but on the effect of the manipulation of its victim – it deceived – and as a result, the beguiled was slain.

As mentioned in the previous verse, the teaching here is taken as an allusion to Gen 3:13. There the deceit of sin is manifested. The woman said, "The serpent beguiled me, and I did eat". Later, Paul, in his epistle to Timothy, stated, "Adam was not deceived, but the woman being deceived, was in the transgression" (1 Tim 2:14). And to the Corinthians he wrote, "But I fear, lest by any means, as the serpent beguiled Eve…" (2 Cor 11:3). The commandment was clear, "Thou shalt not eat", but Satan deceived the woman, Adam disobeyed, sin entered and death followed. Adam's protestations about his innocence were puerile. He had clear instructions about which trees were good for him in the garden. Ample provision had been made for him and for his wife, so they were both at fault. Eve was deceived, but Adam as her head should have stood firm. It did not happen, however, and sin entered bringing with it death.

Care should be taken to place blame where blame belongs. It was not the fault of the commandment, but sin taking advantage of the commandment wrought deception. The commandment pointed to life, but it had no power to give life, or to show mercy on those who fell short of its standards. Sin is here personified again. It takes the cloak of deception upon itself and beguiles its victims. The outcome in the previous verse was "unto death", that is the direction and the goal of sin. In this verse that thought is intensified and the end result is that the one who is beguiled is slain. Obviously Paul's choice of word is for the purpose of expressing sin's power and the dreadful end of all who give in to its deceptions.

12 The question raised in v.7, "What shall we say then? Is the law sin?" is answered here. The reasoning of the apostle has been leading up to this point. Sin is seen to have taken every advantage of the precepts of the law. In Paul's case, putting himself forward as an example, sin was seen to be the real culprit. There was no fault in the law: it was holy, and just, and good. It was God's law and it took character from Him. He was holy and His law was holy also.

There is a change here. The law and the commandment are brought in together. Since the tenth commandment was introduced by Paul into his reasoning (v.7), it seems feasible to accept the commandment as being any precept of the law, and the law as the complete body, the totality of all the parts. The threefold description leaves no room for doubt or for treating the law, either in part or in its entirety, as anything less than a revelation from God. The psalmist said, "The words of the Lord are pure words: as silver tried in a furnace of earth, purified seven times" (Ps 12:6).

Apart from being holy, the law is just. Its righteousness cannot be denied. It may not be able to save or to show mercy to those who cannot keep it, but its righteousness cannot be called in question. To do so would be to cast doubts on the righteous character of God, and any suggestion of that nature is totally reprehensible.

The third aspect of Paul's defence of the law is that it is good. One would have looked for *kalos* ("intrinsically good") here but the apostle uses *agathos*, suggesting what is useful and beneficial. This throws another light on the law. Instead of being a hard taskmaster, exacting the utmost from those who are under it, it is now seen to have good points. It is designed for the blessing of man, not for his hurt. Although in certain instances it has been bracketed with sin in this epistle, sin and the law are poles apart. It is often blamed when in fact the real culprit is sin stemming from the evil root in man. In Paul's view the law is holy, just, and good.

13 This verse is a summing up of the section. From v.7 many facets of the law have been introduced. Its relation to sin has been made clear. Although used by sin as a base from which it wrought havoc and ruin, there was nothing wrong with the law, it was holy, and just and good. So, in conclusion, Paul raises another question, "Was then that which is good made death unto me?" In this, there is a similarity with what has been posed at v.7. There he denied emphatically that the law was evil. Here he rejects forcibly that the law which was good caused his death. It was sin that was the culprit. It used the law to further its aims, but these aims led on to death, which he obviously wants to portray as the inevitable end.

As in v.12, Paul uses *agathos* and not *kalos* for "good". Was that which was designed to be beneficial made death unto him? Immediately he rejects any such idea, "By no means". Such a view was a slur on the character of God. The law was not given to cripple those who were under it. If its tenets were adhered to, it could point to life, but if they were ignored or rejected, the same law condemned and it showed no mercy. It could not lift the fallen.

In pursuance of his argument he goes on to state, "But sin that it might appear sin", meaning, that it might be recognised for what it is. Despite attempts by many do disguise it, when sin springs to life, it is demonstrably evil. Unlike the law, there is nothing beneficial about it. The law can point to life, but sin leads to death. Here Paul brings out the overwhelming sinfulness of sin in that it used the law which was in itself useful, beneficial and good, in order to bring about death. Speaking in a personal way, he says, "it wrought death in me, and it did it through the law which is good". Although the apostle refers to himself in the phrase "by working death in me", he is not necessarily doing any more than using himself as an object lesson to illustrate how the law affects people. He shapes a mould, into which others can fit to show them how sin works through the commandments that sin's surpassing sinfulness might be achieved.

14 What Paul has to say in the first half of this verse is clearly from his experience. He anticipates that his correspondents know full well, just as he also knows, that the law is spiritual. They were all fully aware of this fact. Whatever else might be thought about the law, there was no argument about this aspect of its nature. The word "spiritual" is another word which features high in Paul's vocabulary. He has the monopoly of it. In over twenty occurrences in the NT, only two are outwith Paul's writings. It is an adjective which denotes the quality of things which have their origin in God, which come from God and which are supported and controlled by the Holy Spirit. Earlier in this epistle, Paul expressed his desire to visit the Romans that he might impart to them some spiritual gift (1:11). In this case the qualifying adjective indicated that the gift was not from the material world; it was not that kind of gift; it was in another category altogether. What he wanted to impart was from the realm of the Spirit, a gift that would be characterised by the Spirit's power.

Here Paul states that the law was spiritual. He had already stated that it was holy, just and good (v.12). This could not have been said about it if it had originated in man. Since it came from God, it bore the hallmark of God's approval. His character was associated with it. The power behind it when rightly applied was the Spirit of God. The contrast between the law and Paul, as he sees his own human weakness, is that one is spiritual and the other is carnal (that is, fleshly, indicating the weakness of his fallen nature).

The last three words of the verse amplify what he has to say about being fleshly, he was "sold under sin". He was a slave to sin, totally under its domination. The use of the word rendered "under" stresses sin's control. The form of the words suggests that while he could do little else but sin when sin spurred him on, he was not happy about it. As his argument proceeds, his dissatisfaction with himself for allowing sin to dominate him is apparent. The word "sold" is in the passive voice implying that the desire to sin and the compelling impetus resulting from that desire was not from him. Sin was the driving force that drove him on to practise sinful deeds. There was little he could do about it, because he was a slave to sin, entirely at its bidding. No doubt there was the desire to be free from servitude to sin when its power over him became apparent. He had learned of its tyranny, it was a hard taskmaster, and he was sold to it.

Having described his relation to the law in such graphic terms, it is difficult to imagine that Paul is not reciting his own personal experiences. There are of course, many commentators who think that he *is* doing that, and that he is referring to the time immediately after his conversion on the Damascus road. Newell, who seems to have taken up the view put forward by Kelly and Darby, remarks against this verse, "Now Paul, though his spirit was quickened; and his inward desires therefore, were towards God's law; found to his horror his state by nature 'carnal', 'fleshly, sold under sin'. 'Sold under sin' is exactly what the new convert does not know! Forgiven, justified he knows himself to be: and he has the joy of it! But now to find an evil nature, of which he had never become fully conscious, and of which he thought himself fully rid, when he first believed is a 'second lesson' which is often more difficult than the first – of guilt!"

The view put forward by Newell and others is no doubt valid in many respects, but it leaves many questions unanswered. It is an echo of what Kelly has stated, that unless vv.1-6 are understood and acted upon (and many die without understanding the situation), then the rest of Rom 7 will remain obscure. Against that, the use of the present tense; the many times the apostle uses "I" and "me" and the vivid terms employed throughout seem overdone, if what he is referring to is his own experience during the short period immediately after his conversion. Not only so, but if he went through such a disturbing time before he was delivered, all believers must go through similar experiences before freedom from the law and sin is attained. It seems more reasonable, considering the extent of the variations in believers' experiences of new life in Christ, that Paul is addressing what was a problem with some and could still be with others. He is projecting himself into the worst situation he can think about, addressing all possible angles of what might be, including what he had gone through personally. What he presented to the Romans was the full picture. How much of it was actual and how much was filled in from an imaginary person's experience are difficult to judge, but the end result is beyond question, no one would be in any doubt about the implications of the law and sin in the lives of those who had put their trust in Christ for salvation.

15 This verse carries on the thought of slavery from the close of v.14, "sold under sin". The AV does not make clear the sense of the opening words, "For that which I do I allow not". The rendering of the RV is to be preferred, "For that which I do I know not". The word "do" (*katergazomai*) is of frequent occurrence in the epistle. It has been noted at 7:8 that it carries the meaning of "work out" or "carry through to the goal" as at Phil 2:12. The meaning here is connected with the thought of slavery with Paul putting himself in the place of a slave and projecting the idea that what he works out he does as a slave, sold under sin.

The RV rendering implies that he does not know, or he does not understand what it is he does. Sin is the master and he is the vassal. Why he works out evil he does not know. It is not what he wants to do but he does it nevertheless. The law cannot help him in this state. By pointing out the wrong of his deeds, it only condemns him. It has no answer to the problem of being sold under sin. It is not that he does what he disapproves of every moment of his life. He may be occupied with legitimate things, even "religious activities", but interlaced through them are the dictates of sin. It is a taskmaster and it shows no mercy.

There are things that he wants to do, or would like to do but he does not do them. On the contrary, he does the things which he hates. This may seem a strange admission for Paul, the apostle to the Gentiles, to make. It must, however, be understood in the light of being a slave under sin. Some might consider that he has chosen the worst set of circumstances to get his message across to others who were really in the throws of being under sin's domination, with no help from the law. This is a valid point of view. It is not an autobiography Paul is writing, and yet from his wide experience he is perfectly well aware of the relative ways the law and sin affect others, and even himself. The language he uses is couched in vivid terms. The imagery is dramatic. By the frequent use of "I" and "me", he presses himself into the examples he raises so that the thrust of the message cannot be missed by those who may be in despair. Sin's domination and the law's condemnation of failures are problems of the greatest magnitude for those who have put their trust in Christ and who look for peace to live out their lives for Him.

16 The "If" of this verse is not one of doubt, but bears the meaning, "If, as is the case". The following words in the original are in a position of stress. It reads, "But what I wish not", adding "this I do". The AV does not reflect this. The RV captures the sense, "But if what I would not, that I do". What seems uppermost in Paul's mind as he enters another phase of his argument, is that he does the things that he does not want to do. The things referred to are not planned, they are mechanical, even habitual sins which are in conflict with the law. The verb *poieō* does not suggest considered practices, but a succession of breaches of the law, all of which he wishes he would not do.

There is no question here that Paul disagrees with the law, or that he is in a state of irritation because it condemns what he is doing. His irritation is with himself for doing what he does not want to do. He consents, or better, he agrees with the law that it is good. At v.12 it is noted that he chose the word *agathos* to declare that the law was good. At that point he was stressing the beneficial aspects of the law and without doubt there are many. In this verse he changes the word. He agrees that the law is good (*kalos*). There is a moral excellency in the law. Intrinsically it is good and noble. The character of God is reflected in it and it can therefore be trusted to point in the direction of life. There is nothing wrong with the law, the problem lies with the weakness of human nature.

Paul's agreement that the law is good militates against those who hold that the chapter refers to the unregenerate. It is not an admission that would be expected from the unregenerate that the law was morally good and noble. To admit that and carry on as before would be self-contradictory. The internal evidence of Scripture indicates that those who extolled the virtues of the law were in a happy relationship with God. For example, David's assessment of a good man is that "his delight is in the law of the Lord and in his law doth he meditate day and night" (Ps 1:2). This attitude to the law is reflected in the apostle's comments in this chapter where he states, "For I delight in the law of God after the inward man" (v.22). He has nothing but praise for the law. His problem was not the accusations of the law against him when he broke its commandments, but with his repeated breaches of its plain precepts.

Notes

7 "I had not known (*ginōskō*) sin", "I had not known (*oida*) coveting". Sin in its heinousness was not within his experience until the law pointed an accusing finger at him. He was not aware of what was involved in coveting until he was confronted with the commandment.

Epithumia ("lust", "strong desire") is obviously used by Paul to describe great desire for things that were unlawful.

8 *Aphormē* ("occasion") is used in 1 Tim 5:14, "Younger women...give none occasion to the adversary to speak reproachfully". The six other occurrences of the word in the NT are all in Paul's writings. The word denotes a military base from which attacks are launched. The commandment is the base from which sin launches its attacks. If the base were not there, sin would be powerless. Hence, Paul states, "apart from the law sin is dead".

The AV gives "for without the law sin was dead". This rendering implies a connection with Paul's experience. Since there is no verb in the original (*hamartia nekra*, "sin dead"), the verb "is" should be supplied to make the closing statement of the verb a general one, "for apart from the law sin is dead".

9 The "I" is emphatic, but the verse should not be taken as exclusively Paul's experience. What he has to say has universal application.

Chōris ("without") is better rendered "apart from".

Morris remarks, "He is alive in the sense that he has never been put to death as a result of confrontation with the law of God".

10 In *autē eis thanaton* ("this to death"), *autē* is in a place of emphasis. Death here is not simply the result of having come to the end of life. It has many facets and no doubt this is how Paul intended it to be taken here, in the same way as life has more to it than being alive.

12 *Hōste* ("wherefore", better, "so then") introduces the conclusion arrived at. There is a contrast with v.11. Sin is vile, evil and of no good, but the law is the opposite, holy, just and good.

13 *Kath' huperbolēn* ("exceeding", "excessively") is used adverbially to indicate the extent of the sinfulness of sin that it is surpassingly sinful. Robertson makes an interesting comment, "The excesses of sin reveal its real nature. Only then do some people get their eyes opened".

14 The use of the plural "we know" here merely indicates that what is being intimated is a generally accepted fact.

The contrast here is that the law is spiritual but Paul (using the emphatic "I") is carnal. The word for "carnal" (*sarkinos*), is variously translated and understood. It is rendered, fleshy, fleshly, fleshen, made of flesh. The Corinthians were accused of being *sarkinos* ("fleshy") to the extent that they could not be addressed as spiritual (1 Cor 3:1). They were carnal, (*sarkikoi*, "fleshly", 1 Cor 3:3). Vine makes an interesting observation. He states, "*Sarkikos* is fleshly in the ethical sense, in contrast to *sarkinos* which is fleshly in the material sense, i.e. consisting of flesh. It is said of human nature rather than character". Paul here is stressing that he (and of course all others) are fleshy, that is, made of flesh and dominated by it as by the weakness of his fallen nature. This is in contrast to the nature of the law. It is spiritual, having its origin in God.

15 "I allow", "I practise" (*prassō*, "to be engaged in", "to be busy in") points to activity in pursuing the things he would like to do, but did not do.

"I do" (*poieō*, "to do", "to effect") refers to the habitual doing of the things which he hates.

"I know not" (*ginōskō*) shows that he did not need to be told; his knowing was the result of experience.

"I would not" (*thelō*, "to will", "to exercise the will", "to wish") is the will which proceeds from inclination, rather than determination. Here the things he was inclined to do, these were the things he did not do.

16 "I do" (*poieō*), as in v.15.

"I consent" (*sumphēmi*, "to allow", "to assent") is from *sun*, "together with", and *phēmi*, "to speak with", "to say yes".

(c) *The two natures in the believer made manifest (vv.17-25)*

v.17 "Now then it is no more I that do it, but sin that dwelleth in me.
v.18 For I know that in me (that is, in my flesh,) dwelleth no good thing: for to will is present with me; but how to perform that which is good I find not.
v.19 For the good that I would I do not: but the evil which I would not, that I do.
v.20 Now if I do that I would not, it is no more I that do it, but sin that dwelleth in me.
v.21 I find then a law, that, when I would do good, evil is present with me.
v.22 For I delight in the law of God after the inward man:
v.23 But I see another law in my members, warring against the law of my mind, and bringing me into captivity to the law of sin which is in my members.
v.24 O wretched man that I am! who shall deliver me from the body of this death?
v.25 I thank God through Jesus Christ our Lord. So then with the mind I myself serve the law of God; but with the flesh the law of sin."

17 The previous verse gives the apostle's conclusion that the law is good. The logical outcome of this declaration of approval is what he now sets out. "Now then", or better, "But now" or, "So now", it is no more that I do it, "but sin that dwelleth in me". The point is now reached in the great struggle where the flesh in the believer and the new nature are seen to be so separate, and sin is acknowledged to be the product of the flesh. Hence in the flesh dwelleth no good thing, and although there is often the desire to do good, the power to carry it out is absent.

It is not clear what Paul meant in this verse by "it". Using the word for "do" (*katergazomai*), so often found in this epistle, we learn in the context that what he works out is sin, and that would seem to be what he meant by the phrase, "no more I that do it". What the apostle seems to be saying here is that he, the Paul who wants to do what accords with the law, has another resident dwelling within him. It is sin and he does not approve of its presence. It is an interloper and it is this intruder that is causing the harm.

The apostle is not attempting to provide an excuse for sinning. That would run counter to his whole line of reasoning. If responsibility could be shifted so that the blame for sinful acts could be laid at the door of sin, the sinner would have a solid defence. What Paul is stating is that he has discovered that there is a bitter root dwelling within him. It resolutely clings to its residence and is making its presence felt. The real Paul genuinely wishes to live apart from its influence. But how to do that is his problem, and of course, the problem of every believer. He cannot eject the interloper, it is there and will be there while he is in the body, but what to do to render it powerless is what he has to discover.

18 Paul's consciousness that no good thing dwelt in him was either revealed to him as an apostle of the Lord Jesus Christ, or gained by experience. The acknowledgement goes beyond what he asserted in the previous verse, namely, that it was not he who worked out sin, but the bitter root of it which dwelt in him. To clarify the matter and save any misapprehensions arising, he quickly inserts a parenthesis, "that is, my flesh". The fallen nature which he inherited from Adam is the real source of his trouble.

What he is now saying is that he cannot do the things which he approves because of the flesh which is in him. In the previous section (vv.14-17), he admitted that he could not stop doing the things he disapproved of because he was carnal. He was never able to perform what he wanted to do in the manner that he would like to have done them. He was never free from the interference of the interloper, that part of him foreign to his real self. He had a will to do good. The power to will was not his trouble, but the absence of power to do what he willed was the real problem. He could honestly say that if he had the power he would never had sinned again. But when he set about carrying through his best aspirations to meet the law's just demands, he found he could not do so, or else, what he did do fell far short of what the law required.

There seems to be an allusion to Gen 6:5 in this verse. Before the flood "God saw that the wickedness of man was great on the earth and that every imagination of the thoughts of his heart was only evil continually". The declaration was repeated after the flood, showing that the nature of man had not changed, although with Noah and his family there had been a new beginning. Despite this, God said, "for the imagination of man's heart is evil from his youth" (Gen 8:21). There was no redeeming feature in him. In creation "God saw everything that he had made...was very good" (Gen 1:31). But after sin entered, it was a different situation. Paul's reasoning in Rom 7 bears out the truth of the declarations of the past. His conclusion is, "For I know that in me (that is, in my flesh) dwelleth no good thing".

19 In the original, the verse runs, "For not what I wish, I do, good, but what I wish not, evil, this I practise". From this it is seen that the first "not" governs the whole sentence. Regardless of what the wish was, the outcome was the same, it was not what he wished, or willed to do. The second "not" relates only to "evil", and within the sentence stresses that what he did not want to do, was the very thing he practised. The sad feature about this verse is that on its own it portrays a hopeless situation. Despite a real desire to do good, things do not work out and the wish to refrain from evil is not fulfilled, because of what he does.

In this verse the apostle continues to interchange the words which the AV renders by "do". In the previous verse it was *katergazomai*. Here the first mention of "do" is *poieō* and the second is *prassō*. There are no doubt shades of meaning involved in "working out", "doing", and "practising", but taken together they demonstrate that whatever activity is involved for good or ill, the context must be looked upon as christian experience. This is not, however, a doctrinal portrayal of utter hopelessness. If it were so, new life in Christ would be found sadly wanting and such a suggestion cannot be allowed to stand for a moment. It is essential, nevertheless, that a full realisation of the weaknesses and evil Christians have to face be taken into account. The experience of Christians, Paul included, is that there are trials and problems in life and these come upon believers from many sources. The power to deal with the law, sin and the flesh will be developed in the next chapter but here the apostle continues to give expression to the problems and the struggles of christian living.

At the end of v.18 the apostle mentioned "good" (*kalos*). In this verse he states, "For the good (*agathos*) that I would". Like the three words for "do" which he has been interchanging, so also has he been using these two words for "good". As to the use of *agathos* here, it would seem that his desire, his earnest wish was to do what was beneficial. The practical good which was so much a part of the work associated with the spread of the gospel was what he wanted to do, but alas, he did not find it so.

20 The opening words would read better, "But if, as is the case, what I would not, that I do". The meaning is clear. It adds another aspect to this involved argument about the constant struggle in dealing with sin. It is no longer the "I", the real Paul, that works out sin (*katergazomai*), but sin which dwells in him. He is not portraying himself as a vile sinner; indeed the whole context would suggest otherwise. Neither is he saying that he is not responsible for the actions which are prompted by sin and condemned by the law. What he seems to be doing is to make a clean division between two entities, the real Paul and indwelling sin.

It is clear that the two, as Paul sees them, are incompatible. There are the struggles of one to be free from domination and the readiness of the other to take advantage of every situation that can lead to sinful actions. Life is seen to be complex. It is a constant struggle. To think that the initial act of faith is an end to all problems is a wrong concept. To propagate that view is misleading, to say the least. The road home to glory is an uphill climb, as Peter makes known, "If the righteous scarcely (with difficulty) be saved, where shall the ungodly and the sinner appear?" (1 Pet 4:18). All is not lost, however, there is power for enablement and that will come out as the argument proceeds.

21 There is a considerable difference of opinion regarding which law was on Paul's mind when he stated, "I find then a law". The rendering of the RV, "I find then the law", making the reference more specific, has encouraged many to think the law of Moses is the law intended. The weight of opinion, however, is in favour of taking the "law" here to be a principle, as it is clearly in v.23. If that is accepted, then the apostle means "the law of sin". The law, or principle, is not to be taken as something which is benign, but a principle which is active in the extreme. It is a law which takes over, given the slightest opportunity. Paul has made it clear in his reasoning that it will transcend the will. Even though there is a will to do good, the law of evil will have its way.

The consequence of the closing statement of the previous verse, "But sin that dwelleth in me" is that Paul states, "I find then a law". He has made a discovery. It is not something he supposes. It is not a hypothetical point. From all the angles he has considered in his argument, the only logical conclusion he can arrive at is that there is a principle which acts against him. It is always in residence. When he would do good, evil is present. The word rendered "present" occurs only here and at v.18. As noted, it carries the meaning of "lying ready at hand", indicating that not only is it present, but it is also ready to spring into life. The "good" the apostle refers to here is *kalos*, that which is morally good and upright, rather than *agathos*, that which is beneficial.

It is interesting to note that the law of Moses is also said to be good (*kalos*). Writing to Timothy, Paul stated, "But we know that the law is good if a man use it lawfully" (1 Tim 1:8). There the apostle means to convey that the law is seen to be good. The force of *kalos* there is that it describes the law from the outside – from the observer's point of view. *Kalos* to the Greek mind expresses beauty, as the harmonious completeness, the balance, proportion and measure of all the parts one with another.

22 The statement, "For I delight in the law of God", clears up any misunderstanding or misapprehensions. Paul joyfully agrees with the law of God. It is not merely a case of giving grudging assent, but that he is extremely happy with it. He is not saying that he has to agree with it because there is no alternative. He is enthusiastic, in joyful accord with God's law. This is the only occurrence in the NT of the word rendered "delight", but there is a similar construction in 1 Cor 13:6 where Paul's joy is recorded. There it states that he rejoices (*chairō*) not in iniquity. Against that he records a typical Pauline touch, "but rejoiceth (*sunchairō*) in the truth". He finds no satisfaction in wrongdoing, but he finds happy fellowship with the truth, which he personifies. Love expresses itself in the truth and Paul is happy to have it as a constant companion.

There is no possibility of the unregenerate rejoicing in the law of God. An unsaved person cannot say that he consents to the law that it is good. It condemns him. The Scriptures do not give examples of the unregenerate rejoicing in the law. On the contrary, David's assessment of a good man is that "his delight is in the law of the Lord and in his law doth he meditate day and night" (Ps 1:2). In another psalm he states, "Blessed is the man that feareth the Lord, that delighteth greatly in his commandments" (Ps 112:1). If it were true that the unregenerate rejoiced in the law, it would be pertinent to ask why he does not go further and acknowledge that he needs to own that he is a sinner as the law makes plain, and seek the mercy of the Lord in the salvation which is made known in the gospel?

The closing words of the verse, "after the inward man", or, "according to the inner man", are further proof that the unregenerate were not on Paul's mind. To delight in the law of God in the inner man is to rejoice in it inwardly, not outwardly as a demonstration of piety. Paul is surely here portraying the renewed heart rejoicing in the law of God. The inward man, which is renewed day by day while the outward perishes (2 Cor 4:16), has a deep appreciation of God's law. It will point out his mistakes. It will do nothing to rescue him if he falls, but as he has already made clear, it is nevertheless holy and just and good (v.12). The suggestion that Paul's delight in the law is a reflection of his attitude towards it in his unconverted days, does not accord with his delight in it "after the inward man".

23 In v.21 Paul reveals that he has made a discovery, "I find then a law, that, when I would do good, evil is present with me". Despite that, he declares in the next verse that his delight is in the law of God. Here in v.23 he uses the word *blepō* ("to see") to describe his mental vision with which he perceives another law in his members. The word rendered "another" (*heteros*), carries the meaning of "another of a different kind".

The different law, that is, different from the law of God in which he delights (v.23), is warring in his members. This law is carrying out a campaign against the law of his mind. This evil principle which he abhors is the same as in v.21, "I find then a law, that when I would do good, evil is present with me". It is highly unlikely that Paul is thinking about another evil principle which is different from the principle of sin. He is not suggesting that he is in bondage to yet another taskmaster, both of which would be striving for mastery over him. It must be the same law which he has already described in v.5 which "did work in our members to bring forth fruit unto death".

Paul's choice of words suggests a conflict. The battlefield is in his mind, a term which, in this context, has a wider application than just the seat of his understanding. It is not the heart. His affections are not in view. It is rather his whole thinking and reasoning faculty. The struggle is an intellectual one. The battle is being fought in that realm and the enemy, which is the law of sin, is striving to bring him into captivity. It seeks to dominate him and lead him away captive. The language is vivid. It is necessarily so to emphasise that even the thinking faculty and the power to reason can be brought into subjection. When that happens, then the body and its members must follow, as they cannot act for good independently of the mind's directions.

The verse states that the law of sin is warring against the law of his mind. This phrase, "the law of his mind" suggests that there is a rule of action in the rational part of his being, and it is this which is in conflict with evil. This active principle of the mind consents to the law of God that it is holy, and just, and good, but it has a struggle. The law of sin (the evil principle) is there. It has a permanent abode in his members. It is the interloper who is in residence and will not leave. It has not won the battle over him but of its power there is no doubt. Nevertheless, his description of the struggle is nearing its conclusion. His handling of it has been dramatic. The language used has been vivid, but anything less would not have conveyed the seriousness of the situation. Determining where the believer stands in relation to the law and sin is of paramount importance and cannot be left to conjecture.

24 This verse introduces the climax to the chapter. It bursts open, as it were, with what looks like a despairing cry, "O wretched man that I am". This cannot be the cry of the unregenerate. The unconverted are not prone to admitting their wretchedness. In a very restricted sense, it would be wrung from someone who has tried to break a habit, but failed. Of the rank and file, however, the pursuit of pleasure, wealth and sin does not yield despair, unless perhaps at the end of life, when the folly of empty living catches up and the reaping time arrives. Even then, death-bed repentances are few.

The cry is not likely to be one which the young Christian would make. The joy of salvation, of the knowledge of the forgiveness of sins and of eternal security lasts a long time. Indeed, with many it lasts throughout their pilgrimage and they do not progress beyond it. It is more likely that this is the cry of the believer who has advanced in the christian life and has found what has been so vividly described in this chapter to be a real struggle. Although Denney states, "The words are not those of the apostle's heart as he writes; they are the words which he knows are wrung from the heart of the man who realises in himself the state just described". This view is not generally held. If the Romans, who were the recipients of the epistle, judged that Paul was using over-dramatic language and flights of fancy just to get his message over, and had not experienced what he states in some measure at least, they could not have been expected to accept untried ministry.

How much was Paul's personal experience is not known. It does seem from his use of personal pronouns that he intended that it should be accepted as his own. If this were not the case he would just have been a narrator of someone else's experience or the conveyor of what he considered to be the struggles of a Christian in his dealings with the law and sin. The cry for deliverance from the body of this death is a heart-rending one. It has to be real and not imaginary, even in part. It has to be the earnest cry of one who is yearning for the answer to the struggles portrayed so vividly. To give credence to his reasoning, Paul has to be featured in the cry of the miserable man who is searching for deliverance from the body of death, the instrument of sin.

25 The answer to the question raised in the previous verse cannot be obtained from a human source. There is, however, an answer, and Paul gives it with great joy, "I thank God through Jesus Christ our Lord". What appeared to be a struggle out of which there is no deliverance is seen here to have its answer. God cannot fail. The victory is His. It is made good through Jesus Christ our Lord. Some hold that this deliverance is partly present and partly when the Lord returns. Vine considers it to be entirely at the Lord's return when the body will be redeemed. Others consider that while in the body, at best the deliverance can only be partial. The bitter root will be there until the end, although with the Lord's help it can be rendered powerless. The next chapter will reveal the secret. There is a power and it is available to God's saints. God has not been outdone by sin. The final victory is His and He will yet be glorified.

The next two words, "So then", bring in the logical conclusion. Although what follows is in its correct place in the manuscripts of the original, some judge it is out of place contextually. The climax, according to some exegetes, is in the expression "I thank God through Jesus Christ our Lord". What follows, regarding the law of God and the law of sin in their thinking is a return to the general argument of the chapter and should not be inserted at the end. This, however, is a risky way to handle the Scriptures. If all manuscript evidence supports the verse in the form given in the AV and other good versions, there it should remain regardless of how it looks in the estimation of some who judge that they know better.

There is a reading which changes "I thank my God through Jesus Christ our Lord" to read, "The grace of God through Jesus Christ our Lord". Not much change is required in the Greek to make the alteration and some have adopted it as being nearer to the tone of the argument. Plummer favours it. He holds that the question, "Who shall deliver me?" draws the answer, "The grace of God through, or by, Jesus Christ our Lord". Against this, however, most commentators hold that there is insufficient manuscript authority to warrant any consideration of a change from the present order.

The apostle portrays himself as a representative believer. There is emphasis on "I myself". He is not putting himself in a position that he is independent of the help of the Lord. That must not be read into what he states about himself. Denney adopts this stance. He writes, "So then I myself – that is, I, leaving Jesus Christ our Lord out of the question – can get no further than this: with the mind, or the inner man, I serve the law of God (a divine law), but with the flesh, or in my actual outward life, a law of sin". Be that as it may, it suits the argument better to accept that Paul here considers himself in two ways. In the first he intimates that he serves the law of God and he emphasises his personal commitment, "I myself". The "mind" here meaning his inner man in all its parts, the real Paul, his thinking faculty, his heart, his will, all of him, gladly serves the law of God. His delight is in it, and with the Lord's help with absolute sincerity he will serve God's law as a bondman. The other part of him, his carnal nature, which he will carry to the end, will serve the law of sin. In stating this he is not making any concessions to the flesh, he is acknowledging its presence and potential. It will never change, it has its own character.

There is a view, which seems most logical, that the reason for the return to the mention of the law of God and the law of sin after the victorious cry was to guard the soul from thinking that the flesh had changed. Kelly supports this view and states that the two natures retain their own characters. The sense of victory does not alter the flesh; it is incorrigible. Darby's comment on the flesh in another setting is weighty. He states, "Flesh is flesh, whether it is refined flesh or vulgar flesh, God cannot walk a step with it". "Deliverance", says Kelly, "does not alter the bent of man's nature, which is the same in all, in the Christian, as in the unbeliever. Meanwhile we learn here that if the flesh acts at all, it can only be to sin. Such is its law".

In the introduction to ch.8, Kelly makes a valuable comment which is really a summary of ch.7. He states, "We have seen in ch.7, first, the doctrine in the opening verses; then the discussion of the manner in which the law works in the soul that is born again but that does not realise the deliverance with which he began, not only conflict under law but the discovery of the two natures, and besides, of one's own powerlessness, though renewed – an experience which closes not in utter wretchedness…but in looking completely out of self to God's deliverance in and through Christ".

Notes

17 Vincent makes the point that "no more" (*nuni ouketi*) is "not temporal, pointing back to a time when it was otherwise, but logical, pointing to an inference. After this statement you can no more maintain that etc".

Robertson gives, "A logical contrast, 'as the case really stands' ".

Morris gives an interesting quotation concerning indwelling sin, "The rabbis could say of sin, 'At first it is like a (passing) visitor, then like a guest (who stays longer), and finally like the master of the house' ".

Commenting on "no more I but sin", Robertson observes, "Not my true self, my higher personality, but my lower self due to my slavery to indwelling sin. Paul does not mean to say that his whole self has no moral responsibility by using this paradox".

"To be saved from sin, a man must at the same time own and disown it" (Denney).

18 "Present" (*parakeimai*), "to be near", "to be adjacent"; by metonymy "to be at hand") occurs only here and at v.21 in the NT.

The verb "perform" is *katergazomai*, "to work out", "to carry the desire into effect".

20 Denney comments, "Paul distinguishes himself sharply as a person whose inclination is violated by his actions from the indwelling sin who is really responsible for them".

21 Commenting on "I find then a (the) law", Vine notes that "law" is probably to be understood as a controlling principle defined by the statement which follows. Vincent states, "The constant rule of experience imposing itself on the will. Thus in the phrases, 'law of faith', 'law of works', 'law of the spirit'. Here the law of moral contradiction". Morris suggests, "This is more than simply an observed sequence, as in the way we might speak of 'a law of nature' ".

For "present" (*parakeimai*) see note at v.18.

22 "I delight" (*sunēdomai*), "to approve cordially", "to rejoice with someone", only occurring here in the NT, finds the apostle joyfully agreeing with the law.

"...according to the inner man" (*kata ton esō anthrōpon*) reveals that Paul who abhors sin, in the depth of his being delights in the law of God.

23 Vincent calls this "the faculty of reflective intelligence". The law of sin, for such it surely is, carries its campaign into the realms of the thinking faculty.

24 "Wretched" (*talaipōros*, "wretched", "miserable") is used of the Laodicean rich. They were "wretched, miserable, poor and blind" (Rev 3:17). Robertson comments, "If one feels that Paul has exaggerated his own condition, he has only to recall 1 Tim 1:15, when he describes himself as a chief of sinners".

Morris notes, "It is all too easy to take our christian status for granted", and quotes Smart, "Let us cease to know that we are carnal, sold under sin – and all too quickly we shall be anchored in complacency".

"The body of this death" teaches that the physical body is mortal, characterised by death, that through which sin operates. Death has a lodgment in the body from its beginning, and claims it in the end.

3. Sanctified and Assured of Eternal Blessing
8:1-39

There are few chapters in the Bible which surpass Rom 8 for its message of victorious living. Since it came into circulation amongst Christians it has proved to be one of the greatest sources of encouragement in existence. The Holy Spirit comes into prominence, being mentioned about twenty times. He is seen to be the power which enables believers to triumph over the forces of evil. After the solemn consideration of the man in Rom 7 who was "sold under sin" and wretched in the extreme, it is a joy to read of those in the eighth chapter who are "more than conquerors". Godet is quoted as saying, "the eighth chapter begins with 'no condemnation' and ends with 'no separation' ". Another has added that in between there is "no defeat".

That Rom 8 is sublime few will disagree. Plummer, quoting William Hodge writes, "For fervour and strength of expression, for rapidity and vigour of argument, for richness in doctrine, for revelation of high and precious mysteries, and for a noble elevation of sentiments, which pervades the whole and bursts out at the end with irrepressible ardour, there are few passages to equal it, even in the sacred oracles and certainly none out of them". This witness is true.

(a) *The law of the Spirit of life and the law of sin and death (vv.1-4)*

> v.1 "There is therefore now no condemnation to them which are in Christ Jesus, who walk not after the flesh, but after the Spirit.

> v.2 For the law of the Spirit of life in Christ Jesus hath made me free from the law of sin and death.
> v.3 For what the law could not do, in that it was weak through the flesh, God sending his own Son in the likeness of sinful flesh, and for sin, condemned sin in the flesh:
> v.4 That the righteousness of the law might be fulfilled in us, who walk not after the flesh, but after the Spirit."

1 The "Therefore" at the beginning of the verse obviously points backwards. The question which arises concerns how far back Paul is going in order to substantiate the conclusion which he is now about to press. The content of chs. 6 and 7 suggests that he must build on what he has stated there. However, if these two chapters are a digression in response to the question at the beginning of ch.6, "What shall we say then? shall we continue in sin that grace may abound?" then the connection would appear to be with the two mentions of "condemnation" in ch.5 (vv.16,18). Vine considers "therefore" connects with ch.7 and is a conclusion of what is set out there. He does note nevertheless, that it could reach as far back as 3:19 where the law is introduced and the sentence is that every mouth should be stopped and all the world become guilty before God.

Regardless of how far back the apostle intended to go to provide the point of connection, and commentators have different views on this, one thing is certain, the reasoning is continuous. It is not a series of watertight compartments, but a free-flowing argument, even if there is a digression here and there to illustrate a point in the passing. He has laboured to establish the truth of the blessing of new life in Christ and how God has made it available to all who will exercise faith in Him.

Condemnation is the sentence on all who will to go their own way and are not prepared to cast themselves on the mercy of God. Dependency on the law will not bring salvation. Works of merit will not avail either. Judgment must follow if the principle of faith is ignored or rejected. Condemnation in any sense will not apply to those who are "in Christ Jesus". Those who are identified with Christ, whose spiritual and eternal position is linked to Him will never face judgment in any form. The Saviour said, "He that heareth my word, and believeth on him that sent me, hath everlasting life, and shall not come into condemnation" (John 5:24). Nothing could be clearer. Paul's word to the Romans is really a reiteration of this momentous statement. It is the sheet-anchor for the soul.

The little word "now" (*nun*) separates the old way of life from the new. The past is inferred and it was under the sentence of death and final judgment. The new one, upon which Paul will now elaborate, is free from every aspect of it, and the great words of the opening verse confirm that "there is therefore now no condemnation…"

The latter half of the verse is considered to be an interpolation and should be omitted. It comes in at v.4 which is its proper place. Darby notes: "The Greek, were it to stand as part of the text, must be translated, 'There is no condemnation for those who, in Christ Jesus, walk not after the flesh, but after the Spirit'". The words are to be understood as descriptive of the walk of every true believer. Having died in Christ, they now walk in newness of life (6:4).

2 The intimation of "no condemnation" gives peace of mind from the beginning. This paves the way for the bringing in of the knowledge of a new law within. In ch.7 it was noted that the law of the mind could do nothing because of sin and the flesh, but now a new power is made known. The new life has a new law. The law of sin and death (7:21-23) involved condemnation. Now the apostle intimates that there is another ruling principle. It is the law of the Spirit of life. There is a power within the believer which transcends all other laws and motivating principles. The indwelling Spirit of God is an active force. It is a power that is inherent in the life-giving Spirit. That power operates as a law in the believer. It is a quickening Spirit. It gives life and it supports life. Morris, quoting Manson, gives an excellent comment on the laws mentioned by Paul. He states, "Moses law had right but not might; sin's law has might but not right; the law of the Spirit has both right and might".

The expression "in Christ Jesus" is repeated, stressing again union with Christ. The law of the Spirit of life in Christ Jesus brought freedom. It is a liberating force. It is a life-giving force. The freedom mentioned here is not a progressive experience. The tense of the verb is aorist, pointing to a time past when this freedom was gained. This was when faith was exercised; when new life was imparted; when the Spirit took up residence in the believer. It is, however, when the power is realised that freedom from the law of sin and death is experienced.

The law of sin and death has been seen in ch.7 to be a crippling power. It was that dominating force that caused Paul to cry out, "O wretched man that I am". Now it is seen to be subservient to a superior power. No longer need it lord it over the believer and control his will. There is now a greater power working in him and for him.

3 The use of "For" ensures that the flow of Paul's argument continues steadily. He now makes it clear that the law had a weakness. It was incapable of accomplishing that for which it was given. It could not bring freedom. It was impotent and the reason for its inability to produce the desired results is stated: it was weak through the flesh. As noted at 7:12, there was nothing really wrong with the law. It was holy, and just, and good. But instead of the flesh responding to its statutes, it rebelled and refused to be subject to them. The commandments only served to encourage sin in defiance of the law's demands.

God, however, was not defeated. Such a thought cannot be entertained. The impossibility of the law to accomplish what was intended did not force God to adopt emergency measures. He had a plan. He did what the law could not do, and He did it by sending His own Son. There was no inherent weakness in Him.

He was divine and His manhood was impeccable. The close link between the Father and the Son is emphasised by the use of *heautou*, ("of Himself", "His own"). It was not an angel He sent, but His own Son and He came into this world as man.

The expression "in the likeness of sinful flesh" has caused difficulty with many. The word rendered "likeness" (*homoiōma*) has occurred three times in the epistle (1:23; 5:14; 6:5). It also occurs in Phil 2:7, "made in the likeness of men", and it is in this sense that Paul obviously uses it here. "Likeness" should not be understood as a similarity. While it is acknowledged that He was different in essence from man, He was truly man, sin apart. There is no doubt much in the expression about His person, the depth of which cannot be plumbed, but there is enough made known in the Scriptures to confirm His identification with man as well as to mark the essential contrasts. The great fact remains, what the law was unable to do, God did, and He did it by sending His own Son in the likeness of sinful flesh.

The purpose of His coming is now made clear. It was that He might deal with the sin question. The RV inserts "as an offering" in italics and this is no doubt involved. The apostle, however, did not say that and it is perhaps better to consider the two words "for sin" as embracing the whole question of sin. The result of His coming was that He condemned sin. All sin, every aspect of it, in the flesh and in every other sphere was brought under the sentence of condemnation, ready for final judgment. This He did by taking upon Himself flesh. His spotless life was a condemnation of sin and His sacrifice at Calvary was the sin offering by which He dealt with the problem of sin to the glory of God. The writer to the Hebrews made this plain when he wrote, "but now once in the end of the world hath he appeared to put away sin by the sacrifice of himself...and unto them that look for him shall he appear the second time without (apart from) sin unto salvation" (9:26,28).

4 This verse commences with *hina*, "in order that". What follows from v.3 and is explained in v.4 is the purpose of God, "in order that the righteousness of God might be fulfilled in us". There is no possibility of failure here. If God's plan involved the sending of His Son into the world, the results flowing from that cannot be in doubt. The RV renders "righteousness" as "ordinance". In this connection, Vincent comments, "Primarily that which is deemed right, so as to have the force of law; hence 'ordinance'. Here collectively, of the moral precepts of the law; its righteous requirement". The word is used in connection with Zacharias and Elizabeth, "And they were both righteous before God, walking in all the commandments and ordinances of the law blameless" (Luke 1:6).

The righteousness of the law is stated to be fulfilled "*in* us". This signifies a work of God which is carried through by the indwelling Spirit of God. There is no thought here of the righteous requirement being fulfilled on a personal basis, either "by" or "through" us. It is by the Holy Spirit "in" us, although there must be a willing response to the Spirit's leading. Some commentators hold that since the righteousness of the law was only met by Christ, then the reference in this verse is to Him. However, since believers are "in Christ", as stated in vv.1,2, it is reasonable to expect that they have part in the kind of response God expects.

A safeguard is introduced by the statement "who walk not after the flesh, but after the Spirit". This describes believers only. The unconverted cannot make their way through the world to the pleasure of God. Those who "walk after the flesh", cannot fulfil the righteousness of the law. Such are alienated from God by wicked works and they live their lives in this world fulfilling fleshly desires. God's standards are not their standards and they therefore draw down upon themselves His condemnation. Those who are "in Christ" are enabled by the power of the Spirit of God to live Spirit-controlled lives to God's glory. Believers are not left to their own resources. If that were the case, the law of sin and death would take over. The law of the Spirit of life in Christ Jesus is the controlling force which enables them to triumph. This is now what Paul is revealing. There is a new power; it is the indwelling Spirit of God.

Notes

1 "Condemnation" (*katakrima*) denotes the sentence and the carrying out of the sentence. From the divine side, once the sentence is passed there is no escape. *Katakrima* occurs three times in the NT; here and at 5:16,18.

In the original, "no" (*ouden*), is the first word in the sentence, stressing that for believers, every single believer, there is no condemnation. Harold St. John states, "No encumbrance, no shadow that can ever mar your title to the inheritance".

2 In the first seven chapters, *pneuma* has been used only five times, and not every time applying to the Holy Spirit. In this chapter the term occurs twenty times, showing that the work of the Holy Spirit is the predominant theme.

There is textual difference as to whether "me" or "you" was intended. Either way it does not alter the sense as the term obviously encompasses every believer.

3 Morris suggests that the phrase, "For what the law could not do" can mean either, "the inability of the law was overcome", or, "what was impossible for the law (was accomplished)". Both aspects should be taken as applicable to the situation.

On "likeness" (*homoiōma*), St. John makes the comment, "He has sent His Son as close to us as He could possibly be, in the likeness of those who were fallen all around Him, and yet for ever and eternally divine". The point stressed is the likeness, not the difference.

(b) *The mind of the flesh and the mind of the Spirit (vv.5-11)*

> v.5 "For they that are after the flesh do mind the things of the flesh; but they that are after the Spirit the things of the Spirit.
> v.6 For to be carnally minded is death; but to be spiritually minded is life and peace.
> v.7 Because the carnal mind is enmity against God: for it is not subject to the law of God, neither indeed can be.

> v.8 So then they that are in the flesh cannot please God.
> v.9 But ye are not in the flesh, but in the Spirit, if so be that the Spirit of God dwell in you. Now if any man have not the Spirit of Christ, he is none of his.
> v.10 And if Christ be in you, the body is dead because of sin; but the Spirit is life because of righteousness.
> v.11 But if the Spirit of him that raised up Jesus from the dead dwell in you, he that raised up Christ from the dead shall also quicken your mortal bodies by his Spirit that dwelleth in you."

5 The previous verse introduced two contrasting thoughts, walking according to the flesh and walking according to the Spirit. This topic is now expanded by setting out a series of contrasts and by associating certain results with each. The first contrast establishes that there are those who are "after the flesh" and those who are "after the Spirit". Since the first class are characterised and motivated by the flesh, they are antagonistic to God. The second class, however, are controlled and motivated by the Holy Spirit and they are therefore in happy accord with His mind.

The second set of contrasts shows that the two classes are diametrically opposed. The first class have their minds set on earthly things. They live for self and time. Their horizons are set no higher than earth. The second class have their minds set on heavenly things. They live for God and for eternity. Their horizons are not restricted to temporal things; they have their minds fixed on things which are spiritual. The unregenerate have all their interests in self-centred things – they mind the things of the flesh. Believers are indwelt by the Spirit and led by Him. Their interests are in the things of God.

The verb *phroneō* ("to mind", "to think") is of considerable interest. Of nearly twenty occurrences in the NT, only three are found outwith the writings of Paul. It occurs five times in Romans but three times in Philippians. The appeal of Phil 2:5 has far-reaching implications, "Let this mind be in you (keep on thinking this) which was also in Christ Jesus". Paraphrased, this would read, "Be characterised by this way of thinking, which (way) was His way of thinking"; His way of thinking is then set out in Phil 2 in the way He emptied Himself and took upon Himself the form of a servant, becoming obedient unto death, even the death of the cross. The term, as used here looks two ways. It describes the way the unregenerate think and consequently act. It also describes the way believers think. They set their minds on the things of the Spirit, and they are therefore in harmony with the mind of the Spirit.

6 Another set of contrasts is introduced in this verse. What results from being carnally-minded is death. The issue of being spiritually-minded is life and peace. As each contrast is set out by the apostle, the gap between the unregenerate and the believer widens. The impossibility of bridging the gap is evident, even if the unregenerate had the mind to do so. In this connection there is no indication in what Paul is declaring that there is any desire for change on the part of the unregenerate. There are clearly two roads. While on the road that leads to death, there seems to be no wish to get off it and it is certain that any attempt to retrace the steps to evade the inevitable end is of no avail.

The mind of the flesh is death. Those who are motivated by the flesh in thought and ambition must take character from its condemnation. It is rebellious and antagonistic to God. The sentence of death is therefore upon it. The unregenerate are in this state positionally. The desires, aspirations and practices of those who are carnally-minded lead to ruin. Death here is not simply the end of life which is the portion of every member of the human race. It is a state of alienation from God, dead in trespasses and in sins, and it is also the final doom which is inescapable for all who die outside of Christ. There is wilfulness in the mind of the flesh which makes no allowance for God or for His claims. God, in fact, is not required in any way.

The mind of the Spirit is life and peace. In the expression the stress is not on the believer, as the AV would indicate, just as the stress is not on the unregenerate but on the flesh in the first part of the contrast. The outcome, however, in both cases is beyond dispute. One is death and the other is life and peace. The unregenerate face the former and believers in the Lord Jesus Christ enjoy the latter. The inevitability of the first is manifest. The impossibility of the second coming into condemnation in any form is just as certain, because the mind of the Spirit is life and peace. Life in Christ has been the apostle's great theme in the epistle. It is the portion of all who exercise faith, and peace with God is the resulting blessing. As stated at 5:1, peace with God is one of the completely-new relationships which have been brought about by the work of Christ. The enjoyment of it comes through faith in Christ, as 15:13 states, "joy and peace in believing".

7   The connecting word "because" (*dioti*, "wherefore", "on this account") links the verse with the preceding one. The statement of v.6, "to be carnally minded is death" is now shown to have a sinister side to it. The apostle declares that the mind of the flesh "is enmity against God". The word *echthra*, used by Paul in Gal 5:20 to describe one of the works of the flesh, is used by Luke in a telling way, "And the same day Pilate and Herod were made friends together: for before they were at *enmity* between themselves" (Luke 23:12). The term denotes hostility and as used here by Paul it highlights the attitude of the flesh towards God and the law of God. It is not merely a situation where the flesh ignores God, it is actively opposed to Him and all that bears His name.

The term "flesh" (*sarx*) is one which carries many shades of meaning in the NT, each of which is determined by the context in which it is found. Here Paul is using it to describe man as he is, characterised by the fallen nature inherited from Adam. It is all that man is without God and without Christ. It is a state of alienation from God, one which is characterised by sin and therefore vulnerable to all kinds of temptation. This is a solemn indictment of man as he is. He does not trust God; he does not want God, and as this verse shows, in his mind he is antagonistic to God, an attitude which manifests itself in open hostility.

The hostility of mind against God is not one which is forced upon the flesh by an outside agency. Although it should be subject to the law of God, which is implied, it takes a rebellious stance and expresses downright hostility. God's law is recognised as a rule which places certain restrictions, apart from showing the right path, and the flesh immediately rebels. Conformity to any standard, whether the law of Moses, or any moral law, is unacceptable. In fact, the closing words of the verse indicate that the flesh cannot be tamed. It will never conform, or be conformed, to the will of God. This does not necessarily mean that all men everywhere are blatantly evil. Although many are classed as "law-abiding citizens", the fact remains, towards God they are hostile. Their hostility may be disguised or covered over, but if dominated by the flesh they are outside of Christ and therefore alienated from God.

8 The opening words of this verse, given in the AV as "So then" would be better understood by "And". This makes the verse a straight-forward conclusion of what has just been stated, that the mind of the flesh is enmity against God. It stands to reason that those who are antagonistic towards God, showing it either in open hostility or by covering rebellion over with good works, are not in a condition which brings God pleasure. Indeed, it is quite the reverse. They invite His wrath by despising the goodness of His grace and the provision He has made in Christ.

In vv.5-8 it is worth noting the different allusions Paul makes to the flesh: in v.5 "they that are after the flesh"; in vv.6,7 "the mind of the flesh"; in v.8 "they that are in the flesh". This last reference contrasts sharply with the opening verse of the chapter, "There is therefore now no condemnation to them which are in Christ Jesus". There is no intermediate state. One is either "in the flesh" or "in Christ". To be "in the flesh" is to be "out of Christ" and that position is one which leads on to ruin. It is earthly, sensual and devilish, with no prospect for the future, other than wrath and judgment.

9 The position of "ye" in the original is emphatic. It is as if Paul wished to give a quick assurance to the Romans that they were not "in the flesh", having just stated that all in that state could not please God. Regardless of how many in the world were characterised by the phrase; it did not apply to the Romans. The contrast between "in the flesh" and "in the Spirit" is sharp. Whatever is sublime about being in the Spirit, the opposite is the case about being "in the flesh". There is no question of intermediate states here. It is not a mixture of what is of the Spirit and what is of the Adamic nature. There is no possibility of these two forces coming together. They have nothing in common. They are mutually exclusive.

The statement, "if so be that the Spirit of God dwell in you", does not suggest a doubt. The better rendering is "since", or, "as is the case". It is a confirmation of the fact that the Holy Spirit indwells the believer. He does not indwell the unregenerate. No matter how pious men and women might be, the crucial factor applies to all, and that is, a saving faith in the Lord Jesus Christ. There is no point in a scale of attainments or of profession at which the Spirit enters. Merit has no place in this matter. God operates on the principle of faith and He does not enter into negotiations or bargaining situations with any. When a person is born of God the Holy Spirit enters and that person is then "in the Spirit" in the same way as they are said to be "in Christ" (v.1).

The closing words of the verse should not be taken to mean what is characteristic of Christ. Paul is not setting forth Christ here as an example to be emulated. That would not be in keeping with the teaching of the passage. He is stressing that any who have not the Spirit do not belong to Christ. They are not "in Christ". The Son of God and the Holy Spirit of God are seen here to be integrally related. Indeed, it is held by many that the verse is an indication of the doctrine of the Trinity.

The closing phrase, "he is none of his", or, literally, "is not of him" is a solemn statement. It is one which would cause offence to the professors if it were addressed to them personally on a human level. Nevertheless, if the Holy Spirit is not in residence, there is no living connection with Christ.

10 At the end of v.9 the apostle studiously avoided any reference to the Romans. He used the term "any man", or better, "any one". Now he returns to the personal approach and states, "And if Christ be in you", establishing a contrast with the preceding statement. What he is now making clear is that "the Spirit in you" and "Christ in you" are to all intents synonymous expressions. The position is similar to what Paul wrote to the Ephesians, "strengthened with might by his Spirit in the inner man; that Christ may dwell in your hearts by faith" (3:16,17). There is a close relationship between the Son and the Holy Spirit, although they are distinct Persons. The personality of the Spirit is a doctrinal fact. He is not merely an influence which creates a godly atmosphere in certain situations.

That the body is mortal cannot be denied. It still carries the sentence of death in it. After conversion, however, the believer is no longer "dead in trespasses and in sins". There is emancipation from that aspect of death. The unconverted are in that condition but the believer has life in Christ and this is recognised by God. Not only so, death as a state of judgment when life is over is not the portion of those who are "in Christ". In the next verse he will show that there is a glorious future even for these mortal bodies; the "mortal shall have put on immortality" (1 Cor 15:54), and it is then that "Death is swallowed up in victory". Here, however, Paul is stating the fact that sin is the culprit and because of sin the body is dead.

It is possible that because of the inevitability of death and the undeniable presence of sin, Paul introduces another contrast. The presence of the indwelling Holy Spirit, and the eternal life which He is instrumental in giving, are set against sin and death. Instead of a sense of despair arising at the thought of what sin has brought in, there is one of triumph. It cannot be said that God is making the best of a bad situation. He is altogether in control. As to the righteousness mentioned, this should be taken in its broadest sense and not limited to that aspect of it which was reckoned on believing. Righteousness in every aspect, positional, moral and practical should be understood as being on the apostle's mind here. This suits the whole tenor of his argument throughout.

11 The title of the Holy Spirit here is claimed by Vine to be the longest in the NT. If his view is correct, it is not much longer than the title given by Peter, "the Spirit of glory and of God" (1 Pet 4:14). These periphrastic titles, with others in the Holy Scriptures, are most interesting, adding colour and atmosphere to what the writers wished to communicate. The Spirit here is linked with God, whereas the link in the previous verse was with Christ. As noted there, there is a clear reference in the context to the doctrine of the Trinity.

There are only two references to the Lord's name, "Jesus" in the epistle, here and at 3:26. In the first occurrence the context concerns the justice and mercy of God, manifested in His righteousness in saving those who believe in Jesus. The stress is on the strength of faith in those who believe; they are characterised by faith; they are of the faith of Jesus. The phrase is unique. It links the person who believes in a firm way with Jesus, and there is no doubt about the faith which characterised Him. In this verse the Holy Spirit is the pledge that the God who raises up Jesus, the One who went to the cross, will also raise up those who believe in Him. The Holy Spirit, indwelling the saints, is the seal and the surety that the resurrection is a certainty. If Jesus was raised by the mighty power of God, those who are His will follow in due course.

The point that God acted in resurrecting power is repeated in the verse. This time the apostle states that it was Christ Jesus (v.11 RV) who was raised. He is no doubt referring now to the fact that it was the One who was with the Father in eternity past who came down to earth. The use of the title "Jesus" refers to the humanity and humility of the Lord. But, balancing His deity with His humanity, the significant change of title is made. Taking both together, it was the One who came down, who was seen and known in the flesh, who went to the cross and was raised again from amongst the dead.

Those who believe in Jesus will not be left in "the body of this death" (7:24 RV). At the rapture the great change will take place. Sleeping saints will be raised and living ones will be changed when the Lord comes. The great truth of 1 Thess 4:14-17 and 1 Cor 15:51-54 will come to pass. Here the apostle is stressing that the Holy Spirit will be actively engaged in the emancipation of the saints. Whether He will be the agent or the guarantee is not clear from the verse. The preposition used, "through" His Spirit, could also be rendered, "because" of His Spirit. Either way, or both ways, it is true: God will quicken and He will do it through the Spirit. Because the Spirit indwells the saints, the pledge is there and it will be redeemed when the saints are raised.

Notes

4   Morris states that *hina*, "in order that", introduces the divine purpose, and since that purpose

never fails of fulfilment, it points to the result as well. The purpose is that the righteous requirement of the law might be fulfilled in us.

5 "…do mind" (*phroneō*) signifies not just the thought process but what stems from that type of thinking. So those who think according to the base things of the flesh will produce acts which stem from that kind of thinking.

6 The noun form of "mind" here signifies what the flesh has in mind. It is set on death – this is where it terminates; it has no higher view.

7 Vincent comments on the flesh, "It is marshalled under a hostile banner".

"Subject" (*hupotassō*, "to subordinate", "to arrange under") expresses a voluntary condition which is constant. The hostility to God is ever-present.

10 Commenting on "the body is dead" Haldane suggests that there are three deaths, "One is in this life, the other is at the end of life and the third after this life". According to Haldane, believers are delivered from the first and third, but may undergo the second.

11 Denney remarks, "Though the present results of the indwelling Spirit are not all we might desire, the future is sure".

(c) *The witness of the Holy Spirit to new relationships (vv.12-27)*

v.12 "Therefore, brethren, we are debtors, not to the flesh, to live after the flesh.
v.13 For if ye live after the flesh, ye shall die: but if ye through the Spirit do mortify the deeds of the body, ye shall live.
v.14 For as many as are led by the Spirit of God, they are the sons of God.
v.15 For ye have not received the spirit of bondage again to fear; but ye have received the Spirit of adoption, whereby we cry, Abba, Father.
v.16 The Spirit itself beareth witness with our spirit, that we are the children of God:
v.17 And if children, then heirs; heirs of God, and joint-heirs with Christ; if so be that we suffer with him, that we may be also glorified together.
v.18 For I reckon that the sufferings of this present time are not worthy to be compared with the glory which shall be revealed in us.
v.19 For the earnest expectation of the creature waiteth for the manifestation of the sons of God.
v.20 For the creature was made subject to vanity, not willingly, but by reason of him who hath subjected the same in hope,
v.21 Because the creature itself also shall be delivered from the bondage of corruption into the glorious liberty of the children of God.
v.22 For we know that the whole creation groaneth and travaileth in pain together until now.
v.23 And not only they, but ourselves also, which have the firstfruits of the Spirit, even we ourselves groan within ourselves, waiting for the adoption, to wit, the redemption of our body.
v.24 For we are saved by hope: but hope that is seen is not hope: for what a man seeth, why doth he yet hope for?
v.25 But if we hope for that we see not, then do we with patience wait for it.
v.26 Likewise the Spirit also helpeth our infirmities: for we know not what we should pray for as we ought: but the Spirit itself maketh intercession for us with groanings which cannot be uttered.
v.27 And he that searcheth the hearts knoweth what is the mind of the Spirit, because he maketh intercession for the saints according to the will of God."

This section commences with a reminder that the flesh is not a creditor, in anything: it is owed nothing. What is now sought is a practical putting to death of its deeds by the power of the Spirit. So the leading of the Spirit is brought in, not to single out some who respond to His leading but to mark out all who believe, that they are sons of God. The leading is not specific, but general. It is what is true of all who are born again. Into every aspect of their lives the Spirit of God has an entrance to be not a passive resident, but an active force in leading God's saints.

12 The conclusion arrived at here is that no obligation is owed to the flesh. It is not a creditor in any respect and therefore it has no claims. The opening of the verse is better rendered "So then", making what follows the deduction from the previous verses. The character of the flesh and the truth of the indwelling Holy Spirit provide the background for the categorical statement, "we are debtors, not to the flesh". The construction of this expression suggests that its completion demands, "but to the Holy Spirit", or to someone or something else. If we are debtors, not to the flesh, the question automatically arises, To whom then are we in debt? This, however, is left open by the apostle. The main point of his argument is that the flesh is owed nothing and there he leaves the matter.

The reference to the saints as "brethren" is a warm touch. It is not a term which is loosely used in Scripture. It always conveys the idea of having much in common. There is never any thought of class distinction when the word is used. Indeed, later Paul will exhort the saints to be "kindly affectioned one to another with brotherly love, in honour preferring one another" (12:10). So here, it is "brethren" who are reminded that there is no obligation to the flesh. If they lived and served with each other as brethren, the flesh could be ruled out as having any power over them. The closing words of the verse, "to live after the flesh" are a timely warning. Although his appeal is to brethren, Paul is not suggesting that there is a choice. To live, or not to live, after the flesh is not an option. There is no provision for following a course dominated by the flesh, and no obligation either.

13 In the previous verse the apostle took common ground with the believers and stated, "We are debtors, not to the flesh". He now turns from "we" to "ye" and issues a warning. He is not inferring that there is a danger of believers suffering the fate of the unregenerate and being lost, because death is the end of all who live "after the flesh". But since the flesh has not been eradicated, there is always the danger that some allowance will be made for it to spring into life. Paul has made it clear, there is no good in it. It is incorrigible, and it is a fact that all who live by it will die. The warning therefore to believers is a solemn one. The question to be faced is: why tamper with that which leads to death in those who live after its dictates? The warning is strengthened by the inclusion of the word *mellō* ("must"), stressing absolute certainty.

The latter half of the verse brings in the Spirit of God. "If ye through the Spirit do mortify the deeds of the body, ye shall live". The verb is in the active voice and implies some action on the part of believers to put to death the deeds, the practices of the body. The body here stands for the instrument through which the flesh operates. The deeds (or, misdeeds) of the body have to be killed off. Decisive action is called for in this case. No scope is allowed for mercy on any grounds. The lesson of king Saul's disobedience as described in 1 Sam 15, in sparing what God had condemned to be destroyed, is a classical example of what is involved here. Undoubtedly life, both in the reality of it and the quality of it, is what is enjoyed when the deeds of the body are put to death. Although personal action is called for, the help of the Spirit of God is pledged. Believers are not left entirely to their own resources. There is a power which is available to those who "live after the Spirit".

14 There are no exceptions implied in the opening words, "For as many". The rendering "For all who" is more explicit and emphasises that it is the portion of all believers to be led by the Spirit of God. There is no thought of compulsion. The idea of being driven by the Spirit does not suit the context. There is co-operation from those who are being led, they are willing to be led and they allow themselves to be drawn along. This does not mean that those who are led by the Spirit have ceased to be free agents. Freedom is not surrendered when the gospel of God is believed and Christ is accepted as Saviour. The statement is to be understood in a general way. It is what characterises believers. It is acknowledged, however, that also embraced is the gentle leading of the Spirit, working within and all around the saints, encouraging them in the path of service and towards the person of the Lord Jesus Christ.

The apostle has just given assurance that there is a divine power to put to death the deeds of the body. Another aspect of the Spirit's power and presence is now introduced. All who are led by the Spirit, who make use of His power in mortifying the flesh, these are the sons of God. The proof of position and relationship cannot be denied, since what has been stated cannot be true of the unregenerate. There is emphasis on the pronoun "these" suggesting "these and none else". It is not the relationship of children which is being stressed, but that of the responsible adult, that of "sons". It is not that the Spirit constitutes us "sons", but that by His leading is furnished the proof, the evidence that those who are led by Him, and only those, are sons of God.

15 Once again the apostle uses the negative form in stating his case. This time he asserts that the Romans had not received the spirit of bondage, referring obviously to the time of their conversion. The tense of the verb is aorist, so it was not a process spread over months or years, but a definite point in the past. There is a measure of appeal in what Paul makes known, as if to expect an agreeable reply. It was not a spirit of bondage they received when they believed. Those who remain in their sins, who are "after the flesh" as he has been teaching; they are the ones who are in slavery.

There is a considerable difference of opinion amongst commentators as to whether the word "spirit" in the two occurrences here refers to the Holy Spirit. The AV favours "spirit of bondage" and "Spirit of adoption", but the RV and JND use the lower case for the initial letter in both instances. From a contextual point of view, since the Holy Spirit has featured prominently in Paul's reasoning, it seems right to accept that the two mentions in the verse apply to the Holy Spirit. On the other hand, it seems reasonable to follow the AV and take the first mention to read "ye received not the spirit of bondage (slavery) again to fear". Bondage was not what the message of the gospel intimated when they were converted. Whatever they were enslaved with prior to conversion, even if it were sin with its fear of condemnation and judgment, it was swept away and a new relationship was entered into through the power of the Holy Spirit. The Holy Spirit did not make people slaves, but in amazing grace He was involved in making them sons. At that point it was not the spirit of bondage and fear that prevailed, but another one altogether.

There is, however, an obvious contrast. Prior to conversion there was servility. To whom or what they were servile is not the point. It is the fact that they were in bondage and there was fear attached to it. After they were saved, a new relationship was established. As sons of God, servility and fear were not in question. God did not treat them as would a ruthless earthly master, but instead they were accorded full rights of sonship and every freedom without fear.

Adoption, as it is taught in the NT, is vastly different from what is understood by the use of the word in the world. In that sphere the birth-tie is never there, however much kindness and love are bestowed upon the adopted child. In the divine realm, the birth-tie is there, because all who believe are born of God, they are children of God, and as such they are in the family of God. The blessing of adoption given to Christians is one of son-placing. The full rights of a son are bestowed upon all who believe. Under the law saints were like under-age children, they were under a tutor, a schoolmaster. As Paul teaches elsewhere, this condition was "unto" Christ (Gal 3:24). The law could never bring in such a blessing. It came in with Christ as a result of His work on earth. Although there is a sense in which the believer has no rights in the family, since it is all of grace and merit does not feature in it, the same grace of God bestows full sonship privileges. Those who are sons will one day be with the Saviour at the public manifestation of the sons of God (8:19).

The Holy Spirit is said to cry, "Abba, Father" in Gal 4:6. Here it is the saints who give expression to the cry. The Spirit in them enables them as sons of God to cry, "Abba, Father". It is the cry of the infant, a trusting filial cry. It is the proof of relationship, one which expects the loving care and consideration of the Father. One, indeed, which does not doubt that the Father will respond. The Lord used the same words in the garden of Gethsemane (Mark 14:36), one of four instances when an Aramaic expression is recorded by Mark. The other three are: "Talitha cumi" (5:41); "Ephphatha" (7:34), and "Eloi, Eloi, lama sabachthani" (15:34). Why Mark should record four Aramaic expressions is an interesting question, but as far as Paul's use of one of them is concerned, there seems little doubt that he wanted to stress the filial relationship of sons of God.

16 The rendering of the opening words of this verse in the AV, "The Spirit itself", is not accurate. It should read as in the RV, "The Spirit himself". The Holy Spirit is the third person in the Godhead and should be acknowledged as such, not as a mere influence as maintained by some. The reason for the AV rendering is probably because *pneuma* is neuter in Greek grammar and the pronoun *auto* agrees with it grammatically, hence our translators rendered "itself" instead of "himself".

The Spirit is said here to "bear witness with our spirit". There is no separate word in the original for "with"; it is derived from the *sum* in *summartureō* ("to bear witness with"). There is a view amongst commentators that the verb *summartureō* should be understood in the passage to mean, "The Spirit himself bears witness *to* our spirit" and not "*with* our spirit". In support of this it is held that believers cannot stand unaided alongside the Holy Spirit and bear witness with Him before God that they are children of God. This view, however, is rejected by many commentators. The rendering of the AV and the RV is held to be an accurate translation of the word in question, signifying that the Holy Spirit, aiding and in harmony with the spirits of believers, bears witness that they are children of God.

Having established the dignity of saints in the previous verse, that they are sons of God, Paul now brings out that they are also children of God. This expression confirms relationship. Believers are in the family of God by reason of the new birth. The title "sons of God" is peculiar to Paul. John does not use the title "sons of God" (where it is given in the AV, it should be "children of God"). John does, however, refer to believers as "children of God", twice in his Gospel, and four times in his first epistle. Paul refers to "children of God" on four occasions, three times in Romans (8:16,21; 9:8), and once in his epistle to the Philippians (2:15). The Jews never knew the intimacy of this relationship. They were no doubt a favoured nation, but they were never part of God's family. This was reserved for those who would believe the gospel in the age of grace.

17 Having established the family relationship, Paul now goes on to describe some of the benefits. The children are heirs. They have therefore a title to an inheritance. This is not to be understood as what comes to children by way of hereditary succession. Rather is it what is bestowed upon them as sharers in what is the rightful inheritance of Christ. The thought of an inheritance was all-important to the Jew. Possession of an allotted portion in the land, ground allotted by God and held down for Him, was the ultimate as far as the children of Israel were concerned. In the NT, however, the allotted possession is different. It is not ownership, something to be passed on from generation to generation, but what God has given in grace, a sharing with Christ in what is His, not only His as the Son of God, but what He has won by reason of His work on earth.

The statement, "heirs of God" is remarkable. How God could make it possible and remain true to His own nature is a matter of great wonder. That He should take redeemed sinners into such a relationship is a cause for unending praise. It is, no doubt, the outcome of the work of Christ. Apart from that, it could never have come to pass. In addition, states Paul, we are "joint-heirs with Christ". Whatever is His will be shared. The details are not revealed. In the ages to come, however, all will be made known. In the meantime, the dignity and joy of having such a title bolsters the spirit and encourages the children of God to live for Him in this scene of Christ's rejection.

The phrase, "if so be that we suffer with him" does not imply a condition or a doubt. The word *eiper* ("since") is a strong term. It indicates that suffering with Christ is the normal experience of believers. No doubt in apostolic times, to be a Christian was tantamount to being identified as one who should be persecuted. If Christ suffered, those who are His cannot expect different treatment. The world is hostile to God. That hostility was directed against Christ. It follows therefore that those who are His will suffer also. Paul makes this plain in several of his epistles. To the Corinthians he wrote, "For as the sufferings of Christ abound in us, so also our consolation also aboundeth by Christ" (2 Cor 1:5). To Timothy, he advised, "If we suffer, we shall also reign with him" (2 Tim 2:12). As to his own attitude to suffering for Christ, Paul wrote to the Philippians, "That I may know him, and the power of his resurrection, and the fellowship of his sufferings, being made conformable unto his death" (3:10).

The AV rendering of the last clause is a little misleading. In the original it reads, "we suffer with (him), in order that (*hina*) we may be glorified with (him)". Present suffering results in future glory. The plans of God for His people may seem strange. That those who are sons and children of God have to expect suffering on their way to glory is an extraordinary situation. When it is remembered, however, that it is suffering with Christ now and glory with Him in the future, the position is not as bizarre as some would judge. Considering what He suffered to bring us to God, what is expected by way of return is little by comparison. The reward for faithfulness is certain, God will be no man's debtor.

18 Having introduced the thought of coming glory in the previous verse, it might have been expected that Paul would have continued on that line. Instead, he holds on to the thought of suffering. The trials and the sorrows of the present life are too real to be ignored. Regardless of the joy of being lifted out of a world of pain and suffering, even for a little while, the return to it cannot be avoided. In the apostle's day, persecution of Christians was to be expected and that situation had to be addressed. Peter recognised the seriousness of it and his counsel has come down the ages to encourage the oppressed in every age. He wrote, "If ye be reproached for the name of Christ, happy are ye; for the spirit of glory and of God resteth upon you" (1 Pet 4:14).

In saying, "For I reckon", Paul was not expressing an opinion. This is a considered judgment. The word has in it the idea of assured knowledge. He has used the word several times already in the epistle. In his appeal to man's reasoning he wrote, "And thinkest thou (do you really consider)...that thou shalt escape the judgment of God?" (2:3). As he advanced his argument, he wrote, "Therefore we conclude that a man is justified by faith without (apart from) the deeds of the law" (3:28). These, and many others examples, are instances of the apostle's use of a word which he judged gave the fullest expression to the point he was stating. Here, his considered judgment brings in a striking contrast – the present sufferings and the glory which shall be revealed in us.

The sufferings of the present time should not be limited to apostolic days. Of the word "time" (*kairos*) Trench says it is time contemplated not simply as a succession of moments. It is what characterises the present age. Between Pentecost and the rapture, the intervening years constitute the present age and it is one of suffering. Undoubtedly each generation will experience different features of it, but the overall situation is the same. Nevertheless, as far as Paul was concerned the present age is in marked contrast with the age to come. Details of the future were not what the apostle was dwelling on; it was enough that the reality of present suffering should be set against future glory. Obviously he was not thinking of the distant future necessarily. At this stage, the thought of glory which is on the horizon suits his application better. It is the certainty of it which matters.

Here then, Paul asserts that the sufferings of the present age are not worthy to be compared with the glory to come. The word for "worthy" (*axios*) is interesting. It comes from *ago* ("to weigh"). It is held by many to refer to the beam of a set of scales which is horizontal when the weights are equal on each side of the pivot. Present sufferings and future glory cannot be brought into equilibrium as far as Paul is concerned. The weight of glory far exceeds the present sufferings and the beam of the scales cannot therefore reach the horizontal position. A similar thought was expressed to the Corinthians. To them he wrote, "For our light affliction, which is but for a moment, worketh for us a far more exceeding and eternal weight of glory" (2 Cor 4:17).

The glory which is about to be revealed is not something to be arranged for the occasion. The glory is embodied in the person of Christ. It is there, awaiting its public manifestation. It will be revealed in us and to us. The verb "shall be" (*mellō*) Paul has used several times in the epistle. It denotes certainty: in v.13, "If ye live after the flesh, ye shall die". There is no doubt about that; it is a divine decree. Here the future glory is in question, and it shall certainly be revealed in us. The preposition *eis* may also carry the thought of "to us". It is not simply a case of being privileged onlookers; we shall participate in the revelation of the glory of the Lord Jesus.

19 The conjunction "For" continues the subject of Paul's reasoning from the previous verse. Present suffering and future glory are now applied to creation. It is clear that the apostle's view of the ravages of sin has a wider horizon than mankind. The effect of the fall of Adam had spread throughout creation and it therefore awaits eagerly the day of its redemption. The apostle uses an interesting word to describe the eagerness of creation to realise its deliverance from the bondage of sin. It has the literal meaning of stretching out the head just as an athlete would do at the finishing line in a race. It also suggests that the concentration is so intense that all else is forgotten. The picture is a very vivid one, and it was obviously intended to stir up undivided thoughts of coming glory in the minds of those to whom the apostle wrote.

The waiting of creation is not casual. The word used to describe the waiting is intensive. It bears stress and suggests earnestness, as if to make known that creation knew its only hope for emancipation lay outside of itself. It is an interesting word, one which Paul uses several times in other epistles. Perhaps the best-known usage is Phil 3:20, "For our conversation is in heaven, from whence also we look ('assiduously', Thayer), for the Saviour, the Lord Jesus Christ".

The day of redemption is coming. The aspect which Paul has in mind here is the manifestation of the sons of God. This is a lovely thought. The unveiling of the glory involves the sons of God. This links with what he has already stated about sons (vv.14,15). It is a further encouragement for all who have a placing as sons, to know that when Christ is revealed, they will be manifested with Him. In that glorious day God will declare that He has many sons, all of whom will bear a likeness to His own Son. The certainty therefore of the day of manifestation is added as a further proof that the sufferings of this present age are not worthy to be compared with the glory which is about to be revealed.

20 There is an obvious allusion in this verse to Gen 3:17,18. The cursing of the ground as a result of Adam's sin and disobedience, the proliferation of thorns and thistles; these and much more are proofs that a blight fell upon creation when the tragedy of Eden's garden took place. The evidence of a groaning creation is all around, although not many are prepared to admit that it is all because of sin. Every part of creation has been permeated by the curse and as a result it groans under its bondage. Man, of course, is powerless to ease creation's burden. It will not be cured until the man of God's choice takes up the reigns of government and rules in righteousness.

Creation is said here to be subjected to vanity. It had no chance to reach its potential. There came in a sense of frustration as it failed to achieve what its Designer had planned for it. The vanity of which Paul speaks reflects the failure of creation to develop. It is after all tied up in the same parcel as mankind, and, when man fell, creation in all its aspects fell with him.

It is not as if creation willingly subjected itself to the futility which resulted from Adam's sin. Here Paul personifies nature and he makes it clear that it was not its desire to be brought under the curse. The tense of the verb is aorist, showing that the subjection to vanity was not a process, it was at a definite point in time. When Adam sinned, he not only plunged his posterity into ruin, but creation as well.

Being subjected to vanity is seen here to be by reason of "him" who subjected it. There are differences of opinion as to who is referred to in this connection. Some hold that it was Adam and some that it was Satan. Most commentators, however, hold that it was God, believing that neither Adam nor Satan had such far-reaching powers. This is borne out in the next verse which brings in hope, an anticipation which could never be associated with either. It is consistent with the character of God that He would act in the way that He did. Man fell and God allowed the results of that to permeate the whole of creation. In no sense, however, was God defeated. Even in the garden, intimation was given of a time of reversal. The second man, the last Adam, would triumph over the serpent and bruise his head, even though in the doing of it His own heel would be bruised.

21 There are manuscript differences as to whether the conjunction at the beginning of the verse should be "that" or "because". The AV favours "because" (*dioti*) and the RV gives "that" (*hoti*). There is very little difference one way or the other. The AV rendering suggests that v.21 with its argument follows on from v.19. The RV seems to imply that Paul was stressing that, in addition to the children of God (v.17) being glorified, creation will also come into the good of divine blessing.

The RV carries the reference to hope into the beginning of this verse. Hope in Scripture is not a nebulous quality. It has in it a certainty of fulfilment. It is not as the world understands, having nothing which can be identified as a foundation for what is hoped. Hope in Scripture is not irrational. It takes the Scripture as the very word of God and believes implicitly in the character of Him whose word it is, that He will bring all to pass in His own good time. Paul personifies creation here and makes it hope, looking forward to the time when it will be set free from bondage and when it will shine out in all its glory. Corruption will be no more. What characterises creation at present will no longer prevail. Decay and death hold sway now, but the time of emancipation is fast approaching. Instead of bondage it will be liberty. Creation will match man in the great day of manifestation.

It is not only the children of God who will enjoy liberty but creation will blossom forth in all its splendour. What Isa 11 and 65 so graphically portray will then come to pass. The world in particular has never seen creation as it was intended to be, but when the liberty of the glory of the children of God is revealed, then the restrictions on creation caused by sin will be removed and the magnificence of God's handiwork will be displayed to wondering eyes. As far as the prophetic programme is concerned, Paul passes over impending events. There is no mention of the rapture of the church or of tribulation on earth. As an inspired penman, his remit at this stage is to declare the certainty of coming glory and its effects.

This he does with his usual consummate skill. Creation will be delivered: it will not be left in bondage. It could not be said to be earnestly looking forward to the manifestation of the sons of God if its own emancipation were not involved.

22 Once again Paul appeals to the knowledge of his correspondents. He has done that repeatedly in the epistle, varying the part of speech on occasion to gain greater stress. (See at 2:2; 5:3; 6:9.) Here he appeals to the knowledge which comes from observation and experience. It was an obvious fact that the whole creation groaned. He does not isolate a small part of creation to prove the point. He states that it is common knowledge – creation in all its parts is groaning and travailing.

The RV rightly introduces "together" after the second verb. Creation groans together. All its parts are sighing. They are all affected and therefore they are in sympathy with each other. They have all been touched by sin and they have in consequence a common affliction. The RV renders accurately *sunōdinei* as "travaileth in pain together". Creation has been subjected to vanity (v.20), and what it brings forth is with birth-pangs. It travails in pain. The reference to "now" infers that the troubled state of nature has never known freedom since the fall of man. It still does not know deliverance, but it has an earnest expectation, waiting for the manifestation of the sons of God (v.19).

Paul's choice of words here is significant. Creation groans together and travails in pain together. These are birth-pangs, not death-pangs. There is pain at present, but something new, the like of which has never been seen before, will come forth. God will not be defeated. He knows the troubled state of what He created and He will rectify the situation in His own way and in His own good time.

23 Having made the point that creation groans and travails, Paul widens that and adds, "And not only so", as if to say, "And that is not all, believers also groan". They did so in apostolic times and they have continued through every generation until the present. Paul was not above the suffering. Apostles were not exempt. As he states here, "we ourselves groan within ourselves". Just how much the unconverted groan with creation is not contemplated here. Certainly it cannot be said of them that they are earnestly looking for the manifestation of the sons of God, and therein lies the tragedy. Creation will know deliverance, but the unconverted have only judgment and condemnation ahead.

The apostle, and all believers, have the firstfruits of the Spirit. He is the earnest, the pledge of great things to come. This indicates that the full harvest has not arrived, but the quality of the firstfruits is an indication of a bumper harvest. The expression, "firstfruits" should not be understood as a limited portion of the Holy Spirit now, and all of Him later. It is the pledge that the harvest will be of the same kind. The foretaste of the Spirit's presence and power now, marvellous as it is, is but a pledge of the many blessings which will be the portion of believers when they come into the good of what was won for them at Calvary.

Despite the bright prospect of the future and although we have the firstfruits of the Spirit, we groan (see Denney). It is true that "if any man hath not the Spirit of God he is none of his" (v.9). In that condition, there can be no earnest looking for the day of redemption. The unsaved have nothing to hold on to as far as the future is concerned, and no indwelling Spirit to encourage wider horizons than living for time and pleasure. As far as believers are concerned, whether despite having the Spirit or because they have the Spirit, they certainly groan, but the prospect could not be brighter, the day of redemption is coming. Already believers have adoption, the placing of sons (vv.14, 15), but they know that the work begun will be completed in its entirely in the great day ahead. For that there is an earnest expectation, in the same way that creation yearns (v.19). The body will be redeemed. All the effects of sin will be removed, not as a temporary measure, but a permanent release from bondage.

24 The introduction of salvation is an encouraging feature of Paul's case at this stage. Despite the groaning and the reasons for it, it is good to know that all is settled with God and the future is secure. Nevertheless, Paul does not leave the matter there: he introduces hope, a topic of frequent occurrence in this epistle. Many hold that hope is the key word in Romans and according to its wide usage, this must be accepted as having merit for acceptance.

Later Paul will speak of the God of hope (15:13). It is the only occurrence of the expression in the NT. It signifies that God is the author of hope, the source of hope, a hope which is not mere expectancy, but carries with it the assurance of faith. God Himself is characterised by hope. He never despairs because He is over all and all power is with Him. He never fails and there is no likelihood that He will give up His saints as hopeless.

Here the apostle notes that hope that is seen is not hope. This means, "why hope for something that has already been realised. If that for which hope stands is possessed, why continue to hope for it?" Possibly Paul is bringing to the attention of his correspondents that they must keep looking to the future. In no way have they to interpret circumstances which may be pleasant in the short term as fulfilling God's overall plans. There is nothing permanent in this scene for God's people. They are passing through and while doing so, should keep alive the hope that the God of hope has planted within them. That which is hoped for is certain of fulfilment and is held out to be on the horizon. The attitude of the faithful as recorded in Heb 11:13 is worthy of consideration in connection with what Paul is making known, "These all died in faith, not having received the promises, but having seen them afar off, and were persuaded of them, and embraced them, and confessed that they were strangers and pilgrims on the earth".

25 The apostle seems to be saying in this verse, "But if we hope for that which we do not see we are doing well, this is what hope is all about". However, he does not really say that, although it could be read into the verse without doing despite to it. What he does is to add patient waiting to the expression, "but if we hope for that which we do not see". If we do not have it but are living in anticipation of receiving it, the character of spirit while waiting is all-important. It could be one of fretful impatience, a constant complaining to God and to fellow-believers about the rigours of the way and the seeming delay in realising the things hoped for.

Paul no doubt anticipated that there could be grumbling of some sort and so he uses a word which is full of meaning. He has introduced it already to great effect (2:7, 5:3, 4) and he will use it again. The word *hupomonē* means conquering patience. It implies that all that life can throw up against the believer, the one under pressure, will not only bear but turn it into profit. It is the spirit which no circumstance in life can defeat. This patience is characterised by the same strong word ("wait", *apekdechomai*) as already used in v.19. It is an intensive compound, a word charged with meaning, stressing the spirit that accompanies patience while holding on for God.

26 The opening word of this verse, rendered "Likewise" or, "In the same way", links up what follows with what has gone before. There are two views, however, on what Paul meant by the use of the word. Some consider that believers are sustained by hope (vv.24, 25) and likewise they are sustained by the Holy Spirit. Others consider that "Likewise" should link two actions of the Holy Spirit, firstly as in v.23 where they are noted as having His help as they groan under life's troubles, and secondly, His further help as He sustains them in their infirmities ("infirmity", RV). The latter view does not necessarily infer that the Holy Spirit is not involved in hope. If His exclusion were pressed too far, the result would be hope which is human and help which is divine. It is better, therefore, to accept that Paul intended "Likewise" to cover the Holy Spirit's support in the groaning, His encouragement in hope, and His help with the infirmity of the saints.

The word rendered "help" (*sunantilambanomai*) only occurs twice in the NT, here and at Luke 10:40. In its use by Luke, the sense comes out clearly. In the home at Bethany, Martha petitioned the Lord to bid Mary to help her. The inference was that she could not cope with the household chores on her own, she required help. So here, in this world, believers cannot cope with life's problems without help, in this case, divine help. There is weakness, even in the strongest. In this verse Paul links himself with all other believers, "the Spirit helpeth our infirmity". The infirmity should be considered as singular, meaning a general condition, rather than plural (as in the AV), inferring the different aspects of weakness which manifest themselves.

The RV rendering, "We know not how to pray as we ought" could be taken to mean that we do not know how to pray. This does not appear to be what Paul meant. The order of the words in the original reads, "for what we may pray, as it behoves, we know not". This suggests that Paul was making known that life's needs are so complex it is quite beyond anyone to interpret them adequately. There is not doubt that we do not know how to express ourselves. Apart from inability to interpret what is the will of God and therefore what is best for us, there is the limitation of language to put what is being petitioned into words. If the believer were left unaided, the outcome would be tragic. It could be thought that those with a ready turn of speech had an advantage over those whose power of expression was poor. God, however, has made ample provision to level things out. He understood Hannah's prayer, spoken in the heart, although Eli thought she was intoxicated (1 Sam 1:13-16).

There is no thought in the apostle's mind that because of what he has stated, prayer should cease and the whole matter left to the Holy Spirit to intercede for all saints, all the time, whether they had a distinct burden or not. This idea is in total conflict with the teaching of the Holy Scriptures, as stated in Luke 18:1, "Men ought always to pray and not to faint". The Holy Spirit is here to guide. Prayer should be expressed in the best terms available to those who pray and in an attitude befitting coming into the divine presence. Extenuating circumstances may produce exceptional prayer and a righteous and loving God will understand, but these are not the norm for believers.

The groanings associated with the intercession of the Holy Spirit are those which He draws forth from the saints. They cannot really be ascribed to the Spirit, as a divine Person is not affected by things, although obviously moved by the needs and the weaknesses of God's people. It is the Spirit who helps believers to cry to God. He is the other Comforter whose coming was intimated by the Lord. It is He who will intercede in perfect harmony with the mind and will of God. Although despair often overwhelms God's saints, it should never be looked upon as inevitable. It should be remembered that the Spirit is associated with the groanings and He intercedes with a God who cares and who will answer according to His will and the best interests of His people. Paul prayed three times that the thorn in the flesh might be removed. His prayer was answered, not according to what he requested, but what was best for him, "my grace is sufficient for thee: my strength is made perfect in weakness". The Holy Spirit therefore makes intercession. The word *huperentunchanō* ("intercession") is found only here in the NT. It is therefore reserved for the Holy Spirit. It is a great comfort to know that it is He who will go to God to present the petitions of the saints.

27 There is a contrast suggested in the opening words of this verse. The omniscient God searches the hearts. He who knows the mind of the Spirit, also knows the turmoil in the hearts of His saints. The groanings which are there are not ignored as being of no consequence; they are acknowledged for what they are, interpreted and presented by the Spirit of God.

The statement, "He that searcheth the hearts", is of frequent occurrence in one form or another in the OT. It is possible that Paul thought of the time when the sons of Jesse were paraded before Samuel and the Lord had to correct the prophet's thoughts, "Look not on his countenance...for man looketh on the outward appearance, but the Lord looketh on the heart" (1 Sam 16:7). It is more likely, however, that the apostle was thinking of Ps 139, which begins, "O Lord, thou hast searched me and known me". The psalm is one of the clearest passages in the OT on the omniscience and omnipresence of God. It was held by the Jews as the jewel amongst all the psalms because of the grandeur of the language and the loftiness of its substance. It would therefore come readily to the apostle's mind. He thought in terms of the Scriptures and when he expressed himself it is clear that the letter and principles of the Word had influenced his thinking. The next chapter, ch.9, is one of the clearest examples in the NT of how a writer used the Scriptures to provide an authoritative framework for his message.

The omniscience of God is demonstrated in this verse, and like His other attributes, it confirms His deity. It is one of the characteristics of His nature of which He has been pleased to give glimpses in the Scriptures. It declares that God knows everything. The apostle's awareness of the attributes of God shines through his writings and this reference in 8:27 is an example of how it is woven into the fabric of his thoughts.

God knows what is in the mind of the Spirit. To another assembly Paul wrote concerning the role in communicating the mind of God, "for the Spirit searcheth all things, yea, the deep things of God" (1 Cor 2:10). Some versions follow the rendering of the AV and give "because he maketh intercession". This infers that God fully knows what is the meaning of the unutterable groans of the Spirit *because* He makes intercession "according to God". Other versions give "that" instead of "because". The original, *hoti*, can be understood in either way and it is therefore better left open.

The words, "the will of" are not in the original but it is generally agreed that they should be supplied. However, the phrase reads literally, "because, according to God, he supplicates on behalf of saints". The expression "according to God" is in a position of emphasis. In 2 Cor 7:10 the "godly sorrow" which works repentance is literally "sorrow according to God". Hence interceding according to God may mean with divine understanding and sympathy; as only a divine Person can; or in a manner consistent with deity. (See also Eph 4:24 where the new man is created "after God" in righteousness and true holiness.)

Such intercession is doubtless according to the will of God and it is for saints. All the children of God are included. A special class is not contemplated. Even the humblest may take courage that they are amongst the saints, on an equal footing with the rest as far as the will of God and the intercession of the Holy Spirit are concerned.

Notes

14 Vine makes an interesting point, "In his standing, a believer is a child of God; in his state he should be a son of God, and only as he gives evidence that he is a son of God, can he really claim to be a child of God".

20 The word "vanity" (*mataiotēs*, "folly", "no profit") is in a position of stress in the original. It reads, "For to vanity the creation was subjected". Denney suggests that the idea is looking for something one cannot find; hence of futility, frustration and disappointment.

(d) *The providence and purposes of God (vv.28-39)*

- v.28 "And we know that all things work together for good to them that love God, to them who are the called according to his purpose.
- v.29 For whom he did foreknow, he also did predestinate to be conformed to the image of his Son, that he might be the firstborn among many brethren.
- v.30 Moreover whom he did predestinate, them he also called: and whom he called, them he also justified: and whom he justified, them he also glorified.
- v.31 What shall we then say to these things? If God be for us, who can be against us?
- v.32 He that spared not his own Son, but delivered him up for us all, how shall he not with him also freely give us all things?
- v.33 Who shall lay any thing to the charge of God's elect? It is God that justifieth.
- v.34 Who is he that condemneth? It is Christ that died, yea rather, that is risen again, who is even at the right hand of God, who also maketh intercession for us.
- v.35 Who shall separate us from the love of Christ? shall tribulation, or distress, or persecution, or famine, or nakedness, or peril, or sword?
- v.36 As it is written, For thy sake we are killed all the day long; we are accounted as sheep for the slaughter.
- v.37 Nay, in all these things we are more than conquerors through him that loved us.
- v.38 For I am persuaded, that neither death, nor life, nor angels, nor principalities, nor powers, nor things present, nor things to come,
- v.39 Nor height, nor depth, nor any other creature, shall be able to separate us from the love of God, which is in Christ Jesus our Lord."

28 From v.28 to the end of the chapter the providence and the purposes of God are made known. God's determination to bring to glory all those whom He has called is clearly stated. Present suffering does not alter this, but on the contrary is shown to be the forerunner of the glory yet to come. Robert Lee, quoting Prof D. Smith writes, "The worth of a man's religion is determined by the help which it affords him in dark days. And this is the peculiar glory of Christianity that it is a faith for the sorrowful". Few verses have done as much to encourage the sorrowful as 8:28.

The whole teaching of the epistle thus far builds up to the majestic closing of this section. The work of Christ is the triumphant closing note. Challenges issued to all created intelligences to lay anything to the charge of God's elect find no reply, since the death and resurrection of Christ make all things secure. Hence, nothing can separate from the love of God which is in Christ Jesus our Lord. Present security and eternal union are a fitting conclusion to such a gospel of grace.

The knowledge of the saints mentioned here is one of five occurrences of the expression in the epistle. It signifies that in the saints there is a knowledge derived from intuition that what follows it factual. This is, "that to them that love God, all things work together for good" (RV). The expression "them that love God" occurs only here in the epistle, and while it is descriptive of believers generally, it indicates that only those who have the love of God in their hearts and who are living in the good of it, accept that all things are being made to work together for good.

There is considerable variance of views amongst commentators regarding "all things work together for good". Some hold that it would be better to render the phrase, "God maketh all things work together", which is true, but there is very little manuscript authority for it. Others maintain that it should be, "He maketh all things work together", meaning that it is the Holy Spirit who is the active force, since He is the subject of the two previous verses. The problem with this view is that v.29 refers to God and a sudden change of that magnitude is not to be expected in the flow of Paul's argument. Regardless of how this phrase is understood, it comes back to the basic fact that God is in command and all things are within His control. There are no free radicals in God's universe.

The word *agathos* ("good") suggests things that are good and useful. The expression "all things" which Robert Lee states occurs 22 times in the Scriptures, means that, however contrary they may seem to the believer, they are fitting into place in God's ways and in His own time for good. Jacob did not see this when he exclaimed "all these things are against me" (Gen 42:36). As far as he was concerned, all things that affected him had fallen out of God's control. As it turned out, God had worked in a remarkable way for his blessing, the good of his family and, in the long term, the nation that in His purpose would spring from his loins. It is always a good exercise to look back over life and see how God has ordered events for His glory and the good of His saints. Despite the seeming chaos in the world, it is still a God-controlled world. His limits may appear to be stretched at times, but He never lets nations or men go beyond what He decrees.

Those who love God are now described as "those who are called". The term "called" occurs eleven times in the NT and of these seven are attributed to Paul. It signifies the action of the divine; it is the call of God, not of man, nor even partly of man. The word "called" is nowhere used in the epistles of those who have merely heard the gospel; it always refers to those who have been saved. The call therefore has been effectual and it is in accordance with the eternal counsels of God. His grace in the gospel has called those whom He has foreknown and they love Him, not through any merit of their own, but because He first loved them. Eternal security is therefore an undeniable fact.

29 To be called according to His purpose, leads to a consideration of the divine procedure from eternity past to the eternal ages of the future. Salvation originated with God and it will be consummated by Him also. Human merit plays no part in it, but grace brings in the undeserving. The pervious verse had stated that God works all things for good to them that love Him. Their love is not to be interpreted as the reason why God loves, rather it should be understood as the effect of His love. Why God should so set His love on any is a mystery, but those who experience it gladly respond by loving Him.

It is to be regretted that so many battles have been fought over these two verses. Trying to make the sovereignty of God and the freedom of man compatible has proved impossible for many. Two extremes have resulted, neither of which meets all the requirements of Scripture. Extreme Calvinism has left it impossible for man to be considered a free agent in any sense. Arminianism has advocated the fullest freedom and has left no room for the sovereignty of God. Lee quotes Rabbi Duncan on the subject. He bluntly declared that Calvinism was all house with no door and Arminianism was all door and no house.

Prescience is one of God's attributes. In v.28 Paul referred to them that love God. He now proceeds to show how these saints feature in the divine plans. Firstly, they were foreknown (*proginōskō*, here; 11:2; 1 Pet 1:20). The aspect of foreknowledge to which Paul refers here can hardly be the general fact that God knows all things before they come into existence. Neither is it foreknowledge which results from a divine decree; this is declaring that if He decrees that a things shall be, He foresees that it will be. The aspect of foreknowledge here is linked to those He loved; those He marked out; those He chose beforehand. In this connection Kelly's comment is worthy of consideration, "It is important to observe that the apostle does not speak of a passive or naked foreknowledge, as if God only saw beforehand what some would be, and do, or believe. His foreknowledge is of persons, not of their state or conduct; it is not *what*, but *whom* He foreknew".

The next link in the chain is predestination. The word is *proorizo*, "to set the boundary beforehand", "to appoint beforehand to some particular end", "to mark out beforehand". It focuses attention on the destination of the persons who feature in God's plans. He does not seek anyone's permission before He acts. God is not subject to fickle human choices or approval. It is not chance or an emergency measure to make the best of a bad job; it is what God pre-determines and carries out according to His purposes. Predestination is according to His good pleasure and the counsel of His own will (Eph 1:5,11). He determines to do what He wills and He does it in the way that He determines. He wants to do it and He does it. There is no argument as to free-will placing restrictions on God. What He foreordains is according to His eternal purposes in Christ.

The purpose of predestination is now stated; it is that believers are to be conformed to the image of His Son. The change involved in being conformed is not a mere similarity; but a taking part, a conformity to the person of Christ. The word *summorphos* ("conformed") occurs only here and Phil. 3:21, where it is translated "fashioned like". In that passage Paul is dealing with the nature of the change in the believer's body at the rapture. It will be no longer a body of humiliation as it is now, but one fashioned like unto His body of glory. In our verse the change is twofold. There is a genuine conformity to Christ now; as Morris states, not "that believers should muddle along in modest respectability", but a real Christlikeness, reflecting His graces in every aspect of daily living.

At the rapture the complete change will take place. There will be no flaws in the resemblance then. It will be a permanent conformity to the person of Christ. The reason for the great transformation is given. It is that He might become the firstborn of many brethren. The title "firstborn" is one of rank and dignity. It does not mean born first. Esau was born first but Jacob was the firstborn. There are other references in the NT to Christ as being firstborn, but here the thrust of Paul's teaching is that He will have the pre-eminent place amongst the many brethren who are conformed to His image and who will share His glory.

30 The calling mentioned here is not the call of the gospel to all men to forsake their sins and turn to Christ for salvation. It is not mere "invitation", it is the calling of those who were foreordained; it produced the desired result, for all who were called were justified. From the human standpoint, when it is realised that the calling is a link in the eternal chain, foreknowledge and predestination are readily accepted. The first two links of the chain are the secrets of the heart of God, disclosed but not explained, which believers accept by faith. The call of God however, is appreciated by the senses; but the very fact that it was heard in the soul confirms that divine purpose was in operation before it could become effectual. If God called us then He foreknew us.

The many facets of the great work of justification have already been set out. Those who have been called have been justified by faith (5:1), justified by blood (5:9), justified by grace (5:16). The death of Christ has resulted in an eternal security which is unassailable. Now the apostle can place justification in the chain. This great link not only reflects the glory of God but assures those who believe that the righteousness reckoned to them in time will stay with them throughout eternity.

Denney's comment has been deemed by many to be worthy of quoting. In connection with the phrase "and whom he justified, them he also glorified", he states, "it is the most daring anticipation of faith that even the NT contains: the life has not to be taken out of it by the philosophical consideration that with God there is neither before nor after". The glorifying in its fullest sense is still future. Paul, however, looking back and looking forward contemplates the great plan of God and the believer's place in it by grace. Nothing has affected God's foreknowledge and predestination, or His calling and justification. It is certain therefore that the glorifying which is still to come will not fail either. In the face of that certainty Paul can assure his correspondents that they have the good of that now. It is theirs as a present possession and it is only a short step ahead for full realisation.

31 Once again Paul uses the expression which is characteristic of this epistle.

It is put in the form of a question, "What shall we say then to these things?" The apostle, in the presentation of his arguments, seems to feel the need to ask at certain points, "What can we deduce from the foregoing?" When he raises the question he invariably gives the answer himself. The question here is answered by another question, "If God be for us, who can be against us?" The matter could be left there as there is no power that can defeat the power of Almighty God. The apostle, however, goes on to show why there is no possibility of any created intelligence challenging the provision God has made, or the righteousness of the God who made it. All that God requires to do is to point to Calvary, "He that spared not his own Son". There is the proof, if proof be needed of God's interest in His saints.

There are times when believers begin to wonder if God is really for them. The complexities of life and its many trials cause doubts to arise. The eye of faith is encouraged, however, when confronted by seemingly impossible odds, to look to the ground which can never shift, the love of God is displayed in the gift of His Son. If God did not spare His own Son, all else is of little significance. Any challenge to the omnipotence and righteousness of God is doomed to failure before it is issued.

It looks as if there is an allusion to Ps 118 in the question, "If God be for us, who can be against us?" The psalmist said, "The Lord is on my side; I will not fear: what can man do unto me?" Since Ps 118 is the closing portion of the Hallel it would come readily to Paul's mind when he dictated the epistle. The psalmist had every confidence, "The Lord is on my side; what can man do unto me?" It certainly looks as if Paul had the same assurance when he wrote to the Romans, "If God be for us, who can be against us?"

32 There were two rhetorical questions in the previous verse. A third rhetorical question is now raised, "how shall he not with him also freely give us all things" This third question follows the remarkable statement, "He that spared not his own Son, but delivered him up for us all". This is the proof that God is for His saints. The apostle had unfolded the dealings of God for and with His saints from foreknowledge and predestination through to glorification. A triumphant challenge, "If God be for us, who can be against us?" allows Paul to give the proof of God's interest in His own. If God did not spare His own Son but delivered Him up for us all, everything else is of little significance. If God is prepared to go to the ultimate and deliver up His Son, what He will do for His saints can never be in doubt.

It is held by many that Paul had the mount Moriah experience in his mind when he dictated this wonderful statement. It is certainly reminiscent of Abraham's readiness to deliver up his son Isaac (Gen 22:16). However suggestive that might be, Isaac was not sacrificed. The knife was withheld at the crucial moment. In the sacrifice of God's own Son, there was no holding back, Christ was delivered up for us all. In this verse there is no suggestion that Christ was delivered up by the envy of the Jews, or by any other human agency. He was delivered up by God the Father.

There are restrictions in the givingness of God. He freely gives. There is no grudging with Him. There is no withholding. He gives "all things". Nothing that can be for the good of His saints will be kept from them. Paul includes himself with all who believe; no one will be missed out. The inclusion of the two words "with him" indicate that the rewards of the sacrifice of Christ will be shared with those who will be conformed to His image. God who was unsparing in the giving of His Son, will be unsparing again; giving "all things" to those who are named in the next verse as "God's elect".

33 Vine suggests that this verse and the next two verses contain metaphors from the court of justice. This is an interesting submission, especially when the main characters in court cases, the accuser, the accused, the judge and the executioner are considered. These, Vine asserts, are indicated in the three rhetorical questions in vv.31-35 of the four characters portrayed, however, the accuser and the executioner have no part to play. As far as believers are concerned, no one can assail their position because God has justified them and they will never come into condemnation.

In *Written for our Learning* there is a suggestion that there are two allusions to the OT in this verse. The first one refers to the title, "God's elect". The second one refers to a challenge made by Isaiah, "He is near that justifieth me; who will contend with me?" (50:8). The title "elect" as used here, brings together what is involved in the terms of v.30. Those who were foreknown and predestinated are the chosen of God; they are the elect. This is not a term which is exclusive to the NT. The Lord Jesus was obviously referred to by Isaiah when he wrote, "Behold my servant, whom I uphold, mine elect in whom my soul delighteth" (42:1). The Jews also associated this title with the Messiah. As the Saviour hung upon the cross, the people and the rulers derided Him saying, "He saved others, let him save himself if he be the Christ, the chosen (elect) of God" (Luke 23:35). As a nation, the people of Israel were also known as the elect. Isaiah wrote of them, "My people, my chosen (elect)...they shall show forth my praises" (43:20,21).

In the NT the elect are a new class and some wonderful things are recorded about them as the chosen of God. If God, of His own volition, within the scope of His own attributes and counsels, determines to make a choice, then He will not be influenced or deterred by any power external to Himself. As proof of this, the closing verses of Rom 8 pose questions and give answers which show that God's elect are inviolable. There is none to condemn, separate, or lay anything to the charge of God's chosen ones. No creature can hinder the outflow of God's love to those He has made the objects of it. In answer to the question raised, "Who shall lay anything to the charge of God's elect?" the apostle replies, "It is God that justifieth". There is no case to answer.

The second allusion to the OT is also to the prophecy of Isaiah. The chapter from which it is take commences with a declaration from God that He had not rejected Israel; their sufferings were the outcome of their own sins. The sufferings of the Messiah at their hands and at their instigation, are stated, "I gave my back to the smiters and my cheeks to them that plucked off the hair" (50:6). Nevertheless, this rejected One is seen to be justified by the Lord God and there is no one who can condemn Him. As for the people, there is blessing for those who will fear the Lord and obey the voice of His servant. God is gracious and He remembers those who are the objects of His love. Paul was not unaware of this when he wrote to the Romans and issued his challenge, "Who shall lay anything to the charge of God's elect? It is God that justifieth".

34 The imagery of the court room continues in this verse. Many take the opening words, "Who is he that condemneth?" to apply to the closing thought of v.33, so that it should read, "It is God that justifieth, who is he that condemneth?" It is true that if God justifies, no one can condemn the persons who are justified and the matter is settled for ever in their favour. As the apostle goes on to show, the facts of Christ's death, resurrection and ascension are essential as being unassailable proofs that God acted righteously in justifying. His justice was not sacrificed because of His mercy. In view of the sacrificial work of Christ at Calvary, God can afford to be merciful and still retain His righteousness.

The statement that Christ is at the right hand of God is an obvious allusion to Ps 110:1. This verse from the Psalms is one of the most quoted portions of the Scripture in the NT. It is taken up by Peter, Paul and the writer to the Hebrews and used in many ways to extol the person of the Lord Jesus. It declares the approval of God. He it was who said, "Sit thou at my right hand, until I make thine enemies thy footstool". This was never said of angels, as Hebrews makes clear, "But to which of the angels said he at any time, Sit thou on my right hand, until make thine enemies thy footstool?" (Heb 1:13). So here, the power and authority of the position at God's right hand is noted. The apostle had to record this as the fitting outcome of the work of Christ.

The practical result of being at the right hand of God is that Christ makes intercession for us. It is a remarkable climax to all that has been set out as the privileges of the elect. Their cause was not only undertaken at the cross by a once-for-all sacrifice, they have also become the objects of a perpetual ministry of the One who accomplished it. His experience gained during His life on earth has fitted Him for the work He is now carrying out as a faithful high priest, interceding before God for the saints, those redeemed by His own blood.

35 The opening words of this verse, "Who shall separate us from the love of Christ are answered in v.39, "…nor any other creature, shall be able to separate us from the love of God, which is in Christ Jesus our Lord". The word rendered "separate" occurs only twice in Romans, here and at v.39. It signifies "to create a space". When this is contemplated in connection with the love of Christ, a possibility of being separated from that love is a frightening consideration. It cannot be, however, as He Himself said, "I give unto them (my sheep) eternal life and they shall never perish, neither shall any man pluck them out of my hand. My Father, which gave them me, is greater than all; and no man is able to pluck them out of my Father's hand" (John 10:28,29).

A list of things which might separate us from the love of Christ is now given. Each one has meaning in itself. "Tribulation" (*thlipsis*) has the general meaning of strong pressure. The nature of any particular pressure is not stated here, but obviously what is involved are the trials of life which bear down upon God's saints at different times and in different ways in daily living. "Distress" (*stenochōria*), refers to straightened circumstances. The word is peculiar to Paul, occurring at 2:9 where it is rendered "anguish" and twice in 2 Corinthians where it is rendered "distresses". It suggests the hardships which befall men and women. Pressure may be external and distress may be internal. Both are serious afflictions, but when considered against the love of Christ, they do not have the power to separate.

Persecution was certainly rife in Paul's day. Famine (or, hunger) was always a possibility in apostolic times. "Nakedness" conveys the thought of a lack of clothes, a lack of the basic requirements of life and destitution may result. "Peril" suggests danger, and "the sword", signifying the ultimate sacrifice, was never far away in the early days of the church's history, and indeed at other periods also when saints suffered for their faith. But the great comforting fact remains that the trials which Paul lists, despite their severity, even if they culminate in death, will never separate saints from the love of Christ.

36 This verse contains a quotation from Ps 44:22 LXX. It follows seven things which Paul lists as being possible means of separation from the love of Christ. Taken together they give a comprehensive and formidable picture of unfavourable circumstances. From what Paul lists in other epistles about his sufferings for the testimony's sake, it is clear that he had experience of the first six. The last one, the sword, he would face at the end of his earthly pathway. How near he was on several occasions to death is recorded in Acts, especially the situation where he was left as dead after being stoned (Acts 14:19). It was perhaps this experience that he referred to in 2 Corinthians when he claimed to have been caught up to the third heaven (2 Cor 12:2). The apostle therefore was not conveying to the Romans things which were in his imagination; he had actual experience of them and yet he was convinced that not one could separate from the love of Christ.

The reference to the OT is Ps 44:22. What appears to be a statement about suffering and slaughter without a ray of hope is turned by Paul to a note of triumph. If it were the case that Christians were killed all the day long and counted as sheep for the slaughter, the fact that it was for Christ's sake would make it all worthwhile.

The psalm from which the quotation is taken describes a period of national distress and while it acknowledges some of the great things God had done for the nation, the sufferings of the time then present were a mystery to the people. They claimed they had not forgotten God and yet they were martyrs for Him. The psalmist did not know that some of the words he penned to describe the people's despair would be taken up in a future day to describe the sacrifices of another company. For Christ's sake they were being killed all day long and considered sheep to be slaughtered. The love of Christ was real, but the trials to be faced were real also. Unlike the people described in Ps 44, the believers in Paul's day had the joy of knowing that all their afflictions were opportunities to share in the sufferings of Christ. For that privilege they were prepared to glory in their tribulations.

37 The opening word "Nay" (*alla*), is perhaps better rendered "But", to introduce something contrary to what might have been the expected effect of the forces of opposition just stated. The apostle, however, will not allow the possibility of defeat to stand for a single moment. He states "in all these things we are more than conquerors". He overlooks nothing. Not one of the trials he has listed has any power to break the bonds of the love of Christ which unite the Saviour with the saints.

Instead of succumbing to tribulation in all its aspects, Paul triumphantly declares that "all these things" are turned to advantage. There is no sense of defeat, all is complete victory, as he states, "we are more than conquerors". It has been noted that the word rendered "are more than conquerors" (*hupernikaō*) which occurs only here in the NT, has no English equivalent. Indeed, Morris comments, " 'We are more than conquerors' is an inspired piece of translation. It emphasises the totality of the victory that God gives His beloved". Vine also makes an interesting note. He writes, "As Chrysostom says, 'This is a new order of victory, to conquer by means of our adversary' ". Considering the intensity of the trials outlined in the two previous verses, the conclusion that Paul arrives at does seem contrary to reason. But it is true. God gives grace and enablement to turn what seem to be impossible odds into a conquering triumph which will bring glory to Him and reward to His saints.

The secret of success is contained in the phrase, "through him that loved us". One might have expected Paul would have stated, "through him that loves us", thereby declaring a love that is ever-present. The verb, however, is in the past tense, which no doubt turns our attention to the cross, or even, as some consider, to eternity past. Since it is a timeless love, it goes on for ever. Any thought of an inherent ability in the saints to turn adversity into triumph must be discountenanced. The grace and the power are from a divine source. Here Paul states, "It is through Him that loved us", no doubt referring to Christ and His work on the cross. The help of an indwelling Spirit and the love of God, however, cannot be ruled out; as all members of the Godhead have an interest in the saints. The Holy Spirit makes intercession on earth and the Lord makes intercession in heaven. The saints are therefore well represented.

38 Paul's persuasion was not an opinion. It was far more than that. It was a conviction based on assured facts. Sometimes he expressed his persuasion as a conviction impressed upon him by the Lord. Later in the epistle he writes, "I am persuaded by the Lord Jesus" (14:14). Further on in the epistle he admits to being influenced by others. "And I myself also am persuaded of you, my brethren, that ye also are full of goodness" (15:14). The verb is perfect passive, signifying here (and in the two examples given) that he was impressed by forces outside of himself and that the result was permanent; he was not likely to change. So he writes, "I have been persuaded", and he lists ten contenders which could possibly separate saints from the love of God.

The ten items raised by the apostle seem to be set out in four pairs and two singles. Each one is preceded by *oute* ("nor"), which keeps stressing the negative. There is no possibility that any one of the factors listed can separate. Taken singly, not one more than another has the power to alter the status of those who have put their trust in Christ. The believers therefore should have no fear; they are, as the previous verse states, "more than conquerors".

The first two contenders are death and life, and Paul states categorically in the next verse what is true of all, "they have not the power to separate". Death is an obvious enemy. Unless the coming of the Lord intervenes, it has to be faced. There is no easy way of avoiding it; it is the common lot of every creature. Paul himself acknowledges its terror in his writings although he himself had come to terms with the thought of it and could write to the Philippians, "For to me to live is Christ, and to die is gain" (1:21). Nevertheless, what has been aptly described as the king of terrors and the terror of kings need not terrify the saints, it cannot separate from the love of God which is in Christ Jesus our Lord.

While life may seem to be a feature which is not antagonistic, the expression has to be taken in its widest sense. It is the opposite of death, and if death has no power, then life has no power either. Life with all its temptations and trials is a formidable force. Not everything about life is serene. As far as believers are concerned, it is while they are alive that they have to contend with all that life brings and will do to them. Despite that, it cannot affect the final issue, it has no power to separate.

The reference to angels may seem strange, unless Paul was referring to the angels who had left their first estate and had fallen. Since there is hostility suggested, it is highly unlikely that he was referring to angels who served God and who fly to do His bidding. There is a sense, however, in which the danger of angel worship might be involved. It was so with the Colossians, something Paul condemned (Col 2:18). However, Paul has chosen to leave the matter open and there it has to be left. In the same way, "principalities" are not defined. There could be demons in the heavenlies or earthly potentates. Some consider that the angels portray the heavenly aspect and principalities the earthly one. Elsewhere in Paul's writings "principalities" ("rulers") are noted as spirit beings. To the Ephesians he wrote, "For we wrestle not against flesh and blood, but against principalities" (Eph 6:12). Whatever the apostle had in mind, it is clear that his persuasion was that the powers of darkness, heavenly or earthly, could not separate from the love of God.

The fifth contender to be considered as a possible antagonist is "powers". Paul here personifies the word to give it the sense that no matter who or what has been invested with power it will not rob God's saints of their union with Christ. In this present age or in the age to come the status of the believer is inviolable. That there is might involved in "powers" there can be no doubt. It may at times overwhelm some and cause them to stumble, but it will never separate. Literally, Paul is saying that "powers" (*dunamis*) are not able (*dunamai*) to separate. The "powers" lack the power to come between the saints and the love of God in Christ Jesus our Lord.

39 Having referred to things present and things to come, time in all its aspects, the present and future, the apostle moves on in this verse to consider space. The two words chosen imply what is limitless. The heavens are infinite and the heavenly bodies for number are beyond computation. The vastness of the universe, however, cannot separate the Lord from His saints, neither can it rob them of the sense of His presence. The psalmist was persuaded that there was no place in the universe which was outwith the presence of God. He wrote, "If I ascend up into the heaven thou art there: if I make my bed in hell, behold thou art there" (Ps 139:8). Paul had the same persuasion. Space, infinite though it was in its vastness, could not sever the tie which bound him and his fellow-believers to the Lord.

The depths to which the apostle refers conveys the thought of the great unknown. It has to be considered in relation to the universe, and not the earth. There are limits to the earth, but the universe appears to know no boundaries. Whatever was in the mind of the apostle in his choice of words, there seems little doubt that he introduced them as a climax. His unfolding of the gospel in its many facets and in all its fulness is brought to a triumphant conclusion. Those who believed its message and were justified on the principle of faith are assured of an unbreakable and eternal link with the One who made it all possible. Nothing that God has created can sever the bond. No matter how much power is invested in anything in the universe, in the end it is as nothing compared with the infinite power of the Creator. It is that power which will keep the saints in the love of God which is in Christ Jesus our Lord.

Notes

26 "Infirmities" (*astheneia*, "weakness") is better "infirmity" (singular).

28 Paul's use of the word "purpose" here is not just a general statement about God's plans. It signifies God's decision from eternal ages that there would be a calling out as a result of the sacrifice of Christ. Those who are called are not called on the ground of merit, but on account of God's good pleasure.

29 Christ is the image (*eikōn*) of the invisible God (Col 1:15). He is the exact expression, the true representation of God. As the perfect expression of the invisible God, absolutely so, He could say, "He that hath seen me hath seen the Father". As used of believers here the word suggests something more than a mere likeness to Christ. There will be a conformity to Christ. Believers will have bodies fashioned like unto His body of glory.

32 Denney comments, "The argument of selfishness is that he who has done so much need do no more; that of love, that he who has done so much is certain to do more".

35 "Persecution" (*diōgmos*, "chase", "pursuit", from *diōkō*, "to pursue"), when used in an evil sense, means "to persecute".

37 On the phrase "more than conquerors" (*hupernikōmen*), Denney comments, "A word probably coined by Paul who loves compounds with *huper*".

V. The Justification of God (9:1-11:36)

There are many views regarding the place of Rom 9-11 in the argument which Paul advances in his epistle. Some hold that it is a parenthesis, others that it runs parallel with what is conveyed in chs. 3-8. Some commentators consider that the three chapters have little connection with the major theme and therefore stand alone. However, although the three chapters appear to be a digression from the main theme, there is continuity of thought. They are not an excursion into another subject; they are an integral part of the overall argument.

At the beginning of the epistle Paul established that the gospel was not an emergency measure introduced by God because His plans and purposes were thwarted. Regarding the gospel, the apostle states, "which he had promised afore by the prophets in the holy scriptures" (1:2). As his argument develops, Paul shows clearly that God's dealings were not innovative, as he states, "But now the righteousness of God without (apart from) the law is manifested, being witnessed by the law and the prophets" (3:21). The principle which all would have to accept in order to get right with God was one which had already been declared in the OT (Hab 2:14) and made clear by Paul, "The just shall live by faith" (1:17). There was no unrighteousness with God in calling out Gentiles and Jews by the gospel. Those He called had no righteousness of their own as He made clear, "There is none righteous, no not one" (3:10). Justification was on the principle of faith and not on works of merit.

The Jewish nation, however, had a long tradition behind it. To a great extent the Jews believed that the promises of God were intended for Abraham's natural descendants and that they would be fulfilled in them by their own works. Paul's irrefutable logic in ch.4 proved that this was not the case; justification was by faith. The apostle knew there were objections by the Jews to what he was propounding. Not long after his conversion he was engaged in dialogue with them concerning the fact that Jesus was the Christ. In the synagogues of the various towns that he visited he advanced his arguments. He was aware that it might be claimed that if God was blessing the Gentiles, and not through the Jew, then God had gone back on His promises to Israel. Some might have maintained that there was therefore unrighteousness with God; that Scriptures were not trustworthy, and indeed the character of God was at stake. To meet these objections, the apostle sets out to establish the truth of the sovereignty of God in ch.9. God is not answerable to anyone. Furthermore, man has a will of his own which he exercises. Nevertheless, in relation to his salvation it is his duty to come in the way of God's appointing. This Paul develops in ch.10 where he unfolds the possibilities of faith. As to the future and the establishment of the kingdom of Israel, this has been postponed. The Messiah was rejected and the nation will have to wait and suffer nationally until God's timing brings them again to blessing. This theme is the subject of ch.11.

To meet Jewish objections was not an easy task for Paul. The nation of Israel had been prepared by God for great things. There were privileges and glories which marked them out as a special people, but they had violated the law, persecuted the prophets, and had crucified their Messiah. The condition in which they found themselves was not attributable to unfaithfulness on God's part, but was chargeable to themselves. The gospel was presented to them nationally as is clear from the early chapters of the Acts, but they refused its message, and so the gospel went out to the Gentiles.

Paul's argument in chs. 9-11 is clothed in OT thought. By quotations and allusions he proves there was no change of heart with God. He had not gone back on His promises. What He was doing was perfectly consistent with His character: there was no unrighteousness with Him. The real cause was the hard and impenitent heart of the people on whom He had bestowed such blessings in the past.

Although the charge may be laid that the promises of God had failed, Paul shows in ch.9 that God had not promised that every single Jew would be saved. They were all responsible as individuals to believe. Nevertheless, as ch.9 makes clear, God's promises are being fulfilled at present, a remnant is being saved by grace. In addition, God will yet fulfil His promises, He will save all Israel as ch.11 asserts. There is no unrighteousness with God. His integrity is flawless. This is what Paul defends in Rom 9-11.

1. God's Sovereign Choice
9:1-29

(a) *Paul's sorrow of heart (vv.1-5)*

v.1 "I say the truth in Christ, I lie not, my conscience also bearing me witness in the Holy Ghost,
v.2 That I have great heaviness and continual sorrow in my heart.
v.3 For I could wish that myself were accursed from Christ for my brethren, my kinsmen according to the flesh:
v.4 Who are Israelites; to whom pertaineth the adoption, and the glory, and the covenants, and the giving of the law, and the service of God, and the promises;
v.5 Whose are the fathers, and of whom as concerning the flesh Christ came, who is over all, God blessed for ever. Amen."

1 In saying, "I speak the truth in Christ", it has to be remembered that Paul was presenting his case as to his fellow-countrymen. It was how they would understand the expression that must be taken into account. It is not the equivalent of saying, "I speak as a Christian", that would not be accepted favourably by the Jews. It is not an oath, but a solemn asseveration, consciously as being one with Christ, that he is speaking the truth. It is similar to the OT form used by Elisha to Elijah. "As the Lord liveth and as thy soul liveth" (2 Kings 2:2,4,6). To give further emphasis, he adds, "I lie not". As he embarked on an explanation of God's dealings with the Jews, he judged it essential to remove all doubts about his own integrity.

To complete his solemn introduction he brings in the Holy Spirit. His conscience was enlightened and controlled by the Spirit. He was speaking with a good conscience. Paul is not really saying that his conscience was bearing him witness. His conscience was confirming what he was saying in the Holy Spirit. Although Paul was the one who was doing the speaking, it was the Holy Spirit who was guiding him. He spoke the truth in Christ; the Holy Spirit bore witness with him, so that two divine persons and his own conscience are involved. It is a striking way of making a solemn asseveration of the truth. It would be an unreasonable and bigoted person who would question the veracity of what he was about to say, since the divine support enlisted would ensure that he spoke in the fear of God.

2 Here Paul expresses how deeply he was involved in the matters he was about to raise. He was not delivering a message to the Jews as one who was a mere onlooker. Although his fellow-countrymen were in open hostility to God and had crucified the One who had proved conclusively that He was the Messiah, Paul could not separate himself from his link with the nation. He was a Jew and as he considered the way his fellows were going, he was filled with great heaviness and continual sorrow in His heart. He had an unceasing pain. There was no relief for it. His grief and discomfort were endless and it was because of the plight of the nation. The people had rejected God and God had cast them off. They were not better than the Gentiles (3:3). In their blindness they had opposed Paul and his brethren in every possible way. To Paul's credit, he never gave up feeling for them and trying at every opportunity to point them to Christ as the only one who could save them.

3 From this point Paul embarks on a series of allusions and quotations, using the Scriptures to advance his argument. The first allusion to the OT in the chapter is undoubtedly to Exod 32:31-32, which describes the earnestness of Moses as he pleads for the Israelites. In the narrative Moses confesses, "Oh this people have sinned a great sin, and have made them gods of gold". As a result of their idolatry, God declared to His servant, "Whosoever has sinned against me, him will I blot out of my book". The plea from Moses was, "Yet now, if thou wilt forgive their sin; and if not, blot me, I pray thee, out of thy book which thou hast written". Paul in his day, followed the example of Moses and he declared, "For I could wish (if it were possible) that myself were accursed from Christ for my brethren, my kinsmen according to the flesh".

The desire that Paul expressed, "I could wish that I myself were accursed from Christ", demonstrates the depth of feeling in God's servant for his fellow-countrymen. He was not simply relating the experience of someone else, he was deeply involved personally. He was prepared to bear the curse of God and to be dealt with judicially, which would mean separation from Christ, if only he could do something for his brethren, his kinsmen in the flesh. This of course was impossible, for once in Christ, means in Christ for ever. The climax at the end of ch.8 was that nothing can "separate us from the love of God, which is in Christ Jesus our Lord". Nevertheless, like Moses, Paul's deep concern for his people compelled him to declare his readiness to make the supreme sacrifice.

The desire which Paul declared was that he might change places with his kinsmen so that they would be saved. If it were possible, he would be prepared to be lost if they could be brought to Christ. It is unusual for Paul to refer to his kinsmen in the flesh as his brethren. Most often the word is used of his brethren in Christ. Nevertheless, it shows that his Jewish background was strong. To cut himself off from his roots was not an easy matter. He was a Jew, but his new relationships took precedence. He was by grace one of a new community, the church, and all who were members of that body were his brethren.

4 Having spoken of his kinsmen in the flesh, the apostle goes on to describe them by their national name, "who are Israelites". This is the first in Paul's list of privileges which marked the Israelites as being different from all other nations. They were honoured to be styled as descendants of Jacob who had his name changed by God to "Israel", meaning "a prince of God". Paul's sorrow of heart leads him to consider the peculiar features which were the rich heritage of this strange people. To be called "Israelites" was a title of honour, as demonstrated in the Lord's description of Nathaniel, "Behold an Israelite indeed, in whom there is no guile" (John 1:47). The Jews had a noble ancestry, but as Paul knew so well, it did not influence the nation for good. National pride held on to the name but beyond that there was little or nothing to boast about.

The second national advantage which Paul sets out is adoption. The children of Israel had been brought into the position of sonship, to them belonged "the adoption". This has not be to confused with the situation described in ch.8 whereby believers as individuals are noted as having received the Spirit of adoption (8:15). When Moses was given the command to go down to Egypt and confront Pharaoh, he was directed to say, "Thus saith the Lord, Israel is my son, even my firstborn" (Exod 4:22). This was remarkable grace. Israel was a nation of slaves, ground down by cruel taskmasters and yet God acknowledged them as His firstborn. Many years later the prophet Hosea confirmed the message Moses received in ch.11 of his prophecy, "When Israel was a child, then I loved him and called my son out of Egypt". Paul's mind, conditioned by years of studying the Scriptures, no doubt thought of Moses and Hosea when he wrote, "Israelites, to whom pertaineth the adoption". The nation occupied the privileged place of firstborn amongst all the nations of the world.

The Israelites also had "the glory". There was no other nation which had the Shekinah. It dwelt over the mercy-seat of the tabernacle; clear evidence of the presence of the living God with His people (Lev 16:2). When Solomon came to the end of his prayer at the dedication of the temple, the glory filled it (2 Chron 7:1,2), confirming the presence of the Lord with Israel. The heathens had their temples but only Israel could claim to have the glory. Here Paul does not elaborate on how the glory was perceived or manifested: he simply states that to Israel pertained the glory and there he leaves the subject to be considered by those he addressed.

Not only had the Israelites the adoption and the glory, but they also had the covenants. A few manuscripts give the singular, in which case the covenant referred to would be the covenant of Exod 24, referred to by some as the great covenant. Morris refers to a Jewish habit of distinguishing within the Exodus covenant three covenants, those at Horeb, in the plains of Moab and at Gerizim and Ebal. Most commentators, however, agree that the plural of the word was what Paul wrote and the covenants therefore refer to those made with Noah (Gen 9:9), Abraham (Gen 17:7-12), and Moses (Exod 24:8) and with Joshua and David at later dates. These solemn undertakings were lodged with the people of Israel, committed to their custody to be observed and maintained. In this, the nation was highly privileged; no other nation was in covenant relation with God.

The fifth privilege was the giving (or receiving) of the law. The body of legislation was unique, and although the possession of it was highly-prized by the Jews, it was in fact their greatest accuser. As argued so forcibly in ch.2 of this epistle, the ones who made their boast in the law and sought to teach others were the very ones who broke its precepts and dishonoured God. Nevertheless, when the question was asked, "What advantage then hath the Jew?" the answer was given, "Much every way: chiefly because unto them were committed the oracles of God" (3:1,2).

The service of God, or as the original simply states, "the service", refers to the tabernacle and temple services. The writer to the Hebrews confirms this, "Then verily the first covenant had also ordinances (ceremonies) of divine service and a worldly sanctuary" (Heb 9:1). In particular, the temple service was highly esteemed by the Jews, although the Jews were accused by the Lord of turning it into a den of thieves (Matt 21:13). Corrupt practices outweighed its religious significance.

The promises of God permeated the Scriptures and they pledged God to bless the nation in many different ways. The great promise to Abraham, repeated to others, stated, "I will establish my covenant between me and thee and thy seed after thee in their generations for an everlasting covenant, to be a God unto thee and to thy seed after thee" (Gen 17:7). Promises like this were held tenaciously by the Jews. They were privileged to have as a nation what God pledged. Not one promise of God has been broken, but by reason of the nation's apostasy many of His pledges have been deferred. God has passed over many generations but will fulfil them in the golden age when the Messiah whom the Jews rejected will take up the reins of government and rule in righteousness.

5 The illustrious forebears of the Jewish people are next on the list of privileges peculiar to Israel. The patriarchs, Abraham, Isaac, Jacob and others were revered by the Jews. God had manifested Himself to them in special ways and there was no other nation on earth that could claim to have such a heritage. Sadly the examples of the fathers had not been reflected in the ways of their descendants. The great ones of the past had been betrayed.

The greatest blessing of all completes the list. From the fathers the Anointed of God had come. Despite the failure of the descendants of the patriarchs, God's purposes had not been thwarted. The promised Messiah had come and His genealogy was strictly in accordance with the royal line preserved by God. Satan had tried to break the line. Godless men and women under his control had tried to corrupt it, but without success. And so Paul is able to record with thanksgiving, "The fathers, of whom concerning the flesh, Christ came". However He was not the exclusive possession of the nation of Israel. John makes this clear, "He came unto his own, and his own received him not. But as many as received him, to them gave he power to become the sons of God, even to them that believe on his name" (John 1:11,12).

There is considerable difference of opinion on whether the statement "God blessed for ever" refers to Christ. Many believe that the doxology here was to God the Father, on the grounds that there is no portion of the Scripture which states explicitly that Christ is God. According to these commentators, there are many passages which come near to stating that Christ is God, but they do not say so explicitly. To uphold this view, however, would seem to violate the text here. It is Christ who came into the world and as Paul considers the incarnation, he bursts out in a note of praise. The doxology is a short one, the second of four in the epistle, but it is a suitable climax to the list of privileges which were the portion of the Jews, although they had squandered them over the years. Paul is asserting deity to Christ at this point, enhancing the thought that Christ came into the world as a Jew, descended from the fathers; it called for praise, however short. Taking all things into account, it seems clear that Paul meant that the Christ who came in condescension, was "over all, God blessed for ever".

Notes

2 The combination of these two words "sorrow and pain" indicates the anguish through which Paul was going. With the addition of "continual" the unceasing nature of his discomfort is stressed.

3 Moule gives, "I could almost pray to be accursed". The wish brings out Paul's concern but it was an impossible one. Deep down he could never wish to be estranged from Christ but set against the plight of his fellow-countrymen it is understandable. Had his wish been granted, it still would not have availed anything.

For "accursed" (*anathema*), see 1 Cor 12:3; 16:22; Gal 1:8,9.

5 Regarding the privileges of the Jews and in particular to the coming of Christ, Morris gives an interesting quotation by Cragg, "It is disastrous to be blind, but to be blind to the crowning glory of one's own heritage is a tragedy which words alone cannot convey".

(b) *The sovereign right of God to choose whom He will (vv.6-13)*

> v.6   "Not as though the word of God hath taken none effect. For they are not all Israel, which are of Israel:
> v.7   Neither, because they are the seed of Abraham, are they all children: but, In Isaac shall thy seed be called.
> v.8   That is, They which are the children of the flesh, these are not the children of God: but the children of the promise are counted for the seed.
> v.9   For this is the word of promise, At this time will I come, and Sara shall have a son.
> v.10 And not only this; but when Rebecca also had conceived by one, even by our father Isaac;
> v.11 (For the children being not yet born, neither having done any good or evil, that the purpose of God according to election might stand, not of works, but of him that calleth;)
> v.12 It was said unto her, The elder shall serve the younger.
> v.13 As it is written, Jacob have I loved, but Esau have I hated."

6 As Paul's argument enters a new phase, he sets out to prove the righteousness of God in choosing whom He will. The character of God and the concern of His servant should be kept in mind: God is not a tyrant who will arbitrarily cast aside some and lift others for blessing. He is a merciful God. Indeed the verb, "to have mercy" occurs seven times in chs.9-11 and only once in the rest of the epistle. Similarly the noun occurs twice in these chapters and only once in the rest of the letter. In like manner, Paul should not be looked upon as one who is taking pleasure in the plight of the Jews. He writes as a broken man, burdened with sorrow and anguish.

In anticipation of criticisms which will be made against God for not fulfilling His promises to Israel, the apostle begins by defending God's word. The purpose of God had not failed. The promises He had made to Israel were intact. Harold St. John describes it graphically. He likens Israel to having carried the privileges in a vase for hundreds of years. As time went by the hands grew weak and finally with a jolt the vase is dropped and the privileges fall to the ground. They are not, however, lost, according to St. John. He states, "There is not a single privilege but what is vested in the church spiritually...Israel had them in the flesh; we hold them in the Spirit; and when the church goes up, she will hand all these back to Israel and she will have them again untarnished and complete". This is an interesting thought and certainly one which suggests that God's purposes have not been thwarted by Israel's failure.

The term "Israel" was never intended to be understood as the description of a nation in the same way as Egypt or Greece or Rome. God was not tied to a people who occupied Palestine and relied on that as their claim to divine favour. If God had meant that, there were others whose claims as descendants of Abraham were equally valid. Paul's statement therefore that they are not all Israel who are of Israel is a categorical one, which he will set out to prove in the verses which follow.

7 It might be argued that the bringing in of the gospel with the offer of blessing to the Gentiles was a failure on God's part to fulfil His promises to Israel. It would seem that the privileges given to the nation were in the end of no value and that Israel's unique position was lost for ever. This view is shown to be false.

In a series of quotations from the OT Paul meets the objections of those who thought they had grounds for complaint against God. In a vindication of God's ways with Israel in the past, the apostle raises the point of natural descent and quotes Gen 21:12. The Jews were without question Israelites by natural descent, but to take a stand on that was a grave mistake. The Jews were undoubtedly Abraham's seed, but Abraham was also the father of Ishmael and the sons of Keturah. If natural descent was what counted, then Ishmael and the others had an equal claim. The promise of God, however, was not based on that; it was made in accordance with His sovereign choice, His own election of grace.

The quotation made by Paul in support of his submission is from Gen 21:12. Although Abraham pleaded for Ishmael, God declared plainly that His sovereign choice was Isaac. With this the Jews had no complaint. Ishmael had no place and he was therefore set aside. God in His mercy, however, had other blessings for Ishmael, but as far as the promises were concerned which would eventually lead to the bringing in of the Messiah, Ishmael had no place in God's plans. Isaac was the child of promise. Through that line the true seed would come. The argument therefore at this stage proved conclusively that descent from Abraham was not an automatic title to divine favour. Ishmael was also a son of Abraham and his descendants had a valid claim for recognition if natural descent was all that mattered. What Paul was stating was that it was possible to have a title which was flawless and yet not be one of the children of promise. God was not therefore bound to the Jewish nation. They were not all Israel, which were of Israel.

8 The words "That is" introduce the explanation, "They which are the children of the flesh, these are not the children of God". The children of Hagar and Keturah were Abraham's seed, but they were not God's choice. As far as Ishmael was concerned, he was the outcome of Sarah's mistake because she thought that she was past the age of child-bearing (Gen 16:2). The promise given to Abraham in Gen 15 that his seed would be as numerous as the stars in the heavens did not look like being fulfilled through Sarah. The human reasoning which resulted in taking matters out of the hand of God at the time, had dire results then, and in succeeding years was the cause of constant problems for the children of Israel.

The Genesis account makes it clear how Isaac was born. He was not the child of the flesh. He was not born according to the laws of nature. His mother was well past the age of child-bearing when he was conceived. He was, nevertheless, the child of promise and through him the royal line would be established which would eventually bring in the Messiah.

The descendants of Isaac are those who are reckoned to be the children of promise. The children of Ishmael are the children of the flesh, but since Isaac was born as a result of promise, so his children are characterised by the same expression: they are the children of promise. Apart from the sovereignty of God, however, they had no claim for divine favour. The choice of God did not depend on the flesh, but on His own inscrutable ways. The children of Israel were not children of promise simply because they were descendants of Isaac. The privilege was reckoned to them. Apart from the intervention of God, Abraham and Sarah would never have had a son. In the same way, the children of Abraham through Isaac and Jacob would have had no place as a privileged nation apart from the mercy and sovereign choice of God.

9 In pursuance of his defence of the righteousness of God in His dealings with Israel, Paul develops the thought of divine sovereignty. In another reference to the OT he brings in Sarah. The choice of Sarah to be the one who would bring in the child of promise was entirely the prerogative of God. No one dare question His right to do as He pleased. God was a law to Himself and if He chose to effect a miracle by using Sarah that was His privilege. He was not answerable to man or to any created intelligence for His actions: His ways are inscrutable.

When Sarah's age is considered, the objection based on natural descent becomes untenable. Had it not been for the intervention of God there would have been no natural descent for the Jew to boast about. Ishmael could have boasted. He was born of the strength of the flesh. His title to natural descent was flawless. That could not be said about Sarah nor, in a lesser sense, about Abraham. The Jew was therefore cast upon the God of promise. If there was to be acceptance with Him it had to be on the basis of being one of Abraham's spiritual children; mere natural descent was of no value.

10 The argument of v.9 is now reinforced. The apostle moves on from dealing with the descendants of Abraham to a consideration of the children of Isaac. The opening words, "And not only this", indicate that v.9 did not complete his argument; he will enlarge upon it by bringing in Rebecca and her two sons. A very remarkable situation took place at the birth of the two boys. Esau who was born first, was not the firstborn. That place of rank was given to Jacob the younger son. Paul's argument is that these two boys were conceived at the same time and their father was Isaac. They were twins and although Esau was born first, God's sovereign choice fell upon Jacob. The Jews might dismiss Ishmael as being different from Isaac as they had different mothers and Hagar was a bondwoman, but they could not use that argument against Esau.

Here Paul refers to "our father Isaac". In that he links himself with his fellow-countrymen. As a Jew himself he had to acknowledge that Isaac was the father of Esau and Jacob. Not only so, by introducing Rebecca the apostle makes it clear that in the case of Esau and Jacob there were not two mothers, Hagar and Sarah, but one, Rebecca. As Gen 25:21 reveals, she was barren and was the subject of Isaac's entreaty with the Lord that she might have children. Ishmael was the subject of scheming. Isaac was the subject of promise and his two sons were the result of prayer. As Paul's argument develops, it becomes obvious that God was not influenced by considerations outside of Himself. God was not limited by the laws of nature. Rebecca was beyond child-bearing age but she had two sons. In the working out of His plans therefore it is clear that God was not bound. His almighty power and His sovereign choice together shaped the future of the nation of Israel and the other nations which would spring from the line of Abraham.

11 The AV gives this verse as a parenthesis. It is not clear that Paul intended a digression here as v.12 does not follow on naturally from the end of v.10. However, the substance of v.11 is clear and very much the substance of the overall argument. It looks like an anticipation on Paul's part of a Jewish objection. It might be argued that Esau proved himself to be a carnal, worldly man and that Jacob, despite his scheming, was the better of the two. This view is dismissed by Paul. God's choice was made independently of works of merit. He did not wait to see how Esau and Jacob developed before He made His choice. Before the boys were capable of having done good or evil, before their characters were manifested, preference was given to Jacob. The choice was not made on the ground of works, it was based on the purpose of God in election. The choice was made before Esau and Jacob were born.

God's purpose is stressed. Human merit played no part in it. As the apostle states, it was "according to election…not of works". Those who were the subjects of His election were also the objects of His mercy. If it could be proved that works of any kind were involved then God's choice was limited: it was not free and His mercy was not free either. But the calling of God was not influenced in any way by forces outside of Himself. It was all according to His sovereign choice that His purpose in election might stand. Jacob's life-style played no part in God's choice. That was made before Jacob was born. The calling which is mentioned here is not the call of salvation, but is the activity resulting from His purpose in election. He brought to pass in the lives of the chosen what He determined to do in eternity past.

12 In his argument Paul moves from the possible objection of the Jew on the grounds of natural descent to the doctrine of election. The history of the nation declared that Rebecca had two sons by Isaac. On a claim for recognition as descendants of Jacob, Esau had to be taken into account. He could not be ignored as having no claim; he was as much a son of Isaac as Jacob.

Moreover, because Esau was the elder son in any claim for recognition on the grounds of natural descent primacy was his. Esau's position, however, was settled before he was born, as Paul notes, before either of the boys had done anything good or bad. There was no question of merit in the election. God's choice of Jacob was in accordance with His own purpose.

The word of the Lord to Rebecca was that there were two nations in her womb and that the one people would be stronger than the other people. To this was added the statement recorded by Paul, "The elder shall serve the younger" (v.12). As far as Jacob and Esau were concerned, the choice of Jacob as the firstborn in rank was not according to what he had done but that the purpose of God in election might stand.

God's purpose in giving Rebecca an explanation of what would transpire in the lives of her two sons, still unborn, is not obvious. As the time of their birth approached it would be expected that Rebecca's horizon would be limited to planning her family responsibilities. With the advantage of hindsight from the later chapters of the lives of Esau and Jacob, the partiality shown in the home because of preferences, would account in some measure for the warning of God beforehand. Despite Rebecca's scheming, however, God's ordering of events came to pass, "the elder served the younger". No amount of scheming on man's part can alter the decision of the will of God. It had to be admitted that God was true to His word. He had already made it clear that it was His choice which had been exercised in relation to Esau and Jacob.

13 The argument of the apostle on the subject of the election of God continues with a quotation from the prophecy of Malachi. The words which Malachi records and which Paul quotes, "Jacob have I loved, but Esau have I hated", have caused much difficulty over the years. Many have made attempts to soften the word "hated". Others have used the verse to attack the character of God. As far as *Romans* is concerned it is essential to consider it in the light of Paul's argument in the context, although a brief consideration of the Malachi passage will undoubtedly be of help in understanding the overall position. In this connection the reader is referred to the author's work, *Things Written Aforetime* (p.200).

In Malachi's day doubts were being expressed about God's love for the nation of Israel. "I have loved you, saith the Lord. Yet ye say, Wherein hast thou loved us?" (Mal 1:2). Malachi's burden therefore was to supply the proof of God's love by going back in the history of the nation to Jacob and showing that God loved him not for any merit in him, but because of His election in grace. Esau was not embraced in that love, and was stated to be hated. This has been attributed to the Hebrew way of describing the situation when a person was not loved; hate was the only alternative; there could be no middle ground. See Gen 29:31; Deut 21:15, and compare Luke 14:26 with Matt 10:37.

Some have advanced that Paul is dealing with nations and not individuals, since the word of the Lord to Rebecca was that there were two nations in her womb and that one people would be stronger than the other people (Gen 25:23). There seems little doubt that Paul had both in mind, the individuals as well as the nations they represented. This accords with the thrust of his argument. He is combating what could be raised against God by the Jews that He had not fulfilled His promises to the nation. Whether the expression "Esau have I hated" means "hated" or "loved less" does not affect the apostle's argument. What he had asserted was that "they are not all Israel, which are of Israel" (v.6), and those who could trace their ancestry back to Jacob or Abraham had no more claim upon God as of right than the descendants of Ishmael and Esau. The point which Paul makes is that the Jews have no cause for complaint. If God chooses one and rejects another it is His prerogative and in doing so He will be found to be entirely righteous and consistent throughout.

As to the question of whether reprobation is inferred in the statement "Esau have I hated", and many claim that this is the main text in the NT on the subject, the Scripture is clear: "Have I any pleasure at all that the wicked should die… and not that he should return from his ways and live?" (Ezek 18:23), and again, "For I have no pleasure in the death of him that dieth, saith the Lord God" (Ezek 18:32).

Notes

13 Denney makes the point, "it would not be right to say that Paul here refers the eternal salvation or perdition of individuals to an absolute decree of God which has no relation to what they are or do, but rests simply on His inscrutable will".

Morris quotes Nygren, "Men think that if everything rests in God's hand and depends on His will, there is nothing that rests with men; so there can no longer be talk of his responsibility or guilt. Paul does not admit that alternative. He can affirm both points at the same time…And in the present argument he is not concerned with how the two points relate to one another".

(c) *The sovereign right of God to show mercy (vv.14-18)*

> v.14 "What shall we say then? Is there unrighteousness with God? God forbid.
> v.15 For he saith to Moses, I will have mercy on whom I will have mercy, and I will have compassion on whom I will have compassion.
> v.16 So then it is not of him that willeth, nor of him that runneth, but of God that sheweth mercy.
> v.17 For the scripture saith unto Pharaoh, Even for this same purpose have I raised thee up, that I might shew my power in thee, and that my name might be declared throughout all the earth.
> v.18 Therefore hath he mercy on whom he will have mercy, and whom he will he hardeneth."

14 Once again the characteristic question is asked, "What shall we say then?" In view of what has been stated about God having chosen whom He would, "Is there unrighteousness with God?" This question is answered tersely, "God forbid",

"Not at all". An unjust God is quite beyond all thought. More than once in this epistle Paul has faced up to the possible accusation that God is unjust. Earlier he had posed the question, "Is God unrighteous who taketh vengeance?" (3:5). This follows the categorical statement, "...let God be true but every man a liar" (3:4). It has to be faced, if God is not just, He ceases to be God, and even the Jews who opposed the apostle vehemently, would not deny that fact. Based on that, Paul's overall argument is that if anything is advanced that makes out God to be unjust, then it is false and must be rejected immediately.

In Abraham's pleading for Sodom, he posed the question, "Shall not the judge of all the earth do right?" This undeniable fact was known to the Jews. Paul had already put it back to his objectors, "Is God unrighteous...God forbid, for then how shall God judge the world?" (3:6). Since this was beyond question, the objector might then argue that it was what Paul was advancing which was wrong; for if what the apostle stated was true then God was indeed unjust. That God had rights was not denied, but the exercise of His right to choose whom He would for blessing was unacceptable to the objector. That God should choose Gentiles and set aside the bulk of the nation of Israel was considered unthinkable.

The way that Paul sets out to deal with the problem is clear: he will quote the Scriptures in support of his argument. The very oracles of God in the possession of the Jews will testify that what he is advancing is correct. The Jews could have no argument against the word of God. They were the custodians of Holy Writ and if its precepts revealed that it was God's right to bestow mercy or withhold it, that was His prerogative. Neither Jacob nor Esau had a claim on God for mercy and to argue for one or the other missed the point of Paul's argument – God was sovereign, so objections against His freedom to exercise His choice could not be sustained.

15 The question raised in the previous verse, "Is there unrighteousness with God?" challenged any to provide convincing proof that God had acted unreasonably. From the passages of the Scriptures already quoted, Paul had shown that the election of God was not inconsistent with His righteousness. God was perfectly just in choosing whom He would and there was no one who could prove that the exercise of that right was wrong.

The apostle will now argue from the Scriptures to prove His point. He quotes from Exod 33:19 LXX, "For he saith to Moses, I will have mercy on whom I will have mercy, and I will have compassion on whom I will have compassion". In the matter of worshipping the golden calf, the children of Israel had sinned grievously. They deserved to be cut off and if God had turned away from them He would have been altogether just in doing so. As it was, had it not been for the pleading of Moses, judgment would have befallen them. God had said, "Ye are a stiff-necked people; I will come into the midst of thee in a moment and consume thee" (Exod 33:5).

Against the background of sin and idolatry, Paul introduces what God said to

Moses about His right to show mercy and compassion. If God had acted as He was entitled to act, Israel would have been sorely punished. Instead of that, He demonstrated to the people that He was a gracious God, full of mercy. This mercy, however, was not earned. There was nothing in any to merit it. As far as the situation recorded in Exod 33 was concerned, what was deserved was judgment. But, God chose to show mercy by exercising His right to show it to whom He would. He was not tied to act mercifully to certain people. It was not a case of God exercising His freedom to be compassionate to the pious or to the prominent or to any class. He was perfectly free to exercise His right to bless whom He would. Paul, therefore, in His argument from the Scriptures and the history of Israel confirms what he has already stated, that in the gospel now being proclaimed, man has no rights, all depends on the mercy of God and it will be shown without national distinction. Jew and Gentile will be on level ground, no one more or less deserving than any other. The blessing bestowed on those whom God would justify would all be in accordance with His free unmerited favour.

16 The example of how God shows mercy and compassion is followed by a denial that man's efforts are involved in any way. The will of God, demonstrated in His sovereign choice, is never arbitrary. Although He retains His liberty to act as He sees fit, His actions are never unrighteous. God has rights which are unquestionably divine and they are far beyond any rights of men to challenge. Paul therefore states unequivocally that the mercy and compassion of God are not influenced by human will. The sinner who desperately craves for mercy cannot call it down of his own volition. Trite sayings might suggest the mercy is "on tap", but that is obviously not the case, as this verse so clearly demonstrates. The will of man has no power to move the mercy of God at the time and in the direction he chooses. The verse states, "It is not of him that willeth".

Not only so, but the apostle adds, "nor of him that runneth". Human effort is unavailing. Striving, whether to do good works or religious observances, does not influence the divine will. If these could, even in small measure, Paul's argument in vv.6-13 would be seriously flawed. If it were remotely possible for mankind to contribute anything to earn salvation, the result would be catastrophic. Those who could not supply the required human effort would be lost eternally. The sacrifice of Christ which provides the basis for God's dealings in mercy would be superfluous at some point. No longer could it be described as salvation at the highest cost. It would be a mixture of grace and works. Such a thought, of course, is preposterous, but it is precisely what Paul has been combating from the beginning of his epistle. There were those in abundance amongst his own countrymen who believed that their will and their efforts had a part to play in acceptance with God. In dismissing such claims the apostle could not be more emphatic, it is all "of God that showeth mercy".

17 The argument of Paul takes on a new significance with the reference to

Pharaoh. The mercy shown to Israel gives way to a consideration of the hardening process. God's dealings with Pharaoh were well-known but what was not considered was that the same hardening process applied also to the Jews. Their history proved that despite being constantly reproved they hardened their hearts.

The personification of Scripture is an interesting point. Paul could have said that it was God who addressed Pharaoh but he gives that place to the Scriptures. It is possible that since he was making so many quotations from it that he decided to stress its inspiration and authority. Although the Jews respected their traditions many of which had superseded Scripture, there was still the threefold division of the Word with them – the law, the prophets and the *hagiographa* ("the writings", 13 books in the English Bible). They professed to honour the precepts, but as Stephen proved in his defence before the council, while they were careful about the letter, they were at odds with the spirit of the Word.

The hardening process has in it things which are difficult to understand, but God cannot be charged with acting capriciously. When He exercises His right to harden any person it is a judicial act on His part and that judgment must be in accordance with His righteousness. Invariably there is a hardening of the heart before God steps in to harden judicially. The Scripture is clear that Pharaoh hardened his own heart repeatedly despite the warnings given to him, until eventually the prerogative of hardening or repenting was removed from him and he was inflicted with the judicial hardening of God.

The part of Scripture selected by Paul from the account of God's dealings with Pharaoh unfolds another aspect of the hardening process. Moses was sent to the Egyptian monarch to let him know that he was to be an object lesson for all the earth, and not for that generation only. So it has become, that Pharaoh's hardening of his heart has been a familiar warning for thousands of years.

The use of the quotation from Exodus is proof that mercy is not merited and it stresses that hardening is not unrighteous.

18 The opening words of this verse, "Therefore hath he mercy on whom he will have mercy" are the conclusion of the statement made in v.15, "I will have mercy on whom I will have mercy". From what Paul has set out, leading up to this point in his argument, it is clear that God's right to exercise His will and bless according to His own choice was unchallengeable. To meet a possible objection from the Jews, Paul then proves that God's sovereignty shown in the OT was not only in mercy but also in hardening. The Jews, with their knowledge of the Scriptures, should have known that, but to make it clear, the apostle gives two quotations and one comprehensive allusion, all from the book of Exodus.

The allusion in v.18 is in two parts. The first part refers to the mercy shown to the Israelites when they deserved nothing but judgment because of their idolatry in the matter of the golden calf. If God had cut them off He would have been perfectly just. The nation should therefore have been for ever grateful to Moses for his pleading on their behalf and to God for listening to the pleas of His servant.

If the Israelites were shown mercy when they deserved judgment, there should be no complaints from their descendants about the Gentiles being shown mercy by a merciful God.

The latter half of the verse "and whom he will be hardeneth" is an obvious allusion to God's dealings with Pharaoh. The Scriptures do not state that God hardens any man who has not first hardened himself. As far as Pharaoh was concerned, he hardened his heart on six occasions before his heart was hardened by God. He was warned that God could have struck him and his people with a plague that would have cut them off, but God spared him in order to show His power and that His name might be declared throughout all the earth (Exod 9:15,16). This action on God's part does not minimise the fact that Pharaoh had repeatedly hardened his own heart. The Egyptian monarch's sin brought retribution eventually. God gave him over to the consequences of his own sin and he became a hardened man. Pharaoh had been given every opportunity to do what was right but he refused and what followed was only to be expected. Despite that, he was given further chances to repent, but these were ignored and the final blow fell on the Egyptian nation. As far as the Jews were concerned, their hardening should not have been a surprise, for they deserved to be set aside.

Notes

15 Of the synonyms, *eleos* and *oiktirmos*, rendered "mercy" or "compassion", *eleos* is an active compassion which strives to relieve the misery it sees in others, while *oiktirmos* feels pity but does not necessarily do anything about it. The two verbal references in this verse to showing mercy are *eleeō* and the two references to showing compassion are *oikteirō*. This is exactly as it is in the LXX.

16 The verb "willeth" is from *thelō*, "to will". Regarding the synonymous verbs, *boulomai* and *thelō*, the former seems to designate the will which follows deliberation, the latter the will which proceeds from inclination, notes Thayer.

Moulton observes that "runneth" involves exertion, pushing oneself to the limit. Righteousness is not obtained by pushing to the limit of striving.

(d) *The wrath and the mercy of God (vv.19-29)*

> v.19 "Thou wilt say then unto me, Why doth he yet find fault? For who hath resisted his will?
> v.20 Nay but, O man, who art thou that repliest against God? Shall the thing formed say to him that formed it, Why hast thou made me thus?
> v.21 Hath not the potter power over the clay, of the same lump to make one vessel unto honour, and another unto dishonour?
> v.22 What if God, willing to shew his wrath, and to make his power known, endured with much longsuffering the vessels of wrath fitted to destruction:
> v.23 And that he might make known the riches of his glory on the vessels of mercy, which he had afore prepared unto glory,

v.24 Even us, whom he hath called, not of the Jews only, but also of the Gentiles?
v.25 As he saith also in Osee, I will call them my people, which were not my people; and her beloved, which was not beloved.
v.26 And it shall come to pass, that in the place where it was said unto them, Ye are not my people; there shall they be called the children of the living God.
v.27 Esaias also crieth concerning Israel, Though the number of the children of Israel be as the sand of the sea, a remnant shall be saved:
v.28 For he will finish the work, and cut it short in righteousness: because a short work will the Lord make upon the earth.
v.29 And as Esaias said before, Except the Lord of Sabaoth had left us a seed, we had been as Sodoma, and been made like unto Gomorrha."

19 In the preceding verses the apostle has shown that God does what He wills to do. If He exercises His sovereignty to show mercy or to harden, that is His prerogative. This, however, raises many questions in the human mind, several of which the apostle anticipates and sets out to answer. The first one is, "Thou wilt say then unto me, Why doth he yet find fault?" The objector is asking, "Is it reasonable for God to blame us for doing what simply fulfils what He has decreed?" If what was said to Pharaoh is taken into account, the objector might add, "If the mercy and the hardening of God are for the purpose of causing His name to be proclaimed throughout the earth, is it reasonable to find fault with those who are merely pawns fulfilling what God determined to do?" If there is hardness in the human heart, why should those whose hearts have been hardened, be blamed for their condition?

The second part of the question which Paul anticipates coming from an objector is, "For who hath resisted his will?" The aspect of God's will contemplated here is not His gracious design but His determinate counsel. This is all-powerful and overrules every human action. From Paul's use of the Scriptures to answer anticipated objections it is clear that he has the Jewish position in his mind. The Messiah had come and had been rejected. Appeals to the people to reconsider their ways had failed. The hardening which followed had resulted in the gospel being preached to the Gentiles. The purposes of God had not been thwarted by the hardening of Israel. The course of the river of mercy had been blocked, but it flowed in another channel and brought mercy to the Gentiles. Any objections therefore from a Jewish source had no substance. They merely displayed an ignorance of basic facts. The creature is not in a position to challenge the Creator. This Paul will now prove from the Scriptures. Not only so, but objections to the exercise of God's sovereign rights will be met by a reminder of the sinfulness of man and the longsuffering of the God of mercy.

20 In his anticipation of the questions the objectors will ask, Paul turns to the Scriptures to answer them. He alludes to the prophecy of Isaiah to support the argument he will put forward that the creature has no right to question the Creator. In effect the creature is demanding that God answers on the basis of the way the creature thinks. This of course is not only naive but insolent in the extreme. If God is God, then the creature has no right to challenge what He does or what He says. Even if God condescended to give an account, the creature would be forced to acknowledge his limited ability to comprehend. God has no need to consult anyone. He neither needs advice nor listens to objections. If the good pleasure of His will results in man's blessing there is no entitlement to seek a motive for His actions. If He determines to harden, objections against His will cannot be sustained. There can be no inconsistencies with God.

The question, "Who art thou O man?" reflects Paul's indignation that the creature should have the temerity to question the Creator. The challenge is the height of absurdity. For puny man to reply against God is audacious to the point of blasphemy and Paul repudiates it. To make his point absolutely clear, he turns to Isaiah and from the example of the potter and the clay he carries his argument forward.

In Isa 29 the prophet deals with a situation in which the people were smug about their own wisdom. They pretended they were acting like wise men of God but they were hypocrites. They were attempting to turn things upside down, putting man before God. The God who created the world and brought forth man from the dust of the ground was being treated as far less than almighty God. In Isaiah's mind it was a case of the clay saying about God, "...shall the work say of him that made it, He made me not? or shall the thing framed say of him that framed it, He had no understanding?" (Isa 29:16).

In Isa 45 the prophet reveals how God will use Cyrus, as yet unborn, to do His will. The king of Persia will let the nations know that there is no God like Jehovah. It is this Gentile monarch who will give the command to rebuild Jerusalem. The Jews might object, but Isaiah replies, "Shall the clay say to him that fashioneth it, What makest thou? or thy work, He hath no hands?" (Isa 45:9). The details of Isaiah's example may be different from those confronting Paul but the principle is the same: that which is created cannot challenge the Creator. If God is called to account, that action assumes that the one who calls Him to account is superior. To think that anyone is greater than God is absurd. If God can be called to account He ceases to be God. It is little wonder then that Paul's ire is raised as he repels any objections that might be raised against the rights of God to bless, or harden, according to His sovereign will.

21 The possibility that some may think that God creates only to destroy arbitrarily comes before the apostle's mind. To answer the objections which he envisages may arise, he constantly refers to the OT. As far as Paul is concerned the Scriptures are vibrant with meaning and he applies them with great force. Having defended the sovereignty of God in the illustration of the potter and the clay, he turns from Isaiah to Jeremiah to counteract what may be another objection.

The allusion to Jer 18 has been roundly condemned by some commentators. Some have referred to it as bad analogy on Paul's part, saying that people are not clay and are due at least some consideration of their rights as individuals. The power of the potter over the clay is looked upon as despotic which leaves the vessel in tyrannical hands with no redress whatever. This view assumes that God creates for one purpose or another and disposes according to whims which are unrighteous. Such a suggestion does despite to the character of God and cannot be accepted as being what Paul meant in his allusions to the writings of the prophets.

After stating that the potter had a right to make from the same lump one vessel to honour and another vessel to dishonour, the apostle introduces a hypothetical question. He makes clear that there is a difference between what God has a right to do, being sovereign, and what He did, being longsuffering. As far as the Jews were concerned, the reference to making vessels unto honour and others to dishonour from the same lump must have reinforced the previous statement that not all who are Israelites by birth are Jacob's true descendants, and not all who are Abraham's seed are Abraham's children.

When Jeremiah went to the potter's house he learned a lesson. He saw the potter working at the wheel and he learned that the potter had a plan in his mind when he began to work. He had the power to shape the clay into whatever vessel he wanted to create and, if it did not turn out according to plan, to discard it and start again. The message for Israel was clear, "Cannot I do with you as this potter?" saith the Lord (Jer 18:6).

The Jews of Paul's day needed the same lesson. They were not in a position to argue with God. They had prepared themselves for destruction by their sin and wilfulness. God had endured with much longsuffering the vessels of wrath. But the question arises, "Who can object if God wishes to show mercy to those selected beforehand for eternal glory?" If the Jews had an objection about supposed unfairness on God's part in passing over the nation, they had only themselves to blame. Their own prophets had given repeated warnings that God would turn to the Gentiles.

Some commentators hold that the vessels are in two classes, one for noble use and the other for common or menial use. This view certainly takes away from the stark contrasts which have been introduced by Paul in the previous verses. Vessels to honour included Moses and Jacob and vessels to dishonour undoubtedly embraced Pharaoh and Esau. It seems more likely that Paul was defending God's right to take from the same lump, the human race, some for mercy and others who proved by their obdurate refusal to heed His word, that they were vessels fitted for destruction. The fact is that all are sinners, all are guilty before God as has been proved earlier in the epistle. If some argue that God is unjust because He did not extend His grace to them, they place themselves in an impossible situation. They refuse to respond to God's overtures of mercy and cry for justice. If, when that justice is introduced, they find themselves cut off, they have only themselves to blame.

22 This verse and the next two verses present a few problems. In some points the apostle's train of thought is obscure, a difficulty which is not eased by the grammatical structure of the verses. The opening "if" is not followed by an appropriate clause, and so the conditional sentence is not complete. Certainly the rendering of the AV helps by introducing "What" into the text. If that is not acceptable, then a reply would seem to be required at the end of v.24, as the thread of Paul's argument runs through the three verses. The point would then be, "If God...what would your answer be to that?" Some commentators hold that the apostle did not need to finish the sentence because the "if" is unanswerable; suggesting that what follows in the three verses would silence any objector.

Although the verse states, "What if God, willing to show his wrath", it does not mean that God is bound to give a reason for His actions. Because He chose to show His wrath and declare His power in the vessels of wrath, he tolerated them with great longsuffering. With great patience He bore with those who were fitted (or, were ripe, prepared) for destruction. The form of the verb *katartizō* used here, if in the middle voice, signifies that the vessels of wrath fitted themselves, or made themselves ripe for destruction. (If the verb is passive, the responsibility for the action would be unspecified.) The onus should not be placed on God. There are many passages in the Scriptures which state that God takes no pleasure in the death of the wicked (see, for example, 2:4), but as in the case of Pharaoh to which Paul has alluded, it is obvious that there were repeated demonstrations of impenitence before God in government hardened Pharaoh's heart.

The phrase, "to make his power known" seems to require a noun or a noun clause to complete the sense, but instead of adding that God came down on the vessels of wrath in judgment, Paul stated that God "endured with much longsuffering". It is not therefore a case of saying that those in view were destined for wrath, but rather that they were characterised by wrath. None who find themselves in a lost eternity will be able to say that they are there through no fault of their own. It will be demonstrated to them that they had ample opportunities in life to get right with God but that they spurned every chance to repent and believe the gospel.

Paul does not say who fitted the people for wrath, the verb may be either passive or middle voice. Some say it was God, some say it was Satan, but if the word "fitted" carries the force of the middle voice it is more likely that the vessels of wrath fitted themselves for destruction. AW Tozer makes a valuable comment in this connection, "God's justice stands forever against the sinner in utter severity. The vague and tenuous hope that God is too kind to punish the ungodly has become a deadly opiate for the consciences of millions. It hushes their fear and allows them to practise all pleasant forms of iniquity while death draws every day nearer and the command to repent goes unregarded. As responsible moral beings we dare not so trifle with our eternal future".

The tense of "endured" is aorist, pointing back to the specific example of Pharaoh, rather than making it a reference to a continuing practice of God. He bore the repeated evidences of impenitence with longsuffering. Many opportunities were given to the Egyptian monarch to repent, but such a change of heart was not forthcoming. Nevertheless, as far as the Jewish nation of Paul's day was concerned, the phrase "fitted for destruction" JND was certainly applicable to their position before God. Their obdurate refusal to conform themselves to the privileges and standards which were committed to their trust placed them in a hopeless situation. God's patience had run out. The parable of the wicked husbandmen which the Lord told during His last visit to Jerusalem, contained the expression, so full of pathos, "This is the heir, come let us kill him, and seize on his inheritance". That expression described the attitude of the Jews perfectly. In answer to the Lord's demand as to what should be done to the wicked husbandmen, the Jews pronounced their own sentence, "He will miserably destroy those wicked men, and will let out his vineyard to other husbandmen, which shall render him the fruits in their season" (Matt 21:41). The Jews fitted themselves for destruction and although Paul does not define what was entailed in the word, it is obvious that it means eternal loss. It does not denote annihilation, that is, loss of being, but rather loss of wellbeing throughout eternal ages.

23 The apostle takes his argument a stage further in this verse. What he had to say about wrath is balanced by what God has made known about mercy. It was revealed that God endured with longsuffering the vessels of wrath that He might make known His power. Now Paul states that God is making known the riches of His glory in vessels of mercy. It would have been a sufficient cause for thanksgiving if He had made known His glory, but "the riches of his glory" shows that there is an abundance with God; there is no limit to His glory. That it should be manifested in vessels of mercy is a great wonder. It was a great delight to Paul to tell it out. Writing to the Ephesians he made known "the riches of the glory of his inheritance in the saints" (1:18), and he prayed that the Ephesians might be strengthened…in the inner man "according to the riches of his glory" (3:16).

The expression "vessels of mercy" implies that those to whom God shows grace stand in need of it. No matter how much mercy is required, the limitless resources of God are there to meet the need. It is not merely a declaration of mercy to the needy, but the bringing of it to those who respond to His gracious offer. The contrast between the vessels of wrath and the vessels of mercy is striking; one is fitted for destruction and the other is prepared unto glory.

The vessels of God's mercy are said to be "afore prepared unto glory". This is understood by some to mean that the vessels of mercy are the subjects of God's electing choice. In view of what the apostle has been saying about God's sovereignty and His right to exercise it, there seems little doubt that there is a reference to election in connection with the vessels of mercy. Since, however, Pharaoh's rebellious ways on earth are inferred in connection with vessels of wrath, it is reasonable to assume that the responses made by vessels of mercy in life are taken into account for the future. Those who are born of God are prepared by God, that through their experiences in fellowship with the Lord they will be fitted for glory. Peter no doubt had this aspect in mind when he wrote of the virtues which guaranteed an abundant entrance into the everlasting kingdom of our Lord and Saviour Jesus Christ (2 Pet 1:11). The entrance into heaven is never in question, but a richly-furnished one depends on how the christian life is lived on earth for the glory of God.

24 Since "whom" is a relative pronoun, what follows in the verse is a relative clause, with the antecedent being the vessels of mercy in the previous verse. The reference to "even us" embraces Paul as well as the others who are the objects of God's mercy. These are the ones whom God has called. As always with Paul, the "calling" has been effectual. Paul's argument here does not contemplate anything arising from chance. There is no question of anyone, Jew or Gentile, being saved by default. No allowance is made by the apostle for the possibility of any not embraced in the call of God finding eternal security at the end.

The apostle is adamant that those who are called, are called out from amongst the Jews and the Gentiles. Jews were not called out because they were Jews, and Gentiles were not called out because they were not Jews. The fact that God had cast aside the Jewish nation did not mean that this provided an open door that admitted every Gentile into blessing. The vessels of mercy were called out from Jews and Gentiles according to the sovereignty and grace of God. There was no advantage in being a member of any race. The gospel of God was a worldwide message and there were no privileged classes as far as beneficiaries were concerned.

25 In the next five verses Paul gives quotations from Hosea and Isaiah to confirm that the calling of Gentiles was in God's mind from OT times. He also proves from the Scriptures that the call of God would not include all Israel. God would take out vessels of mercy from amongst Jews and Gentiles. The prophets are called in to supply the proof of what Paul was declaring. If the objectors were alleging that it was Paul's personal views he was advancing, the chain of scriptural quotations given will demonstrate that it is really God who is speaking and not Paul.

The first quotation given is from Hos 2:23. It is a free rendering of what Hosea announced and the order given by Paul is inverted to suit his purpose at this point. Hosea laboured amongst the ten tribes, but because of their apostasy he was given the commission to announce to Israel that they were *Lo-ammi* ("not my people"). They practised the same things as the idolatrous Gentiles amongst whom they lived. They lived like heathens and to all effects were heathens themselves. They were as Gentiles, and it was fitting that Paul should refer to Hosea to support his argument that the OT testified to the fact that Jews and Gentiles would be taken out as vessels of mercy.

In Paul's argument there was hope for at least some amongst the idolatrous people of Israel. And if amongst a disowned people there were vessels of mercy, it follows that God's grace would call out vessels of mercy from amongst the Gentiles who did not have the privileges of those who were in apostasy. Thus, although Hosea's task was not a pleasant one, nevertheless he still had a message of hope. It is this that Paul takes up. If God wills to show mercy, those to whom He shows it will be restored. There are those who will be called "my beloved" and "my people" who were previously at a distance from God. The point of Paul's argument, however, is to stress that this is not new. It had been in the Scriptures for years that God would call out from amongst Jews and Gentiles. It is the call of God and the love of God that matter. It is not privileged birth nor the lack of it that gives the title to being the people of God, it is God's choice of vessels of mercy, and He has chosen to call out from amongst the Gentiles as well as calling out from amongst the Jews.

26 The prophet Hosea is quoted again by Paul. He makes the two verses from Hosea's prophecy run together, although he reverses the order of what the prophet wrote. Hosea's unfaithful wife, Gomer, had three children, all conceived in whoredom. The second child was called *Lo-ruhamah* ("Not pitied", or, "Not my loved one"), and the third one was named *Lo-ammi* ("Not my people"). Hosea, instead of disowning his unfaithful wife, brought her back and restored her to favour. The names were changed and came to mean "my pitied one", or, "my loved one", and "my people". This situation was symbolic of Israel's state. The moral and spiritual decline is reflected in the names given to Gomer's two children. The ten tribes, to whom Hosea prophesied, sowed the seeds of their own destruction and the sentence pronounced upon them was given in the unmistakeable symbolic names, *Lo-ruhama* and *Lo-ammi*.

The apostle Peter quotes Hos 1:10 in his first epistle (2:10). The context of 1 Peter is quite different from Rom 9, but the quotation from Hosea's prophecy is just as applicable. Jews who had embraced Christianity and had been scattered by persecution and other causes might have had lingering thoughts of loss through leaving Judaism. Any regrets, however, should have been dispelled by the wonderful revelation through Peter about the privileges of the royal and holy priesthoods under Christianity. This should have been a comfort to Jews and an encouragement to the Gentiles who had never been in such a relation with the only true God. It could be said of the Jews literally, and in a general sense of the Gentiles, that in times past they were not a people, but they were now the people of God, which had not obtained mercy, but now have obtained mercy (1 Pet 2:10). In this, the apostle Peter was quoting Hos 1:9 to consolidate the position and assure the believing Jews in particular that God was prepared to acknowledge that He had a people again. That mercy, however, which was shown to the Jews was also shown to the Gentiles who were prepared to come in the same way, obtaining the mercy of God on the principle of faith.

Paul's reference to Hos 1:10 was for a different purpose. He was not writing to put at rest the minds of converted Jews. He was addressing Jewish objections about the alleged unfairness of God in by-passing the nation which they claimed had a special relationship with Him. But the apostle, in quoting Hosea, gives the answer. In the very place where it was said, "Ye are not my people", that is, most likely, in the place (and idolatrous condition) where they lived and acted like Gentiles, "there shall they be called the children (sons) of the living God". There was hope therefore for those in the nation who were prepared to come in repentance and cast themselves on the mercy of God. Nevertheless, Jews and Gentiles were on the same footing. It was the divine call that would bring them into the blessing of being called "sons of the living God". To the Gentiles in particular this was something new. To be in a relation with the living (and true) God was indeed a great blessing and it was theirs despite Jewish protests.

27 Paul is obviously anticipating in this verse a cavil from the Jews that he was patently wrong in his argument that Israel should be restored, since all but a few in the nation had rejected Jesus of Nazareth as being the promised Messiah. The prophet Isaiah is quoted to prove that the present exclusion of the mass of the nation from blessing was not new, but reminiscent of what had happened in the past. From their own Scriptures by the word of a revered prophet, the apostle shows that it was not a new thought that only a remnant should be saved. Isaiah had used a phrase which had become proverbial of Israel, based probably on Gen 22:17, that Israel should be as the sand of the sea for number; yet, he adds, "only a remnant shall return", that is, to the mighty God (Isa 10:21).

The fact that the Israelites were large in number is not an indication that large numbers will be saved. A remnant is no doubt small by comparison. The reference to the remnant by Paul and Isaiah should not be interpreted as being "some accidental leftover" (Lenski). The very fact that the bulk of the nation consistently refused to respond to the overtures of God implies that there was a remnant which would obey the call of God and turn to Him for mercy. If the Jews in Paul's day argued that there had been a turn of events about which they had no warning, or knowledge, the prophetic Scriptures were plain: they were without excuse.

In Isaiah's day the Assyrians were raised up to punish the Israelites for blatant sin and idolatry. The king of Assyria compared his idols with the idols in Jerusalem and concluded that his were greater. This was the situation that cried out for retribution. The outlook was bleak, but there was hope, the remnant would be saved.

Having therefore proved the point from Scripture that the calamity which faced the nation was not the fault of God, Paul turned the resentment of the Jews against themselves. Their national status was not as sacred as they thought. The prophetic Scriptures condemned them. Their only hope was to turn to God as individuals and believe the gospel of God which was already being proclaimed far and wide by men and women who had themselves turned to God from idols to serve the living and true God.

28 This verse seems to indicate that there is no possibility of slackness on God's part in bringing all things to a satisfactory completion. Whether Jew or Gentile, when it comes to final retribution God will not fail and all His actions will be consistent with the righteousness of His character. The verse, however, is a difficult one to understand.

What is cut short is not clear. How far Paul intended the historical implications of Isaiah's day to apply to his argument is not clear either. Denney remarks, "It is doubtful whether anyone could assign meaning to these words unless he had an idea beforehand of what they ought to or must mean". The views of most commentators are also obscure. This is borne out by the obvious difficulties of most exegetes in their attempts to give a clear interpretation of the verse. For example, Vine comments, "That God finishes His word (*logos*) means that He brings it to an end; that He cuts it short would seem to indicate the summary and decisive character of the Divine action". Plummer, however, is more lucid. He states, "The sense is that God will righteously and speedily terminate the destruction, or consumption, or sentence of divine displeasure against His people. And this consumption was to be exercised on the descendants of Abraham".

From what Haldane says about the verse, it seems that he was quite clear about its meaning. He states, "This refers to God's judgments poured out upon the Jews for rejecting their Messiah. They were then cut off manifestly from being His people. He cut short the work in righteous judgment. The destruction denotes the ruin and desolation of the whole house of Israel, with the exception of a small remnant". He maintains that this, not having taken place in the re-establishment of the Jews after the Babylonian captivity, must necessarily be understood to take place in the times of the gospel.

There is no doubt that Paul was concerned about the plight of his countrymen. He was aware that the righteousness of God would be expressed in retribution. The judgment was deserved and no objection to the setting aside of the nation, and to its being superseded by a calling of individuals in a new era, could be sustained. The vessels of mercy would be called out from amongst Jews and Gentiles according to the sovereign choice of God.

29 Another quotation from the Scriptures is introduced. As Isaiah made known in the past, had it not been for the Lord of hosts the nation would have suffered the same fate as Sodom and Gomorrah. If the objectors in Paul's day were honest with themselves they would have acknowledged that only the grace of God had saved the nation from extinction. In the previous verses, there was at least a remnant considered. In this verse the apostle changes the reference to a remnant in the quotation from Isaiah's prophecy and limits what was preserved to a "seed". Possibly the thought was in his mind that although there were few survivors, it was nevertheless the power of the Lord of hosts, the Almighty God, that had kept the nation from being wiped out altogether.

The first chapter of Isaiah's prophecy presents a dark picture of the state of affairs in Israel. Sacrifices were being offered in abundance but the God to whom professedly they were being offered had to make known through the prophet that He was tired of burnt offerings. The blood of bullocks, lambs or he-goats brought Him no pleasure. From Isaiah's message Paul applied the lesson to the Jews of his day. They were no better than their forefathers. They deserved to be treated like Sodom and Gomorrah and if God had not decided to preserve a seed, they would have been cut off entirely.

There was no room for complacency on the part of the Jews. The sinfulness of the nation warranted judgment. They relied on God's support and yet they claimed that He was not acting fairly with them. They considered they were in covenant relation with God and that He had no right therefore to pass them by and go to the Gentiles. This attitude was what Paul addressed. As Isaiah said, the Israelites could be as the sand of the sea for number but that weighed little with God. He would still fulfil His promise in accordance with His righteousness and He would save a remnant. In addition, He would show mercy to the Gentiles, and from amongst them He would call vessels of mercy. There was no inconsistency with God. He had not changed and He had not gone back on His word. What He was doing was already intimated in the prophetic Scriptures.

Notes

19 Lee suggests that there is a three-fold objection in this verse:
1. If God is sovereign, then He cannot find fault with me for being a sinner, for I am as He made me.
2. I cannot resist His sovereign will, therefore I cannot help myself.
3. How can He find fault with me for doing what I was predestinated to do?
Paul answers these objections in vv.20,21,22-24.

20 Haldane: "That God does all things right there is no doubt, but the grounds of His conduct He does not now explain to His people. Much less is it to be expected that He would justify His conduct by explaining the grounds of it to His enemies. No man has the right to bring God to trial".

21 Plummer observes: "If He raises Paul to honour and glory that does not show that Nero's condemnation is not just. Honour and dishonour point to the happiness or mercy, the glory or the shame, that shall be finally awarded to man according as their characters shall be at the last".

22 Lee comments: "Observe that when Paul speaks of 'vessels of wrath' he simply says, 'fitted' (i.e., 'marked') for destruction. He does not say that God fitted them! Whereas when he refers to the 'vessels of mercy' he says 'whom He had afore prepared unto glory'. The fact is, men fit themselves for hell, but it is God who fits men for heaven".

26 "The question may be asked, How is it possible for Paul and Peter to take a passage which predicts restoration for Israelites and apply it audiences in which Gentiles predominated? The answer is simple; the same principle operates throughout" (Hendrikson).

2. Israel's Past Disobedience
9:30-10:21

(a) *Human responsibility – Israel's failure (vv.30-33)*

> v.30 "What shall we say then? That the Gentiles, which followed not after righteousness, have attained to righteousness, even the righteousness which is of faith.

> v.31 But Israel, which followed after the law of righteousness, hath not attained to the law of righteousness.
> v.32 Wherefore? Because they sought it not by faith, but as it were by the works of the law. For they stumbled at that stumblingstone;
> v.33 As it is written, Behold, I lay in Sion a stumblingstone and rock of offence: and whosoever believeth on him shall not be ashamed."

30 The last four verses of the chapter are introduced by Paul's characteristic phrase, "What shall we say then?" Taking into account what he had set out, it certainly appeared to the Jew that there had been a complete reversal of God's ways with the nation. To be so highly privileged for centuries and then be rejected in favour of godless Gentiles was more than the Jewish people could accept.

The contrast which Paul develops in the closing verses is not between Gentiles as a whole and the Jewish nation. Even the Jew knew that from amongst the mass of Gentiles certain ones had come into favour, although even a small number of Gentiles was enough to stir up Jewish resentment. The apostle's purpose here is to establish the principle on which Gentiles, though they be few in number, had attained to righteousness. He is not even thinking about the remnant taken out from amongst the Jews who had attained to righteousness in the same way as the Gentiles, styled earlier in the epistle as "vessels of mercy". His aim is to show how the Jewish nation had missed out and how Gentiles were finding acceptance with God.

It is clear that Paul is not finished with the subject of righteousness. It has been the dominant theme of his epistle, the central plank of his theology, although, perhaps, the aspect he is dealing with here is confined to having a right standing before God. The Gentiles as a whole did not pursue righteousness. They had their own gods, and the Scriptures bear record that the God of Israel, the only true God, was of no real concern to them. As Paul has been making known, what has changed is that from amongst the mass of Gentiles, God was calling out vessels of mercy, who were obtaining a right standing before Him by believing the gospel message. God was being justified in the response from vessels of mercy, Jews and Gentiles, who were prepared to acknowledge that the only righteousness God would recognise was that which had been won by the sacrifice of Christ at the cross of Calvary.

31 In the previous verse Paul stated that the Gentiles, although they did not pursue righteousness, attained to it on the ground of faith. The Jews, however, despite pursuing the law of righteousness, did not attain to it. That there was earnest endeavour on their part cannot be denied, but what they sought eluded them. The reason why they failed to overtake it is given in the next verse; briefly stated it was because they went about it in the wrong way, not because they had been set an impossible task. Even before the flood Noah had this testimony, "Thee have I seen righteous before me in this generation" (Gen 7:1). Hezekiah knew what was required, as his prayer makes known, "O Lord, remember now how I have walked before thee in truth and with a perfect heart, and have done that which is good in thy sight" (2 Kings 20:3). Of Zacharias and Elisabeth it was said, "They were both righteous before God, walking in all the commandments and ordinances of the Lord blameless" (Luke 1:6). It is clear that various people at different times could rise to what was acceptable to God, but sadly, the mass of the Jewish nation failed miserably.

The expression "law of righteousness" may be understood in several ways. It could mean a general rule or a general principle which if observed could produce a righteousness before God. It could also mean what results from keeping the law of Moses. It is most likely that it is the latter that Paul had in mind as he will show that it was the way in which the Jews pursued the law that was wrong. In effect they held that God was under a certain obligation to account them righteous by reason of their national status and on account of their system of religious observances. But, as made known by the Lord, particularly in Matt 23, a chapter of woes, they concerned themselves with things that were insignificant and omitted the weightier matters of the law, judgment, mercy and faith.

32 The opening word "Wherefore" is an argumentative question. Paul seems to be asking, "Do you want to know why you did not attain to righteousness? I shall tell you, you sought it not by faith, but, as it were, by works". The Jews had a zeal of (for) God, but it was not according to knowledge (10:2). They refused the ground that God was working on. The Gentiles recognised that the God of heaven was extending mercy on the principle of faith and they grasped the opportunity gladly. The Jews held steadfastly to their works, seeking earnestly to compel God to accept them on the ground of merit. To this end they endeavoured in their own way to keep the law but it was to no effect.

The way the Jews went about trying to establish their own righteousness resulted in their stumbling. The stumbling-stone was Christ. The acceptance of Jesus as Messiah called for faith. The Jews were not prepared to receive Him, preferring to hold on to their preconceived ideas about a Messiah who would come up to their standards. As far as their assessment of Jesus of Nazareth was concerned, He did not answer to their requirements. They sought righteousness by works of law and spurned God's overtures of grace. Acceptance of the Saviour of Israel who had come in accordance with the Scriptures was called for but there was no national response. There were individuals who recognised that the long-awaited day of redemption had arrived, but they were only a spiritual remnant. Nevertheless, on the principle of faith these believers were justified. They did not seek a righteousness of their own, but were happy to have it reckoned to them by the grace and mercy of God. The righteous standing they had pursued under Judaism, but which they never attained to, was received by confessing Jesus as the Christ and accepting Him as their Saviour.

33 Having introduced the stumbling-stone over which the Jews stumbled, the Scriptures referred to complete the thrust of the argument. The apostle joins two OT passages together, part of Isa 8:14 and part of Isa 28:16. Isa 8 has a very strong message of warning for both houses of Israel to turn away from confederacies with other nations and turn to Jehovah, the Lord of hosts. If they failed to heed the warning, Jehovah would be a stone of stumbling and many would stumble over it and fall. Isa 28 presses a similar lesson, but adds that all who trusted in the Lord would find Him a tried stone, a precious corner stone, a sure foundation.

Although the Jews might contest Paul's application of the passages he quoted, there is no doubt about the apostle's understanding of the situation. His firm conviction was that Jesus of Nazareth, as He was known by the Jews, was the promised Messiah. If there had been a time when he thought otherwise, that was no longer the case. His eyes had been opened to see that the prophet was referring to the Messiah and not to anyone or anything else. Although the prophet has many wonderful things to say about the Messiah and the kingdom He would introduce, Paul's point is to select some reference which will amplify the thought of stumbling. A refusal to accept Jesus as Messiah would result in calamity. Instead of being a Saviour He would be a rock of offence, an insurmountable obstacle with dire results for eternity.

The section closes with a wonderful statement, "whosoever believeth on him shall not be ashamed". Instead of bringing this stage of his argument to a close with a warning of coming judgment, Paul brings in a message of hope. There was no need to be faced with shame by being confronted with the error of their ways in a coming day. The door of opportunity was still open. Faith in the One of whom the prophet spoke would ensure that they would never be ashamed or filled with remorse. The righteous standing with God, so earnestly desired and sought after, could be obtained through simple faith, a trust that involved acceptance of the One who was crucified at Calvary and whose resurrection from the dead and ascension to God's right hand was being proclaimed worldwide.

Notes

30 On the phrase "which followed" (*diōkō*, "to pursue," "to follow eagerly"), *The New Bible Commentary* comments, "He uses racecourse imagery to contrast Gentiles with Israel. The former, though not even 'in the race' (who did not pursue righteousness) have, nevertheless reached 'the finishing line': they have obtained a right standing with God. And they have obtained it, Paul makes clear, because of their faith. Israel, on the other hand, though actively engaged in the race, has not reached the goal of that race".

(b) *The righteousness of God exemplified (vv.1-10)*

> v.1 "Brethren, my heart's desire and prayer to God for Israel is, that they might be saved.
> v.2 For I bear them record that they have a zeal of God, but not according to knowledge.

> v.3 For they being ignorant of God's righteousness, and going about to establish their own righteousness, have not submitted themselves unto the righteousness of God.
> v.4 For Christ is the end of the law for righteousness to every one that believeth.
> v.5 For Moses describeth the righteousness which is of the law, That the man which doeth those things shall live by them.
> v.6 But the righteousness which is of faith speaketh on this wise, Say not in thine heart, Who shall ascend into heaven? (that is, to bring Christ down from above:)
> v.7 Or, Who shall descend into the deep? (that is, to bring up Christ again from the dead.)
> v.8 But what saith it? The word is nigh thee, even in thy mouth, and in thy heart: that is, the word of faith, which we preach;
> v.9 That if thou shalt confess with thy mouth the Lord Jesus, and shalt believe in thine heart that God hath raised him from the dead, thou shalt be saved.
> v.10 For with the heart man believeth unto righteousness; and with the mouth confession is made unto salvation."

1 The term "Brethren" refers to Paul's brethren "in Christ" and not to his link by nature to his fellow-countrymen. The difference, and indeed the distance, between these two relationships is immeasurable. Nevertheless, the earnest desire and prayer of the apostle is that the gulf between them might be bridged by the salvation of his brethren in the flesh.

The desire of the heart which Paul expresses indicates the warmth and reality of his feelings for the Jews. The word *eudokia* is frequently used of the way God feels for men and women, especially when they turn to Christ in faith. It indicates favour, good pleasure and delight. A classical example of its use is found in Phil 2:13, "For it is God which worketh in you both to will and to do of his good pleasure (*eudokia*)". Regarding the gospel, the favourable reception given to man by God may be a mystery, but it is gloriously true. The warm welcome to all who believe on the Son is not a fictitious theory; it is a solid fact. God takes delight in those who take sides with His Son and something of that warm feeling is seen in Paul. He wants to show the benevolence of God to his fellow-countrymen but he knows there is only one way they can come into the good of it; they must believe the gospel.

The word *deēsis* used for "prayer" here is not the normal term. It carries the meaning of entreaty or supplication. It is not exclusively a religious word as it is used to address man as well as God. It suggests prayer for particular benefits and in that sense would be better translated as "petition". It is suggested that the fundamental idea in *deēsis* is a sense of need – a particular need – and a sense of helplessness. Since Paul could not bring his fellow-countrymen to repentance and faith in Christ by his own efforts, his dependence on God for their salvation is evident in his pleas on their behalf. There is warmth in Paul's personal testimony of his desire for Israel's salvation. This, however, is contrasted with the zeal of those for whom he prayed as they zealously tried to establish their own righteousness.

2 Paul's testimony is not based on hearsay. He speaks from first-hand knowledge of the zeal of the Jews for God. There was a time in his own life when he was characterised by the same zeal and had been as zealous as any for the defence of the Jewish way of life. He gave the proof of that to the Philippians by stating credentials which were entirely flawless by Jewish standards (Phil 3:5,6). Paul's testimony to the great tragedy of Jewish zeal, however, was that it was not according to knowledge. The credit he was prepared to give only acknowledged the earnestness of their desire to serve God, it did not support the way they went about it.

The AV gives "zeal of God" which infers that the Jews drove themselves forward under the impression that God approved of their efforts. The rendering of the RV is "zeal for God", suggesting that they firmly believed that what they did was done on God's behalf. Either way their zeal was misplaced. Their enthusiasm knew no bounds as demonstrated in their persecution of the Lord, and His apostles and those of their own nation who had turned from Judaism to Christianity. They were lacking in the correct knowledge. The Scriptures, which they professed to believe, clearly testified that Jesus was the Christ, but they shut their eyes and closed their ears to the obvious. The zeal which they had for Judaism propelled them in the wrong direction and created in them a nation of zealots, bent on their own destruction.

Nevertheless, Paul's earnestness for his fellow-countrymen that they might be saved is clearly evident, as is their earnestness to earn acceptance by their works. Sadly, as a nation the Jews were far away from having any part in the apostle's experience and his earnest desire, so clearly stated to the Philippians, "I count all things but loss for the excellency of the knowledge of Christ Jesus my Lord...and be found in him, not having mine own righteousness, which is of the law, but that which is through the faith of Christ, the righteousness which is of God through faith" (Phil 3:8,9) JND.

3 The ignorance which the Jews had of God's righteousness, coupled with a misplaced zeal was a fatal combination. Judaism had degenerated into a blind fanaticism which ignored every warning of divine displeasure. Here Paul states that the Jews earnestly sought after the establishment of their own righteousness; it was an obsession with them. This desire was so fixed in their minds that they failed to see that they were going in the wrong direction. It was impossible for them to establish their own righteousness in their own way, but they chose to pursue it. In this way they were culpable; their ignorance could not be excused.

The righteousness of God which Paul introduces here refers back to all that he has said about it in the epistle. He has made it clear that the basis of having it reckoned on the principle of faith was won by the sacrifice of Christ at Calvary. The righteousness which enables men and women to have a right standing before God was not of works. Striving had no part in it. Zeal, however, sincere in itself was misplaced and therefore of no value. Consequently, the apostle states that the Jews did not submit themselves to God's righteousness. They ignored the overtures of God towards them, preferring to go their own way. In this, of course, they were guilty of blatantly rejecting every offer, willing to remain in ignorance of how to obtain a right standing before God.

4   There are various views of what Paul means by the expression, "Christ is the end of the law". It could mean that Christ (and all that the name of "Christ" implies), is the end of the law as a way of attaining righteousness, or it could be taken that Christ is the goal of the law as far as righteousness is concerned. The problem in the verse is understanding what Paul means by "end" *(telos)*. The word is capable of being translated in different ways and indeed is so variously rendered in the Scripture that it is difficult to arrive at a decisive meaning in this verse, based on the usage of the word itself.

In view of what is stated at 9:30 and 10:2,3, it is clear that the death, resurrection and ascension of Christ, brought an end to any possibility of attaining righteousness by the law. If it were even remotely possible to acquire righteousness by law-keeping, then there was no need for Christ to die. Since, however, God raised Him from the dead and seated Him at His right hand, He is the end of the law for righteousness to everyone that believeth. There is no need for another way of acquiring righteousness. In fact, to advance another code of religious practice would undermine the work of Christ and that could never be countenanced. Righteousness did not come by the law. If it had, then Christ died in vain, as Paul made clear to the Galatians (2:21).

There is nothing wrong with the law. Paul argued vigorously in its defence earlier in the epistle, although he had to admit that "a man is justified by faith without (apart from) the deeds of the law" (3:28). Nevertheless, his firm conviction was, "wherefore the law is holy, and the commandment is holy, and just and good" (7:12). The fault did not lie with the law; it lay with those who used it as a means of seeking to establish their own righteousness before God. The Jews failed to admit that righteousness on the principle of faith was God's appointed way. They had decided that the state of being right before God was acquired by works and they refused to deviate from that despite every appeal and warning to the nation to the contrary.

5   The first passage Paul quotes from the OT in support of his argument about justification by faith is Lev 18:5. It is taken from the introduction to the law of holiness and chastity, a section of the Scriptures well-known to the Jews. Within the scope of a few verses in Lev 18 there are the oft-recurring reminders, "I am Jehovah" and "I am Jehovah your God". These imply that the injunctions were meant by the Lord to be carefully weighed up before Him. The introduction to the law of holiness makes plain that the people were not to do what they observed and what they did in the land of Egypt, neither were they to do what they would see in the land of Canaan to which they were going. There was no obligation to conform to the influences around them, because they belonged to Jehovah their God. The obligation they were under was to do His commandments. If they observed them, they would live in them. Sadly, the history of the nation records that the statutes and judgments were soon ignored or broken.

The AV and the RV render the first portion in the catena or chain of OT references as indirect speech, "Moses describeth..." or, "Moses writeth that". There is good authority in support of a direct quotation, such as, "Moses writes about the righteousness of the law, 'the doing man shall live by it' ". Since the apostle's defence is based on the Scriptures which were in the possession of the Jews, it is preferable to take his OT references as direct quotations. They would then have added force over oblique mentions.

The injunction given by Moses suggests that the law was the aggregate of statutes and judgments given by the Lord. While this is true it is obvious from Paul's statement, "Moses describeth the righteousness which is of the law" that it reflected the character and the grace of God. If anyone set out to obey every statute and commandment of the law, that person would still have to take into account the character and the grace of the God who made such a revelation. The law, however, considered as the aggregate of commandments had no power in it to give life. Paul made this clear to the Galatians, "for if there had been a law which could have given life, verily righteousness should have been by the law" (Gal 3:21). It should have been obvious to the Jews that since they could not attain to the standards demanded by the law, they needed a Saviour. This, however, did not seem to have been taken into account by the nation as the people pursued righteousness believing it to be attainable by their own works of merit.

In Paul's approach to righteousness, he does not separate it from faith. The righteous man does not live before God because of his righteous conduct, but because of his faith. The apostle has already quoted Hab 2:4 in this epistle (1:17) and he quotes the same verse to the Galatians (3:11), "the just shall live by faith". That faith recognises the merit of the person and the work of Christ. It is a faith that accepts the word of God in its entirety. From this point in his argument, Paul will go on to emphasise faith, stressing the principles, "whosoever shall call" (v.13): concluding with "So then faith cometh by hearing, and hearing by the word of God" (v.17). The first passage in Paul's list of quotations laid down an undeniable fact: if a person desired to have a life which was perfectly in accordance with God's requirements, that person would have to conform to every precept in every respect, every moment of every day, all through life. Even the most religious Jew knew that was beyond human attainment, but it did not deter the Jews from going their own way about it, all the while expecting God to add His approval to their system of works.

6 The righteousness which is of the law (v.5) is now contrasted with the righteousness which is of faith. There is no question of there being two sets of works, one under the law and other under faith. Labouring in faith is as unacceptable as working under the law. The righteousness of faith which is introduced in this verse means that righteous relationship with God which is reckoned as a result of unmerited favour on God's part and gained by man on the principle of faith. Works in any shape or form do not enter into it.

The righteousness which is by faith is here personified. Instead of quoting Moses as saying, "Who shall ascend into heaven?" it is the righteousness of faith which "speaketh on this wise". Within three verses there are three short quotations, each interspersed with explanatory comments. They are not exact quotations either from the Hebrew or from the LXX but free renderings. A consideration of Paul's allusions to the OT will reveal that he was so conversant with the Scriptures, that his everyday speech was interlaced with scriptural phrases. In addition, it was a rabbinical practice to run passages of Scripture together. Clearly, Paul was influenced by this as is also evidenced in 3:9-18 where he lists eight references to the OT.

The first quotation in this verse, "...say not in thine heart, Who shall ascend into heaven" carries with it an explanatory note, "that is, to bring Christ down from above". This note forms no part of Deut 30:11-14. It is rather a fresh revelation which gives meaning to the words of Moses. The commandment of the law-giver had no doubt been read thousands of times, but until Paul wrote, it was never understood that Christ would come to earth and return to heaven. Nevertheless, the principle of the commandment was the same as declared by Paul. There was no need to look hither and thither, in heaven or in the deep for direction from God; the word was nigh at all times. It may be that Paul was saying, "Do not think that Christ must be brought back to earth", or he may be saying that it is wrong to think that it is necessary for Christ to be brought down, since the word is nigh thee, even in thy mouth and in thy heart. It is perhaps better to take the latter meaning, since there is stress on "say not in thine heart", a Hebrew phrase meaning "to think" (see Deut 15:9; Matt 24:48; Luke 12:45). The apostle seems to be saying, "Why think on something so highly improbable when the word is so close, as to be actually in the heart and mouth".

7 The second quotation from Deut 30 is given in the form of another question, "Who shall descend into the deep?" This is given in the RV as, "Who shall descend into the abyss?" The word rendered "abyss" (*abussos*), is used in Luke 8:31 by the demons who besought the Lord that He would not command them to go out into the deep (abyss). Elsewhere in the NT the word is found only in the Revelation. It is most likely that Paul used the expression here to describe the abode of the dead, in contrast to his reference in the previous verse to heaven. The reference to the sea is not unusual. The LXX gives "abyss" in some places for "sea" where the thought of its being fathomless is involved (see Ps 107:26). Amongst the Jews, the expressions used by Paul were apparently proverbial ones to describe what was impossible. What he is saying is that it would be folly to think about grappling with the impossible when the word is nigh, even in the mouth and heart.

The purpose behind Paul's question, "Who shall descend into the deep?" is given, "that is, to bring up Christ again from the dead". This is an expansion of what Paul introduced by the phrase in the previous verse, "Say not in thine heart". The righteousness of faith does not think that impossible situations have to be surmounted to acquire the blessing so earnestly desired. Christ has died and He does not need to die again. He came to earth in humiliation and that does not need to be repeated. He descended into the realms of the unseen world and rose triumphantly from the dead, ascending to the Father's right hand. That was the seal of His finished work. To think about repetitions of these, or any other unnecessary and impossible situations, when the means of obtaining a right standing were ever present was the height of folly. Even if there were any who could ascend to heaven or descend into the deep, what would be the purpose, Paul seems to suggest, since God has done it all by sending His own Son to deal with the sin question and open up the way to Himself? That way Paul will describe in the next few verses.

8 The third quotation from Deut 30 is introduced by a question, "But what saith it?" that is, What does Scripture have to say about the matter of obtaining righteousness by faith and not by the works of the law? The question raised by Paul is answered by himself, "The word is nigh thee, even in thy mouth and in thy heart: that is the word of faith, which we preach". It should be noticed that in quoting from Deut 30 the apostle does not state the words of Moses, "that thou mayest do it". The argument he is presenting does not call for human effort: it concerned the word of faith which recognised the inability of man to obtain the blessing of the gospel on any other principle than that of faith.

As it was in the days of Moses, so it is in NT times. God has not set mankind a difficult task. In the mercy of God, even the simplest can come into blessing. The choice of words, "even in thy mouth and in thy heart" confirms that law-works and deeds of merit, however small or great are not necessary; God has brought the means right to each person – no one needs to lift a limb to do anything. The message calls for faith in response to the preachers. Those who were heralds of the gospel were telling it out constantly. No restriction was placed on them to hold it back for a more favourable opportunity. Every day was a day of good tidings and the apostle here confirms that the heralds of the cross were telling it out freely.

The "word of faith" could be construed to mean the body of doctrine in the christian message. It would not do despite to the text to consider the expression that way. It is more likely, however, that since Paul has been stressing at considerable length the contrast between the principle of law and the principle of faith, that he is continuing on that theme here. It is the whole vital matter of faith which is being established. There were fundamental features in the gospel which were beyond the capabilities of man to enhance in any way. The message was simple and straightforward, but it was also profound. It could not rightly be dismissed as being beneath the greatest minds. It was designed by God to meet the needs of all mankind, from the simplest soul to the greatest intellect. The gospel was indeed God's artless, unencumbered plan.

The Deuteronomy background to Paul's argument at this point is worthy of consideration. The Israelites who had heard the covenant details at Horeb had died in the wilderness because of their unbelief. A new generation was about to cross Jordan into the promised land and it was to them that Moses re-stated what had been delivered to the previous generation. The challenge given to the people of Israel which called for total commitment to God was not beyond their capabilities to grasp. It was achievable. What Moses delivered in his address was relevant to their daily lives and was quite within the reach of the people. It was neither up in heaven nor beyond the sea; the word was indeed nigh them. If they listened to the law as it was expounded to them and they stored the knowledge of it in their hearts and minds then its precepts would always be before them to help them obey what the law commanded.

From Paul's reference to Deut 30 it is clear that what he stated was the same in principle as what Moses had declared to the Israelites, with the exception of any references to the law. Nevertheless, God put no obstacles before the children of Israel and, in the new age of grace, He could not have made the way of salvation any simpler. It is in fact so simple and straightforward that many have stumbled when the word of the gospel has been made known to them. In Isaiah's description of millennial blessings he writes of the "way of holiness", and states, "The wayfaring men, though fools, shall not err therein" (Isa 35:8). Similar conditions apply in connection with the gospel of grace.

9 This wonderful verse of Holy Scripture, so often quoted by preachers of the gospel, follows the reasoning of the apostle that there is neither need for miracles nor looking for inscrutable things to find out what God is saying. The word of faith is in the heart and in the mouth. Nevertheless, that word of faith was not answered by a mere mental or verbal assent, it would have to be a firm conviction before it became an effectual work in the soul. This is what Paul emphasises now.

The opening word of the verse, "that", could mean that what follows in vv.9,10 is what comprises the "word of faith", or it could mean, "That is to say, if thou shalt confess…" or, "Because, if thou shalt confess…", suggesting as some commentators do, that Paul is giving the reason for the "word of faith" being preached. Both are acceptable, but the former in the nature of the case seems to be preferable. In practice, myriads down the age have been saved through taking Rom 10:9 as the content of the "word of faith".

Although it would be expected that "believing" would come before "confessing" the order given by Paul suits the order he has given of "mouth" and "heart" in v.8. Some look upon confessing and believing as the outward and inward expressions of the work of salvation and there is no doubt much merit in that. The confessing of Jesus as Lord as envisaged by Paul is a public acknowledgement of total commitment to Him. Mere mental assent does not equate with the confession of Jesus as Lord. This is a universal requirement. It is as applicable to the Jew as it is to the Gentile and it cannot be modified to suit national prejudices. Although it is possible for anyone to say, "Jesus is Lord", that in no way fulfils what Paul is stating here. To the Corinthians he wrote, "…no man can say that Jesus is Lord, but by the Holy Spirit" (1 Cor 12:3), no doubt meaning that such a confession was not made in truth apart from the Holy Spirit.

Belief in the heart is more than a mere mental concession to the fact of resurrection. If confession with the mouth means more than merely saying, "I believe", or, "Jesus is Lord", believing in the heart that God has raised up Christ from amongst the dead must also have deeper implications. Paul has already established the necessity of internal transformation in connection with circumcision, it had to be of the heart and not of the letter (2:29). This word from the apostle was confirmation of what had already been laid down in the OT. Moses called for circumcision of the heart (Deut 10:16), as did Jeremiah (4:4). The words used by the apostle were not indicative of something novel; they were correctly-applied terms from the Scriptures.

From what can be learned from history, the confession "Jesus is Lord" became a test of the reality of faith for many in apostolic and post-apostolic times. To hold fast to that belief meant martyrdom for many believers, including several of the early "fathers". Here, however, Paul makes it clear that confession with the mouth and belief in the heart that God raised Christ from amongst the dead will result in salvation. There is no doubt about that. Belief in the resurrection is vital, as Paul made clear to the Corinthians, "If Christ be not raised, your faith is vain (empty, futile); ye are yet in your sins" (1 Cor 15:17). Belief in the resurrection also involves belief in the ascension and the fact that Christ is alive. It would be an empty faith if it held that the Lord was raised, only to return to the grave.

10 The content of this verse is an expansion of the previous one. Belief in the heart leads to the attaining of righteousness. It is the first link in the long chain of experiences in the christian faith. It is the groundwork upon which God builds. When a sinner is justified, the floodgates of blessing are opened wide and God comes out in wondrous grace. The new life within, divine life in the soul, cannot be contained in secret: it will manifest itself. Here, Paul declares that confession will follow. It is often said that a dumb faith is no faith at all – a saying which has much merit.

It is significant that there is no mention of law-works. What has been declared is universal with no concessions for the Jews. All must come in faith and that faith must be wholehearted acceptance of what God has made known in the gospel. God can read the heart of man. Only He knows the reality of belief in the heart. To others, however, it has to be confessed and it is testimony to the saving grace of God that is recognised by mankind as proof that a divine work has been wrought in the soul.

What has been set out in the first part of the chapter has been a wonderful unfolding of the grace and thoughtfulness of God. The fact that there is no need to do some great thing to receive the blessing is beyond compare. Some are offended by the simplicity of it. Like Naaman the leper who turned away in a rage when given a simple cure, they want to do something to earn salvation. But that is not God's way in the gospel. Plummer, quoting Chrysostom, describes it well: "There is no long journey to go, no seas to sail over, no mountains to pass to get saved. But if you be not minded to cross the threshold, you may even while you sit at home be saved".

Notes

1 Some manuscripts give "on behalf of them" instead of "for Israel". If writing principally to Gentiles in Rome, this would lay less stress on Jewish status.

Denney suggests that his heart's desire (*eudokia*) is that in which his heart could rest with complacency. His prayer and his heart's desire are in their interest with a view to their salvation.

2 Vine, quoting J Armitage Robinson, points out that *epignōsis* is "knowledge directed towards a particular object, perceiving, discerning". Here the sense is more in the nature of adequate knowledge. The zeal the Jews had was not according to adequate perception and discernment of God's righteousness.

8 *Rhēma* ("the word") is not common with Paul (only eight times, whereas he uses *logos* 88 times). Here it carries the meaning of that which is spoken, what is declared.

10 To believe in the heart that God had raised up Christ from the dead is not merely the acceptance of something that was common knowledge. God had seen to it that there was ample testimony to verify that (e.g. "seen of above 500 brethren at once" – 1 Cor 15:6). It is the sinner's acknowledgement that God has accepted the work of His Son and therefore if He has done that, what will He not do for the sinner? (see Rom 1:4-6).

(c) *The gospel offered to all without discrimination (vv.11-15)*

>v.11 "For the scripture saith, Whosoever believeth on him shall not be ashamed.
>v.12 For there is no difference between the Jew and the Greek: for the same Lord over all is rich unto all that call upon him.
>v.13 For whosoever shall call upon the name of the Lord shall be saved.
>v.14 How then shall they call on him in whom they have not believed? and how shall they believe in him of whom they have not heard? and how shall they hear without a preacher?
>v.15 And how shall they preach, except they be sent? as it is written, How beautiful are the feet of them that preach the gospel of peace, and bring glad tidings of good things!"

11 As Paul continues his argument he turns again to the Scriptures for support. He has already referred to Isa 28:16 at 9:33 where he added a few words from Isa 8:14 to highlight the unbelief of the Jews. It is clear that he is now anticipating objections from his fellow-countrymen that the universal appeal of the gospel he preached had no divine approval. To counter this, he brings in Isaiah again to show that even one of their own prophets had a wider horizon in view than the

Jewish nation. Isaiah had proclaimed quite clearly, "He that believeth shall not be ashamed" (LXX).

The apostle makes a slight change in the quotation by inserting the word "Whosoever". Isaiah's announcement, "He that believeth" was wide enough to make it one of general application. To remove all doubt, Paul changes this to "Whosoever" or "Everyone" (*pas,* a favourite word of Paul's), thereby stressing that the promise was not confined to one nation, but that in the mercy of God it had universal possibilities for faith. This is perfectly in keeping with the outlook of Isaiah. He spoke of the blessings that come through faith and that the faith principle was not the sole possession of any one nation.

The apostle Peter also quotes Isa 28:16 in 1 Pet 2:6, but for a different purpose. Whereas Paul quotes only part of the verse, Peter gives it in its entirety. He shows that to those who believe, Christ is precious and they will not be confounded (ashamed), but to those who do not believe and are classed as disobedient, He is a stone of stumbling. The different approaches of these two inspired penmen to the Scriptures illustrate how the word of God is used under the influence of the Holy Spirit to give guidance in the various circumstances of life. Isa 28:16 itself shows evidence of the influence of other portions of the Scriptures. The prophet Isaiah gives three words: "tried", "precious" and "solid" (AV "sure"). These are the same as recorded in 1 Kings 5:17 of the huge stones of the temple, although Isaiah gives them in reverse order. Paul no doubt caught the spirit of that. Referring to Isa 28:16 he asserts that whosoever believeth on Him shall not be put to shame, he shall be as immovable as the tried and solid rock, the Saviour on whom he rests by faith.

The passage from the OT which the apostle quotes makes no mention of confession, but emphasises faith. This suits Paul's appreciation of what is basic to the gospel. It is faith which Paul has been stressing all the way through. This is the response which is expected from those who hear the Word. If they hear and do not respond in faith they have only themselves to blame if they miss the blessing. God cannot be faulted in any way if men and women are lost eternally through their own folly.

12 Paul's statement that there is no difference between the Jew and the Greek is a very bold one. In fact, the Jews and the Greeks were poles apart in every respect. They were both zealous for their cultures, but these were entirely different from each other. What the apostle is stating, however, is that there were situations in which there were no differences. Already in the epistle he has stated that "all have sinned and come short of the glory of God" (3:23). In dealing with the sin question, "Christ died for the ungodly". Jews and Greeks were both embraced in this. Both were ungodly and therefore under the same condemnation. Here, however, both can come into blessing, for in the matter of salvation there are no distinctions.

Paul's argument goes on to establish the truth that there is one God. The Jews might claim sole possession of the true God and the Greeks might serve other gods altogether, even an "unknown god", as Paul observed at Athens (Acts 17:23). As announced in the gospel, all distinctions are removed, "the same Lord is rich unto all that call upon him". The reference here may be to God or it may be to Christ. Since v.9 states that it is Jesus who is confessed as Lord, it is more likely that it is Christ who is referred to in this connection.

The thought that the Lord is rich unto all that call upon Him settles any doubts about His capabilities of satisfying everyone's needs. God is not impoverished by giving liberally to all. Neither are believers the losers by having put their trust in Him. It cannot be that the unsaved have more, despite the fact that the pursuit of wealth is characteristic of their way of life. Those who call upon the Lord can expect to receive the Lord's bounty. This should have been a warning to the Jews that the longer they resisted the gospel, the more they were losing by way of blessing. It should also have been a welcome relief to them that at last they could be delivered from the constant demands made upon them by the law. It was certainly a day of good tidings for them and for the Greeks.

The thought of calling upon the Lord should not be restricted to an initial call for salvation. Calling upon the Lord should be made a habit of life. Those who believe in Him for salvation will also need Him throughout the christian life, and He will answer when they call.

13 Paul was not the first apostle to quote from Joel's prophecy to validate a basic fact of the gospel. On the day of Pentecost Peter preached and he gave a lengthy quotation from Joel 2 in his address. To account for what had happened, the phenomenon of the coming of the Holy Spirit on the disciples so that they spoke with other tongues, Peter declared, "This is that which was spoken by the prophet Joel". Peter did not claim that what had taken place was a fulfilment of Joel's prophecy; that had still to come. Nevertheless, the only prophecy in the OT which could account for what had happened was Joel's and it was to that book that Peter was guided by the Holy Spirit. God was making known through His servant that an age had begun which would bring blessing to all who would call upon the name of the Lord and believe the message, whether Jew or Greek.

The argument which Paul has been advancing to show the universality of the scope of the gospel is taken a stage further in this verse. He has just quoted from the writings of the law-giver, Moses, and from one of the major prophets, Isaiah, and now he quotes from one of the minor prophets, Joel. As what Joel has to say about the day of the Lord is not applicable to the gospel, Paul leaves that out. The principle the apostle wants is the one which can be applied universally, "Whosoever shall call upon the name of the Lord shall be saved", a quotation he makes from the LXX. The apostle had announced the removal of national distinctions and it is Joel that he uses to strengthen his argument. Having called upon Isaiah to prove that God's horizons were wider than one nation, the apostle now makes reference to Joel to confirm what he has stated. One of the great stumbling blocks before the Jews was the scope of the message which was being preached. A gospel which gave equal rights of opportunity to Gentiles was more than they were prepared to accept.

In the earlier part of the epistle, Paul had declared that in the matter of sin there was no difference between Jew and Gentile, for all had sinned and come short of the glory of God (3:23). This was a basic fact of life and it was also fundamental to the gospel. To meet a universal need, it was essential on God's part to provide a universal remedy. The character of God was at stake. If all that God could do was provide salvation for one nation, when sin was universal, there was a sad deficiency in God's ability and there was little hope for the greater part of humanity. But it was not so. Even the OT confirmed that God could meet the need of all, but only those who called upon the name of the Lord would be saved. This wonderful provision is what Paul makes known here.

Although the chapter opens with a declaration of Paul's concern for the salvation of his fellow-countrymen, it is clear from his argument all through that he makes no concessions to their legalism. If the Jews were furious about the Gentiles coming into favour and were prepared to blame God for turning away from the nation, their complaints were groundless. Their own Scriptures condemned them. If they did not grasp the significance of what was happening all around them, it was because they misunderstood what the law said and had not paid sufficient attention to what God had been saying down the years through His prophets. In different ways Paul has been stressing that the Jews had only themselves to blame if blessing was passing them by. They had failed to grasp what the law was really teaching and they also failed to grasp the scope of the gospel which was being preached. They had, as it were, a tunnel vision which saw Israel as being the sole beneficiary of any blessings which God might bestow. The universal scope of the gospel seemed to be beyond their comprehension. In this, of course, they were culpable. The simplicity of the gospel was well within their ability to grasp, but prejudice was blinding them.

14 To meet possible objections against partiality or inadequacy on God's part, Paul has made two quotations, "Whosoever believeth" and "Whosoever calleth". He is led on to consider how faith comes, the process involved and the means used. He deals with the subject by posing four questions, "How shall they call?" "How shall they believe?" "How shall they hear?" "How shall they preach?" He then answers the questions by quoting in the next verse from Isa 52:7, although he might also have had Nahum 1:15 in mind as there is a close resemblance to a statement made in that prophecy. The three quotations given in the section vv.11-15 are given to clarify and authenticate the propositions put forward in vv.10,12 and 14. Properly applied, they left the Jews without excuse.

The reference to calling upon the name of the Lord does not imply a mere cry. It is made out of a sense of real need. It stems from an acute awareness of indwelling sin, a condition from which the one who calls cannot extricate himself.

In addition, by calling on the name of the Lord there is an admission that only He can meet the need. There is no hope in religious observances. Neither is there hiding in a crowd. It is an individual matter between the sinner and the Saviour-God. Here the apostle deals with the subject rhetorically. He poses the question, "How shall they call on him whom they have not believed?" It was pointless to call if faith was not there. Perhaps Paul had the Jews in mind in particular, but as he does not enlarge upon who "they" are, the matter must be left open for the widest application.

Another question is raised, "And how shall they believe in him of whom they have not heard?" The RV correctly deletes "of". The thrust of the verse is not hearing about the Lord but hearing Him, which no doubt means through the preachers. Christ speaks through His servants but if there is no preacher (Paul's third question), then the Lord is not heard. The original gives a participle here, "how shall they hear without one preaching?" The people depended on hearing the voice of God through preachers and if there was no one preaching then there was nothing for men and women to consider. The channel God used in biblical times was the herald, but if there was no one to herald out the word of the cross, people would remain in darkness and perish in their sins.

15 The rhetoric of the previous verse is now brought to a head. The message of the gospel needs to be preached. Not only so, but the heralds of it need to be sent. They do not go forth at their own charges. To be effective they must be fitted to go out as servants of God who bear the gospel of peace and the glad tidings of good things. It is no ordinary message they carry. The issues which stem from it are of the most solemn nature. Those who hear it have either to accept its terms and enter into life, or neglect or refuse it and store up for themselves wrath against a day of wrath (2:5).

Paul obviously anticipated that there would be difficulty in the minds of his readers about the declarations made by Isaiah and Joel. If the good news made known by these prophets had universal application, how would it be proclaimed? In the times of the prophets their world had narrow boundaries. What was beyond Israel and the neighbouring countries was quite unknown to them. When the Saviour came, however, that limitation was removed and the outlook was expanded, for He said, "Go ye into all the world and preach the gospel to every creature" (Mark 16:15). Paul therefore, in his reasoning raises the necessity of preachers, carriers of the glad tidings to every part of the world, that all may hear and all may know.

The chapter in Isaiah's prophecy from which Paul makes his quotation has some interesting parallels with the situation in apostolic times. The prophet sets out directions from the Lord about leaving Babylon. The first six verses of Isa 52 call upon Zion to prepare to awake, to shake off the dust; to dwell no longer on the mistakes of the past, but to look to the future. God was about to intervene and His people would know that He was about to bless them. The good news of

Israel's departure from Babylon is stated in 52:7, "How beautiful upon the mountains are the feet of him that bringeth good tidings". It would seem that the joy of hearing good news of deliverance was so great that even the feet of the messengers were considered to be beautiful. These were the feet that were bringing the glad tidings of peace. It is clear that Paul has the same joy in his heart as he thinks of the gospel going forth. A far greater deliverance from bondage was before him. It was not confined to one nation, but had universal appeal. A golden age had dawned for mankind.

Notes

11 "Whosoever" (*pas*, "all"), a favourite word of Paul's, occurs over 1200 times in the NT, of which over 400 occurrences are in Paul's writings. Whereas he had a very limited outlook under Judaism, his view of mankind under the gospel was universal. His message was for "all".

12 Vine suggests that the word "call" (*epikaleō*, a strengthened form of *kaleō*, "to call") sometimes carries the force of making an appeal. It could practically have that meaning here. (See its use in Acts 25:11, "I appeal unto Caesar".)

"Difference" (*diastolē*) is better rendered "distinction" (see 3:22).

14 Stuart comments: "Calling 'on' is not just the same as calling 'to'. It means the open confession of Him on whom they call and who is to be worshipped. How can there be that without a revelation or testimony first going forth? That testimony was going forth by the gospel but not all had obeyed it".

"A preacher", or "(one) heralding" is from *kērussō*, "to proclaim as a herald", "to announce openly". The stress here is on the actual preaching, rather than on the person who preached.

15 There is good manuscript authority for the omission of "that preach the gospel of peace".

"Beautiful" (*hōraios*) is literally "timely", "suitable". See Acts 3:2,10.

"Preach" is "to address with good tidings".

(d) *Jewish obstinacy in rejecting the gospel (vv.16-21)*

> v.16 "But they have not all obeyed the gospel. For Esaias saith, Lord, who hath believed our report?
> v.17 So then faith cometh by hearing, and hearing by the word of God.
> v.18 But I say, Have they not heard? Yes verily, their sound went into all the earth, and their words unto the ends of the world.
> v.19 But I say, Did not Israel know? First Moses saith, I will provoke you to jealousy by them that are no people, and by a foolish nation I will anger you.
> v.20 But Esaias is very bold, and saith, I was found of them that sought me not; I was made manifest unto them that asked not after me.
> v.21 But to Israel he saith, All day long I have stretched forth my hands unto a disobedient and gainsaying people."

16 Having stressed that the glad tidings were not just an ordinary message, but altogether special, being "good" (*agathos*), the apostle moves on to admit that not all obeyed it. The RV gives "hearken", which emphasises the fact that the hearing of the message was not mixed with faith. There is no denial of the fact that the Jews heard it but they treated it with disdain. The verse is introduced with "but" as in vv.18,19,20 and 21. What Paul is bringing out is that despite the excellence of the message, not all were moved by its appeal. Indeed the "not all" could be taken to mean surprisingly few when compared with the numbers who heard.

To demonstrate that the course of events had not taken God unawares, Paul turns again to the prophecy of Isaiah to support his statement. In the NT there are at least eighty references and allusions to this prophecy and many of them concern Isa 53. Although the division into chapters and verses was not in the original Scriptures, it is worthy of note that there are 27 chapters in the section known as "the prophecies of peace" (40-66). These fall into three sets of nine chapters and Isa 53 is the centre of the middle set and therefore the centre of the prophecies of peace. The German expositor, Franz Delitzsch, writing on Isa 53 states, "All the references in the NT to the Lamb of God (with which all allusions to the passover are interwoven) spring from this passage in the prophecy of Isaiah – the dumb type of the passover now finds a tongue".

Sadly, it is the opening words of the chapter which Paul is led to quote, "Who hath believed our report?" Despite the fact that the One of whom Isaiah spoke prophetically had walked through the streets and lanes of the towns and villages of the land, and had given the clearest possible evidence that He was the Messiah, the response from "his own" had been minimal. During His short life on earth the people refused to accept Him, so much so that John wrote, "But though he had done so many miracles (signs) before them, yet they believed not on him: that the saying of Esaias the prophet might be fulfilled, which he spake, Lord, who hath believed our report?" The apostles John and Paul, in their quotations from Isaiah's prophecy both implied that those who heard ought to have believed. John in particular emphasises that the refusal was despite the many signs that were provided by Christ to authenticate His claims and thereby fulfil the Scriptures which spoke of Him. Paul, by the logic of his argument and his striking quotations from the OT, pointed in the same direction. Despite the many proofs of His identity, and the grace which He showed in His tireless ministry, He was rejected by the very people He had come to save.

17 The conclusion which the apostle arrives at is that faith cometh by hearing and hearing by the word of Christ (most MSS). In this chapter the subject of faith has been set out in different ways (see vv.4,6,8,9 and 10). Now the means by which it is made known is declared, it comes by hearing and hearing by the word of Christ. This may mean the word of the messengers concerning Christ or it may be Christ speaking through His messengers. Both meanings are acceptable. The stress is not on the preachers but on what the hearers heard concerning Christ or from Christ that would make them consider their position before God.

This verse is important in that it relates three matters of importance to the understanding of the chapter: faith, hearing (translated "report" in v. 16) and the (spoken) word of Christ (AV "God"). We learn that faith "cometh" of (*ek*) hearing (or a report) whereas hearing is by (*dia*) the word of Christ. We conclude that when divine truth, here concerning Christ and His resurrection, is set before the soul, faith "cometh" out of that circumstance. Only when God acts to convey "a report" to man can there be an intelligent acceptance that this report is of God, i.e. can faith come. On how that divine work is wrought Paul does not elaborate save to point out that human communications do not constitute "a report": the report is by the spoken word (*rhēma*) of Christ. Paul therefore expects that the preacher would speak as the oracles of God and convey orally a report about Christ. That spoken word of God is received by faith; it is therefore "the word (*rhēma*) of faith" according to v. 8.

Since the signs and wonders done by the Lord in the midst of the Jewish people were not done in a corner, they were without excuse. They had constantly demanded signs, and while the Lord did not respond to their demands, the evidence that He had come from God, both in what He said and in what He did was there for all to weigh up. The message being preached following His death and resurrection was not something cobbled together by man; it carried the same authority as that which had gone before the crucifixion. God was behind it. The Holy Spirit was in it in power. Many were crowding into the kingdom who had neither privilege nor earthly title, but the nation to whom it was offered first remained obdurate. Like the elder brother of the prodigal, they chose to remain outside.

18 Again the strong adversative "But" is used to meet any contradiction to what has just been stated about the way faith comes. The double negative (*mē ouk ēkousan*) in the rhetorical question which follows anticipates a positive answer. It is a derisory one which rejects any suggestion that the Jews did not hear. If they insisted that they did not have the opportunity to hear, Paul's answer is again from their own Scriptures, this time from Ps 19:4.

Ps 19 considers what the heavens declare. The sun, moon and stars have their message, "…their voice is gone out into all the earth and their words to the end of the world" (19:4 LXX). Creation is an untiring witness to the existence and presence of God and its voice is loud and clear to all mankind in every corner of the world. Its testimony is unbroken. At all times, "day unto day it uttereth speech, and night unto night sheweth knowledge" (19:2). Everywhere the heavens span the earth and everywhere the message is the same.

It must not be thought that Paul is teaching that creation told out the same gospel that he was preaching. What he is saying is that creation's message, while co-extensive with the gospel of God, is a foreshadowing of the grace of God in the gospel. The rhetorical question then, is answered, "Yes verily". The Jews heard and the Gentiles heard it also. The testimony of God in creation touched the Gentiles and now they were being embraced worldwide in the gospel. There were no distinctions and its scope was universal. In his letter to the Colossians Paul makes this point known when he writes of the glad tidings "which ye have heard and which was preached in all creation under heaven, whereof I Paul am made a minister" (Col 1:23) RV or Newberry.

In the light of Paul's quotation from Ps 19, any objection from the Jews that they had not heard was not valid. God had spoken in creation and Gentiles recognised it despite the fact that they did not have Israel's privileges. In addition, the gospel of the grace of God had not only been preached openly in Jerusalem, Judaea, Samaria and throughout neighbouring countries; its universal message was going forth throughout the whole world. The universality of the message was clearly foretold in the Scriptures and the Jews had no cause for complaint.

Obviously Paul did not mean that the gospel had already gone to the ends of the world as it was then known. It was, however, spreading at such a rate that the form of words was quite permissible in their description of the progress of the universal message. The Jews who had been in Jerusalem on the day of Pentecost and heard it preached had returned to the lands from which they had come, but they carried the news with them. In this way and by travelling merchants and itinerant preachers, the word of the gospel was making great advances. Not only so, but it brought home to the Jews that Judaea no longer held exclusive rights within its boundaries to be the place where heavenly communications were received.

Regarding the reference to this verse in the OT, Kelly makes the following comment: "The apostle quotes from Ps 19, a striking and most apt illustration of the universality of God's testimony. The heavens belonged to no land in particular, nor do the sun and stars shine for Israel alone. They are for man in the earth at large according to the beneficence of Him whose rain falls on just and unjust and whose sun is made to rise on evil men and good. Just so, the gospel goes forth in the grace of God without restriction. God is not indifferent, if the Jews were, to the Gentiles".

19 Again the word "But" is introduced. The apostle supposes now that there was a possibility that Israel did not understand. He had dealt convincingly with the question, "Have they not heard?" Now he asks, "Did not Israel know?" Were the Jews ignorant of the purposes of God to bless the Gentiles? Was this unfettered and free proclamation of the gospel a surprise to them? Had it taken them unawares? The psalms had given testimony in answer to the question, "Have they not heard?" Paul now turns to the law of Moses to prove once again that God always had the Gentiles in mind for blessing and the Jews should have known that this was His plan.

The quotation Paul takes up to prove his point is from Deut 32. The chapter is a sad indictment of the nation of Israel given in the form of a song of Moses. It could be looked upon as the lawgiver's valedictory, as all that remained for him to do after the song was to pronounce his blessing upon the people before he ascended Mount Nebo to die. The language of the song is beautiful, even in English, as for example the opening words, "My doctrine shall drop as the rain, my speech shall distil as the dew". Nevertheless, the song does not cover up anything as Moses traces the longsuffering of God with Israel whose vanities provoked Him to anger.

The response of Jehovah to the vanities of the Israelites is the point the apostle takes up, "I will provoke you to jealousy by them that are no people, and by a foolish nation I will anger you". Here was an intimation that God would turn away from a privileged nation and would extend His mercy to others. The Gentiles who would come in for blessing were nothing in themselves. In no way could it be construed that they did anything to merit being blessed by God. It was simply an evidence that His love could not be hemmed in, it would overflow and embrace others, even Gentiles despised by Israel. To express jealousy and anger as a result would not alter the outcome.

The thrust of the quotation from Deut 32 by Paul is evident. If Jews complained that they did not know, this reference to their history was a reminder that previous generations had spurned the grace of God and He had turned to the Gentiles. In the gospel He was doing it again. It was predicted in the Scriptures, even in the book which they professed meant so much to them. They were without excuse.

20 Having appealed to the psalms and the law in support of his argument, the apostle now turns to the prophets. In Paul's reasoning, he is now stressing that the Gentiles who had been occupied with false gods and idols were now finding the true God through the gospel. The Jews on the other hand, despite all their enlightenment were stubbornly refusing the same gospel. In the goodness of God it had been offered to them first, but they had rejected it and the preachers who carried it, with the result that God then turned to the Gentiles. When they heard it, many of them turned away from idolatry and found the true God. How this happened is depicted in the Acts of the Apostles. God fulfilled His promise; the message of the gospel was proclaimed to the nations and many were blessed with salvation.

Paul states that Isaiah was very bold when he said, "I was found of them that sought me not; I was made manifest unto them that asked not after me". The prophet's boldness means that he spoke without reserve and without regard for the risk involved in stating things which were offensive to the people amongst whom he ministered.

Despite the privileges of the Jewish people, separated by God from the idolatrous nations around them, and given an economy far beyond anything possessed by other nations, they still maintained an obstinate unbelief. Although a covenant relationship with Jehovah existed, and He blessed them in so many different ways, His purpose to bring in the Gentiles for blessing was always there. This fact is clearly brought out in Paul's quotations from the psalms, the law and the prophets, especially Isaiah, from whose writings the passage is taken which tells how God "was found of them who sought me not".

The verse quoted, taken from the LXX, declares that Gentiles would seek God and would find Him. Indeed, others would find Him who did not actively seek

Him. In making this known, Isaiah was certainly a brave man. As a Jew he was acting in a way that was contrary to his own national inclinations. It would perhaps have given him more pleasure to acknowledge a resurgence amongst his own people, but since this was not forthcoming he had to recognise the Gentiles would respond where the Jews had failed. Paul's reference to the situation in Isaiah's day was a reminder that history was repeating itself.

21 For the fifth time the apostle introduces what he will say by "But". Having spoken about Gentiles finding God, he then states, "But to Israel he saith". This may mean, "But about Israel he saith", or, "With reference to Israel he saith". It is the intimation of the longing of God in His entreaty for the people He had made into a great nation. He is seen in Isaiah's prophecy and again here in Romans as stretching out His hands all day long to a disobedient and gainsaying people. But the longsuffering of God and His patient grace were met by an ungrateful and rebellious nation. They refused to be persuaded that they were on a wrong course and that their practices were in fact an abomination to God.

The Jews did not like to hear of Gentiles coming into blessing. As for themselves, Isaiah makes it clear in 65:3-7 that God abhorred the things they were doing. Being highly privileged they had no excuse for their way of life. The prophet stated that they sacrificed in gardens on altars of brick, a form of words chosen to show that even if they observed the letter of the law and offered at the temple on proper altars, they were still very far from God in heart and spirit. Isaiah's references to dwelling amongst the tombs and feeding on swine's flesh are solemnly descriptive of the defiled condition of the people, however much there was of self-complacent conformity to the outward letter of the law.

In Isaiah's day, his bold declaration about the Gentiles finding favour with God was evidently prophetic. Since he contrasts the readiness of the Gentiles and the reluctance of the Jews to respond to the appeals of God, he is obviously not thinking of the millennium, as in that day the Jews with the Gentiles, will, enjoy the favour of God. While Paul clearly applies the words of Isaiah to the attitude of Gentiles and Jews to the gospel, the conditions described by the prophet are seen to be developing during the time when the Lord was here on earth. The statement, "He came unto his own, and his own received him not" (John 1:11), is indicative of a change. Many other passages in the four Gospels and in the Acts of the Apostles give similar intimations, until Paul and Barnabas finally declare at Antioch in Pisidia, "Lo, we turn to the Gentiles". From that point, the outstretched hands of God finally dropped as far as Israel as a nation was concerned. The day of national privilege was over.

Notes

16 Plummer states that possibly Isaiah's lament was based on the fact that so few of the Jews obeyed the call to return to their own land from Babylon. The Lord Himself deplored the unbelief of His time (Luke 19:42). Now Paul makes the same observation, "But they have not all obeyed", i.e. so few have. Isaiah foretold that the Jews would not accept the divine origin of the message. As it was in his day, so it was with the gospel.

18 The word "sound" (*phthongos*, "utterance", "a clear distinct vocal sound") is also used in 1 Cor 14:7, "And even things without life giving sound, whether pipe or harp, except they give a distinct sound, how shall it be known what is piped or harped?"

Paul uses "words" (*rhēmata*, "that which is spoken", "the coherent word").

"A foolish nation" is Paul's description of the Gentiles. As far as an understanding of anything of a spiritual nature was concerned, they were senseless (*asunetos*). Nevertheless, they found God.

21 "Disobedient" (*apeithounta*, "disobeying", present participle of *apeithō*, "to refuse to believe"). The Jews were a people who would not be persuaded.

"Gainsaying" (*antilegō*, "to speak against", "to contradict", "to adopt the opposite view") should be contrasted with 10:9, "confess" (*homologeō*, "to speak in accordance", "to adopt the same terms of language").

3. *Israel's Present Remnant of Grace*
   11:1-10

> v.1 "I say then, Hath God cast away his people? God forbid. For I also am an Israelite, of the seed of Abraham, of the tribe of Benjamin.
> v.2 God hath not cast away his people which he foreknew. Wot ye not what the scripture saith of Elias? how he maketh intercession to God against Israel, saying,
> v.3 Lord, they have killed thy prophets, and digged down thine altars; and I am left alone, and they seek my life.
> v.4 But what saith the answer of God unto him? I have reserved to myself seven thousand men, who have not bowed the knee to the image of Baal.
> v.5 Even so then at this present time also there is a remnant according to the election of grace.
> v.6 And if by grace, then is it no more of works: otherwise grace is no more grace. But if it be of works, then is it no more grace: otherwise work is no more work.
> v.7 What then? Israel hath not obtained that which he seeketh for; but the election hath obtained it, and the rest were blinded
> v.8 (According as it is written, God hath given them the spirit of slumber, eyes that they should not see, and ears that they should not hear;) unto this day.
> v.9 And David saith, Let their table be made a snare, and a trap, and a stumblingblock, and a recompence unto them:
> v.10 Let their eyes be darkened, that they may not see, and bow down their back alway."

Having portrayed Israel as being a disobedient and gainsaying people whose resistance to the righteousness of God as declared in the gospel warranted their cutting off, the apostle now shows that God has not rejected them completely. They certainly deserved to be cut off. Despite being given many chances, they remained obdurate. Paul's burden in this chapter, however, is to show that although the people of Israel have been set aside, it is neither total nor final. In

God's grace there is a remnant with implications which are far-reaching. There will be blessing in the present and a guarantee of national restoration with worldwide blessing eventually.

In a broad division of the chapter, vv.1-10 show that the casting-off is not complete, and vv.11-32 show that it is not final. The subject of God's sovereignty in His electing grace is prominent. In the previous chapter man's free will has been set out in the strongest terms. Now Paul seeks to put God's sovereignty and man's free will into perspective. Harold St John is very bold in his view. He states, "There is no passage from 9:30 to the end of ch.10 where we get more fully stated what is called the 'free will of man'. Ch.9 – Calvinism pure and simple; ch.10 – Arminianism. Ch.11 takes the two things and puts them together as far as human knowledge will go". In another statement he remarks, "God is sovereign, and if He is sovereign, no man has any right to question what He does. If I question it, I presume to be greater than God. Secondly, a thing is right because God does it. God has His own standard and the thing that He does is right because He does it in the inflexible purity of His nature". In this connection, Wm MacDonald states, "When we say that God is sovereign, we mean that He is in charge of the universe and that He can do as He pleases. In saying that, however, we know that, because He is God, He will never do anything wrong, unjust or unrighteous. Therefore, to say that God is sovereign is merely to allow God to be God".

Paul's argument will show that the Jews have indeed a place in the providence and plans of God. To prove this, the apostle does not rely on dogmatic assertions, but rather brings in the Scriptures to support his claims. The fact that the Gentiles had come into blessing might cause Jews to wonder if there was any advantage in being members of a chosen race. If they had been discarded, as Paul had made known, they might well want to know what the future held for them. The apostle in anticipation of Jewish questions makes it clear that God has not been taken unawares by their rebellious ways; He has been working out His plans despite Israel's failure. In the past, as the Scriptures foretold, there was a remnant. In the present there is still a remnant according to God's election of grace. In the future there will still be a remnant until the time when national revival awakens the nation.

The truth of election is raised again. The righteousness which Israel sought so earnestly but did not obtain as a nation, was realised by the elect, the remnant which was chosen by grace. As for the mass, God gave them up to their stubbornness, a condition which was self-induced before God cast them away. In turning to the Gentiles, however, as the apostle explains, this had the added effect of provoking the Jews to jealousy (v.11). Harold St. John, in one of his telling illustrations, explains it this way, "Thus the Jewish train has been shunted into a siding, and the church express comes thundering through and the Jew says, 'I wish I were on that' ". The opportunity for individual Jews in the sidelined nation to leave has been open for nearly two thousand years, but the nation itself will remain sidelined until God brings it out, and that will not be until "the fulness of the Gentiles be come in" (v.25).

Newell makes a telling comment, "The whole question of Rom 9, 10 and 11 is one of reconciling God's special calling and promises of Israel, the earthly people, with a gospel which sets aside that distinction, sets aside Israel's distinctive place for the present dispensation; and places the Gentiles in the place of direct divine blessing, once enjoyed by Israel".

Newell further states, "Unless we clearly see that Paul in this chapter is not discussing church truth, we shall become hopelessly mired. The apostle is not declaring here the character, calling, destiny, or present privileges and walk of the church – none of these things".

1 The opening words of this verse, "I say then", or better, "I say therefore", intimate that Paul is now about to state his answer to any suggestion that God was unrighteous in His dealings with Israel. Their stubborn ways, and their rejection of Christ and the gospel had resulted in the inevitable judgment of God being passed upon them. Nevertheless it did seem that God had broken His promise, for the psalmist had said, "For the Lord will not cast off his people" (Ps 94:14), and Samuel the prophet had declared, "For the Lord will not forsake his people for his great name's sake" (1 Sam 12:22). These and other promises were held tenaciously by the Jews. To their minds any breach of them would cast a doubt on the integrity of God, and what Paul had been teaching might be interpreted that way.

To answer any possible objections, the apostle begins by repudiating any thought that God had thrust away His people. Indignantly he states, "By no means", and in proof of that he cites himself as an example of the grace and faithfulness of God. Vehemently he declares "I also am an Israelite". He was as much an Israelite as any other member of that nation and it was logical to accept that if all were cast off he was pronouncing judgment on himself. If it were true that God had rejected every member of the race then he must also be included in the rejection.

To underline his link with the nation Paul adds another two proofs to what he had already stated. He was of the seed of Abraham and of the tribe of Benjamin. Both of these claims carried weight with the Jews. Abraham, the exemplar of faith, was venerated as the father of the nation, and with him Paul had a link as a direct descendant. It was to Abraham that God gave promises and any suggestion that God would sever His tie with the one whom He called His friend was totally reprehensible. In addition, that Paul could trace his lineage through to Benjamin was another fact of great substance. This was the tribe that remained loyal to Judah and the apostle's link with it gave the utmost credence to his Jewishness. He was fully entitled therefore to express his horror of any thought of rejection.

2 There are two words in the opening sentence of this verse which have caused considerable discussion and differences of opinion for generations. These two words are "people" and "foreknew". Regarding the reference to "his people", to all appearances this seems to have the same force as "his people" in v.1, where the term applies to the entire nation of Israel. In support of this view, Morris states, "Paul is referring to 'the people he foreknew', not 'those of his people whom he foreknew' ". This stance is also adopted by Vine and others. Haldane, however, is quite adamant that this was not what Paul was advancing. He states, "The term 'people' in the preceding verse refers to the whole of Israel as the typical people of God, but is here restricted to the elect among them who were His true people, and are distinguished as 'his people whom he foreknew' ". This stance is also adopted by Plummer and others.

Regarding the words "he foreknew", Wm Kelly has the footnote in his commentary, "It is a mistake to call this an election before the world's foundation which is only said of Christians, of the church. Israel were chosen in time". In effect, Kelly is introducing yet another aspect, that the whole nation is in view but that the mention of the foreknowledge of God here does not imply that the choice of Israel as a nation was made in eternity past. The remnant according to the election of grace was, of course, another matter.

Regarding God's foreknowledge, it should not be taken as meaning His prescience of future events. The purpose of God must be taken into account because every future circumstance is ordered and fixed by Him. Since therefore all things are the subject of divine purpose, He knows everything that He has purposed. There is no possibility therefore of a turnaround in relation to Israel. Their stubborn and rebellious ways cannot be looked upon as a surprise to God. He chose the nation and therefore any thought of a complete rejection cannot be countenanced. In this connection, Denney comments, "*hon proegnō* (whom he foreknew), must contain a reason which makes the rejection incredible or impossible". It must therefore be accepted that God does not change His plans or His purposes, although He may defer putting them into effect.

In this verse, however, it is not implied that God foreordained the whole nation to be saved. It is not taught in the Scriptures that God accepted all the descendants of Abraham through the line of Isaac and Jacob in a national salvation. Israel nationally was chosen by God as a people in whom His purposes would be worked out and He will never go back on that. He has not rejected Israel completely. Not every single Israelite has been cast off nor ever will be. A remnant of grace will be preserved in every generation until the time yet future when a national revival will take place.

From the beginning of the people's history there has always been a remnant. This includes the ones who are spoken of in v.4, "I have reserved to myself seven thousand men who have not bowed the knee to the image of Baal" and to those who are referred to as "a remnant according to the election of grace" (v.5). In support of his claim therefore that God had not cast off Israel completely and that there was indeed a remnant, Paul takes up the case of Elijah the Tishbite when he pleaded with God against Israel. From Elijah's point of view, things had come to such a sorry pass that he was the only faithful one left in the nation. His complaint against Israel was that apostasy had swept everyone away, and outwardly that appeared to be the situation. Against this state of affairs in the history of the nation there could be no argument by the Jews in Paul's day, although they would staunchly reject any suggestion that history was repeating itself.

3 The plea which Elijah made against Israel is found in 1 Kings 19:9-18. The prophet had fled from Jezebel and under a juniper tree he poured out his complaint to God. As he saw it, departure from the true God was total. Israel had abandoned the God of their fathers, and everything that was holy was the subject of remorseless attack. Although originally there had been only one altar (Deut 12:13,14), the division of the nation had created more. The prophet therefore refers to what existed, the altars were pulled down and the prophets were slain. Such were the terrible conditions which existed when Ahab and the wicked Jezebel were at the head of the nation. Elijah's assessment of the situation, however, was one of extreme pessimism. He left God out altogether, even to the point of believing that he was the only faithful person left and his life could be taken at any time.

Under the juniper tree the prophet requested that he might die, for he was, as he said, "no better than his fathers". Some prayers are not answered, which is just as well, and some reasons for giving up are not reasonable, which is true in Elijah's case, for no one ever said he was better than his fathers. But God is gracious, and He dealt kindly with His distraught servant even to tell him for his encouragement, that he was not alone as he imagined himself to be. Although there were many similarities between the prophet's position and the situation Paul was in, it is clear that the apostle was not pessimistic. Sorrow about the nation's state and his own isolation there might have been but he was not in despair. He saw the whole picture clearly.

4 In the previous verse Paul quoted the words of Elijah on Mount Horeb when he pleaded with God against Israel. In this verse the apostle gives the answer of God to the prophet. He had reserved to Himself seven thousand men who had not bowed the knee to Baal. The kingdom of Israel under Ahab's rule had sunk to a low level in every respect and Elijah could see no hope for its recovery. But God had His faithful servants in the nation and, as Paul stresses, they were reserved for God Himself. They were not many in number but they were enough for God to work through when the time was right to bring them into prominence.

There was clearly a parallel between the conditions which prevailed in Elijah's day and those that marked apostolic times. Paul obviously saw himself in the same situation. The mass of the nation was in apostasy and only a few, comparatively speaking, were turning to the Lord. With this remnant of grace Paul was identified. Unlike the prophet, however, he would not plead against the nation, but rather intercede for them as already stated in the previous chapter,

"Brethren, my heart's desire and prayer to God for Israel is, that they might be saved" (10:1).

There may well be some significance in the number 7000 as far as the numerical symbols in Scripture are concerned, but whatever else is intended, it indicates a positive situation from the divine side. The seven thousand were not "left overs" as a residue after the people had suffered under Hazael, Jehu and Elisha (1 Kings 19:17), they were kept back by God Himself. This aspect is clearly before the apostle's mind when he states "I have reserved to myself". The seven thousand, no doubt at great risk to themselves, had not bowed the knee to Baal, they had remained faithful to God. They were interspersed throughout the nation. They were obviously not a recognisable company, otherwise Elijah would have known about them and Ahab would have searched them out. But seven thousand individuals, in their own spheres, known only to God, were the ones He had reserved for Himself. As for Elijah, if he had enquired of God if there were any more like himself instead of interceding against the nation, perhaps God would have let him into the secret of where and with whom he might have found fellowship.

5 The opening words of this verse establish the similarity between the days of Elijah and apostolic times. The mass of the nation was in apostasy and only a remnant was saved. There is no question in either case of human merit. All who were embraced in the remnant were chosen by God and they were there by His grace. Had it not been for the electing grace of God they would all have been swallowed up by national apostasy. Nevertheless, there was obedience in the few and in them God could take pleasure. Their stance bore witness to the fact that God had not made a mistake in bestowing His grace and love upon them.

Regarding the mass of Israel, there never was a time in the history of the nation when there was complete fidelity to God, or to the truth He had made known. All through the OT from the time the Israelites were called out of Egypt, it is repeatedly emphasised that it is a minority that is faithful. The nation is never looked upon as being saved in its entirety. It has a national future, of that the prophets wrote, but in the past and in the present the truth of the remnant is what is obvious. Apart from Israel, the same principle applies to every nation. There is no such thing as a christian nation. Men and women are not saved because of being members of any nation in particular. It is a matter of having a personal experience with God, which involves an acknowledgement of total unworthiness and the need of the Saviour, Jesus Christ.

Having referred to the remnant in Elijah's day, the apostle moves on to make known that there was a remnant in his time which was according to the election of grace. These were Jews who had believed in the gospel of the grace of God. They were not, however, a separate body from the Gentiles who had also believed the gospel, and who were also the elect of God. For the purpose of strengthening his argument that God had not cast off His people totally, Paul could make known without fear of contradiction that Jews were being saved. This was proof that

God had not gone back on His word. In another epistle the apostle might make known that the middle wall of partition between Jew and Gentile had been broken down (with all that implied), but that is not his purpose here. He is defending the reliability of God's promises to Israel.

It is a great pity that the strength of feeling between opposite schools of thought causes some a constant search for a satisfactory explanation to a problem which has baffled great minds for generations. Some have concluded that election of the remnant is corporate. They assert that Christ is the elect of God, and when sinners put their trust in Him, they are then "in Christ" and they come into the sphere of electing grace. It is then corporately that they become the elect of God. Whatever substance is in this view, it is certainly at odds with what has been taught by most expositors for many years.

It seems to be a case of begging the question to assert that sinners are saved as individuals but that they were elected *en masse*. The reasoning is suspect that decides that men and women, although called out from the world one by one (through the gospel in NT times), should only be considered in the aggregate in the election of grace. However, rather than dismiss the subject entirely, which many are prone to do, or adopt a stance which purports to have the answer to what is obviously a problem area, it seems better to accept what is within reach of the finite mind and leave the rest with the omniscient, omnipotent God whose prerogative it is to choose whom and when He will. Regarding the subject of election, under the heading, *Divine Sovereignty and Human Responsibility*, Wm MacDonald gives a concise and balanced view in the introduction to Rom 9 in the *Believer's Bible Commentary* (pages 530-532). What that author has to say on the subject is worthy of consideration.

6 In this verse the subject of grace and works is introduced again. Vine makes the interesting observation that this is the fifth time in the epistle that Paul refers to the distinction between these two words (see 3:24-28; 4:1-8; 9:11; 9:30-10:13). Here he is asserting that the existence of the remnant is due to the grace of God and has nothing whatever to do with works of merit. It will be noted that Paul does not supply a verb in the clause and one has to be inserted to give the sense. If the remnant was chosen by grace, there is no place for works. Any thought of earning favour by holding to the Jewish religious system is immediately rejected.

The use of "otherwise", or perhaps better, "if it were", indicates that it is pointless to talk about grace if works features to any extent. Introduce works and grace changes its meaning; it is no longer grace. Paul seems to say that his understanding of what grace means would have to be drastically altered if it had any element of works attached to it. Not only so, but God's choice of the remnant is an eternal one according to His grace. Works, however, would imply that God's choice was on the basis of His foreknowledge of deeds performed, and that strikes at the root of what is involved in the foreknowledge of God. This is a matter Paul takes seriously. Looking back or looking forward, there is no place for works. Nothing is clearer in Paul's theology than that grace means grace and must never be tainted in any way by human merit. As to the latter half of this verse, it is generally agreed that it lacks manuscript authority to support its inclusion in the text. Nevertheless, "It is at once too difficult, and too *deeply* related to the context, to look like the insertion of a scribe" (Moule). Its presence emphasises that in the matter of divine choice too, grace and works are, in their very nature, mutually exclusive.

7 The opening words, "What then?" call for an answer as to how the argument stands. They are an abbreviated form of the characteristic expression used frequently in this epistle which throws the matter under discussion back on the reader. Here the apostle follows up the question himself with a categorical statement, "Israel hath not obtained that which he seeketh for". Despite an earnest and prolonged search, spread over many generations, the righteousness so desperately desired was not obtained.

The latter half of the verse divides the nation. The elect, the remnant according to grace (v.5), are credited with having obtained what Israel sought so long without success. The rest, the non-elect, were blinded (or, hardened). Although Paul does not say so specifically, it is clear from his argument in the preceding chapters that the state of being right with God is what is still before his mind. The part of the nation described as the election (or, elect) received the blessing through believing the gospel in exactly the same way as Gentile believers received it and were reckoned righteous by faith.

Since one part of the nation has received what was so earnestly pursued by all, the question then arises, "What of 'the rest'?" Nothing could be clearer than the sentence pronounced upon them "the rest were blinded", or better, "the rest were hardened". Since the passive voice is used, the hardening obviously is the judicial act of God. It is the inevitable result of rejecting His overtures of grace. If mankind constantly refuses to accept God's offer they will fall away to a hardened state that leads on to perdition. To neglect or disparage God's mercy is to actively oppose the Almighty. Not only so, the idea that a decision to get right with God can be put off to the end of life ignores the fact that a callus of unbelief is formed on the heart by spurning God's offers of grace. God cannot be blamed for judicially allowing the hardening process to work out its ultimate end.

Although Morris considers that "the rest" could mean "the rest of men", Gentiles as well as Jews, the context suggests that Paul's argument is dealing only with Israel at this point. Nevertheless, to assume that the elect remnant of Israel who are saved under the gospel is a separate entity from Gentiles saved under the same gospel is quite wrong. Likewise, "the rest" of Israel are in the same condemnation as "the rest of men" who spurn the gospel of the grace of God.

8 Once again Paul supports his argument by an appeal to the Scriptures. The quotation he makes is a free one. The first part seems to be taken from Isa 29:10

with possible references in latter half to Isa 6:9 and Deut 29:4. Whatever lessons Paul had in mind in his allusions to the OT, it comes out clearly in 11:8 that God had given to "the rest" in Israel a spirit of slumber ("stupor", RV). They fell into a condition where there was no spiritual response. They were entirely culpable for putting themselves into this state, and they had no complaint against God if indeed He allowed their unbelief to progress to the point of spiritual stupefaction.

The prophet Isaiah recorded six woes in chs. 28-33 of his prophecy. They were directed against Israel because of their occupation with things which were false. Isa 29, to which Paul alludes, contains a woe against false religion. The people had blinded themselves and fallen into a stupor, having rejected the truth. The situation in Isaiah's day was serious and Paul here is emphasising that things had not changed. They were still serious, indeed more so, as God's patience had run out and "the rest" of Israel were in the process of being cut off. Blindness to what was obvious and closed ears to the voice of God permeated the nation with the exception of the remnant. What had happened over generations in the past had persisted "unto this very day" (RV). The hardening in all its aspects had reached its high-water mark, even as Paul wrote.

9 Having called upon Moses and Isaiah to confirm that judicial blindness was the inevitable result of unbelief, Paul in this verse turns to David. He quotes from Ps 69:22,23, with a possible allusion to Ps 35:8. In these psalms David writes of the persecution he suffered at the hands of his own people, and warns that Israel would be judged because of the persecution of the righteous. It is clear that Paul sees a parallel in his day. The situation was not new. History proved that pursuing a rebellious course was a national trait.

The verses from Ps 69 chosen by Paul had very serious implications for the Jews. Many of the psalmist's predictions had been fulfilled in the experiences of the Lord and now the psalm is made to speak again. The "table" in symbolic language suggests the privileges given to Israel by God. That He had sustained the nation in a variety of ways was beyond doubt, but the privileges had turned sour and the very blessings on which they depended and about which they boasted had become a snare, a trap and a stumblingblock. As the psalmist stated, what should have been for the welfare of the nation would come to a bleak end.

The trap and the snare spoke of danger that would come upon the nation suddenly and unexpectedly. As Paul wrote, the dark clouds were already beginning to gather over the land. Within a few years the Roman taskmasters would take a terrible toll and leave the land desolate. This Paul calls a recompense. It was a retribution that was inevitable. The nation had been well warned.

10 This verse carries through the completion of the quotation from Ps 69. The seriousness of the situation causes Paul to multiply words. It seems now to be a petition addressed to God to consolidate the blindness that he had already mentioned in v.8, and to bring upon the nation heavy burdens. The psalmist had been moved to make similar requests in his day, and although conditions were bleak they were not final. The high-water mark was reached in apostolic times and the price was about to be paid for years of national folly.

The bowing down of the back is a peculiar expression. It is not clear what was on Paul's mind by introducing it. It is taken from the LXX and may mean that in retribution, instead of enjoying privileges, they would have to endure heavy burdens. Vine suggests that the youthful activity indicative of the favour of the Lord gives place to a figure of decrepitude of age. The vigour of a vibrant nation is replaced by a decrepit people with neither power nor influence.

Notes

4 The phrase "the answer of God" (*ho chrēmatismos*, "the oracular response") occurs only here in the NT.

5 "Even so then" (*houtōs oun kai*, "therefore also", "so too"), applies what happened in the past to the present. Denney comments, "...*ho nun kairos* is the present regarded not merely as a date but in some sense a crisis".

7 "Were blinded" (*pōroō*, "to harden", "to cause a callus to form", "unimpressible", see 2 Cor 3:14). "Hardeneth" in 9:18 is *sklērunō* ("to make stubborn", "to harden").

4. Israel's Future Restoration
11:11-36

(a) *Israel's restoration means blessing for the world (vv.11-15)*

> v.11 "I say then, Have they stumbled that they should fall? God forbid: but rather through their fall salvation is come unto the Gentiles, for to provoke them to jealousy.
> v.12 Now if the fall of them be the riches of the world, and the diminishing of them the riches of the Gentiles; how much more their fulness?
> v.13 For I speak to you Gentiles, inasmuch as I am the apostle of the Gentiles, I magnify mine office:
> v.14 If by any means I may provoke to emulation them which are my flesh, and might save some of them.
> v.15 For if the casting away of them be the reconciling of the world, what shall the receiving of them be, but life from the dead?"

11 After taking a very firm stance against Israel in his quotations from the OT, Paul carries his argument a stage further. The question he poses, "Have they stumbled that they should fall?" is answered by an emphatic "God forbid" ("may it not be", "by no means"). There is no doubt that they had stumbled as he had already made clear (9:32,33). The point in question now is, "Was it God's purpose that they should fall never to rise again?" Paul's denial, so trenchantly put, makes it clear that Israel's downfall did not exclude recovery; indeed the coming of salvation to the Gentiles, in which it resulted, was intended to awake the Jewish nation to a sense of what might yet be theirs in Christ.

The Scriptures are brought in again to strengthen the apostle's argument. Allusion is made to Deut 32:21, a portion which has already been quoted at 10:19. Previous generations had spurned the grace of God and He had provoked them to jealousy by turning to the nations. History was repeating itself. Israel's unbelief was the Gentiles' opportunity. The Jews had stumbled over Christ and had fallen. In their obstinacy they had tried in vain to establish their own righteousness and as a result hardening had followed.

Although the situation for the Jews was serious, their fall had worked out for the good of the Gentiles. The very blessing that had come to them was intended to provoke the Jews to jealousy. It was not a jealousy of hatred against the Gentiles, but one intended to cause the Jews to seek for restoration and salvation. The verse in Deut 32, to which Paul alludes, makes it clear that the Gentiles were nothing in themselves. The Israelites were to be provoked by a people who were a "no people". Nevertheless, in the mercy of God they would be blessed and this bestowal of divine favour was intended to stir up the Jews to seek the blessing which was being offered to the Gentiles. There could be no argument from the Jews; it had all happened before and it was happening again before their eyes.

12 What Paul announces in this verse has an element of hope in it. He begins, "Now if (if, as is surely the situation) the fall of them be the riches of the world, and the diminishing of them the riches of the Gentiles, how much more their fulness?" Having established in the previous verse that there was a national fall, the apostle builds on that. God's grace cannot be hemmed in because of the failure of man. It will go out, and here Paul states that it will go out in the widest sense; it will reach out to the whole world. There is no thought of frugality. The gospel of God would go out in fulness of blessing to all mankind.

Not only so, if the diminishing of Israel has resulted in such riches to the Gentiles, the question arises, "how much more their fulness?" What blessings for the Gentiles may not be mediated to them through an Israel basking in the fulness of divine favour? There is little doubt that the unbelief of the Jews had resulted in a diminution. It is not necessarily numerical, but a loss of status among the nations. With the favour of God removed and a scattering of the people amongst the nations of the world, the diminishing was a solemn reality. Set against that loss, however, was the contrast: the fulness of Israel would come in God's good time. To contemplate that day was a comfort and an encouragement to national pride, but since it carried no guarantee for individual Jews in any generation during the gospel age, the only hope for each one was personally to turn to God, and believe the gospel concerning His Son, Jesus Christ.

The "fulness" of which the apostle speaks obviously stands in contrast to the "diminishing". Although there has been a diminution of the nation in the governmental dealings of God, all that has been taken away will be restored. To suggest that God in the end will be satisfied with less than that cannot be countenanced. In this verse there is a sense of triumph. It is not all loss because of Israel's fall. The whole world, with the Gentiles considered specifically, would know of the riches of God's grace as intimated in the gospel.

13 If the Gentiles at Rome were thinking that Paul was concentrating too much on the Jews, what follows puts matters into perspective. The Gentiles were never out of his mind. It was necessary that the Jewish position should be clarified, but Gentile blessing was involved in the outcome. With this in view the apostle lets the Gentiles know that he was speaking to them; they were as much a part of the plans of God as the Jews.

The claim to be an apostle of the Gentiles does not suggest that it was exclusive to Paul. There were others in the work also. He was however, a chosen vessel, as the Lord made known to Ananias, "to bear my name before Gentiles, and kings, and the children of Israel" (Acts 9:15). This special commission from the Lord was a duty about which he was very conscious, so much so that he wrote to the Galatians, "the gospel of the uncircumcision was committed unto me" (2:7). And again to the Ephesians, "that I should preach among the Gentiles the unsearchable riches of Christ" (Eph 3:8). There is no thought, however, of exalting himself in this ministry. On the contrary, the next expression confirms that service was the all-important point, not his part in it.

The word *diakonia* ("ministry", AV "office"), chosen by the apostle, does not denote service of an exalted nature. It could be used to describe the mundane. Nevertheless, the fact that it concerned the gospel, and in particular the gospel as it was addressed to Gentiles, made Paul consider that his input could bring glory to it. If in its preaching it reached beyond Gentiles and brought blessing to Jews, that was indeed a glorious result. His discharge of his ministry was resulting in conversions and that in itself was bringing glory to the Lord.

14 The ministry to the Gentiles is noted here as having another implication. The opening words, "If by any means", have been rendered by some "in the hope that". Certainly the idea is here of an earnest desire to see his fellow-countrymen turning to Christ. If somehow by his ministry to the Gentiles he could arouse his own to envy, some might be saved.

The reference to his fellow-countrymen being his flesh is unusual. No doubt the purpose is to stress his close natural links with Israel. The stirring up to jealousy has the end in view that some might be saved. The salvation of all Israel is not the point in this verse. He recognises that his is not to see the multitude of Israel gathered in, but longs that "I might…save some". To that end he will labour, "striving according to his working, which worketh in me mightily" (Col 1:29). Those who will be saved will have to come as individuals and in the same way as the Gentiles. The gospel was a universal message. It did not have separate values for Jews and Gentiles. If all had sinned and come short of the glory of God, as intimated earlier in the epistle, the way of salvation was also intimated in general terms, "For whosoever shall call upon the name of the Lord shall be saved" (10:13). The inclusion of the word "some", however, is a clear indication that Paul realised the magnitude of the task that faced him, and what could be achieved by his contribution was indeed a joy to his own heart.

15 Continuing his theme, Paul writes, "For if (as is the situation), the casting away of them (Israel) be the reconciling of the world". This statement acknowledges that he had come to the point of recognising that Israel had been cut off. The word for "casting away" used is different from that which occurs in vv.1,2. Here it carries the thought of loss. It is used only once more in the NT and that is in Acts 27:22 concerning the loss of a ship. The thought of Israel's rejection leads Paul on to the implications of that. He sees it as the reconciling of the world. If one channel is blocked through unbelief, another one will open and God's blessing will flow to the Gentiles. The apostle is not stating that the whole world will be reconciled. He is declaring that the scope of the gospel is worldwide and all who will believe can be reconciled to God. Writing to the Corinthians he made the position clear, "Now then we are ambassadors for Christ…be ye reconciled to God" (2 Cor 5:20).

The apostle's thinking stretches out to the future. The question arises that if Israel's rejection brings in its wake an offer to the world of reconciliation to God, what will be the situation when Israel is accepted? Figuratively, the nation at present is dead. God has thrust Israel away from Himself. Out of it a remnant is being saved in every generation through the gospel, but national revival is yet future. When the nation is restored to its place again at the head of the nations, that will indeed be a great day for the world. Of that time Micah wrote, "And many nations shall come and say, Come and let us go up to the mountain of the Lord and to the house of the God of Jacob, and he will teach us of his ways, and we will walk in his paths, for the law shall go forth of Zion, and the word of the Lord from Jerusalem" (Micah 4:2).

Notes

11 Denney renders *mē eptaisan hina pesōsin*, "surely they did not stumble so as to fall?" He adds, "The subject is the mass of the Jewish nation, all but the elect remnant. The contrast here between stumbling and falling show that the latter is meant of an irremedial fall from which there is no rising".

12 For "fall" (*paraptōma*) see v.11.

"Diminishing" (*hēttēma*) is literally a "defect", "a shortcoming", "degeneration". Armitage Robinson, paraphrases, "If the Gentiles have been enriched (by the blessings of the gospel) through the very miscarriage and disaster of Israel, what wealth is in store for them in the great Return, when all Israel shall be saved – when God hath made the pile complete?"

(b) *Lessons from the olive tree (vv.16-24)*

v.16 "For if the firstfruit be holy, the lump is also holy: and if the root be holy, so are the branches.
v.17 And if some of the branches be broken off, and thou, being a wild olive tree, wert graffed in among them, and with them partakest of the root and fatness of the olive tree;
v.18 Boast not against the branches. But if thou boast, thou bearest not the root, but the root thee.
v.19 Thou wilt say then, The branches were broken off, that I might be graffed in.
v.20 Well; because of unbelief they were broken off, and thou standest by faith. Be not highminded, but fear:
v.21 For if God spared not the natural branches, take heed lest he also spare not thee.
v.22 Behold therefore the goodness and severity of God: on them which fell, severity; but toward thee, goodness, if thou continue in his goodness: otherwise thou also shalt be cut off.
v.23 And they also, if they abide not still in unbelief, shall be graffed in: for God is able to graff them in again.
v.24 For if thou wert cut out of the olive tree which is wild by nature, and wert graffed contrary to nature into a good olive tree: how much more shall these, which be the natural branches, be graffed into their own olive tree?"

16 Having introduced the prospect of a radical change in Israel in the future, which he likens to life from the dead, Paul now gives two illustrations to support his claim. The first part of the verse is an allusion to the consecration of dough as described in Num 15:17-21. The offering of the firstfruit ensured that the lump, and indeed the whole harvest was consecrated to the Lord. This meant that the lump, the whole batch, or in the widest sense, the harvest, was in fact a gift given back to the people by the Lord. Israel's history was not without examples. The remnant which returned from Babylon pledged themselves to walk in God's law. Included in the things that they promised to observe was the bringing of the firstfruits of their dough to the chambers of the house of their God (Neh 10:37). Ezekiel also drew attention to the necessity of giving the firstfruits to God. He wrote, "Ye shall also give unto the priest the first of your dough, that he may cause the blessing to rest in thine house" (Ezek 44:30).

The inference is clear from the illustration of the firstfruit being holy and the mass being holy also. Those who were coming to God through the gospel were holy; they belonged to God. Paul's argument is that God will also claim the harvest; Israel as a nation will yet be saved. This is still obviously future, but God has not relinquished His claim. As for Paul's reasoning on this point, the Jews would not find fault with it; they were well aware of what was implied in the giving of firstfruits to God and His claims therefore on the harvest also.

The second illustration is taken from nature. This is introductory to a consideration of the olive tree and the lessons to be drawn from it in connection with Israel. Since he is defending God's right to claim the lump (the mass of Israel), having taken to Himself the firstfruits (the converted Jews and Gentiles),

Paul now goes back to the beginning. The father of the race was Abraham. He was the root. If therefore the root was holy, the branches were holy also.

17 Having introduced the thought of the root bearing branches, Paul now proceeds to use his illustration to apply some warnings. He begins by saying that some of the branches were broken off. In this he is clearly referring to Jews. Not every Jew is implied as obviously the godly remnant is still linked to the root which is holy. Only "some", as he states, were broken off. Nevertheless, regarding the nations, Christ had come to His own (things) and His own (people) had rejected Him (John 1:11). Further opportunities to get right with God were given in the gospel, but these were rejected, and so God turned to the Gentiles (Acts 13:46). As a people, they were broken off from their place of privilege and testimony.

The apostle now turns to address the Gentiles. He selects a representative. Putting stress on the pronoun, he states, "Thou, being a wild olive tree, wert graffed in among them", that is, among the believing remnant. Into the place forfeited by the unbelieving Jews, this typical Gentile is now introduced and he becomes a fellow-partaker of the root and fatness of the olive tree.

The reference to the olive tree is an obvious allusion to Jer 11:16,17. The prophet states, "The Lord called thy name, A green olive tree, fair, and of goodly fruit: with the noise of a great tumult he hath kindled fire upon it, and the branches of it are broken. For the Lord of hosts, that planted thee, hath pronounced evil against thee, for the evil of the house of Israel and of the house of Judah". What therefore Paul was introducing was not new as far as Jews were concerned. One of their own prophets had already made known that both houses of Israel had fallen away from being the green olive tree as planted by God and had come under His judgment. In the apostle's mind, the final separation had taken place.

Paul has come under severe criticism from commentators because of his illustration of the wild olive being grafted into the good olive tree. According to many, this is not the practice in horticultural circles and what Paul has set out is absurd. Harold St. John states that one commentator remarked that inspiration did not save Paul from bungling. He adds that Dr Moffat commented, "I apologise for the awkwardness of the whole thing, but Paul had all those limitations of a city-bred man and had not sufficient interest in plants and flowers even to ask how they treated the olive trees that fringed the roads along which they tramped". It now appears, however, that Paul was not as far adrift as the commentators allege. Harold St. John's research into the subject revealed that the practice of grafting in wild olives to good olive trees was fairly common in Palestine in Paul's day. Old olive trees were pruned and wild olives were grafted in to enrich the old stock, thereby causing the sap to flow again.

In connection with the grafting process an interesting observation is made by Morris regarding the writings of the Talmud. In them reference is made to Ruth the Moabitess and Naamah the Ammonitess (the mother of Rehoboam) as "two goodly shoots engrafted into Israel". Although the rabbis did not start writing the Talmud until the fourth century AD, there was in circulation in Paul's time a vast body of oral law and of rabbinical commentary which probably included what the Talmud recorded years later. It is probable that in apostolic times, Paul's illustration was not as far out as many commentators have alleged.

Many consider that there is no problem for Paul to face since he states himself that the wild branches were grafted in "contrary to nature" (v.24). He knew all the time that what he was saying was not in keeping with horticultural laws, but the illustration explained how Gentiles could be brought into the privileges enjoyed exclusively by the nation of Israel. The difficulty to be faced, however, is that it is not consistent to claim that what Paul advanced was sound practice and then say that the same situation was contrary to it. The answer to this may lie in the fact that v.23 states, "for God is able to graft them in again", which relieves Paul of any accountability in the whole matter. God is not bound by natural laws.

Hendrikson advances the view that the true solution is probably wholly different. He writes, "To begin with, it is not true that in v.24 Paul, in calling something 'contrary to nature' is even indirectly referring to a method of horticultural grafting. And secondly, with respect to the first attempt to rescue Paul, those who endorse it seem to forget that Paul in writing about grafting and regrafting is under no obligation to adhere to the rules and practices of nature grafting. He is talking about grafting in the spiritual realm. Gentiles had come in from the outside and had been spiritually grafted in amongst the Jews. Only in this manner had they come to share the nourishing sap from the olive root".

18 A warning is now issued. The casting away of the Jewish nation did not mean that Gentiles were any better. There was no ground for boasting. Paul is emphatic in his condemnation of any such tendency. In effect he says, "Stop doing this, there is no reason for adopting an arrogant attitude to the Jews because they have fallen from the place of privilege". In speaking of the branches, it is not clear whether Paul means only the Jews who held fast to the old ways, or whether he included those who had embraced Christianity. Although in Rome anti-Semitism was developing in apostolic times, there is no evidence that it affected the assembly there. Either way the apostle's warning is clear, there were no grounds for Gentiles to "boast against" the Jews. Any grandiose ideas of superiority were baseless.

Regardless of how the Gentile believer looked upon his position, he could not alter the fact that the root was Jewish and at the best he was only the wild olive. God had not uprooted the tree and planted another one. Abraham as the root had not been removed. He was still the root of the olive tree. If by the grace of God Gentiles had come into favour, this did not mean that the wild olive was rooted and the olive tree drew its fatness from it. The line of faith began with Abraham and he had not been supplanted. In His public ministry the Saviour made known to the Samaritan woman, "Salvation is of the Jews" (John 4:22). In that respect the Gentiles were indebted to them, even though the mass of the nation had been cast off.

19 The apostle anticipates a reply. Into the mouth of a typical Gentile believer he puts an answer, making him say, "The branches were broken off that I might be grafted in". Since there is no definite article before "branches" it appears that Paul was taking cognisance of the fact that not every Jew was cast away; the remnant remained. The emphatic "I" makes the glorying egotistical. The Gentile raised by Paul in his argument maintains that God broke off the branches so that he could be grafted in, the inference being that the Gentile saw his inclusion as the direct cause of what happened to the Jews. Any such idea was of course sheer arrogance and far removed from the true situation. The Jews were broken off from the olive tree because of their unbelief and into the place of privilege and testimony Gentiles were brought by the grace of God. Merit had no part in it.

20 There is possible irony in Paul's opening words here. He seems to say, "Well, imagine that now", or perhaps, "Hold on, that is not the complete picture". The true story is that the branches were broken off because of unbelief, not because Gentiles were superior to Jews and therefore any better suited to represent God. Here Paul makes it clear that the only ground of acceptance is faith. Earlier in the epistle he has stated that faith excludes boasting (3:27). Faith and boasting are diametrically opposed. Trust in the living God and personal pride in one's standing and achievements cannot exist side by side. It was a stubborn refusal on the part of the Jews to accept salvation by faith which resulted in their rejection. It was on the ground of faith that Gentiles were brought in, and that excluded works of any kind. To come to any other conclusions about the rejection of Jews and about Gentile standing would be totally wrong.

Paul's counsel therefore to any Gentile believer who is disposed to be highminded is to fear, or perhaps better in this case, to stand in awe. The psalmist wrote, "Stand in awe and sin not" (Ps 4:4). Some good authorities render it, "Tremble and sin not". To lose the awareness of God's interests in such vital matters was fatal. It was a critical time in the history of mankind. The most highly-privileged people in the world were being side-lined and total strangers to the covenants of promise were being brought in. For the objects of God's grace to boast against the rejected people and to boast about themselves was presumptuous in the extreme, and certainly an attitude which would invite the displeasure of God.

21 There is no mistaking the implications of this verse. God had not spared the natural branches. Descendants of Abraham whose genealogy could be traced back to the patriarch were cut off. Their credentials naturally speaking were flawless, but these had not saved them. The warning to the representative Gentile believer has therefore tremendous implications, "take heed lest he also spare not thee". The Gentile was a stranger. He had no background of dealing with Jehovah reaching back for hundreds of years. There was nothing he could point to which equated with what the Jews possessed. His coming into favour was entirely on the ground of grace. If he ignored that and became high-minded he was presuming on the mercy of God. To do that was the height of folly. The warning was clear, "If God spared not the natural branches, take heed lest he also spare not thee".

22 The imaginary Gentile Paul has been addressing in the past few verses is now called upon to take note of the goodness and severity of God. These two characteristics are held in perfect balance by God. His goodness is not dispensed at the expense of His severity. His severity is not inconsistent with His goodness. The righteousness of His character is beyond question. Mankind should recognise that God in His severity is not hard, and in His goodness He is not soft. Already in this epistle the goodness of God has been declared. It is that goodness which is marked by forbearance and longsuffering, a goodness that leads to repentance (2:4). By way of contrast the word occurs again in relation to mankind, "there is none that doeth good, no not one" (3:12).

The severity of God is seen to be towards them that fell. The word "severity" (*apotomia*), implies a cutting off. Because of unbelief, His patience having been exhausted, God's sternness was at last manifested. The unbelievers in the nation, those who consistently despised the riches of His goodness, finally stumbled and fell. In v.11, the apostle noted that it was not a case of falling, never to rise again. The situation was certainly disastrous, but Israel would rise again in a day yet future and that would result in universal blessing. The severity of God, seen in this verse as applied to the unbelieving nation, is a present judgment. Israel had been cut off from its place of privilege and testimony on the earth.

Addressing the representative Gentile, Paul speaks of the goodness of God towards him. This is made known in the gospel which was being preached to all mankind. Although the severity of God was directed towards the Jewish nation, behind it His kindness was being declared in the gospel of His grace. There was hope for every individual Jew, but there was only one way. Paul had taken that way and others in the nation had also welcomed the chance to get right with God. The door of mercy was still ajar, wide enough to let individuals enter into blessing. Nevertheless, the fact in the generic sense, which Paul is announcing here, is that the Jewish nation had been cut off.

Still dwelling on the principle of Jews and Gentiles considered generically, the two divisions of mankind, a warning is given. Continuance in goodness is essential, otherwise a similar fate awaits the Gentile; he also will be cut off. The point here is not eternal security. Already in ch.8 that has been announced; there can be no separation from the love of Christ. What is intended here is a warning that God cannot be expected to act severely towards the Jew and then deal leniently with the Gentile. The righteousness of His character would certainly come under censure if that were to be the case. Two situations exist, the Jewish position and the Gentile position. The Jews were given a lengthy time of probation but failed. The Gentiles are now on trial. They cannot expect different standards. God in His righteousness will apply the same rule of measurement to them and it behoves Gentiles to remember that fact, "otherwise they also shall be cut off".

23 Reverting to the Jews again, Paul makes it clear that the position is not irrevocable. As far as the future is concerned there will be a national mourning followed by a national revival. The prophet Zechariah declared that God "will pour upon the house of David and upon the inhabitants of Jerusalem the spirit of supplication and they shall look upon me whom they have pierced and shall mourn for him" (12:10). John also writes of this time, "Behold he cometh with clouds; and every eye shall see him, and they also which pierced him: and all kindreds of the earth shall wail because of him" (Rev 1:7). When this great work of national repentance is completed then will the branches be grafted in again "into their own olive tree". As Paul makes known, God is able to do this. It may be contrary to horticultural practice to graft in branches that have been cut off, but what will happen is not determined by that. Paul is here declaring that in the spiritual realm God is able to do that which seems impossible in the natural.

As to the present, from the branches cut off through unbelief, there are individuals who recognise the folly of their ways. Under conviction of sin they believe the gospel and accept Jesus Christ as Saviour. Since they "abide not still in unbelief" they are grafted into the olive tree from which they were cut off. They become part of the believing remnant and with other born-again believers take up again the position of privilege and testimony, albeit in a new relationship altogether. However, the main thrust of the apostle's argument in the context is not directed towards salvation or the church. It is occupied with the olive tree, the testimony of Israel on earth, followed by Gentile testimony on earth as a result of the casting away of Israel through unbelief. Profession therefore comes into consideration. Gentile testimony, as it is seen in Christendom, is no better than that of Israel in an earlier dispensation.

24 Paul addresses the representative Gentile again. He was part of an uncultivated olive, a tree of little value and wild by nature. He was cut out of that and grafted into the good olive contrary to nature. At this stage of the apostle's argument, recognised horticultural practice is not the point. What he is advancing is the ease with which God accomplishes His purposes. There can be no disputing the fact, "God is able". If therefore a Gentile, a stranger to the covenants of promise and having no claim upon God for mercy, can be brought into the spiritual blessings inferred by the root and fatness of the olive tree, how much more shall God show grace and compassion to the people who have been peculiarly His own since patriarchal times.

In the natural realm, the thought of engrafting branches may seem inconceivable. In the spiritual realm, however, if God has displayed His divine power by grafting in the Gentile to the tree of privilege, what He will do for the restoration of Israel is little by comparison. Here the apostle refers to "their own olive tree". This is something the Gentile should never forget. The grafting in of the Gentile is an inestimable privilege. How long Gentiles continue in the place of privilege depends on themselves. The apostle makes the condition clear, "If thou continue in goodness". Failure to do so will result in being cut off, just as it was in the case of the nation of Israel. Gentile profession must prove that it is real, otherwise cutting off will follow, and unlike the Jewish position, there is no hope held out for restoration. The Gentile will never again be grafted into the olive tree.

Notes

15 *Apobolē* ("rejection"; from *apoballō*, "to cast aside") is used here but a different word from vv.1,2, meaning, "to thrust away from one's self".

(c) *Israel's restoration was prophesied (vv.25-32)*

> v.25 "For I would not, brethren, that ye should be ignorant of this mystery, lest ye should be wise in your own conceits; that blindness in part is happened to Israel, until the fulness of the Gentiles be come in.
> v.26 And so all Israel shall be saved: as it is written, There shall come out of Sion the Deliverer, and shall turn away ungodliness from Jacob:
> v.27 For this is my covenant unto them, when I shall take away their sins.
> v.28 As concerning the gospel, they are enemies for your sakes: but as touching the election, they are beloved for the fathers' sakes.
> v.29 For the gifts and calling of God are without repentance.
> v.30 For as ye in times past have not believed God, yet have now obtained mercy through their unbelief:
> v.31 Even so have these also now not believed, that through your mercy they also may obtain mercy.
> v.32 For God hath concluded them all in unbelief, that he might have mercy upon all."

25 The opening statement, "For I would not, brethren, that ye should be ignorant" is one which Paul uses six times in his epistles. He has already used it at 1:13. Obviously by introducing the expression he has something important in his mind which he feels his readers ought to know, as for example things pertaining to the coming of the Lord in 1 Thess 4:13. In the six occurrences he always refers to his readers as "brethren". This removes any thought that he is disassociating himself from his brethren by what he is making known. Here in v.25, the apostle's concern is that his readers should not be ignorant of "this mystery", which is, as he explains, "that blindness in part is happened to Israel until the fulness of the Gentiles be come in".

The mysteries of the NT do not describe events or aspects of truth which are incomprehensible. They concern secrets which God makes known to His people when the time is right to reveal them. They are new and unexpected developments in the ways of God known to Him but kept from His people until the appropriate time arrives for their disclosure. These mysteries are beyond the unaided human mind to discover but they are not inscrutable. When God by His Spirit reveals the truth of any mystery, the spiritual mind can quickly grasp what is involved.

The apostle has written much in this epistle about remnants. The character of the remnant which he deals with in this verse has often been referred to as "the heavenly remnant". This is because it concerns Israelites who are saved through believing the gospel and whose hope is therefore a heavenly one, as distinct from the earthly hopes of Israel. By putting their trust in Jesus Christ they lose their national standing and give up their earthly hopes, but they enter into higher and better privileges as members of the church which is His body.

The fact which is the subject of this mystery is that "blindness in part is happened unto Israel". It was not a mystery that God would smite Israel with blindness. Paul had just made known that Moses, David and Isaiah had all prophesied that God would smite Israel with blindness (vv.8,9). That this blindness would not affect the whole nation but would continue while Christ built His church – that is the secret which is now made known. This state of affairs will last until the fulness of the Gentiles comes in. That point of time is when the last Gentile is saved through the gospel of the grace of God, and when that gospel ceases to be preached at the Rapture. Gentiles who respond to the preaching of Jews after the rapture come into another category, which is not the subject of Paul's argument at this point.

There is a word of warning in the verse, "lest ye should be wise in your own conceits". Initiating the Gentiles into the secret that the hardening of the mass of Israel had its limits, that it was neither total nor final, was intended to keep them humble. God was giving them their day of opportunity. There was nothing meritorious about them. They were as described by the Lord in His answer to the Syrophenician woman, "It is not meet to take the children's bread, and to cast it unto the dogs" (Mark 7:27). Her reply reflected an understanding of the true character of God, "Yes Lord: yet the (little) dogs under the table eat of the children's crumbs". There was something for those who were prepared to bend down and take what had first been offered to Israel.

26 There is difficulty with the connection of the opening words "And so". Some take them to introduce the conclusion of what Paul has just said about Israel's hardening being partial. Others consider them to be the introduction to her future deliverance: "all Israel shall be saved and there shall come out of Zion the Deliverer". Denney considers that "And so" has the force of "And thus". He also considers that "all Israel shall be saved" is an independent sentence. The most likely meaning seems to be that since the hardening of part of Israel was not final and that there was a limit to the day of grace for Gentiles, the time had to come when the hardening would give way to restoration. Then it can be said, "All Israel shall be saved". This does not necessarily mean that every Jew will be converted; salvation will still be an individual responsibility. Paul is thinking of the nation as a whole, and her part in God's plans for the future.

The hardening of Israel in part was a mystery beyond the scope of man's mind to know, apart from divine revelation. However, God had made known Israel's ultimate restoration and Isaiah is here called upon to authenticate it: "There shall come out of Zion the Deliverer; and shall turn away ungodliness from Jacob".

Isa 59:20 LXX gives, "And the deliverer shall come for Sion's sake and shall turn away ungodliness from Jacob". Reference has already been made to Isa 59 at 3:15-17 and Paul will make three more references to that chapter in Eph 6:14,17 and 1 Thess 5:8. The apostle here is concerned only with the fact that the Deliverer is coming and that ungodliness shall be turned away from Jacob. There is no mention of the enemy coming in like a flood or of the Deliverer putting on righteousness as a breastplate. It is sufficient for the apostle's purpose at this point to record the intervention of the Lord and the effect on Jacob. Vincent notes that the Hebrew for "deliverer" is *goel*, "the avenger", "the kinsman redeemer". Vine suggests that the literal rendering of the Hebrew is: "There shall come a redeemer for Zion and for them that turn from transgression in Jacob".

27 This verse gives the other half of the quotation from Isa 59, with a possible quotation from Isa 27:9 LXX, "Therefore shall the iniquity of Jacob be taken away". The covenant referred to is the new covenant to be made with the house of Judah and the house of Israel as described in Jer 31:31-34. It will be an unconditional covenant. It will not depend on obedience from those embraced by it; but on the basis of the blood shed at Calvary. This aspect, however, is not uppermost on the apostle's mind here, but, as is clear, it is what will be done from the divine side, resulting in the taking away of the sins of the people of Israel.

The question of Israel's sins cannot be overlooked. If Israel will have a leading role to play amongst the nations in the future, the sin question in particular will have to be addressed. Here Paul does not dwell on national confession and mourning but on what God will do, He will take away sins. The overriding theme in the epistle had been justification. Even here, the justification of God, as seen in Israel's restoration, is evident. The groundwork for the taking away of Israel's sins has been laid at Calvary. On the ground of the sin-atoning work of Christ there, God will be entirely righteous in taking up Israel again and in the removal of their sins.

28 Having made known certain facts concerning the present position and future restoration of Israel which previously had not been revealed, Paul now shows that the fresh revelations were perfectly consistent with God's character. The first point he raises relates to the gospel. As far as the gospel is concerned the Jews were enemies. This does not mean that it was because of the gospel they were enemies. It means "with reference to the gospel they were enemies on account of you". Because of the disobedience of the Jews and their attitude to the gospel, God turned to the Gentiles. Paul is not inferring that God was taken by surprise and that the bringing in of the Gentiles was an afterthought. The rejection of the Jews was not a tragedy in that sense, but rather was part of the plans of God which had in mind mercy for the Gentiles and which came into effect by the attitude of the Jews to the gospel.

The apostle moves on to another consideration. God had not discarded Israel altogether. In relation to the gospel which the nation rejected, they are enemies, the objects of God's hostility. However, when Paul considers the choice of Israel to be the people of God they are no longer seen as enemies but as the objects of God's love. The fact that the Jews had treated the gospel with disdain did not cancel out His love for the nation.

This reference to the election should not be taken to mean choice in connection with salvation in the present dispensation of grace. It means that God chose the nation for the working out of His purposes. Despite failure, Israel is still the object of God's love because of the promises He made to the fathers. God's covenant relationships with Abraham, Isaac and Jacob brought in their descendants and although they were marked by unfaithfulness, God bore with them for the patriarchs' sakes.

The situations described in chs.9-11 are not inconsistent with the central theme of the epistle which is justification. They demonstrate from other viewpoints that God is indeed just and the justifier of the ungodly.

29 Another aspect of the consistency of God is introduced. Despite the fact that Israel, by refusing the gospel, had become the object of divine hostility, God's original intentions for the nation had not changed. The people of Israel had turned against Him but He had not gone back on His promises. If God calls and makes gifts, He will not change His mind and cancel what He has done. God is immutable. There is never a moment when He has remorse. After He has called He will not rescind that as if to admit that He has made a mistake. All His actions are in accordance with His eternal counsels and these never change.

The context demands that the gifts mentioned here are not general to all mankind, but relate specifically to the nation of Israel. The apostle made much of the privileges of the Israelites at the commencement of His consideration of the Jewish position. He wrote, "to whom pertaineth the adoption, and the glory, and the covenants, and the giving of the law, and the services of God, and the promises; whose are the fathers, and of whom as concerning the flesh Christ came" (9:4,5). No other nation had such gifts. If God had called them back, the immutability of His character would have come under censure. But such a thought Paul will not allow. What God gives is not subject to change or recall and that is a principle which covers all His dealings with mankind.

30 The dominant theme of this verse and also the next is the mercy of God. The apostle takes up the Gentile position and shows how it came to pass that God could extend mercy to them. In doing so, His action is seen to be consistent with His divine purposes. In view of what Paul has set out earlier in the epistle, there can be no question that in times past the Gentiles believed not God, they were disobedient. Nevertheless, God in grace has shown them mercy. Through the unbelief (or, disobedience) of the Jews, the way has opened up for Gentile blessing.

There is no question of merit here. The apostle does not say that in times past the Gentiles were disobedient but now have become obedient. The contrast is clear: in times past disobedient, they now have obtained mercy. Human achievement has no place in this. The grace of God is behind it. The Jews were disobedient and forfeited their place of privilege. God then used their disobedience to work blessing for the Gentiles. It is all of mercy. Historically, as ch.1 of the epistle reveals, the Gentiles were no better than the Jews. They were deserving of judgment but such is the grace of God, He found a way to extend His mercy to the undeserving. He is still making it available to all mankind through the gospel.

31 There are several distinctions between the relative positions of Jews and Gentiles as set out in vv.30,31. In v.30 the periods of time considered in relation to both are past and present: disobedient Gentiles in the past; disobedient Jews and mercy to Gentiles in the present. In v.31 the time aspect considers disobedient Jews and mercy to Gentiles in the present, but mercy to Jews in the future. Jews and Gentiles are seen to have two things in common, both were disobedient and both were cast on the mercy of God. Neither can say that God was obliged to show favour. They were both in the same plight and undeserving of divine mercy.

The point the apostle seems to be stressing to the Gentiles is that there has been disobedience on all sides and therefore entitlement to mercy is non-existent. Nevertheless, while in the present day of grace Gentiles have the priceless opportunity of hearing and obeying the gospel, the day will come when Jews nationally will arise, as it were, from the dead (v.15) and mercy will be shown to them. Any thought therefore that God is unfair or that He has lost control cannot be sustained.

32 The conclusion Paul arrives at here is striking. Having dealt with disobedience in relation to the Gentiles, and separately with the disobedience of the Jews, he now brings them together. He states that all have been shut up under disobedience. The reference to "them all" means that no one can escape from the net which shuts up every man and every woman in unbelief. None can claim that the sentence, "all have sinned and come short of the glory of God" has loopholes, and that there were some, somewhere in history, who had merited God's favour. In all of Paul's writings, and none more so than the epistle to the Romans, it comes out with the utmost conviction that salvation is never earned. Never for a moment does Paul concede that favour is a right or a reward; it is all of grace.

The verb "hath concluded" (*sunkleiō*) carries the meaning of being enclosed on all sides. It is used in Gal 3:22, "The scripture hath concluded all under sin". A cognate word is used in Luke 5:6 to describe a great multitude of fish inclosed in a net, shut in with no hope of escape. Here Paul makes known that God in His own mysterious ways has so ordered circumstances that the disobedience of all, Jews and Gentiles alike, shuts them up on all sides without escape by human merit. All are imprisoned in sin and unbelief.

The great purpose of God in it all is declared: it is that He might have mercy on all. This does not mean universal salvation. That is not taught in Scripture. As to the present age, nothing can be clearer than the universal scope of the gospel. It makes no differences of any kind; all are embraced in its outreach. In it God displays in a wondrous way His great mercy. As to the future on earth, when Israel is restored, God will show mercy to all nations in the millennial age. Even then, despite universal peace and splendour, the Scripture does not teach universal salvation; sin will still evidence itself. As to the view that in eternity all will be saved, this is a vain hope which endeavours to throw a cover over sin. There is no way round the statement, "It is appointed unto men once to die, but after this the judgment" (Heb 9:27). It behoves men and women to heed the advice given by the Saviour in His ministry, "Agree with thine adversary quickly, whiles thou art in the way with him" (Matt 5:25).

Notes

15 "Mystery" (*mustērion* "a secret which would remain such apart from revelation") is from *mueō* "to initiate".

"Blindness" (*pōrōsis*, "hardness", "a hardening") is from *pōrō*, "to petrify", "to harden". (*Pōros*, a callus, a stony concretion).

26 "Ungodliness" (*asebeias*) is a plural, so literally "ungodlinesses").

27 For "I shall take away" (*aphaireō*, "to remove"), see use of the word at Heb 10:4.

29 "Without repentance" (*ametamelētos*, "not subject to recall"), only here and 2 Cor 7:10 in NT.

"Calling" (*klēsis*) is not the sense of vocation, but is the call, the authoritative invitation of God.

30 "Mercy" ("to have compassion on") is to be distinguished from *oiktirmos*. Trench in *Synonymns of the New Testament* maintains that *eleos* is an active compassion that desires to relieve the misery of others. *Oiktirmos* is not used in vv.30-32.

(d) *A fitting doxology (vv.33-36)*

> v.33 "O the depth of the riches both of the wisdom and knowledge of God! how unsearchable are his judgments, and his ways past finding out!
> v.34 For who hath known the mind of the Lord? or who hath been his counsellor?
> v.35 Or who hath first given to him, and it shall be recompensed unto him again?
> v.36 For of him, and through him, and to him, are all things: to whom be glory for ever. Amen."

33 The last verse of the chapter contains the expression of praise which is generally recognised as a doxology. It is clear, however, that the build-up to the final word commences at this verse with the outburst, "O the depth of the riches…" Having traced the righteousness and mercy of God with Jew and Gentile throughout the epistle, the apostle finds himself in such a position of indebtedness that he cannot contain his praise. It seems obvious that he finds he cannot proceed any further until he has discharged the obligation placed upon him to render the praise that is due to God.

Commentators are divided regarding the force of the word "depth" here. There is little doubt that it suggests what is unfathomable, and therefore inexhaustible. The point at issue is whether it refers to three attributes, riches, wisdom, and knowledge, or to two, wisdom and knowledge. Since the original text can be interpreted to support both views, it is perhaps better to take both approaches into account to get the fullest sense of appreciation of these wonderful aspects of God's character. The riches of the wisdom and knowledge of God cannot be calculated. Considered in the other sense, the words could be rendered, "O the boundless riches and wisdom and knowledge of God". God is rich beyond human thought and He knows everything that ever was, is, and shall be. His wisdom leads Him to chose what ends are best and what are the most suitable means to achieve the ends He determines.

In the verse the apostle has two more observations to make. The first one concerns His judgments. They are not merely legal determinations although the earlier ministry in the epistle would support that, but all His providential dealings, a view which the whole epistle would support. These judgments are beyond human finding, they cannot be searched out. Regarding His ways, they are beyond tracing. They are footprints which cannot be tracked down. Taking both of Paul's observations together, the picture is clear. No amount of searching or tracking by human ingenuity will penetrate realms which are infinite. The wisest course when faced with what is unfathomable and inexhaustible is to do the same as Paul and bow before God in adoring worship.

34 Although Paul was a chosen vessel to reveal aspects of truth which had been kept secret by God, he was forced to declare that he was dealing with things which were past finding out. The abundance of the revelations given to him did not provide more than a very limited understanding of the ways of God.

He was initiated into many of the secrets of God, but he is the first to admit that he was only on the edge. The outworking of the attributes of God were far too wonderful for him. His only recourse was worship and praise.

In this verse there is a free quotation of Isa 40:13 LXX. The meaning, however, is clear. God does not require counsel or advice from any created intelligence. Hence, the prophet Isaiah and the apostle throw out the challenge, and there is no answer to the question they pose. God works to His own counsel and is not answerable to anyone. He is not beholden to angels or men for what He does. In the context of Isa 40, the prophet states that the nations are as a drop of a bucket and are counted as the small dust of the balance. It is no small wonder then that Isaiah asks, "To whom will ye liken God? or what likeness will ye compare unto him?"

The choice of a passage like Isa 40:13 to clinch his argument was certainly a master stroke on Paul's part. The Jews, who were familiar with the Scriptures could not fail to be impressed by the logic of the apostle's reasoning. Whether they were disposed to believe it and have a change of heart is another matter. Nevertheless, for those who had bowed the knee in repentance, the words of Paul's doxology would certainly be heart-warming and inducive of praise to the God of all grace.

35 The apostle raises another rhetorical question, "Who hath first given unto him, and it shall be recompensed unto him again?" No one has ever made an advance to God that obliged Him to make repayment. No one has ever placed God in a situation where God was beholden to him. The thought of the eternal God floating a project which needed funding of some sort from another source does not bear thinking about. All that men and women have, and may be moved to give to Him, came from Him originally.

God is not unmindful, however, to respond to those who are willing to give to Him, as Paul wrote to an assembly in his day, "God loveth a cheerful giver" (2 Cor 9:7). That, however, is not the point the apostle is making here. What he is establishing is that no created intelligence can take up a position for a moment which suggests that there is equality with God. Any one assuming to be God's creditor is on dangerous ground. Such presumption is the height of folly. And yet there are many who choose to ignore that there is a great gulf fixed which can never be bridged by works of any kind. God will be no man's debtor.

36 The answer to the rhetorical question of the previous verse is now given, "For of him, and through him, and to him, are all things". Paul's conclusion is that God is the originator of everything and he cannot think of anything of which He is not the author. Bringing all things into existence was not left to agents which might imply that other hands had left their imprints on creation. Through Him all things were established. Nothing was left to others whose wills might be independent of His own. In the end all things were to Him. There is no possibility that God will lose control, neither will He abdicate and leave the responsibility for the consummation of the ages to others to tie up the ends. Having therefore dealt with the deep things of God in the epistle, Paul's view of deity leaves him with one recourse: he can only bow in the presence of Almighty God in worship.

The doxology in this verse is the third of four in the epistle. The other three are found at 1:25; 9:5; 16:27. They are not without a sense of progression. The observation, however, is of interest, since in such a wonderful epistle there are only four clear doxologies.

The first doxology involves creation. At 1:25 the apostle records, "The Creator, who is blessed for ever. Amen". The second doxology concerns incarnation. At 9:5, the apostle states, "of whom as concerning the flesh Christ came, who is over all, God blessed for ever. Amen". The third doxology concerns preservation. Having considered God's ways with Israel and the future He has in store for that nation, Paul records here, "For of him, and through him, and to him, are all things: to whom be glory for ever. Amen". Finally, to close the epistle, having considered the righteousness and wondrous ways of God, the apostle records a fitting consummation at 16:27, "To God only wise, be glory through Jesus Christ for ever. Amen".

Notes

33 Vine suggests that vv.33-36 may be set out in chiasmic or crosswise order. Some consider the verses to be a hymn, while others see poetic structure in them. Whatever way they are considered, they are a most remarkable outburst of praise.

VI. The Righteousness of God Displayed (12:1-15:13)

In the first eleven chapters Paul has set out the great doctrinal facts of the gospel. From various points of view the righteousness of God has been considered. Throughout, God's dealings with Jews and Gentiles have been seen to be entirely consistent with the righteousness of His character. No charge can be made against Him. Even His severity is tempered by His mercy, for although He has concluded all in unbelief, it is to the end that He might have mercy upon all (11:32).

In the main, the doctrinal part of the epistle ends at the close of ch.11, but the subject of the gospel and the righteousness of God does not terminate there. His righteousness has been displayed. The gospel has to be worked out in the lives of those who have believed its message. The believer is placed under an obligation to demonstrate that the truth can be read in christian living. The exhortations which commence at ch.12 are all entirely consistent with the doctrine of the gospel set out in the earlier part of the epistle. The scope of this will be before God, the church and every section of society. This all shows that the new way of living cannot be confined to a corner. It has to come out and be displayed in the widest sense, so that its message will be carried to every part of the world.

Analysis need not be forced. Paul's thinking is clearly identifiable. He considers the Christian first of all in relation to God in 12:1,2. The believer must be properly regulated there to be right before men and women. As a follow-on to that, the apostle seems to have the church in view in vv.3-8, where he considers spiritual gifts and how they are regulated. Christian living is then widened out, firstly in relation to believers in vv.9-13, and then in relation to unbelievers in vv.14-21.

1. The Christian's Attitude toward God, the Church and the Brethren 12:1-21

(a) *Towards God (vv.1-8)*

- v.1 "I beseech you therefore, brethren, by the mercies of God, that ye present your bodies a living sacrifice, holy, acceptable unto God, which is your reasonable service.
- v.2 And be not conformed to this world: but be ye transformed by the renewing of your mind, that ye may prove what is that good, and acceptable, and perfect, will of God.
- v.3 For I say, through the grace given unto me, to every man that is among you, not

v.4 For as we have many members in one body, and all members have not the same office:
v.5 So we, being many, are one body in Christ, and every one members one of another.
v.6 Having then gifts differing according to the grace that is given to us, whether prophecy, let us prophesy according to the proportion of faith;
v.7 Or ministry, let us wait on our ministering: or he that teacheth, on teaching;
v.8 Or he that exhorteth, on exhortation: he that giveth, let him do it with simplicity; he that ruleth, with diligence; he that sheweth mercy, with cheerfulness."

1 The word "therefore" marks a significant point in the epistle. What the apostle will press for must be seen in the light of all that has gone before. Another crucial stage was marked by the word "therefore" at the end of ch.4, where the apostle states, "Therefore being justified by faith, we have peace with God" (5:1). Another conclusion is reached at the end of ch.7 which leads Paul to make a wonderful statement, "There is therefore now no condemnation to them which are in Christ Jesus" (8:1). So here at the commencement of the practical section, the responses called for must be in keeping with the great truth of the gospel and the righteousness of God.

"I beseech" (*parakaleō*) can be variously translated. In the context here it is better to consider the word as being much less than a command. The apostle is urging believers to respond willingly from within themselves rather than be influenced or even forced by apostolic authority to conform. The appeal is made to brethren stressing christian relationships, and it is based on the mercies (*oiktirmōn*) of God. W E Vine in *Expository Dictionary of New Testament Words* draws a distinction between *oiktirmos* and *eleos,* both of which are translated "mercy" in the NT. Here Paul uses *oiktirmos*, a more tender word than *eleos,* to give his appeal warmth. The warm compassions of God give the apostle's plea the proper condition for its acceptance.

The appeal to the believers is to present their bodies a living sacrifice. It is not a challenge to everyone to do extreme acts of heroism, as might be expected from the heathen towards heathen gods. It is rather a living sacrifice, an ongoing commitment of life to God. This sacrifice must be holy. What is required from God's people is not a lower standard than what was required in connection with animal sacrifices under the law. Believers must lead lives that meet the requirements of God and are therefore well-pleasing to Him. The reference to "bodies" may have had a deeper meaning in the apostle's thinking than merely physical bodies. The context suggests total commitment, with the inner man finding full expression through the body in all its parts.

The presenting of the body as a living sacrifice is seen by Paul as the reasonable, logical response of the saints. He is not restricting the resultant action to what is becoming, what in the nature of the circumstances might be expected. He is stressing that it is the outcome of considered judgment. It is intelligent, in complete accord with reason in its deepest sense. The service is spiritual, rather than religious. The verb was used by the apostle to describe how he served God in the gospel. It was with his spirit and he could call upon God to bear testimony that this was the case (1:9).

2 The apostle now moves from a positive attitude to a negative one. Service towards God will not be well-pleasing to Him if it is conformed to the world. It is not a reasonable service which endeavours to balance what God expects with what the world demands. The word for "world" (*aiōn,* "age") signifies the characteristics of humanity, moral or otherwise, at any point of time. Paul describes it clearly at the beginning of his epistle to the Galatians. Writing of the grace of our Lord Jesus Christ, he states, "who gave himself for our sins, that he might deliver us from this present evil world (age)" (Gal 1:4). Since God has passed judgment on all that is of man, and it only awaits His pleasure until the sickle is put in, it is folly to be conformed to what has a very limited future. Conversion implies a turning to God and a turning away from the world and its ways. It is a tragedy therefore when there is a return to what was left behind.

Much has been written about the difference between "conformed" and "transformed". The core words, *schēma* and *morphē,* are also at the centre of the *kenōsis* ("the emptying") in the great Christological passage of Phil 2. There, as here, there are deep waters to swim in. The phrase "And be not conformed" is rendered in the RV "And be not fashioned". Robertson maintains it has the meaning of conforming to another's pattern and he therefore gives the rendering, "Do not take this age as your fashion plate". There is no doubt that Paul meant more than a mere superficial conformity when he wrote the words. To him the world was a scene of evil and corruption and being fashioned to it in any respect was a grievous matter. External likeness to the world's fashions, and habits is clearly condemned. It is an evidence that the influences of the present age are taking over from the powers of the age to come.

The apostle calls for a transformation. It suggests an inward change of such a nature that outward manifestations will result. Matthew and Mark used the word when they made known the intensity of the change that took place on the mount of transfiguration. They wanted their readers to know of the shining out of the Lord's glory, the transcendency of His regal majesty. It is little wonder that Peter wanted to make three tabernacles lest a scene of such brilliance should pass away from him too quickly. Paul uses the word and calls for a radical inward change.

He then deals with how the change be accomplished; it is by the renewing of the mind. The implication is both intellectual and moral. In the natural man the workings of the mind are influenced by the inner state, the corruption that is there by reason of sin. The believer is indwelt by the Holy Spirit and there is therefore a new power within. The means are there for a constant renewing of the spiritual, intellectual and moral faculties. The two words "conformed" and "transformed" are imperatives in the passive voice. The first suggests that the world must not be allowed to influence. The second implies that since the means are there, the change must be allowed to take place. The renewing is in the present tense. It implies that the work of the Holy Spirit is ongoing in the process of renewal. He will constantly update the believer's thinking to meet the ever-changing challenges of the world in which service for God is carried out.

The purpose and the result of the renewal process is that there will be an ability to prove the will of God, that which is good, acceptable and perfect. The great fact of this verse is that the Christian is seen to have all that is necessary to prove what is the will of God in any situation. The discernment is there to be used. Even in the youngest believer the potential is present. It may take time to develop it to maturity, but never should it be thought or inferred that God has left His people to their own devices. He has made ample provision to enable His saints to cope with every contingency and to do so to His pleasure. Clearly the three words, "good, pleasing and perfect" indicate that service for God is not irksome. If it brings pleasure to Him it will have its reward in His servants who labour for Him.

3 Not all agree that Paul's stance in vv.3-8 is churchward, preferring to consider his exhortations to be directed to believers generally. Be that as it may, the gifts described are such that they are better understood as functioning in an assembly setting.

"For" links what follows as a consequence of what has gone before. Perhaps "I say" is like "I beseech", softer than a command. Some consider that apostolic authority is enjoined. This was certainly claimed in the opening verse of the epistle, but whether it was meant to make an apostolic impression on every statement thereafter is doubtful. Here Paul makes known that what he is going to delineate is in accordance with the grace given to him. He commences with the danger of pride finding a place in the thinking of those he addresses. To give advice on that needs grace and he therefore speaks of the grace given to him to address such an important matter.

He addresses "every man that is among you". None is exempt from the peril of lofty thoughts. Thinking more highly than one ought to think is fraught with danger, and especially in the light of the gifts which Paul is about to discuss. There is safety in thinking soberly. A sound mind, occupied with sober thinking, is what Paul calls for. He himself seems to have taken the humble position in the introduction, as if to say, "Apart from grace, pride would have dominated my way of thinking". He makes a play on words, giving three variations of *phroneō* ("to think"), in order to get his message across. Each is to be minded towards sobermindedness.

Sober thinking will not be self-centred but will recognise the measure of faith distributed to each one. The standard for assessing one's own worth and the worth of others is the faith which God has given. This is a spiritual exercise. In connection with faith, capacities may differ, but each believer has the faculty to absorb in measure what is communicated by God through His word. The assimilation of what God is constantly making known is essential for providing the proper fitness for christian service. Faith and trust are the motivating forces in believers, quite different from what motivates the unconverted.

4 Teaching on the subject of "the body" is not as fully dealt with here as it is in 1 Cor 12 and Eph 4. There is no argument here from the apostle as in 1 Corinthians regarding one member of the body saying to another, "I have no need of thee". Obviously the Romans were not taken up with a spirit of independency. Neither is there an explanation of what the body is, how its members are fitly joined together and how each part is nourished. That was for the Ephesians who had reached a spirit of maturity which could appreciate the close connection of believer with believer with a view to the functioning of each part in relation to others in the body.

In connection with the truth of the body it is essential to see that its members have not the same "doing". The word "office" in the AV is an unfortunate rendering of *praxis* (*prassō*, "to practise", "to act"). Indeed the word is part of the title The *Acts* of the Apostles. Paul is saying that the members of the body have different "doings". The gifts differ and the functionings differ also. The word rendered "office" is in the singular and it contains the idea of repetition. The thought of holding down an office is quite foreign to the teaching of the verse.

5 There is no difficulty in understanding the teaching of this verse. Individual believers (however many) are members of the body. This is a great thought. It becomes apparent as such when all the nationalities of the world are taken into account. Although such a scope might not have been to the fore in the Roman situation, there were obviously Jews and Gentiles there and they were addressed as members of one body. Hitherto this had never happened. No scheme in the world's ways could have accomplished it. It was through the work of Christ, as Paul made known to the Ephesians, "Christ Jesus...hath made both one, and hath broken down the middle wall of partition between us (Jew and Gentile)...that he might reconcile both unto God in one body by the cross" (Eph 2:13, 14,16).

Here the members are said to be "one body *in* Christ". This is different from the situation as described in Ephesians and Colossians. There the main thought is of Christ being the head *of* the body with all the members being fitly joined together and nourishment descending from the Head and percolating down through all the members. Here the members are considered as being one body "in Christ", and as such they have unity. If they were not "in Christ" there could be no body and therefore no unity. Any thought of a body in a spiritual sense would have no meaning if they were not "in Christ". The great fact, however, is that believers of the gospel are "in Christ" and are therefore members one of another in the body, sharing the same joys, privileges and responsibilities.

6 Although the grammar of the verse is held to be difficult, "having" being a participle with no related verb, it does seem clear that Paul takes the possession of gift as an established fact. The members of the body have not the same gifts and they have not the same "doings". They have, nevertheless, all been endowed by the Lord with gifts which differ according to the grace given to them. The two epistles, 1 Corinthians and Ephesians, deal with the subject in detail but here the apostle takes it for granted that there are gifts in the members of the body and they differ one from another. How much natural ability or fitness is involved is not the point. What Paul is teaching is that there are different gifts and he will give examples of these and how they are regulated.

The aorist tense of "given" signifies that a point of time is involved. The gift is given at conversion and the necessary grace is given with it. It may take time for the gift with its accompanying grace to become manifest, but it is there potentially and given time it should come out in display. The seven examples which follow are all governed by the basic statement of this verse: the acknowledgment that the members of the body have gifts and there is sufficient grace to exercise them.

The first gift mentioned is prophecy. It is generally agreed that the NT prophets have gone and their function has been taken over by teachers. A prophet in OT times was a teller-forth, not necessarily a forth-teller of the future but a declarer of the mind of God, even for the time then present, the time that the prophet spoke. The prophet was one who came from the presence of God, with a message from God for the people of God. Those who heard the message were seldom in doubt that God was speaking through His servant. Similar conditions existed in apostolic times and the need was there for prophets to speak the mind of God. Until the NT scriptures were all written and the canon completed, the prophets were necessary. Now that the canon is completed, teachers have taken over the prophets' role and are accomplishing the same end.

Here the gift is seen to be regulated; it is according to the proportion of faith. Those who prophesied in apostolic times could not go beyond what the Lord had given them. Neither could they reach out further than the proportion of faith. If they beyond what God had given they were inviting His displeasure. They were required to be faithful, not only to God, but to themselves and to those who were addressed. The discharge of the prophetic message was not a light thing. The proper response from the saints depended on the faithfulness of the prophet to deliver exactly what was given to him.

7 The second gift mentioned in Paul's list is ministry (*diakonia*), which normally signifies service of a general nature. Originally the word described the service of a waiter at tables but later it was applied to service of a menial type. Because of the lowly kind of service implied, many consider that a special gift is not indicated. This view, however, fails to take into account that there are many Christians who serve and are happy to do so, performing the most menial tasks as unto the Lord. That such are fitted for their work and have the ability to raise their service to the level of a noble occupation is difficult to deny.

Paul's advice here is to have service regulated. He does not say that it should be characterised by humility, or any other grace, but by doing the work for which one is fitted. How often it is seen that the one who serves is so closely identified with the service engaged in, that it is difficult to think of that aspect of the work without thinking of the person who does it. It would seem that this is what Paul is advocating, that the worker and the work should be so closely united that one cannot be separated from the other.

Regarding the next gift, there is no argument against teaching being listed. That there were teachers in apostolic times is clear from the Scriptures. A typical example is the record of Acts 13:1, "Now there were in the church that was at Antioch certain prophets and teachers". The ability of a teacher who is gifted and able to bring his audience into the presence of God by his teaching is a great blessing to those who are prepared to listen attentively to the ministry. Apart from the instruction given and the lessons learned, it is a great joy to be able to look beyond the vessel and hear what God is saying. From the human standpoint, the standard is that set by Peter, "If any man speak let him speak as the oracles of God" (1 Pet 4:11).

Here Paul puts in a regulating word. The teacher has to wait on his teaching. He must be characterised by what he teaches. It would be grossly wrong for a teacher to expound the Scripture and not conform himself to what he is teaching. When the Lord taught He was the perfect model of what He taught. When He quoted the Scriptures in the temptation in the wilderness, He was totally conformed to each passage quoted. Those who teach should always keep this example before their minds. Conformity to the word of God is essential, otherwise those who are being taught will fail to appreciate the authority and sacredness of the Holy Scriptures. Regarding the teacher and his teaching, Robert Candlish makes a telling observation. He states, "With no pretention to the gift of discovering new truth, or even to the gift of presenting old truth in a new light, and enforcing it with new strength, you may be skilful in carefully breaking up the truth, and affectionately training the raw and the rude intellect for its reception".

8 The next gift identified by Paul is exhortation. Basically the word means "to call to one's side", "to call near", hence "to comfort and encourage." A classical example of this gift in the NT is Barnabas, a son of consolation. When he saw the grace of God at Antioch he "exhorted them all, that with purpose of heart they would cleave unto the Lord" (Acts 11:23). The exhorter has the ability to encourage others. This gift, however, is regulated also. It would be a strange exhorter who called people to his side and then simply pointed the way forward. If he were characterised by his own ministry, he would gather those together who needed to be led and then lead them forward himself. It is expected of the exhorter that he would lead from the front. Words of consolation need to be put into practice if they are to have any meaning, or effect on others.

The gift of giving is not often considered as a spiritual gift. More often it is looked upon as a responsibility and in measure this is true. That some have been fitted for this work cannot, however, be gainsaid. They are channels through whom the Lord operates to give of their substance as the need arises. In the strange ways of God these servants seldom find themselves in want. God restores to them with interest what they have imparted, and so they carry on with the service committed to them. By the very nature of the gift, it is not one which is seen in public display. People who give, as unto the Lord, do not publish the fact abroad. The recipients may know of their generosity, but that is not always the case as many prefer to remain anonymous. Giving is here regulated by a telling expression, it should be done with simplicity, or, with singleness of mind and purpose. The word is the opposite of duplicity. It carries the meaning of that which is spread out, it has no wrinkles. It indicates that there are no ulterior motives in the giving. Used wrongly, giving can exercise a power to influence, and if the goal is not spiritual, grievous harm may result. Paul's qualifying word is therefore a very telling safeguard.

The choice of word in the AV to describe the next gift is unfortunate. "He that ruleth" has been taken by many to justify the role of the despot. There is no support in the word of God for such a position in the church of God. The word used by the apostle means literally, "to stand before" or "to set before". When as here the verb is in the middle voice, the principal thought is leadership. The person described by the gift is one whose work involves standing before the saints to lead. He must do it with diligence. There is zeal and anxious care in it. This is what qualifies the gift. Paul himself could claim that he had an anxious care for all the churches, which came upon daily (2 Cor 11:28). He knew from experience what was involved.

The last gift in Paul's list is showing "mercy" (*eleos*), which implies a striving to relieve the distressed and the person so moved will do so to the best of his ability. If the word had been *oiktirmos,* the work might have appeared to be confined to having feelings of pity for the oppressed without actually doing anything to relieve their burdens. What Paul is advancing is compassion of a more practical nature. It will not have a grudging spirit. It will not be ready to associate blame with misfortune but will rather seek to relieve with cheerfulness. The spirit of joy which is associated with the working out of this gift is what the apostle is conveying. The word he uses is *hilarotēs,* from which comes the word "hilarity". The bad sense into which the word has fallen is not what Paul has in mind here. He is thinking of an unbounded cheerfulness.

Notes

1 "Present" (*paristēmi*) in the aorist tense here indicates a once-for-all action. Some think it is possibly a technical term for offering a sacrifice. See Eph 5:27 where the word is used of Christ presenting the church to Himself.

The word *logikos* ("reasonable") is used only here and at 1 Pet 2:2, where the RV renders the passage "long for the *spiritual* milk which is without guile" not as in the AV, "of the word".

"Service" (*latreia*) is religious service as rendered by the Israelites. It points Godward. Paul's use of it in 1:9 states that he served God "in his spirit", that is his spirit under the control of the Holy Spirit, and not in the empty ceremonial manner of the Jews. The service here is rational and spiritual and not ceremonial.

2 "Conformed" (*suschēmatizō*, "to fashion in accordance with") is in contrast with "transformed" (*metamorphoō*, "to change the external form", "to undergo a spiritual transformation"). For "renewing" (*anakainōsis*, "renovation"), see Titus 3:5, "and *renewing* of the Holy Ghost", the only other occurrence of the word in the NT.

The Lord spoke of "this age" (*aiōn*), of its cares (Matt 13:22), of its end (Matt 13:39), of its children (Luke 20:34).

3 "Grace" (*charis*, "charm") here means what God has graciously imparted. RC Trench in his *Synonyms of the New Testament* makes an interesting comment about *charis*. He writes, "There has often been occasion to observe the manner in which the Greek words taken up into Christian use are glorified and transformed, seeming to have waited for this adoption of them, to come to their full rights, and to reveal all the depths and the riches of meaning which they contained, or might be made to contain. *Charis* is one of these. It is hardly too much to say that the Greek mind has in no word uttered itself and all that was in its heart more distinctly than in this; so it will abundantly repay our pains to trace briefly the steps by which it came to its highest honours".

Note the play on words in three uses of *phroneō*, ("to think"); *huperphronein*, ("to think highly); *sōphronein*, ("to think soberly"). Hendrickson suggests that Paul is giving a warning against exaggerated self-esteem.

8 "Simplicity" (*haplotēs*, "sincerity", "simplicity, uncomplicated, uncompounded" is used in Matt 6:22, "If thine eye be single"; 2 Cor 8:2, "unto the riches of their liberality". (There is an absence of duplicity or double-dealing in the word.)

For "cheerfulness", see Prov 17:22, "A merry (cheerful) heart doeth good like a medicine: but a broken spirit drieth the bones".

(b) *The Christian in relation to fellow-believers (vv.9-13)*

> v.9 "Let love be without dissimulation. Abhor that which is evil; cleave to that which is good.
> v.10 Be kindly affectioned one to another with brotherly love; in honour preferring one another;
> v.11 Not slothful in business; fervent in spirit; serving the Lord;
> v.12 Rejoicing in hope; patient in tribulation; continuing instant in prayer;
> v.13 Distributing to the necessity of saints; given to hospitality."

9 It is significant that love is placed at the head of this section. It has the effect of a regulator. Its influence permeates the injunctions and exhortations which follow. The four references to the word earlier in the epistle are in themselves striking. Each has left its imprint on the context where it is found and indeed has carried forward in the epistle. It is heartening to read of the way that God commendeth His love towards us (5:8) and to be assured that nothing can separate us, either from the love of Christ (8:35), or the love of God (8:39). So it is that Paul calls for a response, "Let love be without dissimulation (hypocrisy)". Although there is no verb in the original, it is a fair assumption that an optative is intended. Other words for "love" will come out in the chapter, each having its own significance in the context, but here the word is *agapē,* which chooses its object with decision of will and devotes a self-denying and compassionate devotion to it.

The apostle moves to another consideration, "Abhor that which is evil". A present participle is used, possibly with the force of an imperative, "shrinking from the evil". True love would cause this effect. There is no room in it for mere sentimentality. Evil is evil and love's reaction to it is one of abhorrence. R C Trench in his *Synonyms of the New Testament* differentiates between *ponēros, kakos* and *phaulos,* all of which mean evil in its various forms. The word here is *ponēros,* which has the peculiar force of putting others in trouble and taking a delight in doing so. A person who is characterised by *ponēros* is a perverse character who seems never to be happy unless causing harm.

There is of course a safeguard. Paul gives what can be taken from him as an injunction, "Cleave to that which is good". The word "cleave" has the idea of a strong adhesive indicating that one has to make the firmest of ties with "good". It is a permanent fixture. The word chosen by Paul for "good" suggests what is good and useful, what is of practical benefit. To be firmly attached to things that are good and beneficial is a great safeguard and an obvious boon to one's well-being.

10 There follow two other words for "love". In the original language, the first one is *philadelphia,* love of the brethren. With regard to the believers, he is calling on them to manifest a unique love, a love that is peculiar to the christian circle. It was unknown in the world of Paul's day. Men did not consider each other as brethren with such a distinct type of affection. The word might have applied in measure in a family where there were brothers and sisters but outside the family unit it was unknown. Here then is another word raised up by the Spirit of God to give meaning to that bond of affection which exists between those who are born of God.

The second word *philostorgos,* is a compound of *philō* ("love") and *storgē* ("natural affection"). Family affection is the force of it. Believers are privileged to be in the family of God. In that circle warm affection is a uniting feature. It is clear that Paul is pressing for conditions that will bind believers together. The love that is called for has preservative qualities. If believers can count upon warm affection from others it has a settling effect in the assembly. As there are no other occurrences of the word in the NT, there are therefore no examples of its use for comparison.

Paul leads on to another telling but difficult expression: "in honour preferring one another". It has been variously translated. Perhaps the simplest way to understand it is to accept that there should be a readiness to give precedence to others. In the christian assembly it is an unseemly situation to have believers striving for pre-eminence. Paul is obviously calling for the prior place to be given to others. If honour is due, nothing is lost by the believer who is prepared to waive his right to it and defer to another. The apostle is making no allowance for a false humility. This is not the case of competing with each other to see who can be the most self-effacing. Despite some difficulty in the wording of the verse it is clear that this call from the apostle is meant to put a stop to the advance of self. The best way to ensure that the right spirit prevails is to be ready to give place and honour to someone else.

11 The apostle now gives a set of three guiding principles. There are three more in the next verse. The suggestion that the force of the first three is external and that of the second three is internal may have some merit. Certainly the first three principles have a strong sense of activity about them. The present day use of the word "business" makes the AV rendering, "Not slothful in business (*spoudē*)", less desirable than the RV, "In diligence not slothful". In v.8 it was noticed that those who give a lead in the assembly should be marked by zeal. *Spoudē* has an element of haste in it and may be considered as the opposite of slothful. Towards the end of his life, Paul's advice to Timothy was, "Study (be eager, be zealous, strive diligently) to shew thyself approved unto God" (2 Tim 2:15). Here to the Romans Paul is stressing that holy zeal for God and sloth have nothing in common.

To be fervent in spirit is an expression which is not peculiar to Paul. Luke uses it to describe Apollos, "Being fervent in the spirit". From this it is clear that such fervour was identifiable. The word, "fervent" comes from a verb, meaning "to boil". When this describes believers in a spiritual sense, it is obvious that their fervour has bubbled up, or even bubbled over. This is not a condition which can be worked up in the flesh. It is spiritual, the effect of the Holy Spirit within being given His place. It is not confined to apostolic times, but is an obvious manifestation of the Spirit-filled life. In its expression it is seldom if ever ecstatic. Believers who are filled with the Spirit demonstrate it in an unostentatious way, but there is no mistaking the power of it.

There are textual variations in the next clause. Most manuscripts read, "serving the Lord", but there are a few which give "serving the time", or, "serving the hour". The word "serving" (*douleuō*) involves discharging the duties of a slave. The weight of authority supports the idea of always being ready to serve the Lord and to do that in the happy relationship of bondservant to master. Service for the Lord is never irksome or drudgery; it is the highest of privileges. To be in bondservice to time, or the hour, has challenging implications. It will mean the buying-up of every opportunity, never wasting one of life's most precious commodities, the present hour for service.

12 Another three principles are set out. The first one, "rejoicing in hope" is broad in its scope. "Hope" is the key word of this epistle, indeed God is referred to as "the God of hope" (15:13). God is characterised by hope. He never despairs because He is over all and all power is with Him. He never fails and He never gives up His saints as hopeless. "Hope" in the English language can be a very indeterminate word: normally it needs to be buttressed by another word, like "in the sure and certain hope of resurrection". The Christian's hope is based on the living God who is utterly reliable, and whose purposes, however long their fulfilment may tarry, can never finally be frustrated. The apostle here calls for a rejoicing in hope, in virtue of hope in God, "which hope we have as an anchor of the soul, both sure and steadfast" (Heb 6:19).

The apostle's call to show patience in tribulation has certainly been a buttress to the faith of many. Trouble comes in many guises. The word chosen by Paul here to describe tribulation contains the thought of serious trouble. It has in it the idea of pressure, not in a minor sense, but being subjected to a crushing load. The response called for in this situation is patience. The word *hupomenō* does not convey the sense of sitting down and letting the tide of events flow over. It means not only the ability to bear things, but in the bearing of them to turn them into triumph. It is the idea of conquering patience. It is the spirit which no circumstance of life can ever defeat.

Often our attitude to prayer is that we turn to it when all else fails; prayer is the last resource. That is not the way Paul looks at it here. He gives a present participle of the verb *proskantereō*, ("to persist in adherence to a thing"). The word is used of the early believers, "they *continued steadfastly* in the apostles doctrine" (Acts 2:42). Paul's counsel to the Romans did not allow for letting up on the need for constant prayer. It was not a spasmodic exercise as far as he was concerned, but one to be persevered in, using up the opportunities given in daily life to seek the presence of God for guidance and help.

13 The needs of the saints now come before the apostle. In the Rome of Paul's day there were rich and poor, and those who were poor knew what it was to be in want. Paul's counsel to those who had a surplus was that they should be constantly sharing their substance with needy saints. There is more to the word than merely making a contribution. It is implied that by entering into the circumstances of others, there will be an understanding of their needs or even their plight. Sharing is a word of considerable breadth. Paul is not applying it to the rich and restricting its outgoings to passing on largesse. The principle applies to all as even the poor can have something to share with others. Peter dwelt with one, Simon a tanner (Acts 9:43), obviously a brother of humble means. He did not have much but he shared what he had. Later in the epistle, the subject of this verse is taken up on a national scale where Gentiles of Macedonia and Achaia remember the poor saints of Jerusalem (15:26), and Paul takes it upon himself to be the bearer of their contributions. Christianity does not encourage being insular. God expects His people to share what He has first of all given to them.

In the latter half of the verse the AV expression "given to" is not strong enough. The word means to "pursue" and its use here implies the expending of effort to provide hospitality. It does not mean to have a leaning towards that kind of service, but an active pursuit of it. It is not intended to be fulfilled by an occasional social event, but by the expenditure of time and substance to minister to the saints as a need arises. Lydia's attitude is an example of what Paul is pressing for here. Luke wrote that she said to Paul and his companions, "If ye have judged me to be faithful to the Lord, come into my house and abide there. And she constrained us" (Acts 16:15). It has been said that the constraining of Lydia was of the type that would not take "No" for an answer. By using the word "saints" here Paul defends the status of believers. Even if they are the poorest of the poor they are still God's saints and no different in His eyes from the richest in the assembly. Plummer comments, "Poverty, sent on us by God's providence, is a great trial, but no crime. In your straits contrive, if possible, to help your poorer brethren and neighbours. Are you given to hospitality? It is a universal duty. It has been obligatory on all classes of persons under all dispensations".

Notes

9 "Dissimulation" (*anupokritos*) is from the verb meaning "to act a part", "to assume a counterfeit character", "to feign".

"Abhor" is a strong word meaning "to shrink from with abhorrence".

11 Peter, in the virtues listed by him uses "zeal" (*spoudē*, "diligence") in an impressive phrase, "giving all diligence" (2 Pet 1:5). It is wrong to lie back as if the ultimate has been reached.

Some manuscripts have *kairō* ("time"). The weight of MSS evidence favours *kuriō* ("Lord").

12 "Tribulation" (*thlipsis*, "pressure", "compression") is from *thlibō* ("to squeeze", "to press upon").

"Continuing instant" (*proskartereō*) implies a persistence or adherence to a thing.

"Hospitality" (*philoxenian*, "kindness to strangers") is more literally "a love of strangers". See Heb 13:2. "Be not forgetful to entertain strangers", literally "of hospitality, be not forgetful".

(c) *The Christian's attitude towards society (vv.14-21)*

> v.14 "Bless them which persecute you: bless, and curse not.
> v.15 Rejoice with them that do rejoice, and weep with them that weep.
> v.16 Be of the same mind one toward another. Mind not high things, but condescend to men of low estate. Be not wise in your own conceits.
> v.17 Recompense to no man evil for evil. Provide things honest in the sight of all men.
> v.18 If it be possible, as much as lieth in you, live peaceably with all men.
> v.19 Dearly beloved, avenge not yourselves, but rather give place unto wrath: for it is written, Vengeance is mine; I will repay, saith the Lord.
> v.20 Therefore if thine enemy hunger, feed him; if he thirst, give him drink: for in so doing thou shalt heap coals of fire on his head.
> v.21 Be not overcome of evil, but overcome evil with good."

14 With the change of outlook which is introduced at this verse, a word of caution is given. The proper response to persecution from the world is not retaliation, but blessing. Since there is no inherent power in a believer to impart blessing, the meaning must be a calling upon God to bless. If the persecuted Christian pleads with God to bless an oppressor, God will do it in the way He considers to be best for all concerned. The absence of animosity in the saint who calls upon God is implied in Paul's instruction. It would be contradictory to ask for blessing while all the time hoping for revengeful action to be taken.

There is a play of words between "given to hospitality" and "Bless them which persecute you". The word rendered "given" is the same word which is rendered "persecute". The christian attitude to fellow-believers in particular is to pursue hospitality, while the world for different reasons pursues hostility towards them. There is no call to court reproach. To antagonise knowingly the unconverted by ill-advised words or actions under the guise of faithfulness finds no support in Scripture. Persecution will come without inviting it. When the Lord sent forth His disciples He gave them the instruction, "…be ye therefore wise as serpents, and harmless as doves" (Matt 10:16).

The call to bless is emphasised by repeating it. The positive command is coupled to the negative, "and curse not". The Lord taught in the Sermon on the mount, "Love your enemies, bless them which curse you, do good to them which hate you, and persecute you". To this He added, "That ye may be the children of your Father which is in heaven" (Matt 5:44,45). If the tendency to curse should arise in a believer in response to some act of persecution, the safeguard is given in one word, "Bless". If the slightest risk or temptation should arise to depart from blessing, Paul's word should be held firmly, "curse not". To maintain that this imperative means "stop cursing" is too strong. It is better to consider it as carrying the meaning, "Go on refusing to curse". In that way the believer will be drawn more into conformity with what the Lord expected of the subjects of the kingdom, "that ye may be the children of your Father".

15 There are no distinctions in the directions of this verse. It may well be that those who persecute are the same ones who in other circumstances find themselves in need of sympathy. The Christian cannot be selective. Whether we are confronted with rich or poor, pleasant or unpleasant, whether the pleasures or trials of life present themselves, the response must be what is appropriate for the occasion. It must be unbiased. Our Lord entered into the joy of the wedding at Cana, and He was affected by the sorrow around Him at the funeral of Lazarus. The expression "was troubled" is better rendered, "troubled himself", indicating that His emotions were controlled. He wept, but He was not carried away with uncontrollable sorrow. In joy or in sorrow the believer should be able to be on top of emotions, although it has to be acknowledged, the nearer the relationship the deeper becomes the involvement.

It is a well-known fact that it is easier to weep with them that weep than it is to rejoice with them that rejoice. Envy plays no part when confronted by sorrow, but it may not be absent when a cause for rejoicing is presented. It takes a noble spirit to enter into another's happiness and to share the joy, particularly if that person has shown little interest in the joys and griefs of others. The standards of Christianity are high. If the proper response does not come from Christians it is not a correct expectation to look for it from other sources. In addition, today it may be some other person's time for joy or sorrow; tomorrow it may be the believer's lot. It behoves all therefore to know their seasons, the time to rejoice and the time to weep in sympathy.

16 This verse should be taken as a follow-on from v.15. It appears to be an explanation or an expansion of the former. It takes a high and noble spirit to "rejoice with them that rejoice and weep with them that weep". The rejoicing and the weeping are evidences of being able to condescend to men (or, things) of low estate. There is no support from Paul for the eastern practice of engaging professional mourners to give effect to the proceedings. This kind of thing came under the condemnation of the Lord at the house of Jairus. When He saw "the tumult and them that wept and wailed greatly", He said to them, "Why make ye this ado and weep?" The record states emphatically, "he put them all out" (Mark 5:38,39). The apostle is calling for genuine concern for others, a unity of mind, not necessarily only with those of kindred spirit, but for all to whom the breadth of christian grace can be shown.

A literal rendering of the opening words might read, "The same thing toward one another be minding; not the high things minding". This is not a contradiction of Paul's word to the Colossians, "Set your affections on things above". Here he is calling for genuine humility. There is no real thought of condescension, of making a great stoop, much below one's status in life, real or imagined, but rather the readiness to move in the current of the things that are lowly. The fact that a present participle is used suggests that a habit of life is implied. An occasional stoop is not what Paul is advocating. Whether "men" or "things" is the true rendering in the verse is of small moment (the argument turns on whether the masculine or neuter gender is involved). Most agree that it makes no difference which is selected since both are permissible and both make sense in the context. To accommodate oneself to humble people and humble things is sound christian practice; it was the Lord's example.

The closing words, "Be not wise in your own conceits" may be rendered, "Become not wise with yourselves". There is a certain dignity attached to saints, but it is a peculiar dignity, not borrowed from earth. It is neither marked by a chain of office nor by vain personal conceit. It is the dignity of moral and spiritual supremacy, quite different from what worldly dignitaries consider to be appropriate to their office or station in life.

There is a possibility that Paul had Prov 3:7 in his mind when he wrote, "Be not wise in your own conceits". The wise man's counsel was, "Be not wise in thine own eyes". The LXX, which was in circulation in apostolic times, gives, "Be not wise in your own conceits". The similarity is strong enough to indicate a quotation rather than an allusion. It may be that many of the sayings of the book of Proverbs were proverbial and commonplace in the apostle's day. If that were so and they were incorporated in the NT writings, they were lifted from their everyday use to become part of the inspired word of God. The wise man carried the benefit beyond what Paul wrote. "Then shall there be health to thy body and good keeping to thy bones" (Prov 3:8 LXX). In his opinion, the correct spirit is conducive to good health and peace of mind.

17 The injunction, "Recompense to no man evil for evil" must be understood in a universal setting. To return wickedness for wickedness has no support in christian teaching. It is foreign to the example of the One who in His short public life had every cause to retaliate, but "when he was reviled, reviled not again" (1 Pet 2:23). His teaching in the Sermon on the mount set out clearly what was expected of His disciples, "Do good to them that hate you, and pray for them that despitefully use you and persecute you" (Matt 5:44). In addition to this, it is wrong for a follower of the Lord Jesus to spend time plotting a course of revenge. There is no scriptural authority for using such a precious commodity for the purpose of gaining personal satisfaction of that nature.

The order of the words in the original, "To no one evil instead of evil returning" gives added emphasis to "no one". The word here for "evil" is *kakos*, not *ponēros* as at v.9 (where see comment). Trench makes a difference between the two words, "The *kakos* may be content to perish in his own corruption, but the *ponēros* is not content unless he is corrupting others as well and drawing them into the same destruction with himself". Evil may have different shades, but there is no encouragement given to study evil and to become conversant with the different ways it manifests itself. The latter half of the verse shows the believer's true occupation.

The wise man wrote in Prov 3:4 of the things that were good "in the sight of God and man". It is possible that Paul had this in mind when he wrote, "Provide things honest in the sight of all men". The believer is to be watchful against anything in his behaviour that others may fairly think is unchristian. Impeccable behaviour is implied. The believer's life is open to the scrutiny of God as well as being open before men. Paul is not advocating that it is up to the believer to practise what he considers to be good–that might be quite wrong. What is required is that Christians live their lives according to the terms of the gospel and the truth of God as revealed in the Scriptures, and the outcome will be the good which the Holy Spirit can use.

18 This verse takes into account that it may not always be possible to live peaceably with all men. Human nature being as it is, opposition is inevitable. "As much as lieth in you" means "as regards your side" or "inasmuch as it depends on you". In saying that Paul is not diluting the force of the injunction. If peace is not attainable, the believer must ensure that he is not the one responsible for the breakdown. While taking every opportunity to maintain peace, it must never be at the expense of the truth, faithfulness to God must be preserved at all times. To provide things honest in the sight of all men is therefore a very demanding requirement.

The phrase, "as much as lieth in you" does not mean "suffer as much as you can before retaliating". It means that the believer will avail himself of all the means at his disposal to pacify the opponent in whatever form the opposition may take in an attempt to restore harmony. It may mean taking evasive action or fleeing from the scene. At all costs, as far as it depends upon the believer, peace is sacrosanct. This is why the apostle encouraged Timothy to pray even for "kings and all that are in authority, that we may lead a quiet and peaceable life in all godliness and honesty" (1 Tim 2:2). The requirements of the verse are difficult. This world is not an ideal one and sinful men practise sinful deeds. It behoves the believer to remember, however, that as much as lieth in him, he should live peaceably with all men.

19 It is obvious that Paul borrowed the words of Deut 32:35 to reinforce his argument at this point. What the apostle states is tantamount to the reinforcement of a right which belongs to God and which He has no intention of giving up, however much He may use the human vessel to carry it out. At no time, however, can man assume in himself that he is God's avenger. Redress is safe in the hands of God; it is most unsafe in the hands of man. Repayment here, is the extraction of retribution from the evil-doer and that is God's strange work, always remembering that "it is a fearful thing to fall into the hands of the living God" (Heb 10:31).

There are four words in this verse which have to be faced, "avenge...wrath...vengeance...repay". When considered with the exhortation of v.17, "Recompense to no man evil for evil" and that of v.18, "If it be possible, as much as lieth in you, live peaceably with all men", the command of v.19 is clear, no form of retaliation is allowed to the Christian. The boundaries which are set here are set by God and they are for the safeguard of His saints.

The first clause "avenge not yourselves" makes a clear statement regarding christian conduct. The role of the avenger belongs to God. Bringing "right" into a situation is God's prerogative. For a believer to spend time preparing a course of action by way of revenge is wrong, especially in the absence of any guidance from Scripture as to how it should be done. The second clause, "but rather give place to wrath" poses the question, "whose wrath is it?" Is it the wrath of God? There are lengthy arguments in support of each but the view which holds the most acceptance is that the wrath is the wrath of God. It is a giving place to One, who, although acting in severity at times, always acts in righteousness.

The two remaining words, "vengeance" and "repay" are part of the quotation from the OT. The reference to Deut 32:35 re-affirms the righteousness of

God. Although He will act in severity if necessary, there is no vindictiveness with Him. In the days of Moses those who despised the law, died without mercy. The intervention of God in those cases did not reflect that He was unfair, rather it emphasised that He was not lax in His standards. God must act in accordance with His righteousness, and His course of action will always be vindicated.

The distinction between vengeance and wrath should be noted. Wrath takes place within a person. It is a feeling which arises either justifiable or otherwise when an injury has been inflicted or is thought to have been inflicted. This wrath is a settled condition of mind; it does not burst into a conflagration quickly, but while it may be slow to arise it can be lasting in its effects.

Vengeance is the indulgence of wrath, possibly in an act of revenge. The entire subject of wrath and vengeance is so fraught with danger for the Christian that it is essential to leave the matter with God, whose prerogative it is to take vengeance when He judges it is warranted. For others, it is very seldom that redress which is obtained by taking vengeance brings satisfaction. But if redress is sought by bringing God into the situation, and God gives it in His own way, there will be no remorse at the outcome.

The word of exhortation from Paul, supported by the statement of the law through Moses is a most important word of advice to Christians. It is far better to take offence from the one who gave it and by kindness return good for evil. In that way "thou shalt heap coals of fire on his head".

20 The RV gives "but" instead of "therefore" at the commencement of this verse, thereby underlining in greater contrast the truth of v.19 with what follows in v.20. What Paul states here is a quotation from Prov 25:21,22, probably taken from the LXX. The apostle, however, stops short of what is added in both OT versions, "and the Lord shall reward thee". Indeed, the LXX goes further still and adds, "with good". It is possible that Paul withheld a mention of being rewarded with good in the context of this verse as he wanted to add it to his exhortation in v.21 where he links it to the overcoming of evil. It may be that once again, Paul is quoting what had become a proverbial saying. If this is the case it is a fair assumption that the words of Prov 25:21,22 were well-known to Jews. Apart from this, the introduction of a principle from the past serves to re-assert christian teaching.

It should not be taken that the adversary mentioned in the verse should be given something tangible; it is only an indication of the manifestation of goodwill. Neither must it be assumed that the showing of kindness will cause an injurious person to relent; it may in fact have the opposite effect. In addition, it would be wrong to withhold kindness because the indications are that it would be spurned. It is most likely that kindness shown will have one or other of two outcomes; it will either melt or harden.

The exhortation in this verse is not one which emphasises a reward from God to the Christian who acts righteously. It gives a course of action and a reason for following it out. Heaping coals of fire on another's head must not be subjected to conjecture to provide some hidden meaning answering to the literal statement. Speculation is unwarranted. The message of the context is clear; it is God's prerogative to overcome evil because He cannot be overcome by evil. He is prepared, however, to allow His saints to have a part in one of His inevitable processes. He will allow them to overcome evil, but only with good. Beyond that is not permitted.

21 The conclusion which must be arrived at in considering the apostle's argument is that evil must not be allowed to triumph. If the believer responds to evil shown to him, he is merely adding to it and what may only be a spark could become a conflagration. The requiting of evil is a sure way of causing it to grow, which may lead to its growing out of hand. It is clear that Paul is giving a warning that there is the ever-present danger of being overcome by evil if a policy of retaliation is followed. The believer does not have the power to go a certain distance in the pursuit of revenge and then draw out at the appropriate point or time. Once the process of returning evil for evil is put into practice, there is no guarantee that it will stop at a point which favours the one who started it or the one who responded to it. The advice to the believer is clear. It means either, "Stop doing this", or, "Go on refusing to do it".

The word here for "evil" is *kakos* (see note at v.17); the word for "good" *agathos*, which emphasises the good which is practical. The apostle does not enlarge upon this here. Perhaps he meant it to be left to the good judgment of the believer. However, as stated at v.17, it is better to live the christian life in accordance with the teaching of the word of God and leave the Holy Spirit to apply what is best in the circumstances. It is therefore of great benefit to have a sound knowledge of God's word. From that position of strength many examples can be brought quickly to mind by the Spirit which will be the appropriate response for the situation. Nevertheless, God will not leave His saints vulnerable. Even the simplest can count on His help for guidance when it comes to a matter of overcoming evil with good.

Notes

16 "Condescend" ("to lead", "to carry away with") in middle voice is to conform one's self willingly to certain circumstances.

17 "...in the sight of all men" is to be taken with the verb, "providing for". Men's estimate of what is honourable is not the standard.

18 Vincent says of "possible", "Not 'if you can' but 'if others will allow'".

19 Robert Candlish suggests that "Dearly beloved" (an expression of significance in his opinion) breaks in two the series of precepts in the midst of which it stands; it separates the five preceding verses (vv.14-18) from the three which close the chapter (vv.19-21). He claims, "And the division is a right one, not forced or fanciful, suggested by an incidental phrase, but substantial and of real practical importance".

Vincent paraphrases "gives place" as "give room for it to work, do not get in its way".

Note the article qualifying "wrath" (*orgē*), "the wrath" is of course God's wrath.

20 "Coals of fire" is common as a symbol of fire and divine judgment amongst Arabs and Jews. Some consider that it would be strange if Paul used this expression in a good sense.

2. Towards the State and the World
13:1-13:14

There is considerable difference of opinion regarding the authority of the first seven verses of this chapter. Some hold the verses to be an interpolation, since they do not seem to follow on naturally from ch.12, and there is no grammatical connection with 12:21. In addition, it is held by many that the seven verses do not lead on naturally to 13:8, which seems the proper connection with 12:21. Concerning this situation, Morris quotes O'Neill, "These seven verses have caused more unhappiness and misery in the Christian East and West than any other seven verses in the New Testament". Morris also refers to James Kallas and notes that although he is not as severe as O'Neill, he finds the passage alien to the thought of Paul and argues that it is an interpolation.

In *The New Bible Commentary*, the contributor, Douglas J Moo, makes an interesting comment, "Paul does not explicitly connect this paragraph with what comes before it, and this had led some scholars to think it is a later, perhaps post-Pauline addition to the text of Romans. But there is no textual evidence for so drastic an interpretation. The passage fits in the context perfectly well: submission to government is part of that 'good, pleasing and perfect will' (12:2b) that Paul has been outlining and is also a specific example of doing 'what is right in the eyes of everybody' (12:7b)". Hendrikson also addresses the subject, "There are those who regard this section as an alien body in Paul's exhortation. But the mere statement of such a negative position does not constitute proof. The section is not nearly as foreign to the context – whether preceding or following – as some seem to think".

In his commentary on the epistle to the Romans, WE Vine gives a balanced view on the controversy in his introduction to ch.13, "While there does not seem to be any definite connection between this section and what has preceded, possibly the subject of divine retribution upon evildoers leads to the similar responsibilities vested in earthly potentates as ministers of God (v.4). There follows, then, the attitude incumbent upon Christians towards those who are in authority over the state. The injunction to be in subjection to the higher powers, while important in every country, would have a special force in Rome, where the government would rigorously repress any religion which tended to run counter to that of the state, and especially Christianity, for Christians were largely regarded as a Jewish sect, and propaganda considered in every sense to be Jewish would be suspected as being of revolutionary tendency. There was also the danger, no doubt, that Christians might entertain wrong notions of the kingdom of Christ and its present relation to the kingdoms of this world. To Jews, conscious of the covenant relationship of their nation to God, there was a natural repugnance to submit to heathen rulers".

The chapter has two divisions. In vv.1-7 the apostle outlines the Christian's responsibility to civil authority and in vv.8-14 he gives counsel regarding the Christian's attitude to his neighbours. In the first section there is no support for believers to become embroiled in politics. To another assembly Paul wrote, "For our conversation (citizenship, politics) is in heaven from whence also we look for the Saviour, the Lord Jesus Christ" (Phil 3:20). Affiliation to any political party on earth is an anomaly in the Christian. Support for policies which may be dubious, if not totally unrighteous, or active opposition against the party in power, and therefore "the powers that be" in the appointments of God, is quite contrary to what Paul is teaching here as far as the Christian's attitude to civil government is concerned.

(a) *The Christian's attitude towards civil authorities (vv.1-7)*

v.1 "Let every soul be subject unto the higher powers. For there is no power but of God: the powers that be are ordained of God.
v.2 Whosoever therefore resisteth the power, resisteth the ordinance of God: and they that resist shall receive to themselves damnation.
v.3 For rulers are not a terror to good works, but to the evil. Wilt thou then not be afraid of the power? do that which is good, and thou shalt have praise of the same:
v.4 For he is the minister of God to thee for good. But if thou do that which is evil, be afraid; for he beareth not the sword in vain: for he is the minister of God, a revenger to execute wrath upon him that doeth evil.
v.5 Wherefore ye must needs be subject, not only for wrath, but also for conscience sake.
v.6 For for this cause pay ye tribute also: for they are God's ministers, attending continually upon this very thing.
v.7 Render therefore to all their dues: tribute to whom tribute is due; custom to whom custom; fear to whom fear; honour to whom honour."

1 As far as the christian position is concerned, there is no room for argument against the opening statement of this verse. Subjection to higher powers is mandatory. Although Paul is addressing believers primarily, what he is stating is true for all. It is incumbent on every person to be subject to higher authority. The reference to "every soul" is a Hebraism, meaning in the context, every individual. The call "to be in subjection" does not mean servile obedience where all christian dignity is sacrificed. The thought is submission to the civil authorities as those who represent God in the maintenance of law and order in any nation. Whether the rulers realise that they are God's representatives is not the point here. How wisely and fairly they exercise the authority invested in them is not the point either. It is the establishment of a basic principle of life under any national government, democratically elected or otherwise, that submission is the proper attitude.

The reason for submission is given in the latter half of the verse. There is no power but what originates with God and is appointed by Him. This does not mean that God is ultimately responsible for the excesses of any ruling body. Those who rule unwisely will answer to Him and be the subject of His governmental ways. Here, however, the principle is that rule is not a human device and although elected bodies may think so, the true position is that God appoints and He discards according to His will. Daniel had to remind Nebuchadnezzar of this in his interpretation of the king's dream, "…till thou know that the most High ruleth in the kingdom of men, and giveth it to whomsoever he will" (Dan 4:25).

When the Lord was given a question which contained an inference of resistance to civil authority, He replied, "Render to Caesar the things that are Caesar's" (Mark 12:17). Peter followed his Master's teaching when he wrote, "Submit yourselves to every ordinance of man for the Lord's sake; whether it be to the king as supreme; or unto governors, as them that are sent by him for the punishment of evildoers, and for the praise of them that do well" (1 Pet 2:13,14). Here Paul follows the same line of teaching. Although Jews were notoriously bad subjects, and the Romans were inhuman at times in their suppression of resistance, the apostle is not considering breaches of law and order. His call is a general one to respect higher authorities and to be subject to them.

2   The opening word *hōste* implies "and so", or, "consequently". It carries forward the implications of the facts outlined in v.1. In the apostle's treatment of subjection to "the powers that be" in these verses, there are no exception clauses. The areas in which the Christian is forced to take a stand against civil authorities are dealt with elsewhere. At this point, the apostle's burden is to stress divine appointment. His injunction concerns obedience from believers because there is no power but of God: the "powers that be" are ordained of God. Chalmers comments, "It is not the kind of character of any government, but the existence of it which invests it with its claims for our obedience, or at least which determines for us the duty of yielding subjection thereto. Its mandates should be submitted to, not because either law or justice or respect for the good of humanity presided over the formation of it, but simply because it exists".

There can be little argument against the clear statement, "whosoever resisteth the power, resisteth the ordinance of God". The first mention of "resisteth" *antitassomai* means "to set one's self in opposition", the second "resisteth" (*anthestēkotes*) is a different word, translated by the RV as "withstandeth". These two words are synonyms chosen by Paul to stress the wrong of opposing in any way what is instituted by God. The ordinance of God suggests the orderly arrangements of God.

What God has set in order, either before Jews in the law (see Acts 7:53), or before mankind generally in constituted civil government, must be acknowledged. To resist "the powers that be" is in fact to resist what God has set in place. The ordinance of God does not suggest a haphazard situation. That could neither be said of the law nor of what He has set in place before mankind in legitimate government. What the apostle is stating is not a new development as far as God's sovereign ways in relation to the kingdoms of men are concerned. It was also applicable in the OT, as stated in the Proverbs, "By me kings reign and princes decree justice. By me princes rule..." (Prov 8:15,16). What is new is the clear code of conduct given to Christians as to how they as individuals should live as citizens or subjects in the various kingdoms of the world.

It should be observed that Paul does not make any mention about what form civil government should take. It was Hodge who commented, "While government is of God, the form is of men". Plummer also makes a comment in this connection, "God has never made one form obligatory on all communities. He has simply laid down certain principles, applicable to rulers and subjects under every form in which government exists". If therefore there is resistance to the government in power, the apostle makes it clear that judgment will inevitably follow for those who oppose. The word "damnation" is archaic; what is involved is judgment. The apostle does not state, however, whether the judgment is of God or of men. Anarchy in any form is not of God, and it is certain that Christians should not be involved in any attempt to overthrow governments. God can propose and dispose at will and He does not require lawless elements to do His work for Him.

God does not need to act in judgment from Himself. The "powers that be", having been set in place by Him, can legitimately act for Him in punishing those who resist lawful government. Here it is not a question of the rights or wrongs of any government's policies, or the fairness of their judgments, or whether believers should obey God rather than men. Paul is not concerned with that in this context. All that he is teaching is subjection to governments in power and that those who resist will bring judgment upon themselves.

3 Paul now turns to give a reason why governments should be recognised and obeyed. The change of word to "rulers" does not seem to have any special force, other than the fact that authorities are in power to rule. That is their function and if they do not fulfil their responsibilities, anarchy might follow. The instruments through which governments enforce law and order, armies, police and other means, are not there to strike fear into the hearts of law-abiding citizens; they are there for the purpose of restraining evil. The inference in the clause is that they may cause fear in evildoers. They are the ones who have cause to tremble. If it were not for wrongdoers, there would be little or no need for forces of law and order.

The next clause "Wilt thou then not be afraid of the power?" need not be taken as a direct question. It can be taken as a statement introducing the appeal of the closing words of the verse. The apostle seems to be suggesting to the believers that they should consider the situation reasonably and if they want to live in peace in whatever country they may find themselves as citizens, then the way to accomplish that is to submit to the government. In that way there will be no fear of harassment or punishment.

From the divine standpoint, those who rule in the kingdoms of men are responsible to recognise good in those who are their subjects. In the context Paul is not considering the abuse of power. Persecution of Christians had already started in Rome when Paul wrote, but the condemnation of that was not the apostle's purpose at this point. His counsel is that doing good will earn the praise of "the powers that be". The wisdom of Paul's treatment of the subject is obvious. He wants to establish what is the norm. Stable government has many advantages and Christians may be the section of society that will benefit most from it as they bear witness to the saving power of the Lord Jesus Christ. The believer's contribution to a nation's stability is to do good. Elsewhere in the Scriptures, responsibility to remember kings and all in authority in prayer is pressed, but here the stress is placed on good behaviour, something governments can recognise and praise.

4 It is considered by most that the opening statement of this verse belongs to v.3. The subject matter is certainly linked to what has been outlined earlier about that which is good. Be that as it may, the ruler is now seen as a servant of God. The word *diakonos* denotes service in general, even that which is menial in character. It is quite clear what Paul is setting out; before God the ruler has no special standing; he is there to work, regardless of how he attained to the position he has. In his own estimation, the ruler may see himself as an earthly potentate, high above all others, but as Paul notes here, in the sight of God he is a servant and nothing more, and that only while he holds power. The service which he is there to render is for the good of all, especially for the believers who will use the benefits that accrue for the service and glory of God.

The word rendered "be afraid" is in the present tense, suggesting that fear will always be present if evil is practised. There will be continual dread of the sword, a metaphorical way of describing judicial punishment. The right to punish, even to exercise capital punishment, is committed to magistrates as representatives of the governments in power. They do not wear (or, bear) the sword in vain. It is not an empty symbol. The sword is part of the responsibilities which rest with any who assume the role of government.

The apostle repeats the reference to the ruler being a servant. In view of the seriousness of what is being outlined, the apostle obviously judged it necessary to make the ruler's status clear. He is not an independent operator. He may see himself as such and may act as if he is not responsible to anyone for his actions. His role, however, is clearly defined. He is an agent of God to punish evildoers. He is an avenger in the sense that he acts for God in the suppression of evil. The power that is invested in him is for the welfare of the subjects, and in return for their good works, he is expected to praise. Equally so, when evil manifests itself, it is incumbent upon him to wield the sword and to do so with severity if that is warranted.

5 The conclusion of all that Paul has set out in the preceding verses is "ye must needs be subject". There is no other way or rule of conduct that will permit an unsubmissive attitude to the state. What Paul seems to be saying is that in the nature of the case, Christians are compelled to submit. There is no support in Scripture for resistance or political involvement which could lead to being in opposition to the government in power.

Two reasons are given as to why Christians should submit to authority. The first one, wrath, implies punishment. As in the previous verse Paul does not say whose wrath is involved. Some translations give "God's wrath", although there does not seem to be any manuscript authority in support of it. That it is God's wrath, possibly worked out through earthly magistrates, seems clear enough in the teaching of the context. Christians are not above the laws of the land. If they fall foul of the law by reason of departure from the path of right and duty, they have only themselves to blame for the resulting punishment.

The second reason why Christians should be submissive is given. By introducing conscience Paul opens up another field of thought. There is the witness within, which will keep asserting its moral right to be heard when evil is committed. If it should be that conscience is quiet, this could be evidence of a tacit approval of the laws under which the Christian lives and moves for God.

6 The word rendered "tribute" covered the tax levied on a subject people by the conquering nation. It could be levied on lands and property, as noted in Nehemiah's day, "We have borrowed money for the king's tribute, and that upon our lands and vineyards" (Neh 5:4). It could also be levied on people, as reflected in the question put to the Lord by the representatives of the chief priests and scribes, "Is it lawful for us to give tribute unto Caesar or no" (Luke 20:22). Because of being under the rule of an oppressor, taxes of this nature were as a rule hated by the oppressed. However, in accordance with the general terms of Paul's teaching about submission to "the powers that be" it is more likely that he is referring here to taxes in general. Unless governments are funded they cannot function. Taxes are the general way to raise the necessary revenue and ruling bodies are perfectly within their rights to do so. Whether the taxes are right and fair is not the point here; what is pressed is that Christians have no other option but to pay what is demanded from them.

God's interest in the functioning of nations is now stated. The rulers are in fact God's agents. They have a right to demand payment of taxes as representatives of God. Stable governments are what God is looking for in the world and they need funding to exercise civil functions for the people over whom they rule. The word used here for "ministers" (*leitourgos*) is different from the word given in v.4 for "servant" (*diakonos*). As a rule, *leitourgos* is used of priestly service, but it was also used to describe a public servant. It stresses the importance of the person who is engaged in service of an official nature on behalf of the state. Here rulers are seen as God's agents and as such, in the levying of taxes, they have His approval. It does not follow that the rulers are conscious of being God's agents, or in fact are prepared to acknowledge their responsibility to Him as such.

The clause "attending continually upon this very thing" most probably refers to the constant diligence they apply to the business of collecting taxes. Consciously or otherwise they are engaged in the work as God's agents. How fairly they apply the taxes for the benefit of the people is not the point here; it is the principle Paul is asserting. Nations have a right to tax their subjects.

7 The apostle now stresses liability: what is owed must be paid. If governments levy taxes, it places an obligation upon the citizens to meet them in full. The reference to "all" means all who have lawful claims to exact payment of dues. The "dues" cover what is owed by all those who are rendered debtors to pay. There are no escape clauses in this situation.

The four sets of implications extend the indebtedness of believers. The first two still concern taxes but there are differences between them. The apostle states that tribute must be rendered to whom tribute is due. The word for "tribute" (*phoros*) is the same as in the previous verse. It means "tax", such as is laid on a subject nation. The word comes from *pherō* ("to bear"), and implies the burden of taxation placed upon the people. Custom, a tax placed on goods, must be rendered to whom custom is due. No doubt Matthew the publican was engaged in collecting this and other taxes when the Lord called him to His service. Zacchaeus also was a publican, or tax-gatherer, who like Matthew was employed by the Roman authorities. Tax-gatherers were hated by the people, not only as traitors, but by reason of their dishonesty. It was common practice amongst them to exact more than their due, a situation which John the Baptist addressed when publicans being baptised by him asked for his guidance. His advice was, "Exact no more than that which is appointed you" (Luke 3:13). The Scripture does not encourage the payment of more than is due, although for testimony's sake, some may in certain situations suffer themselves to be defrauded.

The apostle moves away from the subject of taxes to assert the rights of civil authorities to be respected, either by fear as the avengers of God (v.4), or for honour as God's ministers (v.6). The principle of rendering honour has already been established in connection with the Christian's attitude towards fellow-believers (12:10). Here Paul looks for an extension of that. It is not a question of rendering taxes with a grudge and conveying that spirit to those who represent civil authorities. There is no indication in Paul's exhortations of the level of civil authority where the official ceases to be classed as God's agent. If a government official goes about his official business, he is entitled to respect as a minister (*leitourgos*) of God.

Notes

1 Hogg and Vine comment on "powers" (*exousia*), "it is first, the freedom to do anything, and then, the authority to do it. Thus God is free to do as He wills" – as in Acts 1:7, "which the Father has put in his own power". It has pleased God to delegate authority to others, as here, superior powers.

In using "are ordained" (*tassō*, "to arrange", "to set"), as Robertson comments, "Paul is not arguing for the right of kings, but for government and order".

2 "Ordinance" (*diatage*, "injunction") is from *diatassō* ("to arrange", "to prescribe"). In the NT it occurs only here and in Acts 7:53, "who have received the law by the disposition of angels".

3 "Wilt thou" (*thelō*) points to the exercise of the will.

6 *Proskartereō* ("to preserve") occurs in Acts 2:42, "they continued steadfastly in the apostles' doctrine"; here it is rendered "attending continually".

Vincent remarks of "ministers" (*leitourgoi*): "The word here brings out more fully the fact that the ruler, like the priest, discharges a divinely-ordained service. Government is thus elevated into a sphere of religion. Hence RV, 'ministers of God's service' ".

(b) *The Christian's attitude towards his neighbours (vv.8-14)*

> v.8 "Owe no man any thing, but to love one another: for he that loveth another hath fulfilled the law.
> v.9 For this, Thou shalt not commit adultery, Thou shalt not kill, Thou shalt not steal, Thou shalt not bear false witness, Thou shalt not covet; and if there be any other commandment, it is briefly comprehended in this saying, namely, Thou shalt love thy neighbour as thyself.
> v.10 Love worketh no ill to his neighbour: therefore love is the fulfilling of the law.
> v.11 And that, knowing the time, that now it is high time to awake out of sleep: for now is our salvation nearer than when we believed.
> v.12 The night is far spent, the day is at hand: let us therefore cast off the works of darkness, and let us put on the armour of light.
> v.13 Let us walk honestly, as in the day; not in rioting and drunkenness, not in chambering and wantonness, not in strife and envying.
> v.14 But put ye on the Lord Jesus Christ, and make not provision for the flesh, to fulfil the lusts thereof."

8 The opening words of this verse have been misunderstood by many down the years. Paul did not mean that it is essentially wrong to be a debtor. Some fall into debt despite their best efforts to avoid it. What the apostle is teaching is that debt should never be left outstanding, but should always be paid as soon as it is possible to do so. This does not mean as soon as it is convenient to do so. The creditor's needs must be taken into account as having a high degree of priority for settlement of debt. In the wider view, it is obviously wrong for Christians to contract liabilities which they are not able to meet. It is wrong to speculate if this involves more than the believer is able to lose without placing family, friends and creditors at risk. The believer should consider the risk factor well before proceeding with projects which involve indebtedness. Apart from pecuniary debt, the clause has wider applications and was obviously meant to cover all obligations, financial, social and moral.

Although Paul has been stressing that all obligations must be met and all debts paid, he is aware of an obligation which is permanent and from which it is impossible to obtain a discharge. The debt of love is one which must be paid daily. It is always owed. It is not an indebtedness from which some are excused. The humblest believer is as much a debtor in this connection as the most pious saint on earth. What is paid at any time does not clear the account; love towards one another, saint and sinner, always remains. Regardless of how much is paid in service to God and man, there is always more ahead which can be undertaken in love. Christians stand continually in debt to God and to one another.

Paul continues to apply the implications of what he has stated "for he that loveth his neighbour has fulfilled the law". To the Jew, a neighbour was a fellow-Israelite. Gentiles and Samaritans were beyond the pale. The Jewish lawyer who asked the Lord, "And who is my neighbour?" was not prepared for the answer he received. The Lord's command, "Go thou and do likewise" implies that neighbourliness does not have restricted horizons. The lesson for the Jewish lawyer was that a true neighbour is one who can be relied upon to act in a neighbourly fashion when the need to do so arises. All who are moved by love to act rise above legal requirements; they are the ones who fulfil the spirit of the law as well as the letter. Nevertheless, it should always be remembered that the Christian can never say, as the Lord could, "I have finished the work thou gavest me to do". Christians stand continually in debt to God and to one another.

9 This verse contains two quotations from the OT. The first one is taken from Exod 20:13-17, or possibly from Deut 5:17-21 LXX. The second one comes from Lev 19:18. In the so-called Sermon on the mount, the Lord summarised the law and the prophets in the words, "Therefore all things whatsoever ye would that a man should do to you, do ye so to them: for this is the law and the prophets" (Matt 7:12). The Jews were reminded of the spirit of the law and what was expected of them if they professed to uphold it. A new force, however, was at work in Christians. To this the apostle had directed attention in the previous verse. He was not merely stressing the observance of what was right and in accordance with the letter of the law, he was insisting that love towards one another transcends that and was therefore a fulfilment of the law's requirements.

In the first quotation from the OT Paul does not give a complete list of what the decalogue stated. What he gives are typical examples of what the law lays down regarding one's obligations to one's neighbours. The part of the decalogue which sets out man's obligations to God is not mentioned. Since the context is dealing with neighbourliness, that side is not required here. Regarding what is quoted, however, there is no possibility that the solemnity of what is listed can be passed over. Apart from the law of Moses, most, if not all, of what is quoted is encapsulated in other national laws and holds a similar degree of seriousness.

The commandments Paul has not mentioned specifically, he covers in the words, "and if there by any other commandment, it is briefly comprehended in the saying, namely, Thou shalt love thy neighbour as thyself", taking in the quotation of Lev 19:18. The importance of this portion of Scriptures is reflected in the fact that it is quoted eight times in the NT. (For comments on these quotations, see the author's work, *Things Written Aforetime*.) Paul is not saying here that all the commandments are summed up in one precept and that all other commandments are therefore redundant. Some have held erroneously that it is not essential to know the details of the law, since love to one's neighbour renders such knowledge unnecessary. Such a view is quite wrong. Love without the guidelines of Scripture would be an energy liable to deterioration into a sentimental gloss. Love finds its avenues of expression within the framework of what God has revealed. If it acts or admires, it does so with good and sufficient reason.

Here then the passage quoted states, "thou shalt love thy neighbour as thyself". As Hendrikson remarks, "It is a certain thing that a person will love himself, and it is also certain that he will do so in spite of the fact that the self he loves has many faults". There are many faults with which love has to contend, but since no one is perfect, there is all the more reason for letting love have its way within the parameters of the Scriptures, always remembering the reflective force of Lev 19:18, "Thou shalt love thy neighbour as thyself".

10 In this verse love is personified. The apostle adopts the same procedure in 1 Cor 13 where in his personification of love he records many of its beautiful features. Although not fully understood in the world, these features are nevertheless admired in all levels of society. Here Paul states that love will do no harm to its neighbour. Harm is quite foreign to the concept of love in the NT. The negative form used here may be in contrast to the demands of the law or may just be a stronger way in Paul's mind of making his point than insisting on doing good. In christian service, however, doing good to one's neighbour will leave no scope for doing harm. It follows of course that doing good must be characterised by love. The good that one would do, if done without love, could be very far removed from a christian grace.

The word "therefore" introduces the conclusion. If love does no harm to his neighbour, it is the fulfilment of the law. The law cannot point an accusing finger at it. Even if the receiver took up a belligerent attitude and refused all the overtures of the giver, love would still not be cancelled out. It would, however, fulfil all love's ends if the giver and the receiver responded in accordance with love's outlook. Regarding this amazing spiritual energy, it certainly "suffereth long and is kind…is not easily provoked…hopeth all things, endureth all things…(indeed) – love never faileth" (1 Cor 13:4-8).

11   The last four verses of the chapter deal with the reasons why the truths just stated should be put into practice immediately. The first reason given refers to the importance of the present time. The word "time" (*kairos*) indicates the significance of the present, because it is characterised by certain important features. The participle "knowing" indicates an understanding of the situation. It implies that those to whom the apostle wrote were well aware of the need to press on with christian living because "now it is high time to awake". The hour had come for work. Time was short. There was no time for slumber. If they were in a state of lethargy akin to being asleep, then they should "awake now".

The hour of opportunity which Paul is stressing is obviously intended to make christian service a matter of urgency. A leisurely approach was out of the question. There was no guarantee of time beyond the immediate present to do what was required to be done. Indeed, Paul moves from "the high time" ("the hour") to a point still closer, as he states "for *now* is our salvation nearer than when we believed".

The aspect of salvation which Paul advances here is the future hope of deliverance. The nearness of it stresses its imminence. The initial salvation involving the salvation of the soul, of which much has been said in the epistle, is here shown to have a consummation. The gap between the time of believing and that of being redeemed bodily was not wide as far as Paul was concerned. That being the case, it follows that each day which passes shortens the gap between initial believing and the day of redemption. What the apostle is advancing here is entirely consistent with what he taught elsewhere. To the Philippians he wrote, "For our conversation (citizenship) is in heaven, from whence also we look for the Saviour, the Lord Jesus Christ" (3:20). To the Thessalonians, having acknowledged that they had turned to God from idols to serve the living and true God, he took account of their eager expectancy "to wait for his Son from heaven" (1 Thess 1:10). The time therefore to do something for God was the present, because of the imminence of the Lord's return. When that happens all opportunities to serve the Lord Jesus Christ in the matters highlighted here will be gone for ever.

12   There is no explanation given of what Paul means by "the night". In apostolic times it seems to have been a common way of describing the world conditions. There are similar terms in 1 Thess 5 and Eph 6, including in both cases references to spiritual armour. There is little doubt, however, about what Paul is teaching. The night of which he speaks is lengthening out and obviously nearing its end. The fact that many years have passed since Paul made this statement does not rob it of its force. Although the night of alienation from God is continuing to lengthen out, behind that, God's day of grace is also stretching out. The darkness may be deepening in the moral sense, but the opportunities to get right with God still abound confirming what Peter states, "The Lord…is longsuffering…not willing that any should perish" (2 Pet 3:9).

The day to which the apostle refers is obviously the day of emancipation for the saints. It is covered by the expression in the previous verse, "now is our salvation nearer than when we believed". The Lord is coming. Paul taught that and at no point in his teaching inferred that anything else had to take place before the coming of the Lord and the rapture of the saints. Because of the certainty of the coming it was of vital importance that the works of darkness should be put away. Since believers have been called out of darkness into His (God's) marvellous light (1 Pet 2:9), and delivered from the power of darkness (Col 1:13), it follows that the works and evil influences associated with that realm should be cast aside once and for all.

The armour of light which Paul encourages the saints to put on is a clear indication that christian service is a warfare. Regardless of age or experience, the way forward for the believer is a battle. The darkness describes a world in opposition to God. Without the righteousness which is declared in the gospel, mankind is left to contend with life according to human standards. Even these differ from one country to another and in many cases are far removed from what is fair and equitable. Civil disobedience on the other hand is endemic and will only be controlled when the reins of government are taken over by the Lord Himself. In the meantime, Paul's call is to don the armour of light. Living in righteousness according to God's standards is the only safeguard for the believer in the moral darkness of this scene.

13 The verse commences, "As in the day-time, let us walk becomingly". This contrasts with "the night" of the previous verse, a condition which is marked by the works of darkness. Believers are not characterised by these things. They make their way through the world in the light of day, in a manner which is comely. Even the unconverted will recognise, however grudgingly at times, that the behaviour of the believers is commendable. The same advice was given to the Thessalonians, "That ye may walk honestly (becomingly) towards them that are without" (1 Thess 4:12). It is part of the testimony to be declared in the world: the message of the gospel and changed lives go hand in hand.

The six features listed by the apostle which are foreign to the believer's way of life are what mark the men and women of the world. These traits are set out in three pairs. Each pair seems to have something in common. The first two are linked to the excesses of strong drink. Drunkenness and revellings go together. They indicate a loss of self-control and are listed elsewhere by Paul as works of the flesh (Gal 5:21). It is to be expected therefore that the apostle would brand them as being entirely foreign to the believer's way of life.

The second pair concern debauchery. Unrestrained lust is indicated. The root of the word rendered "chambering" is the word for "bed". It came to mean the forbidden bed, and what marks one who sets no value on fidelity or chastity. The word rendered "wantonness" (*aselgeia*) is noted by Barclay as being one of the ugliest words in the Greek language. The person it describes makes no attempt to hide his shame, but indeed is happy to flaunt it. Both of these are sins of the deepest dye and should never be seen in the lives of believers.

The final pair of vices in Paul's list are strife and envying. Both of these are found amongst the works of the flesh (Gal 5:20), and are listed by James as marks of the wisdom which cometh from beneath (James 3:16). Both of these vices concern the assertion of self. They are entirely opposed to Paul's advice at 12:10, "In honour preferring one another". Those who are marked by envying and strife will never take second place. To obtain pre-eminence and prestige, they will display a ruthlessness, which is foreign to comeliness.

14 The phrase, "But put ye on the Lord Jesus Christ" is a very strong metaphor. In the Ephesian and Colossian epistles where Paul encourages the saints to put on certain qualities and strip off unbecoming ones, his metaphors are not hard to understand. Here, however, he introduces the Lord Himself as the One to be put on. Obviously he is not meaning simply the graces of Christ. If he had meant christian graces he would have listed them as he did elsewhere. He is most likely calling for a deeper aspect of union with Christ than that which took place on believing. To be clothed upon with the Lord Jesus Christ leaves little room or scope for anything else. Approached from another standpoint, if He becomes the element into which the Christian is absorbed it will be His life that will be manifested in the believer's walk. Christ will be seen in a myriad of different ways in a world where He is in fact rejected.

The existence of the flesh is acknowledged by the apostle. Here he does not identify any particular traits of it but shows it as that for which God finds no place. It is the seat of sin in man and God will not move a step with it. Paul's advice is to take no forethought for it and therefore no scope will be allowed to for to manifest itself in evil deeds. The flesh is there in the believer. The day of deliverance from its presence is coming, but in the meantime Paul's advice is to take no thought for it and therefore make no allowance for it, but be entirely absorbed with the Lord Jesus Christ and a becoming walk in the world will result.

Notes

8 "Comprehended" (*anakephalaioō*) points "to the bringing several things under one". Lev 19:8 is the summing up of all that law demands.

11 Against this verse, Robert Lee comments, "Observe the signs of the times; dispense with spiritual langour; recognise the threefold nature of salvation".

12 "...is far spent" (*prokoptō*, "to cut forward", "to advance") insists that the night of man's day is progressing quickly to its end.

"The day is at hand", Robertson says this is a vivid picture of day-break.

3. *Towards Neighbours and the Weak in Faith*
14:1-15:13

In the two previous chapters, Paul has been stressing the necessity of having love towards one another. Love is to be without hypocrisy (12:9). It never works ill towards its neighbour (13:10). Its influence indeed is far-reaching and that is seen in the apostle's considerations in ch.14 and reaching into ch.15.

Two classes of believers are mentioned. There are those Paul terms "weak" and there are others that he classes as "strong". There have been many suggestions and endless arguments as to who these believers were and what views they held. Perhaps there was wisdom in the stance which Paul took as much more may be gained by considering the principles associated with both classes, rather than identifying them. If they had been identified that would certainly have classified them and made them the subjects of specific faults for ever afterwards. A case in point is the statement of a Cretan regarding his own people. "The Cretans are always liars, evil beasts, slow bellies (lazy gluttons)", to which Paul adds, "This witness is true" (Titus 1:12,13). Happily such disagreeable national traits are not noted as existing in Rome.

The main issue which Paul addresses is scruples. There were those who had certain scruples and who held on to them tenaciously. Their weakness in faith which the apostle mentions may be simply failure to recognise christian liberty. Nevertheless, the firm way they held on to their scruples is taken into account by the apostle. The danger which he foresaw and which he addresses was that those who did not have these scruples might cause serious harm and division by despising their "weak" brethren. Mutual love and respect was what was called for in the circumstances, and to obtain this Paul considers the problem in depth and gives his advice.

(a) *Consideration for the weak (vv.1-13)*

v.1 "Him that is weak in the faith receive ye, but not to doubtful disputations.
v.2 For one believeth that he may eat all things: another, who is weak, eateth herbs.
v.3 Let not him that eateth despise him that eateth not; and let not him which eateth not judge him that eateth: for God hath received him.
v.4 Who art thou that judgest another man's servant? to his own master he standeth or falleth. Yea, he shall be holden up: for God is able to make him stand.
v.5 One man esteemeth one day above another: another esteemeth every day alike. Let every man be fully persuaded in his own mind.
v.6 He that regardeth the day, regardeth it unto the Lord; and he that regardeth not the day, to the Lord he doth not regard it. He that eateth, eateth to the Lord, for he giveth God thanks; and he that eateth not, to the Lord he eateth not, and giveth God thanks.
v.7 For none of us liveth to himself, and no man dieth to himself.
v.8 For whether we live, we live unto the Lord; and whether we die, we die unto the Lord: whether we live therefore, or die, we are the Lord's.

> v.9 For to this end Christ both died, and rose, and revived, that he might be Lord both of the dead and living.
> v.10 But why dost thou judge thy brother? or why dost thou set at nought thy brother? for we shall all stand before the judgment seat of Christ.
> v.11 For it is written, As I live, saith the Lord, every knee shall bow to me, and every tongue shall confess to God.
> v.12 So then every one of us shall give account of himself to God.
> v.13 Let us not therefore judge one another any more: but judge this rather, that no man put a stumblingblock or an occasion to fall in his brother's way."

1 The RV renders the opening words, "But him that is weak in faith". Some versions give, "Now him that is weak in faith". Both views register a link with what has already been stated. The weakness is obviously not a physical one, but a condition which is spiritual. The fact that Paul refers to "him that is weak", does not imply that only one person was involved. The manner of speaking is generic, standing for all that are marked by weakness of faith.

Although there is a definite article in the text before "faith" this does not mean that Paul meant "the faith" as the body of doctrine. Since the context determines whether the definite article should be translated, it is accepted by most commentators that it should not be included in this case. The weakness must therefore be that scruples of some kind or other have warped the understanding of christian teaching. Basic faith in Christ for salvation is not the issue. There is no indication that there is any flaw in that. It is the advance from that stage which is influenced by other issues thereby causing faulty christian living. It is quite understandable that new converts in apostolic times, coming from different cultures, would bring with them certain beliefs and practices with which they had lived all their lives. Time, teaching and forbearance were needed to allow the conscience to deal with things which had no place in christian practice.

The appeal is made to receive warmly all who might be looked upon as "weak in faith". They were not to be made the subject of doubtful disputations, that is, they were not to be subjected to judgments or reasonings in matters which were disputable. The scruples held by the "weak in faith" were not to be made a test of acceptance. They were not to be the subject of debate. The "weak in faith" were not to be put in jeopardy by the strong just to settle some points with which they did not agree, even though these points may be right. Patience and forbearance were called for in dealing with the sensitive matters held firmly by some in fellowship in the assembly.

2 It seems clear that those whom Paul addresses are "the strong" (15:1). They were the ones who were free to eat all things. Although the beliefs of two individuals are contrasted, the apostle is still using the singular form in the generic sense. The lengthy argument embarked on was certainly not about two believers whose views in some matters differed greatly, but for the benefit of quite a few.

The first case cited concerns freedom to eat anything. The faith of the person envisaged is such that he believes what he does is perfectly correct and in accordance with christian teaching. He has no qualms about eating anything. In some respects the position is similar to what existed in Corinth where certain believers ate with good conscience what had already been offered to idols. The principle which guided their actions was that the idol was nothing (1 Cor 8:4). The apostle does not say, however, that the Corinthian problem applied in Rome. In the first instance, there were those who felt free to eat all things, including meat, and those whose scruples about eating meat led them to restrict their diet to vegetables (AV "herbs"). It should be noted that Paul does not at this point outline what is true christian practice: he merely states that scruples about what believers feel free to eat have to be respected.

3 For the peace of the assembly at Rome it was essential that tolerance and forbearance should be exercised. Paul concentrates on the two parties he has designated respectively "weak" and "strong". Whether there were others who were neither weak nor strong is not the point here, the main thrust of the advice is directed at two classes. He first of all addresses an individual as the representative of the strong. This one, who had no scruples about what he ate was not to despise the one who had. The verb rendered "despise" (*exoutheneō*) carries the meaning of treating persons or things as being of no account. It is translated in 1 Cor 6:4, "who *are least esteemed* in the church", but more accurately in the RV, "do ye set them to judge who *are of no account* in the church". The force of this is that there were those who were not in assembly fellowship and had therefore no right to judge in church matters– they were of no account.

The apostle is equally clear in his treatment of those who had scruples. If they confined themselves to a vegetarian diet that was their prerogative, but they had no jurisdiction over those who had no conscience about eating meat. Both classes in themselves obviously felt that they were correct and that the others were wrong. Intolerant attitudes predominated, probably because each party felt strongly about the respective stances taken.

There is a sense in which both parties were returning to a situation where works were having a place. What they did (or did not do) was taking on an importance which was quite out of keeping with what christian teaching set out. The great truth of justification by faith was in danger of being weakened by reason of the rigidity of some in defence of what they did not do and the attitude of others towards them in perhaps flaunting their freedom to do what they pleased.

The apostle is strong in his rebuke of the one who adopted the vegetarian stance. His censorious attitude could not be tolerated. He reminds him that when God received the strong the question of eating did not arise. God welcomed him just as He had welcomed the vegetarian. There was no argument against God's acceptance at that time and there should be no objections against the strong one's freedom to continue to do what he had always done.

4 Although some consider that Paul's challenge is addressed to the weak and strong, and no doubt the principle is applicable to both, nevertheless, in the author's view, the greater problem is associated with the attitude of the weak. (Most commentaries consider the greater problem lay with the "strong" brother's failure to respect the "weak" brother's scruples.) The word "judge" is carried over from the previous verse, indicating that the apostle is still addressing the censoriousness he has condemned. The challenge he makes to his imaginary weak brother shows the weak one to be in conflict with the strong one's Master. By his criticism of the servant of the house, he is in fact directing his judgment against that servant's Master, since the Master has every confidence in his servant.

To his own lord and master the servant stands or falls. It is the master who has the ability to judge his servant's conduct. He has the power to make him stand and it is the master's business to deal with him, should he fall. The view of the outsider regarding the servant's position with his master does not enter into it. The scruples of another do not affect the master's course of action. Indeed, as Paul states emphatically about the strong one's position, he shall be made to stand, for the Lord is able to make him do so.

The apostle here makes it clear that despite the criticism of the strong one's liberty, the Lord will support him. Paul opposes scrupulousness which goes beyond holding certain views to the condemnation of others who are not like-minded. To those who adopt such a self-righteous attitude he warns that the Lord will not desert those whose liberty is challenged. He will cause all such to stand despite the criticism levelled against them.

5   From the subject of food, Paul turns to another matter of dispute, that of the observance of days. Here he acknowledges that one person regards one day different from another; he makes distinctions. There is another person, however, and according to the apostle he considers every day to be the same; he makes no distinctions. Although many seek to identify the days as Jewish, Paul does not identify them here. When he wrote to the Galatians, he left no doubts about what affected them (Gal 4:10,11), and in his epistle to the Colossians he was equally clear about the dangers that faced them in the observance of days (Col 2:16). Here, however, the inference is that the weak one put different values on certain days, but the strong one considered every day to be a day of opportunity for serving the Lord.

The advice that each man should be fully convinced in his own mind identifies a danger. The apostle does not support the adoption of another's views simply to fall into line. A person's convictions must be his own and they are to be held as such before the Lord. If in the course of time and under further teaching, the appreciation of certain aspects of truth changes, then it is before the Lord that the adjustments are made. Enlightenment ought to be under the influence of the Spirit of God and not simply a desire to accommodate what is held by others. This is a solemn rejoinder the apostle makes; one with far-reaching effects.

6 There is a very flimsy manuscript support for the inclusion of the words, "and he that regardeth not the day, to the Lord he doth not regard it". Denney comments that almost all critical editors omit the words. The verse then states that the "weak" brother sets his mind upon certain days and makes a distinction between them. There is no suggestion of being insincere. The person observes some days as being set apart for whatever reason and purpose and he does so as unto the Lord. The omission of the latter half of the sentence does not infer that the "strong" brother attaches no significance to any particular day. His position is that he treats every day the same, i.e. as being of equal importance for serving the Lord. There is stress on "to the Lord". Paul acknowledges that due recognition, indeed honour, is given to the Lord regardless of the stance taken.

A similar line is taken up by Paul regarding what is eaten and what is refused. He does not say what it is that is eaten, although the context might suggest that it is meat. Both the "strong" brother and the "weak" brother give thanks. As they bow their heads over their food, one thanks the Lord for his meat and the other thanks the Lord that he is not eating meat. They are both acting for the glory of the Lord and in that sense the name of the Lord is honoured. There is no question here of the unconverted finding fault with different points of view. There is nothing in what either does which exposes the testimony to criticism, even if the separate views were known outside the assembly. Both weak and strong were genuine in their beliefs and their strong convictions made them act, as they saw it, for the glory of God.

7 What is stated in this verse arises out of the subject of food and the observance or non-observance of days. Although the differences of views in these matters might be allowable, in the final issue, no Christian can ignore the fact that he lives or dies unto the Lord. Paul is not considering here any thought of what a man is amongst other men. He is not thinking of how a Christian's conduct affects those with whom he comes into contact. It is the believer before the Lord and his responsibility to Him that is the real issue of life. Opinions about certain things and independent actions may govern behaviour, but the sobering thought is here made known, that in it all it is the Lord who has be to acknowledged; it is not the pleasing of self that matters.

The same principle applies to death. The Christian does not determine the time or the manner of his death. That is the Lord's prerogative. The option is not given to the believer to continue to serve or to end service. Although the apostle has much to say about death and the believer's attitude to it in 1 Cor 15, he does not enter into that here. Sufficient for the weak and the strong to know that life's span, though it be characterised by scruples and differing opinions, is set by the determinate will of God.

8 This verse confirms the Lordship of Christ. As far as the Christian is concerned there is no time, either in life or in death when he is not bound by that. The previous verse established that the believer does not live unto himself, neither is he free to choose the time or the mode of his death. In life he lives and serves consciously as unto the Lord. Death does not sever that relationship. He is still the Lord's and whatever form service will take after death, it will still be under the Lordship of Christ. This is obviously Paul's burden here. Three times he asserts it in the verse. In view of the different stances taken at Rome which he has addressed, it is obvious that the overriding fact had to be pressed. Regardless of different views, in the end every believer stands in relation to Christ as Lord, a relationship which does not cease even at death.

9 The purpose of Christ's death and resurrection is now given. Paul states that He died and He lives again. The apostle is not saying that He lived and died. That is not the point here. It is His death and His springing to life that is before him. This, says Paul, is that He might be the Lord both of the dead and the living. There is a sense in which Christ was always Lord, but the special force of the point brought out is that His sacrificial death and resurrection establish a new relationship. The words, "For to this end" indicate the divine purpose and this is clearly that He might be Lord both of the dead and the living.

The context indicates the reason why Paul has drawn attention to the death and resurrection of Christ. There were those who had scruples about eating meat and those who felt free to eat as they pleased. There were some who observed certain days and there were others who treated every day alike. Regardless of the different stances taken, Christ is Lord over all and that not only in relation to the living, but over the dead also. Whether saints are weak or strong, they belong to Him. His title to them is that He purchased them by His own blood and in the resurrection He exercises His Lordship over them.

10 Twice in this verse the pronoun "thou" is placed in an emphatic position. To the weak brother, the question is put, "Thou, why judge thy brother?" And to the strong, a similar question is addressed, "Thou, why despise thy brother?" In both there are faults. The vegetarians and observers of days have taken up the position of being judges of their brethren and in so doing have usurped the prerogative of the One who is Lord over all. Similarly, those who feel free to eat meat and treat every day the same have little or no consideration for the scruples of their brethren and in consequence have despised saints who are nevertheless the Lord's.

What the apostle is concerned about is clearly that time and effort spent on defending attitudes and condemning others is valueless, since all will appear before the Lord and everyone's views will then be seen in their true light. The word "brother" is an important one in Paul's estimation. He never forgot hearing it pronounced upon him by Ananias shortly after his conversion (Acts 9:17) and he referred to the incident again when he gave his testimony later before the Jews (Acts 22:13). Here he points out that the weak has to remember that the strong is his brother. And just as pointedly the strong is reminded that the same relationship exists with the weak. It is not just people who are involved in the judging and despising; it is brethren.

Before the saints at Rome the future prospect of judgment is raised, "for we shall all stand before the judgment seat of Christ". There are three passages in the NT which deal with the judgment seat: 1 Cor 3; 2 Cor 5; Rom 14. Only two of these use the descriptive title, the judgment seat of Christ: 2 Cor 5, Rom 14, although the better reading in Rom 14:10 is "judgment seat of God" RV. Since, however, God has committed all judgment into the hands of the Son (John 5:22), the end result is the same. Regarding judgment of believers, the great sheet-anchor for the soul is in the words of the Lord, "He that heareth my word and believeth on him that sent me, hath everlasting life and shall not come into condemnation (judgment) but is passed from death unto life" (John 5:24). Judgment as such for the believer is passed. The sin question was dealt with at the cross and the believer will never be judged at any future assize for sins committed.

At the judgment seat of Christ no questions will be raised about sin. It has to be remembered that when Christ comes, believers will be changed, they will have bodies fashioned like unto His body of glory (Phil 3:21). It would be incongruous to think that in that blessed condition there would be any suggestion of guilt. The question of sin and salvation is settled long before believers appear at the judgment seat. The purpose of the judgment is in another connection altogether. From the two other passages which deal with the subject, 1 Cor 3 and 2 Cor 5, it will be seen that works and not sins will be reviewed.

The subject of the judgment seat is not dealt with at length in Rom 14. Here there is no mention of all being made manifest before the judgment seat, that they may receive the things done in the body, according to what each has done, whether it be good or evil. That is considered at 2 Cor 5:10. Neither is there a reference to works, such as is found at 1 Cor 3:14-15, "If any man's work abide...he shall receive a reward. If any man's work shall be burned, he shall suffer loss". The main thrust in Rom 14 is to correct the judging of brethren since they "are the Lord's" and He will judge all in righteousness at a future date.

11 The Scriptures are now called in to support the apostle's argument. He quotes Isa 45:23, but is not saying that the words of Isaiah refer to the judgment seat. He is stating that judgment as a general principle is inevitable. It may be considered as one great assize, but the Scriptures make it clear that there will be different sessions. Isaiah wrote, "unto me every knee shall bow, every tongue shall swear". That is absolutely certain, but not all will bow and confess at the same time.

The scope of Isa 45 is far-reaching, even beyond the tribulation to the time when all Israel shall be saved. In Isaiah's day there were protests against God that He should use a Gentile monarch, Cyrus, to do His will. This was contrary to the pride of the Jews. Jehovah's action, however, was in accordance with His sovereign rights and so Isaiah uses the figure, "shall the clay argue with the potter, why do you make me thus?" Argument was futile; all the world would know that Jehovah was the true God and there was none else.

Isaiah prefixes the reference to future judgment with Jehovah's oath, "I have sworn by myself". The Hebrew epistle makes it clear that He does that because He can swear by no greater. Paul introduces the verse with different words, "As I live, saith the Lord", possibly meaning, "As surely as I live". This is substantially the same as the oath, especially when the words "saith the Lord" are added. The inevitability of judgment, even though in different forms and at different times, is therefore put to the Romans, that all might refrain from judging their brethren.

12 This short verse is most emphatic on several counts. It states that "every (each, RV) one of us shall give account of himself to God". There are no exceptions. Not only so, but the review is personal. No one is called upon to give an account of someone else's life and works. Each person is answerable to God and not to any other. The scope covers every believer, even the apostle, as he includes himself, "each one of us".

The thrust of Paul's statement is obviously to enforce the futility of spending valuable time and effort in defending scruples and judging others when in the final analysis, each believer will give account of his own works to God. How earnestly one defended or propagated personal views in life will then be seen to have no value in the light of God's estimation of worth. A consideration of a day of review in the future should result in a re-appraisal of life's values. A re-adjustment in time will obviate loss at the judgment seat. There will be no argument then with the divine assessment.

13 Although many consider that this verse introduces a new section, it is taken here as the conclusion of the argument of vv.1-12. In view of the judgment seat and the personal rendering of an account, a change is necessary. To the weak and the strong Paul gives his counsel that judging each other must cease. Judgment is a divine prerogative and one which God has not passed over to others. Once again the apostle includes himself, "Let us therefore", showing that he himself is not above the advice he is giving.

There seems to be a play on the word "judge" in what follows. There is a place for judging, according to the apostle, but it is a personal one. It concerns the strong, and it calls for a decision not to place a stumbling block or an occasion of falling in front of the weak. The exhortation is not a general one about not placing stumbling blocks in the paths of others. It is a specific call not to do anything to cause a brother to fall. The Lord said to His disciples, "It is impossible but that offences (stumbling blocks) will come; but woe unto him through whom they will come" (Luke 17:1). Paul also stressed the seriousness of doing anything likely to cause others to fall. To the Corinthians he wrote, "But take heed lest by any means this liberty of yours becomes a stumbling block to them that are weak" (1 Cor 8:9).

Notes

1 "Receive ye" (*proslambanō*, "to take to one's self") implies not a reluctant gesture, but a warm reception.
2 The word "herbs" (*lachana*) comes from *lachainō* ("to dig"), hence describes what is grown from land that has been dug, i.e. vegetables. Plummer comments, "Disputes about dietetics were not confined to the primitive church".
4 This word "servant" (*oiketēs*) is a household servant. This rare word is possibly chosen to indicate the servant's closeness to his master.
6 "Regardeth" (*phroneō*, "to think") here means setting the mind on a thing, that is one day being different from others.
13 Harold St. John makes a distinction between stumbling block and occasion to fall. He says, "The stumbling block is more a casual thing lying on the road over which a man might trip and fall. But the 'occasion' of stumbling is something that has been definitely put there to make him stumble. The first suggests carelessness and the other suggests malice".

(b) *Consideration for the brother (vv.14-23)*

> v.14 "I know, and am persuaded by the Lord Jesus, that there is nothing unclean of itself: but to him that esteemeth any thing to be unclean, to him it is unclean.
> v.15 But if thy brother be grieved with thy meat, now walkest thou not charitably. Destroy not him with thy meat, for whom Christ died.
> v.16 Let not then your good be evil spoken of:
> v.17 For the kingdom of God is not meat and drink; but righteousness, and peace, and joy in the Holy Ghost.
> v.18 For he that in these things serveth Christ is acceptable to God, and approved of men.
> v.19 Let us therefore follow after the things which make for peace, and things wherewith one may edify another.
> v.20 For meat destroy not the work of God. All things indeed are pure; but it is evil for that man who eateth with offence.
> v.21 It is good neither to eat flesh, nor to drink wine, nor any thing whereby thy brother stumbleth, or is offended, or is made weak.
> v.22 Hast thou faith? have it to thyself before God. Happy is he that condemneth not himself in that thing which he alloweth.
> v.23 And he that doubteth is damned if he eat, because he eateth not of faith: for whatsoever is not of faith is sin."

14 In a very emphatic way Paul makes known that his firm persuasion is that there is nothing unclean of itself. He knows that intuitively, but in addition, quite apart from his own reasoning, he is persuaded in the Lord Jesus. As a result of his union with Christ he is absolutely certain that there is nothing unclean or common of itself. It is when something is associated with what is considered to be unholy that it is judged to be unclean, but nothing in creation is of itself inherently unclean.

Paul is re-asserting his firm conviction about liberty. Although his own views link him with the strong, he is nevertheless careful to stress the necessity of respecting the conscience of the weak brother. Douglas Moo quotes Martin Luther in this connection, "A Christian man is a most free lord of all, subject to none. A

Christian man is a most dutiful servant of all, subject to all". And Moo adds, "By this he meant that even though our liberty in Christ may permit us to engage in a certain activity, we nevertheless may not be wise in doing so".

The AV commences the next clause, "but". The RV gives, "save", and some render "except", suggesting that there is a situation where great care is needed. If someone considers a thing to be unclean, although it is not unclean in itself, then that person's conscience must be respected. The conscience may be misguided or unenlightened, but nevertheless it is what guides the weak brother and it is due the utmost respect. The scruples of the weak brother render certain things to be common in his reckoning. As Paul has made clear, whatever is considered unclean is not in itself unclean, but the scruples which brand it as unclean have to be taken into account. It would be wrong to stumble anyone who had genuine difficulty, although he may be totally misguided.

15 The opening clause puts the onus clearly on the strong brother. He may have difficulty in coming to terms with the fact that something as unimportant as meat should be the cause of a weak brother being grieved. If the strong has liberty there is no value in flaunting it if it causes another brother to stumble. The verb *lupeitai* carries the thought of distress. It is not simply grieving quietly within; the suggestion is there of deep distress and it results from the strong eating what the weak considers to be unclean. Morris quotes Brunner, who warns against "a devout carelessness in doing what one has recognised as right for oneself but which can ruin one's neighbour".

This clause refers back to 13:8-10, which begins, "Owe no man anything, but to love one another", and closes, "therefore love is the fulfilling of the law". If therefore there is no consideration for the scruples of the weak and all food is eaten regardless, the brother so acting is no longer walking in love. As Throckmorton notes, "Paul is consistent in his criterion: one is free to love; one is not free not to love". If the integrity of a believer is at stake, one's liberty has to be seriously examined. The apostle is using the plainest language to register a warning with the strong that the utmost care is needed to live amicably with those whose views are different.

The closing statement of this verse places before the strong the outcome of thoughtlessness. A literal rendering of the first few words is, "Not by the food of thee that man destroy". This infers that something as unimportant to the strong as food is not to be compared with the destruction of a brother. In addition, the interests of the Lord are involved: for that weak brother, Christ died. There is therefore the strongest of contrasts between the length the Saviour was prepared to go to save and the total indifference in the strong to the possibility of the weak brother's collapse. His lack of tolerance could result in the destruction of a brother whose title to eternal life was won for him by the sacrifice of Christ.

16 This verse concludes what has been set out in the previous verses. The "good" to which the apostle refers is the liberty which the strong has enjoyed. Apart from having to contend with the scruples of the weak, the faith and general conduct of the strong are not in question. The exhortation therefore requires that the good of his testimony should not be put in jeopardy by careless or thoughtless behaviour. This liberty could be interpreted by some as a cover for the indulgence of selfish practices, resulting in the strong being railed upon.

There is the possibility that Paul was referring to criticism from outside the assembly if what existed inside had become known. This could result in slanderous comment being directed against all the believers. Some hold that the exhortation has a wider application than merely to the strong, and it is the good of the whole assembly that is at stake. This view may have some merit, but as the verse is introduced by "therefore" and Paul has been addressing the strong, restricting the appeal to the strong seems the more likely option.

17 The announcement Paul makes here about the kingdom of God makes an end of outward observances. There is neither room nor scope for ceremonial rites in the light of this monumental statement. What has gone before in his dealing with the subject of meats and days leads up to the clear conclusion, that adherence to external things has no value. The kingdom of God, the sphere of God's rule, has to do with principles which are spiritual. In its moral aspect it is distinctive, essentially different from anything which is characterised by empty forms.

The Romans needed to be reminded that the scruples which some held and which others scorned were robbing them of the good of spiritual values. Righteousness and peace and joy in the Holy Ghost were blessings to be richly enjoyed. Although righteousness and peace and joy have been considered separately earlier in the epistle, the force of the three words here obviously concerns their practical importance. Instead of having two factions arguing as to whose stance is the correct one, cultivating right relations with each other would bring in peace. They would then have joy in the Holy Ghost. He would be free to bring everyone into the good of all truth, the deep things of God, just waiting to be communicated to them. The kingdom of God is not brought in by man. He can, however, enjoy the blessings of the kingdom if he is prepared to abide by its statutes and judgment.

18 The logical sequence of Paul's argument is clearly seen in this verse. The service which he refers to is bondservice. Whether weak or strong, every believer belongs to Christ and as such is at the disposal of the Master. There is no reference or allusion here to service within the frame of what kinds of meat should be eaten, or to the attitude of the strong as to whether there is consideration for others. What is before the apostle is righteousness, peace and joy and only if these are practised is there pleasure brought to God. This is the kind of service God desires. It is this which is acceptable (or well-pleasing) to Him. This is a strong point in Paul's argument. Scruples and the lack of forbearance do not bring pleasure to God, but righteousness, peace and joy in the Holy Ghost certainly do. When this is thoughtfully considered in His presence, service will be viewed differently. Personal preferences will be laid aside and what pleases God will be seen to be the all-important matter in the christian life.

The word "approved" (*dokimos*), signifies "approved after testing". It is not that Paul is subjecting the saints to the formal scrutiny of men, believers and unbelievers, but that their righteousness, peace and joy are bound to draw from others sincere and unreserved approval. To be approved of men does not mean that the good opinion of others should be actively sought after, but that life should be so lived that an ungrudging acknowledgment of godly living will be forthcoming. The principle is the same as that in Paul's exhortation to the Corinthians, "that they which are approved (*dokimos*) may be made manifest among you" (1 Cor 11:19).

19 The exhortation of v.13, "Let us not therefore judge one another any more", seems to be taken up again in this verse, "Let us therefore follow after the things which make for peace". At 12:13 it was noted that the verb *diōkō* in "given to hospitality" signifies "to pursue". Here the same verb is rendered in the AV "follow after". This rendering, however, does not reflect fully the earnestness in the apostle's appeal. The things that make for peace have to be pursued. Conduct which promotes disharmony has to be modified or changed entirely so that acrimony amongst the saints does not arise.

Edification is not looked upon here as a goal; it is a process. The work of building up each other has to go on continually. The word carries the meaning of house-building, and of its eighteen occurrences in the NT, fifteen are in the writings of Paul. It is used widely in the metaphorical sense throughout Paul's epistles, indicating that the apostle identified many christian graces which, if pursued and worked out by believers, would result in their being built-up. To the Ephesian elders, Paul said, "And now brethren, I commend you to God and to the word of his grace, which is able to build you up (*oikodomeō*)". This exhortation illustrates clearly the apostle's earnest desire to see spiritual growth in the saints.

20 Having established the necessity of mutual building-up, the apostle now warns of the danger of pulling-down. The word chosen to describe this process is met with in building situations to describe structures which are being demolished. It is used in 2 Cor 5:1 to describe the dissolution of the body, this earthly house of our tabernacle, when death occurs. The apostle states therefore that for the sake of meat, of no consequence in itself, eaten or refused, it is certainly not worth the risk of demolishing the work of God. What is involved in the expression "the work of God" cannot be identified exactly. From the context, it could cover the work of God in the weak brother, but God also worked in the strong brother and behind both is the assembly. Whatever was in Paul's mind it is clearly not worth the risk of demolishing "the work of God" for the sake of scruples or the despising of them.

There is obviously no doubt in the apostle's mind that all kinds of food are clean. However it is wrong to eat if there is the possibility of offending anyone. If the weak brother eats and acts against his conscience, that action is an offence to him. If the strong brother eats regardless of the possibility of causing the weak brother to stumble, that also is evil. It is not clear whether Paul is addressing the strong or the weak here. It is better therefore to leave the subject open. To eat or not to eat requires careful consideration in case scruples or the despising of them causes offence. In this case it is confirmed again that people do not live unto themselves. What they do or refrain from doing affects others.

21 Up to this point he had used *brōma* ("food"), but now he refers to *kreas* ("flesh"). It is not clear why he should change and why he should include a reference to wine. Perhaps as he drew near the end of his argument he wanted to be more specific, although it might also indicate that he had a certain situation before him. The general reference which follows would certainly cover all situations and leave no room for finding a reason to ignore his exhortation.

Paul does not say here that it is not good to eat flesh or drink wine. He states that it is good not to eat flesh or drink wine. Occasions might arise in other circumstances where scruples did not exist, and in these situations eating flesh or drinking wine would be permissible. The advice given here covered the situation in Rome. To avoid giving offence or occasion of stumbling by refusing what was legitimate was a noble action. Refraining from exercising one's rights so that the weak would not stumble was highly commendable. The conscience of the weak had to be protected. Encouraging others to do what their consciences disapproved was not conducive to edification.

22 The RV rendering removes the question with which the AV opens the verse. It reads in the RV, "The faith which thou hast, have thou to thyself before God". Paul is not denying the faith of the strong. What he is saying is that the faith which permits the strong to eat flesh or drink wine should not be paraded. It should not find expression in claiming rights; thereby causing the weak to stumble. Faith here indicates a link with God, an invisible but very real relation with the Divine. Rather than boast about it or demonstrate it by visible means such as freely eating or drinking, it is better, in Paul's opinion, to have faith privately before God.

If faith is exercised in due consideration of others, the apostle concludes that such a believer is happy (or blessed). By not claiming rights and therefore making due allowance for the scruples of others, the person contemplated here does not need to judge himself for causing someone to stumble. If by exercising his rights to do what he approves, he may afterwards have to censure himself for having done so, he may lose that blessedness. Happy is the believer who considers the faith of others and quietly before God acts in the light of his own faith for their benefit.

23 Attention is now focused on the weak brother. He is neither free in mind nor in conscience. He is troubled with doubts. To be like the strong and be free to eat without restriction would seem to be the way forward. But if he should eat once, he is condemned, because that action would not spring from his faith. The weak brother has been seen to have scruples which he holds tenaciously. To him they are fundamental issues. If he should break one, he has acted outwith his faith and he stands condemned. This does not mean condemnation in the sense of 8:1, but he is guilty of bringing displeasure to the Lord.

The situation described by the apostle portrays a man who will act against his conscience. He is declaring a freedom he does not have. He is prepared to do something about which he has doubts and which is against his faith. He is not unlike the man who wavers, described by James. That man is double-minded and unstable in all his ways (James 1:8). The motive behind this action is simply to comply with another person's views without being persuaded that they are correct. Since that action did not arise from faith, it is sin. It is important to recognise that Paul's conclusion here concerns the case before him. It may be that what he has stated was not meant as a principle for general application to every situation in life.

Notes

14 "...am persuaded" (*pepeismai*) refers not to Paul's own reasoning. The persuasion is of the Lord.

"Unclean" (*koinon*, "common") is man's estimate of a thing and so renders it unclean; not what it is in itself that so renders it unclean.

18 "In this" (*en toutō*) Robertson notes, "On the principle implied by these virtues", i.e. righteousness, peace and joy.

19 "Therefore" is literally "So then" (*ara oun*), two inferential particles, Robertson renders "accordingly therefore".

20 "Destroy" (*kataluō*, "to loosen down") carries on the metaphor of building, notes Vincent.

21 Some manuscripts omit "or is offended", or "is made weak".

(b) *The appeal for christian unity (vv.1-7)*

The theme of ch.14 continues in the early verses of this chapter. The subject changes slightly with the plea of v.7, following the completion of the prayer commencing at v.5 where the apostle calls upon the God of patience and consolation. He will also call upon the God of hope (v.13) and complete the chapter with an appeal to the God of peace (v.33).

The scope of the chapter widens out to a consideration of christian unity. This takes character from the example of Christ (v.3) and is supported by the plea in v.6, "That ye may with one mind glorify God". The six quotations from the OT are worthy of careful thought. They are taken from the three main divisions of the OT, the Law, the Psalms, and the Prophets. They are examples of the monumental statement of v.4, "For whatsoever things were written aforetime were written for our learning, that we through patience and comfort of the scriptures might have hope". The importance and significance of OT quotations and allusions are considered in the two books, *Things Written Aforetime,* and *Written for Our Learning,* both of which titles are based on the words of 15:4.

> v.1 "We then that are strong ought to bear the infirmities of the weak, and not to please ourselves.
> v.2 Let every one of us please his neighbour for his good to edification.
> v.3 For even Christ pleased not himself; but, as it is written, The reproaches of them that reproached thee fell on me.
> v.4 For whatsoever things were written aforetime were written for our learning, that we through patience and comfort of the scriptures might have hope.
> v.5 Now the God of patience and consolation grant you to be likeminded one toward another according to Christ Jesus:
> v.6 That ye may with one mind and one mouth glorify God, even the Father of our Lord Jesus Christ.
> v.7 Wherefore receive ye one another, as Christ also received us to the glory of God."

1 It is significant that Paul numbers himself with the strong. He could have remained neutral to avoid the possibility of being thought of as having bias, but he comes out strongly as being amongst those not affected by scruples. Possibly he judged that the stance he adopted would make the strong more conscious of their indebtedness. They were under an obligation. The weak were without power (*adunatos*). Their christian faith was not suspect. It was the restrictions they brought upon themselves by the scruples they held that brought about the weakness. Intolerance of their position by others was the problem Paul addressed. What was of little importance to the strong was paramount to the weak and there was a danger of permanent damage being caused to the testimony by lack of understanding on both sides.

In this verse the apostle makes it clear that the strong do not have an option. They are under an obligation. The verb he uses (*opheilō*), clearly indicates how they stood. It could be rendered, "We owe it". The weak were fellow-believers, and the strong had no entitlement to shrug off responsibility for caring for them. Paul addressed a similar exhortation to the Galatians, "Bear ye one another's burdens" (Gal 6:2). Some believers there had heavy loads to bear and it behoved others who were able, to come forward and ease their burdens in whatever way possible.

The exhortation, "not to please ourselves" does not mean that there should be a ban on what brings pleasure. It is understood in connection with the weak.

They must at all times be taken into account if they were affected in any way by actions that are pleasing to others. What Paul is calling for is essentially different from what applies in other societies and religions in the world. Christianity is shown here to be a caring concept. For the sake of others, either to keep them from stumbling, or as here, that the weak might be supported, personal liberty is held in restraint.

2 The implications of this verse are far-reaching. The injunction, "Let everyone of us please his neighbour", if taken to extremes, could place an intolerable burden on the caring element in any christian community. Although the apostle's appeal is to "each one" (RV), and he uses the word "neighbour" to give the widest application to the injunction, the context is still concerned with the weak and the strong. If the weak had to keep introducing scruples, and keep maintaining the right to be conformed to them, they would soon have a controlling influence over the assembly. The others, if guided by a completely literal appreciation of Paul's exhortation, would have to constantly make adjustments to their way of life to accommodate the weak. In view of what could result in chaos it seems preferable to understand what Paul has written as a guiding principle rather than a rigid rule of conduct.

By introducing the word "neighbour", there is an obvious extension here to the principle laid down at 13:10, "Love worketh no ill to his neighbour". The question of debt is raised in that context also, "Owe no man anything, but to love one another" (v.8), which leads on to the verse quoted from the OT, "Thou shalt love thy neighbour as thyself" (v.9). Although the injunction is addressed to the strong, it would be wrong to assume that the weak were entirely free from any obligation to consider their neighbours for good also. As far as they were able, it was incumbent upon them to exercise a caring ministry, even if it were merely appreciation for kindness shown.

The exhortation to please one's neighbour for his good to edification does not mean complying with every whim that the weak may express. Paul was never party to that. He could write to another assembly, "For do I now persuade men (seek their favour), or God? or do I seek to please men? if I yet pleased men, I should not be the servant of Christ" (Gal 1:10). To the Romans, the apostle limits the pleasing of others to that which is "good for his edification". The exhortation assumes that the strong know what is good and beneficial for the weak. The spiritual understand what will lead to the building up of others. This condemns any thought of self-pleasing which ignores the effect it will have on weak believers. The goal of the strong is to lead the weak by spiritual means towards emancipation from the scruples which stifle their faith.

3 Paul now introduces a strong encouragement. The example of Christ is brought in, supported by a quotation from Ps 69:9. It is significant that the apostle did not point to a particular incident in the life of Christ, but directed attention to the whole of His earthly sojourn. This is confirmed by the tense of the verb, "Christ pleased not (did not please) himself". There was no occasion in His earthly life when He did not abide by His Father's will or when He looked to His own interests. It is not surprising therefore that Paul set before the believers such a powerful motive to put the interests of others before their own.

The practice of the apostle to bring in the Scriptures to support his argument is demonstrated again. No doubt it was his rabbinical training that enabled him to turn readily to an appropriate passage and leave it to speak for itself in the context of his writings. The confidence he had in the finality of the word of God to end all doubt or argument is most striking. This is evidenced by the explanation given in the next verse, "whatsoever things were written aforetime were written for our learning".

The psalm from which Paul quotes here is one of great significance. Five times there are direct quotations from it in the NT and it is clearly referred to on eight other occasions. Apart from Paul, the Gospel writers allude to the psalm, and John in particular has at least three allusions in the Revelation to "the book of the living", the existence of which the psalmist makes known. In his advice to the Romans, the part of the psalm which Paul considers to be applicable to the point he has before him, concerns the attitude of mankind to God. The mockery of evil men is directed against any who have a zeal for God and who take a stand for righteousness. The reproaches therefore which are intended to be directed against God are heaped upon those who are identified as God's servants. The supreme example of this unjust and wicked treatment is given here by Paul, "The reproaches of them that reproached thee (God) fell upon me (God's Son)". Nevertheless, despite the reproach, Christ never pleased Himself, but always concerned Himself with the interest of others. Even on the cross, this way of life is clearly seen in His plea on behalf of His tormentors, "Father, forgive them for they know not what they do" (Luke 23:34).

4 The relevance of the OT to the daily lives of Christians is brought out in this verse. Here Paul is stating that everything that was written aforetime, meaning everything that was written in the Scriptures, was written for a purpose. He is not including writings outwith the OT, but what was declared and recorded by the inspired vessels of the past as they were moved by the Holy Spirit. The amazing statement of 15:4 implies that the inspired writers of the past were not only writing for their own generations, but in the wisdom of God and under the guidance of the Holy Spirit were writing for future generations also. Not only so, but it infers that in every age following the completion and circulation of the sacred writings, the recipients of them would be responsible to read them, hear them, consider them and apply them to daily living.

The apostle states that the things written in earlier ages were written for our hope. This is not restricted to the hope of the Lord's return, but to hope in its widest sense. It is to the God of hope that people must turn to fill life's expectations. If believers have their hopes fixed on God, the doubts which assail will lose their significance. Here Paul recognises that the Scriptures are the basis for sustaining the Christian's hope, and in that respect he gladly includes himself.

There are two important points to be faced. Hope is the goal but there is patience and comfort to be derived from the Scriptures also. God uses what is written to encourage His saints. Examples from the past, such as that great cloud of witnesses to which the writer to the Hebrews refers, are a source of encouragement to lay aside every weight and run with patience the race of life which is set before us (Heb 12:1). Christian fortitude is strengthened by the Scriptures, and in the wisdom of God, He has left a storehouse of examples. Here in 15:3 the supreme example is given. Christ pleased not Himself and what that meant for Him was foretold in the writings of the past. There should therefore be confidence in the word of God to supply the answer to every exigency in life.

5 The raising of a short prayer is characteristic of Paul. It is as if the subject before him calls for divine help and rather than wait until later to make the plea, he interjects what he is writing with a prayer, and sometimes with a doxology, as at 1:25. That others should follow his example is suggested in his epistles, as in Eph 6:18, "Praying always with all prayer and supplication in the Spirit". The short prayer here is to the God of patience, the source of the power and the grace to endure. Coupled with this is the fact that He is also the source of comfort. The apostle is not suggesting that believers have these qualities as part of the human framework; he is stating that God is the source of them and is ever ready to impart the necessary help to cope with life's problems.

The use of the genitive is peculiar to Paul. He refers here to the God of patience and comfort; in v.13 to the God of hope and in v.33 to the God of peace. Adolf Deissman called these genitives "the mystical genitives", inferring that sometimes they defy exact and precise definition. Here God is noted as the source of the steady power of endurance which is necessary to continue through to the end, however great the discouragements. It is the refusal to give up, whatever the odds. Without such a grace Christianity becomes a mere sentiment. Being a source of comfort, He has the ability to sympathise and cheer. He is the God who stimulates the believer to brotherly love, as is called for in this context.

The apostle's plea is that God will give likemindedness one toward another. The word *phroneō*, ("to think") never means merely to hold an opinion, but to do so with a view to action, based on the judgment formed; for example, Phil 2:2, "be of the same mind", meaning, with a view to acting accordingly. Here it is a wish for the future. If the believers acted upon it, it would banish ill-feeling, bitterness and recrimination. They would realise that, despite their differences they had a common nature and therefore unity was called for, according to Christ Jesus, that is, a oneness which accords with Christ.

6 The short prayer continues in this verse. It is that there should be one heart and one mouth. This prayer of Paul's shows how earnestly he desired that all possibility of division should be averted. A real danger existed. To avert that danger the example of Christ was brought in and the matter was commended to God. Here the one-mindedness according to Christ Jesus unites in praising God. This implies if there is no one-mindedness, glory to God is not rendered. God's full title in relation to Christ is given. He is the God and Father of our Lord Jesus Christ. It confirms the Lord's genuine humanity and stresses the need to ensure that God is not robbed of the praise that is due to be rendered to Him by His saints.

The expression "one mouth" is used only once by Paul, although Luke uses it many times in the Acts of the Apostles. It is a vivid expression. It does not simply mean many people saying the same thing, the recital of some commonly held religious tenets. It implies the reflection of a stance taken, here the response to what God has done. If the God of patience and comfort comes out to bless and support His saints it behoves them to respond in a similar way that His name might be glorified.

7 The conclusion is given. Assuming that the company at Rome was not only composed of weak and strong but that there were others also, then all are included in Paul's injunction, "Wherefore receive (or, accept) one another". The word "receive" (*proslambanō*) requires a wholehearted acceptance and a warm welcome. It is not suggested that the acceptance of each other will be easy, but the reminder that Christ accepted the believers with all their peculiarities, leaves objectors without an excuse. What Christ accomplished in each one must not be forgotten.

If the reading "you" is adopted instead of "us", then Paul is keeping himself aloof to give his advice its fullest impact on the company. Here he makes it clear that Christ brought glory to God when He received sinners. It is incumbent upon all therefore to remember from where and what they are called. Instead of being taken up with personal things, the example of Christ should put everything into perspective. The good of all the saints must be taken into account.

Notes

1 Paul employs "strong" (*dunatos*, "able", either intrinsically or absolutely for specific reasons) to class himself with the strong to make the obligation his own.

In this case "infirmities" (*asthenēmata*, "weakness", "a deficiency of strength") are the scruples. "Weak" (*adunatos*, "weak", "impotent", "not able") is set here in contrast to *dunatos*.

4 "Patience" (*hupomonē*) does not mean patience in the sense of sitting down and letting the tide of events flow over one. It means the ability to bear things, but in the bearing of them to turn them into triumph. It is a conquering patience.

(c) *Cause for Jew and Gentile to glorify God (vv.8-13)*

> v.8 "Now I say that Jesus Christ was a minister of the circumcision for the truth of God, to confirm the promises made unto the fathers:
> v.9 And that the Gentiles might glorify God for his mercy; as it is written, For this cause I will confess to thee among the Gentiles, and sing unto thy name.
> v.10 And again he saith, Rejoice, ye Gentiles, with his people.
> v.11 And again, Praise the Lord, all ye Gentiles; and laud him, all ye people.
> v.12 And again, Esaias saith, There shall be a root of Jesse, and he that shall rise to reign over the Gentiles; in him shall the Gentiles trust.
> v.13 Now the God of hope fill you with all joy and peace in believing, that ye may abound in hope, through the power of the Holy Ghost."

8 A reason for continuing the subject of vv.5-7 is now given. It is that Christ has become a minister of the Jews in the interests of the truth of God. It is not a temporary state. The perfect tense indicates that Christ continues His service on behalf of the circumcision. What He came to do as far as the nation of Israel is concerned, He will not give up, although the practical expression of it is still future. He came as the Messiah and despite rejection as such, He is still the Anointed and will demonstrate that when He resumes His links with the nation.

The verse opens with the words, "For I say". Some consider this should be expressed in stronger terms, "For I tell you". Denney considers it should be, "What I mean is this–Christ has been made etc". The choice of the word "circumcision" to describe the Jews might underline the fact that He came "unto his own" (John 1:11). He Himself said, "I am not sent but unto the lost sheep of the house of Israel" (Matt 15:24). There may be a thought of covenant relationships suggested in the use of the term "circumcision", but the context rather directs attention to the purpose; it was "for the truth of God". This may be understood as "in the interests of the truth of God". In His service He took upon Himself the responsibility of vindicating the truth of God. All that God had made known through His prophets and was ready to be confirmed and put into effect was taken up by Christ. The truth of God was advanced by Christ and not one aspect of it was left unstated or undone.

In respect of the Jews, the purpose is stated, "to confirm the promises made to the fathers". The verb *bebaioō* ("to confirm") is variously translated. Barclay suggests the thought of "guaranteeing"; Vine gives "establish", and Robertson thinks "to make stand" is a reasonable rendering. What is obvious is that the promises given to the patriarchs could never fall to the ground. They were committed to the trust of Christ. At the right time He came, or as Paul describes it, "When the fulness of the time was come, God sent forth his Son" (Gal 4:4). To the Jewish nation Christ came and He vindicated the truth of God in His ministry to the circumcision.

9 Having upheld the faithfulness of God in confirming His promises to the fathers, the apostle turns from the Jews to the Gentiles. The mercy of God towards them calls for praise. As, however, they were not embraced directly in the promises of old, they had no grounds for boasting against the Jews. Nevertheless, they were in God's mind for blessing as Paul will show in his references to the OT. The fact that God had also the Gentiles in His plans takes away from the national prejudice of the Jews. Their belief that they had exclusive rights to blessing had no foundation. The tendency therefore to insist on the observance of their scruples, coupled with their censorious judgment of Gentile believers had no credence.

The expression, "as it is written" introduces Paul's burden of proof from the OT. The passage he selects to establish the fact that Jews and Gentiles have cause to glorify God for His mercy is Ps 18:49. Blessing for the Gentiles is not the overall burden of this psalm; in fact the nations as such are not considered until v.49. For the purpose before him, Paul draws on the mention of the nations and makes the speaker the Lord Jesus, "For this cause I will confess to thee among the nations". The psalm has a peculiar aspect to it in that it is practically the same as 2 Sam 22. As both portions are said to be the words of a song sung by David for the Lord's deliverance from his enemies and from the hand of Saul, it has been suggested that the duplication results from David's singing of the song at different times as he considered the good hand of God with him.

While the experiences of David are listed in the psalm, it is obvious that a greater than David is in view. The deliverances of David were during his lifetime, necessarily so, but in the case of the Lord, His triumphs were in resurrection; the final victories over His enemies still being in the future. The blessings unfolded in the psalm are millennial; it is then that the nations come into the good of the mercy of God.

In this verse the apostle is showing that the mercy of God for Gentiles was not a last minute emergency measure, but was in fact intimated at various times in the past and recorded in the OT. So it is that Paul proceeds to prove the point from the law, the psalms and the prophets. He emphasises that salvation was of the Jews and that there was therefore an obligation to the Jews placed upon the Gentiles when they came to share the blessings of the gospel.

The aim of the passage is to promote unanimity and harmony; a difficult task when the Jews were clinging tenaciously to anti-Gentile prejudices and the Gentiles were contemptuous of the religious scruples of the Jews. In the gospel Jew and Gentile have been brought together. The quotation from Ps 18 shows that the union was in accordance with the OT, albeit the psalm anticipates the millennial age. Paul strives to prove that the same effect is obtainable in the gospel age, but toleration and understanding were required from both sides if future blessings were to be secured in the present.

10 In the next quotation from the OT in support of his argument, Paul turns to Deut 32:43. He is using a well-known rabbinical practice of running together several portions from the Scriptures in support of his submission that God had always Jews and Gentiles in His mind for blessing. So here, cited from the LXX, he quotes the note of joy which Moses struck, "Rejoice ye Gentiles with his people". In the law, the psalms, and the prophets there are many prophecies which show clearly that God's plans embraced Jews and Gentiles. In the millennial age all nations will rejoice with the Jews that righteousness has at last been established on a worldwide basis, but it will not be as a result of the efforts of man, it will be due to the intervention of God. It will be God's Man who will take up the reins of government on a universal basis. What Paul is teaching is that these blessings were available in the present through the work of Christ, and the good news of it was being declared in the gospel. Jews and Gentiles did not need to wait for the millennial age to be ushered in; worldwide blessing was available in the gospel of the grace of God.

The quotation is from the song of Moses (Deut 32 LXX). The song is a record of the history of Israel and God's dealings with that nation. It is a profound unfolding of the ways of God from the beginning through to the setting-up of the millennial kingdom. In its setting in Deuteronomy the song has a sad note. Immediately after Moses gave the song to the people he was directed to ascend the mountain where he would die, and be buried by God.

The last verse of the song is the verse chosen by Paul from which he takes an excerpt calling on the nations to rejoice with God's people. This foretells the great rejoicing at the end of the tribulation period when Antichrist and his associates meet their end. The Jewish nation will rejoice also when the hand of God with the Jew is recognised and when Christ will reign in millennial splendour. That will be a great time for all the peoples of the earth, but as Paul labours to prove, there are countless blessings in the gospel's universal message; blessings for time and eternity, all available on the principle of faith. If Jews and Gentiles will rejoice together in the future, they should also do so in the present age.

11 The apostle returns to the psalms for this third quotation. Ps 18 has already been called in, now Ps 117, a small psalm of two verses, will be made to yield its testimony to the mercy of God with the Gentiles. It may be significant that this small psalm has been noted by many as the central chapter of the Bible and that it should deal with a call for all nations and peoples to praise the Lord. It is fitting also that Paul should bring it in here. The bigotry of the Jews in the days of the Lord's presence on earth is in sharp contrast to the spirit of this small psalm. Blessing for the Gentiles was something the Jews found most difficult to accept. But here in this psalm and in Paul's brief quotation from it there is the intimation that the grace and mercy of God would not be confirmed to one nation, but would be extended to all mankind.

It has been said that Ps 117 is such a small portion of the Scripture that one might easily overlook it. Not so the Holy Spirit, however. He it was who moved the apostle to emphasise its place in revelation and apply it to an everyday situation, calling for forbearance and understanding between brethren, and in a wider setting, between Jew and Gentile. If all will end in all peoples praising the Lord, all without exception, it cannot be too much to expect oneness in the gospel age. Since all believers, whether weak or strong, belong to Christ, they are indwelt by the same Holy Spirit of God.

Ps 117 is part of the great Hallel. The six psalms of the Hallel are Pss 113-118, and they were sung at certain times of the Jewish year. The six psalms are closely connected in their themes; a fact which would not be lost on the Jews. All of them have strong calls to praise the Lord, especially for His mercy which endureth forever. This small psalm is no exception, but as the Jews sang it, they must have considered that the psalmist was looking forward beyond that one nation to a time when all nations would acknowledge the loving kindness of God and praise Him for it. If the weak brethren at Rome were fair and open-minded, they could not fail to be impressed by Paul's inclusion of a quotation from this psalm to support his call for unity. Although the Gentile believers might not be acquainted with the teaching of the psalm and its place in the Hallel, they could not fail to be impressed with its relevance in Paul's argument.

12 The quotation from Isa 11:10 LXX adds another dimension to what has already been quoted from the law and the psalms. The blessings made known by Paul have been drawn from the OT assurances that Jew and Gentile were in the mind of God for ultimate blessing. In this verse the blessings are seen to be associated with the person of Christ.

The chapter in Isaiah's prophecy from which the apostle takes the quotation is also millennial in character. It commences by referring to One who would come as a rod out of the root of Jesse. This is a reference to the One who would come from the royal line, a branch that would grow out of its roots and on Him would rest the Spirit of the Lord in wisdom, understanding, counsel, might and knowledge in the fear of the Lord.

Although Isa 11 has a millennial outlook, the fulfilment of the prophecy is recorded in the Gospels. When the Lord was baptised in the Jordan, the Spirit descended upon Him like a dove, thereby confirming what Isaiah had prophesied. His royal lineage had already been authenticated in the genealogy given by Matthew, but the voice from heaven and the baptism of the Spirit established beyond doubt that God's Anointed had come in accordance with the prophetic word.

The millennial outlook of Isa 11 notes the change in the animal kingdom. The wolf shall dwell with the lamb, the leopard shall lie down with the kid, the young lion and the calf and the fatling together, and a little child shall lead them, for the earth shall be in full knowledge of the Lord. All of these blessings are due to the establishment of the millennial kingdom by the One who is described in the chapter as the root out of Jesse.

The force of Paul's argument here would seem to be that if all nature will settle down in harmony under the reign of the Messiah, it should not be beyond believers in the present age to accommodate each other and respect each other's principles. Believers in the age of God's grace, indwelt by the Spirit of God, should not be less responsive than mankind in the millennial age. If harmony pervades that scene, it ought also to be in evidence in the church presently.

13 In vv. 5-6 Paul interjects a prayer to the God of patience and consolation. In this verse he raises another short prayer, "Now the God of hope fill you with all joy in believing". This is an important point in the epistle. The argument which began at 1:17 ends here. The subject of faith was introduced and its various facets were addressed throughout until it ends with the expression, "in believing". From v.14 the epistle is taken up with personal matters.

It is characteristic of the apostle to end his argument with a prayer. He does not upbraid anyone or threaten any who may not agree with him. Instead he calls upon the God of hope. Hope is a keyword in the epistle and it reflects the importance Paul attaches to the concept in the christian faith. Indeed, the reference to the God of hope, to the One who is the source of all the longings of the saints for the future, near or distant, is to the God of hope who is utterly reliable, who will never fail. His purposes, however long at times their fulfilment seems to take, can never finally be frustrated. Paul's prayer is therefore that the God of hope will fill with all joy (another of Paul's great concepts) and peace in believing. Joy in the heart soon expresses itself and while peace is an inward state, its presence within is soon read by others. These are two great graces for which Paul pleads from the God of hope and he does so in typical fashion. The measure was not to be a limited one, but one which would reflect the givingness of God, nothing less than being filled with all joy and peace.

The purpose of the prayer with which the great argument of the epistle finishes is "that ye may abound in hope, through the power of the Holy Ghost". Those he addressed were to be filled with hope. Anything less than that was not what Paul requested. The apostle knew that this could not be worked up. Human effort could not provide it, hence the final word is added, "through the power of the Holy Ghost". This great fundamental feature of the christian life could only become available to the saints as it came from God and was made good to them in the power of the Holy Spirit.

Notes

8 For "minister" (*diakonos*), see comments at 12:7.
9 Vine notes, "The double parallel in v.9 should be noticed. (a) 'for his mercy' is parallel to (a) 'for the truth of God'; (b) 'that the Gentiles might glorify God' is parallel to (b) 'that He might confirm the promises given unto the fathers'. This is given in chiasmic or crosswise form (a), (b), (b), (a).
10 Vincent notes the word "rejoice" *(euphranthēte)* is frequently in the NT of merry-making (Luke 15:23,24). See "fared sumptuously" (Luke 16:19).
12 "Ariseth to reign" is a paraphrase of the Hebrew, "stands as banner" (Vincent).
Bengel notes, "There is a pleasant contrast; the root is in the lowest place, the banner rises highest, so as to be seen even by the remotest nations".

VII. Conclusion (15:14-16:27)

1. *The Purpose in Writing – Paul's reasons*
15:14-21

> v.14 "And I myself also am persuaded of you, my brethren, that ye also are full of goodness, filled with all knowledge, able also to admonish one another.
> v.15 Nevertheless, brethren, I have written the more boldly unto you in some sort, as putting you in mind, because of the grace that is given to me of God,
> v.16 That I should be the minister of Jesus Christ to the Gentiles, ministering the gospel of God, that the offering up of the Gentiles might be acceptable, being sanctified by the Holy Ghost.
> v.17 I have therefore whereof I may glory through Jesus Christ in those things which pertain to God.
> v.18 For I will not dare to speak of any of those things which Christ hath not wrought by me, to make the Gentiles obedient, by word and deed,
> v.19 Through mighty signs and wonders, by the power of the Spirit of God; so that from Jerusalem, and round about unto Illyricum, I have fully preached the gospel of Christ.
> v.20 Yea, so have I strived to preach the gospel, not where Christ was named, lest I should build upon another man's foundation:
> v.21 But as it is written, To whom he was not spoken of, they shall see: and they that have not heard shall understand."

14 At the commencement of the epistle, Paul wrote concerning the report of the faith of the saints at Rome. This, he stated, "is spoken of throughout the whole world". From that point he had embarked on a detailed unfolding of the fundamentals of the faith. He had written firmly and without fear of contradiction. Because of the weighty matters he had raised, the saints at Rome might have thought that the apostle had not such a high opinion of them after all. If any fears of this nature had arisen, they are now dispelled, "I myself also am persuaded of you, my brethren, that ye are full of goodness…"

This is not the first time the apostle has mentioned his persuasion to the Romans. In the monumental statement of 8:38 he wrote, "For I am persuaded, that neither death, nor life…shall be able to separate us from the love of God, which is in Christ Jesus our Lord". To use the same word regarding the virtues of the brethren is indeed a remarkable acknowledgement of their spiritual condition. He states that he had taken it upon himself to address them with great plainness of speech to recognise and acknowledge that even of themselves they were full of goodness. They had not arrived at that stage as a result of help from him or any other apostle, they had attained to it personally, no doubt being ever ready to conform to the truth as it was made known to them.

They were replete in goodness. The word used, *mestos* (as at 1:29), conveys the thought of being full to the brim. The contrasting thoughts in the verse add considerable force to the apostle's high praise, "I myself am persuaded...ye yourselves are replete". Not only so but they were filled with all knowledge. As far as the facts of the faith were available to them they had embraced them in their entirety. The practical outcome of that was that they were able to admonish one another. The word "admonish" (*noutheteō*) in the context indicates an ability to teach and instruct. What they had embraced of christian truth they passed on to each other, thereby creating mutual growth.

15 This verse is a model of tact and courtesy. When he states that he is writing more boldly, he is not implying that the saints were deficient in some respects. If what he wrote was in some ways audacious, it was for the purpose of reminding them. The word *epanamimnēskō* (only here in NT) he uses for "putting you in mind" is perhaps better rendered, "As putting you in remembrance" (Robertson). This was not an unusual exhortation as far as Paul was concerned. To Timothy he wrote, "Wherefore I put thee in remembrance" (2 Tim 1:6), and to the Corinthians, "For this cause have I sent unto you Timotheus...who shall bring you into remembrance of my ways" (1 Cor 4:17). Peter also had a similar exercise, "Wherefore I will not be neglectful to put you always in remembrance of these things, though ye know them and be established in the present truth" (2 Pet 1:12). It is always beneficial to bring to the memory of others things which perhaps they know already but which they may be overlooking.

The verse does not say what Paul brought to the remembrance of the Romans. No doubt, however, the great truth of the gospel of God which he has set out in detail is what is in his mind. The verse suggests that the Romans had heard much of what he had written. The gospel they believed was in substance the same gospel Paul had set before them in detail. As Morris notes, "Paul was enlarging their horizons, but he was also reminding them of things they already knew". The epistle was not simply the outcome of a notion he had, but was the result of the grace given to him by God. In humility he states that it was of grace, and yet it did not lack authority, for it was given to him by God. He had a divine commission to write, but he did not boast about that; he was content to be seen as a vessel, taken up by the grace of God for service to His saints.

16 The grace which the apostle claims was given to him is now seen to be for the purpose that he should be a minister of Jesus Christ ("Christ Jesus", RV) to the Gentiles. In Paul's day there were many others who were ministers of Christ, as the opening words of several epistles confirm, but none could claim to be a minister (*leitourgos*) to the Gentiles. The service he had was special, having been given to him by the Lord. On two of the occasions in the Acts where his testimony is recorded, he refers to this special calling. He quotes the words of the Lord to him, "for I will send thee far hence unto the Gentiles" (Acts 22:21); again before king Agrippa, "Delivering thee from the people, and from the Gentiles, unto whom now I send thee" (Acts 26:17).

The apostle's choice of word, *leitourgos,* to describe his service should not be taken as having sacerdotal implications. He has already used the word to describe the officers of the "powers that be"; they are "God's ministers" (13:6). Of all the words available to the apostle to cover his unique service, the one he chose is obviously closest in meaning to the point he had before him, which was "the offering up of the Gentiles". C.E. Stuart suggests, "Special was this service and restricted to him. For just as the Levites had been waved as a wave offering before God by Aaron (Num 8:13), so the Gentiles are here viewed as offered to God, being sanctified by the Holy Ghost, Paul being the official instrument of Christ, the *leitourgos* for that purpose".

There is little doubt that Paul wanted to make clear that the proclamation of the gospel and the offering up of the Gentiles were solemn considerations. His part in it as the *leitourgos* was not to imply a liturgical input, like a priestly service, but to stress the sacredness of the situation. The word *hierourgeō* he uses to describe the ministering of the gospel, has the meaning "to act as a priest", but again, Paul's use is obviously sacrificial imagery for the purpose of emphasising the sacred character of what was being offered to God. There is no support here for a sacrificing priesthood. What is described in the verse is peculiar to Paul and he has no successors in it. Haldane remarks in this connection, "It is not the gospel which is here represented as a figurative sacrifice, but the Gentiles. Believing Gentiles are a sacrifice presented unto God by the apostle through the gospel. The gospel is the means by which the Gentiles are made a sacrifice. It is not in respect to the gospel that Paul considers himself figuratively a priest. It is with respect to the sacrifice, namely the believing Gentiles, who are fitted for presentation as a sacrifice by the gospel. There is now no sacrifice in the proper sense of the word, and the apostles were not priests, except as all believers are priests".

The term, "might be acceptable" is significant. The Gentiles became an acceptable sacrifice to God through faith in the gospel. They were sanctified by the Holy Ghost. He was the agent who set them apart for the pleasure of God. A similar thought is found in 2 Thess 2:13 where Paul reminds the saints that God had chosen them to salvation through sanctification of the Spirit and belief of the truth. Here Paul is stressing that the offering of the Gentiles is only acceptable through the gospel and sanctification of the Spirit. Those who seek to come to God by any other way are unacceptable to Him. There is no hope of finding acceptance by works of any kind. The Holy Spirit is not an agent where self-righteousness is involved.

17 Paul has a cause for boasting. The glorying which he speaks about here is the result of his involvement in the ministry of the gospel and the offering up of the Gentiles. In addition, he realises that he is the object of God's grace which excludes any thought of personal worth or achievement. What he is and what he has done is all a result of the grace and mercy of God, which set him apart for special service.

The glorying which is intimated is in Christ Jesus (RV). It is not in himself. It was the risen Lord who met him on the Damascus road and who in mercy enlisted him for service, especially to the Gentiles. This was the burden of the instruction to Ananias, "he is a chosen vessel unto me, to bear my name before the Gentiles, and kings, and the children of Israel" (Acts 9:15). This special favour was not wasted on Paul. He never forgot the unmerited favour which separated him. This is reflected in the statement, "through Christ Jesus in those things which pertain to God". It is things that are connected with the service of God that provide the entitlement to boast.

18 This verse adds to what has been stated in the previous one. There are certain things about which Paul will not speak. He does not say what they were, but he obviously considers that it is sufficient to classify them all under the phrase, "the things which Christ hath not wrought by me". If any aspect of the work was not done through him, he will not presume to speak about it. In v.20 he acknowledges that there were others who were labouring for Christ and he may be referring to that. If such is the case, he is stating categorically that he will not dare to speak of that. Taking credit for another servant's labours is not in his line of thought. In fact, he thoroughly deprecates such a practice.

Paul's claim "to make the Gentiles obedient" implies that it was what Christ did through him whereby Gentiles were obedient to the gospel. They believed it implicitly and it changed their lives. The effect of the new birth was a departure from former ways and a cleaving to a new order. Paul's input by word and deed was such that Gentiles were saved. It is about this that he will boast, but as to what others accomplished, he would not dare speak of it, lest any thought he was claiming credit he was not due.

19 The first half of the verse is an obvious continuation of the theme of v.18. As Christ worked through Paul by word and deed it was accompanied by signs and wonders and the power of the Spirit of God. Signs gave significance to miracles. They attested that God was conveying some message through the mighty deeds wrought by the apostles. The wonders which accompanied the signs were the effect they had on people. This is clearly indicated by Paul in 2 Cor 12:12, "Truly the signs of an apostle were wrought among you in all patience, in signs and wonders and mighty deeds". The ministry of the apostles was unique. Not only did God add His seal of approval to the message of the gospel but He authenticated the ministry of His messengers. In addition, the power of the Holy Ghost was in evidence. This additional comment would seem to indicate that the Spirit's power was manifest apart from signs and wonders. Perhaps the apostle was drawing attention to the effect of the message with its accompanying signs. There must have been many conversions, all of them remarkable in their own ways of the power of the Spirit to transform lives.

Paul now summarises what Christ had accomplished through him in his years of apostolic labours. He began at Jerusalem. His missionary journeys took him all the way round the eastern Mediterranean countries. The territory reached from Jerusalem to the borders of Illyricum, the eastern shores of the Adriatic. There is no mention of Illyricum in the Acts but there is scope in Luke's historical account for labours of Paul which are not mentioned in detail. The apostle's purpose in mentioning the extent of the area covered is obviously to make known that the commission given to him had been completed. He had not stopped short, either in his travels or in his preaching. He had "fully preached" the gospel of Christ. He is not saying that every country was saturated with the gospel. His strategy was to preach the Word and establish assemblies in the larger cities and towns, and from these the gospel would radiate to the far corners.

20 In apostolic times there was no need to move in to another servant's sphere of labour. The field was so vast and the challenges so great that the pioneering spirit carried the heralds of those days to fresh ground, ever reaching out with the gospel of God. The apostle states that he "strived to preach the gospel, not where Christ was named". Vincent suggests that the correct sense of Paul's striving is "to prosecute as a point of honour", meaning to carry the message forward as a project, carrying it on to a successful termination. As Denney remarks, "...he did it as a point of honour, not of rivalry". Stott, quoting Cranfield, states, "We understand his claim to have completed that trail-blazing, pioneer preaching of it, which he believed was his own apostolic mission to accomplish".

The apostle realised that the Lord had different vessels for different purposes. To the Corinthians he wrote, "I have planted, Apollos watered, but God gave the increase" (1 Cor 3:6). His own calling as apostle to the Gentiles was special. He did not need to build upon another man's foundation. He was content to leave others to their own work as answerable to their own Master.

21 In support of his ministry to the Gentiles, Paul quotes Isa 52:15. Although it is messianic in its scope, the apostle applies it to the service in which he was involved. As he stated in the previous verse, his ministry was not an extension of someone else's labours, but a special assignment given to him by the Lord. Isa 52:15 LXX is made to declare the fact that the Gentiles were in darkness until Paul took the gospel to them. The quotation rounds off the subject which Paul had dealt with at length, confirming that God had something in mind for the Gentiles as well as blessing for the Jews.

Although the end of Isa 52 should be taken with Isa 53, commencing with the words, "Behold my servant shall deal prudently", the chapter has a wonderful unfolding of the work and message of the herald, "How beautiful upon the mountains are the feet of him that bringeth good tidings, that publisheth peace; that bringeth good tidings of good". The herald is pictured as coming on the mountains to proclaim the coming reign of the Lord, words quoted by Paul in 10:15. The quotation in this verse emphasises the effect of the message as it fell on the ears of those who had never heard it before. The Gentiles are seen here to be the objects of prophecy. Although it has a future application, the scripture is fulfilled in measure in Paul's going to the Gentiles with the gospel.

Notes

14 Paul's confidence in the saints at Rome acknowledges that they were full of goodness (*agothōsunē*). The goodness here is practical, not moral. The expression of it, one to another, was full, not just an occasional good deed. Their knowledge was complete (*plēroō*), meaning they had an excellent comprehension of the truth, so much so that they were able to admonish one another.

15 The thought in "more boldly" may even be that Paul was saying that what he had written was daring, bordering on being audacious.

20 "So have I strived" is rendered by the RV as "Making it my aim". The verb can also signify "to be ambitious" (see 1 Thess 4:11, "make it your earnest ambition to be quiet").

21 Morris notes that this is the last of 64 direct quotations from Scripture in Romans in the list given in the UBS Greek New Testament. He admits that this list cannot be taken as the last word on the subject, for the boundary between a free quotation and the expression of one's thoughts in scriptural language is not easy to tie down. In *Things Written Aforetime* 52 direct quotations are noted and in the companion volume *Written For Our Learning*, 36 allusions are noted and commented upon.

2. The Request for Prayer – Paul's plans
15:22-33

> v.22 "For which cause also I have been much hindered from coming to you.
> v.23 But now having no more place in these parts, and having a great desire these many years to come unto you;
> v.24 Whensoever I take my journey into Spain, I will come to you: for I trust to see you in my journey, and to be brought on my way thitherward by you, if first I be somewhat filled with your company.
> v.25 But now I go unto Jerusalem to minister unto the saints.
> v.26 For it hath pleased them of Macedonia and Achaia to make a certain contribution for the poor saints which are at Jerusalem.
> v.27 It hath pleased them verily; and their debtors they are. For if the Gentiles have been made partakers of their spiritual things, their duty is also to minister unto them in carnal things.
> v.28 When therefore I have performed this, and have sealed to them this fruit, I will come by you into Spain.
> v.29 And I am sure that, when I come unto you, I shall come in the fulness of the blessing of the gospel of Christ.

v.30 Now I beseech you, brethren, for the Lord Jesus Christ's sake, and for the love of the Spirit, that ye strive together with me in your prayers to God for me;
v.31 That I may be delivered from them that do not believe in Judaea; and that my service which I have for Jerusalem may be accepted of the saints;
v.32 That I may come unto you with joy by the will of God, and may with you be refreshed.
v.33 Now the God of peace be with you all. Amen."

22 The apostle now gives the reason why he had not been able to visit Rome. The verse opens, "For which cause", or, "This is why", referring in particular to vv.18-19 where he mentions his ministry to the Gentiles. It was his commitment to carry the gospel to the Gentiles that had kept him from fulfilling his desire to visit the capital. It was on his heart to go there but there were areas of service still to be covered and his priority was to see that through to its completion. Undoubtedly the Lord was ordering his circumstances. It was of greater moment to Him that the ground was adequately covered by the gospel message and assemblies were established at critical points than that the apostle's wishes should be fulfilled. Paul recognised this situation. He states that he had been hindered often. The verb *enkoptō* literally means "to cut into", or "to impede one's course, cutting off the way", and therefore to hinder. The verb is in the imperfect tense, implying a succession of hindrances (Wuest). His circumstances were beyond Paul's control and he accepted them as from the Lord. Nevertheless, he wanted the saints at Rome to know that his desire to see them never abated, despite the hindrances.

23 The demand for Paul's special apostolic service in the eastern Mediterranean had its limits. He had done what was required of him and he was free to move on to new territory. There was no more "place" (*topos*, "scope" or "opportunity") in the areas he had covered. Others would no doubt follow and build upon the foundation he had laid. He states that his desire to visit Rome was one he had held for many years. It appeared now that he could fulfil his desire and come to Rome, his pioneering work elsewhere having been brought to completion.

24 The apostle presses on with the subject of v.23. His work being completed in the eastern Mediterranean area, he feels free to move into new territory. His horizon now is Spain, and on his way there he hopes to visit Rome. Not only does he have a desire to see the saints there but he hopes they will assist him to go forward to the goal he has in mind. He is still making it clear that he will not build on another man's foundation; he will pass through Rome and head towards Spain. The phrase, "brought on my way" renders the word *propempō* ("to send forward"). It supports the thought of providing fellowship, prayer, provision, and the necessary wherewithal for travel. It may be that the apostle considered Rome to be a suitable centre for future journeys and being on good terms with the saints there would relieve him of much concern for his own welfare.

The closing phrase of the verse is one of great tact. It may be understood as meaning that he will journey on to Spain "after he had satiated himself with their fellowship". He is not saying that he will exhaust the good of their fellowship and then move on; he is saying that no matter how long he waits in Rome, he will never come to the end of that. At the best, his satisfaction will only be in part, there will remain much more to be enjoyed on another occasion.

25 Having set before the saints at Rome his strong desire to be with them, Paul now reveals his plans for the immediate future. The present tense of the verb *poreuomai* suggests that he is on his way to Jerusalem. It is not a task that can be postponed, for the condition of the saints at Jerusalem makes it a top priority; he must go and minister to the believers. Many suggestions have been made as to why poverty should be so acute. Possibly it was as a result of famine, or the sharing of their worldly goods on conversion, or because of taking a stance for Christ in a hostile community. Whatever the cause, the saints needed help and Paul saw this as a compelling reason to return to Jerusalem instead of heading towards Rome and further afield.

26 The readiness of the saints of Macedonia and Achaia to enter into the circumstances of the poor saints at Jerusalem is most commendable. It was not simply a matter of having fellowship with the believers by easing their poverty a little. It was not a fixed sum money that was being sent. It was the expression of the willingness of the Christians throughout Macedonia and Achaia to give freely and bountifully, not a reluctant giving but the evidence of their good pleasure. The assemblies in these provinces were pleased to help. Their fellowship was cordial, and Paul recognised that for various reasons he had to be involved. The apostle's part in it all is not stated specifically. No doubt it was he who made the need known and possibly it was his ministry on the subject which created the exercise.

Wuest maintains that the contribution was to the poor of the saints at Jerusalem. They were not all poor. If that is the case, the poverty must have made severe demands on the resources of those who were not amongst the unfortunates, and additional help from outside was needed. Whatever the circumstances, it is refreshing to read of the good pleasure of the saints of Macedonia and Achaia to ease the burdens of the fellow-believers, even though they were far away and of a different culture altogether. It is little wonder that Paul boasted to the Corinthians "of the grace of God bestowed on the churches of Macedonia; How that in a great trial of affliction the abundance of their joy and their deep poverty abounded unto the riches of their liberality" (2 Cor 8:1,2).

27 Although the good pleasure of the saints of Macedonia and Achaia is evidence of remarkable grace and consideration on their part, they were not entirely free of obligation. They were debtors to the Jews and were therefore bound to repay the debt in some form or another. Historically, spiritual blessings were associated with Israel. God in His providence had decreed it that way. When the glad tidings of Christianity began to be told out, it was the Jews who were first embraced and who were the messengers chosen by God to make the gospel known. It was through their labours that the Gentiles came into the blessings of the gospel. There was therefore a debt to be repaid and it is gratifying to note that the churches of Macedonia and Achaia responded. Their resolve was a practical one, no doubt helped on by Paul's promptings, but it was a pleasing one nevertheless.

The choice of word to describe the ministry, *leitourgeō*, has been used by Paul in noun form several times (see v.16; 13:6). The use here of the verb implies a priestly connotation and suggests that Paul has lifted the gift of the Gentile churches on to a higher plane. There is of course no sacerdotal implication, but it does seem that the apostle wanted to underline the sacrifice that the Gentiles made. They did not give of their surplus, but as noted elsewhere, it was out of their poverty that they gave (2 Cor 8:2). They owed it to the Jews to make a good response. Spiritual blessings had come to them and to their credit they repaid the debt handsomely. The principle established in this verse has been one which has opened many hearts and purse strings down the years. Many who have received spiritual blessing have responded by repaying in material things. In this way the Lord has ensured that His servants are supplied with what is necessary for their maintenance, and at the same time giving others opportunities to share in the responsibilities of carrying on the work.

28 The apostle now lets the saints at Rome know that when he has accomplished his mission, he will go on by them on his way to Spain. There is no evidence that this plan ever materialised. Although he had a burning desire to open up new territories for the furtherance of the gospel, the only certain place he reached after Jerusalem was Rome. Since the epistle to the Philippians records how the gospel spread rapidly after Paul reached Rome, it is highly probable that others from Rome carried the message on to Spain, thereby fulfilling in measure Paul's exercise about that land.

The reference to sealing fruit to the saints of Macedonia and Achaia has brought out many suggestion from commentators. Some consider that Paul simply meant that when he had ensured that the poor saints in Jerusalem had received the gift, then he would go on to Spain. Vine thinks it indicates the sacredness in God's sight of ministering material assistance to the saints. He considers that the metaphor of sealing conveys the thought of a formal ratification of this ministry of the churches by his faithful delivery of the gift to the saints at Jerusalem. Hendrickson states that the expression "have sealed this fruit to them" is amongst the most controversial in Romans. He goes on, however, to give a lengthy explanation which he summarises, "when therefore the apostle now describes the contribution or collection as 'fruit', he probably means that it must be regarded as a product of the Gentiles' genuine faith and of their sincere gratitude for the willingness of the Jewish believers to share with them their faith in Christ".

Apart from all the different views expressed, the fruit Paul mentions is no doubt the collection, the evidence of grace working in the lives of the saints. When this was handed over by Paul and hopefully accepted (v.31), then the gift was sealed to the credit of the saints of Macedonia and Achaia. This may seem too simplistic, in view of all that the scholars have put forward, but what the Romans understood Paul to mean seems to be a factor that is often ignored.

29 The RV renders the opening words of this verse, "And I know that…". Vine concludes that *oida* means that Paul knew intuitively, he was well aware. Haldane considers that if Paul knew he would come to Rome in the fulness of the blessing of Christ he would know it only from God. Either way there is indicated a note of certainty in what the apostle says. In all his service for Christ he had enjoyed His blessing and he was sure that his experience of the Lord acting through him would be no different when he came to Rome. In the providence of God the way the apostle would arrive in Rome was not what he was considering when he wrote. Nevertheless, the fact that he arrived as a prisoner did not alter the situation, he came in the fulness of the blessing of Christ.

There is not much good manuscript support for "of the gospel" as in the AV. The fulness of the blessing of Christ, however, is all-inclusive and the mention of the gospel is not out of place in the context. The presence of the apostle in Rome, either as a free man in his own hired house (Acts 28:30), or as a prisoner must be a blessing for the saints. What was invested in Paul and what he had acquired by way of experience was quite unique to him. Associated with him there was wealth of spiritual blessing, even to the point of overflowing, which had to be for the good of every saint who was open to receive it.

30 While it is fairly common for Paul to request prayer from the believers in the various assemblies to which he wrote, it is significant that there is no request for prayer in 1 Corinthians or Galatians. The probable reason was the need for both companies to get before the Lord on their own behalf and sort out their many deviations from the truth. Such a situation did not exist at Rome, and Paul can therefore make his plea to the saints to strive together with him in prayer to God.

The appeal is qualified on two grounds. It is "by our Lord Jesus Christ" (RV), and "by the love of the Spirit" (RV). Bringing the Lord and the Holy Spirit into his plea in this fashion is unusual for Paul. The reason for doing so may be to give the utmost authority to the request and to stress the love which the Holy Spirit had brought about in the believers. Since Paul is appealing for prayer in its warmest and truest sense, bringing in all three members of the Godhead is most significant; certainly it underlines the truth of the Trinity. The believers were to "strive together" with him. Praying for Paul would be a spiritual conflict as there were forces of darkness ranged against him. If he needed to agonise in prayer, any others who were sharers in his exercise would require to engage in prayer with the same fervour.

Anything less than a striving would not do for Paul. Indeed formal prayer would neither reflect the Lord's authority nor the love which the Spirit had kindled in the saints. The prayers are "to God for me". A similar request is made to the Thessalonians, "Finally brethren, pray for us, that the word of the Lord may have free course and be glorified, even as it is with you: and that we may be delivered from unreasonable and wicked men" (2 Thess 3:1,2).

31 The subject of the prayer requested is now made known. The apostle desired to be delivered from the disobedient in Judaea. He is not asking to be rescued from their clutches after they had taken him, but to be kept out of their hands altogether. He had the great burden in his heart of going up to Jerusalem and he would go regardless of the dangers. Nevertheless, he knew the perils which would confront him and it is deliverance from these that he sought.

Paul's request is in two parts. Firstly he desires that he might be delivered from "them that do not believe". The RV renders *tōn apeithountōn* as "them that are disobedient", meaning the Jews who had spurned the grace of God in the gospel and were bitterly opposed to those who had embraced it. At 10:21 the apostle had already drawn attention to Israel's disobedience and their refusal to be subject to the will of God, pointing out in a quotation from Isa 65:2 that they were always a disobedient and gainsaying people. The rebellion against God found its expression in the persecution of believers and it was deliverance from this ever-present danger which Paul sought.

The second part of the request is that his ministration for the saints at Jerusalem might be accepted. It was not a certainty that the Jewish believers would accept help from Gentiles. Denney considers that they might even regard the contribution as a bribe, in return for which Paul's opposition to the law would be condoned and the equal standing of his upstart churches in the kingdom of God acknowledged. It was by no means certain that it would be taken as what it was, a pledge of brotherly love. Whether the true state at Jerusalem was as fraught with danger as Denney suggests, is open to question, but there is little doubt that there was opposition to Paul's stand. In particular, the references in the Galatian epistle (see 3:1,17; 5:1-4; 6:12) confirm that not all Jews who had embraced Christianity were sympathetic with Paul's views.

32 The apostle's desire, expressed here, hopes for a thwarting of the opposition of the Jews. If this happened, his coming to the saints at Rome would then be one of joy. This would be the ultimate answer to the prayers of the believers. Not only so, if those in need in Jerusalem accepted the help sent by the Gentiles, this would crown his joy. His journey to Jerusalem would not have been in vain. With the personal danger over, and his ministration accepted he would be refreshed and find rest. The "rest" he speaks of is a mutual one. It was not for himself only, but a rest shared with the saints. He anticipates a time of physical and spiritual refreshment, shared with the believers at Rome.

His desires are prefixed by an acknowledgement of the will of God. If it is God's will, his coming to Rome in joy would come to pass. As it was, the will of God ordained it differently from what Paul envisaged. He did come to Rome, and no doubt with joy, but not with total freedom. He arrived in chains, but in the goodness of God he was spared for a while to minister to all who came to see him and benefit from his ministry.

33 The little prayer to the God of peace invokes peace for the saints at Rome. Paul has already appealed to the God of patience (15:5) and the God of hope (15:13). Now he thinks of the tranquillity, security and serenity which should be the portion of all believers, and so he calls upon God who is the source of peace to supply it. In what is sometimes referred to as the Lord's last will and testament, He said to His disciples, "Peace I leave with you, my peace I gave unto you; not as the world giveth, give I unto you" (John 14:27). As far as the world's peace is concerned, it means the absence of war and strife, and sometimes to obtain it a person has to be isolated from society, or insulated from outside influences to the point of being a recluse. Peace according to the Scriptures is not like that. It stresses right relationships between God and man and between man and man. Peace in the NT is a completely new relationship which has been brought in through the work of Christ. Haldane remarks, "In the OT God is called 'the Lord of hosts', but in the NT, having made peace by the blood of the cross of His Son, He is pleased to call Himself 'the God of peace' ".

This is not the only occasion where Paul calls on the God of peace. Writing to the Thessalonians, he called upon the very God of peace to sanctify them wholly (1 Thess 5:23). And to the Philippians he gave a reminder that if they put certain christian graces into practice, the God of peace would be with them (Phil 4:9). At the close of Rom 15 the call upon the God of peace follows the apostle's plea for prayers on his behalf. Usually, peace forms part of the salutations at the beginning of his epistles, but here it is a closing note. Although the appeal was on behalf of the saints at Rome, it is clear that the one who made the plea needed the peace of God every bit as much as they did.

Notes

23 The region to which Paul was referring is not clear in his reference to "parts" (*klima*, "a region", "a district"). This is the only occurrence in the NT of *epipothian*, (*epipothia* "a strong desire").

24 The second reference to "journey" (*diaporeuomenos*) in the verse has the prefix *dia*, meaning "journey through". It is clear that Paul's plans at this stage were to pass through Rome on his way to Spain.

"Filled" (*empiplēmi*) is "to be satisfied" or "satiated".

25 "Minister" (*diakoneō*, "to assist", "to attend upon") underlines the purpose of his visit to Jerusalem.

26 The "contribution" (*koinonia*, "fellowship") or gift was proof of the common love between believers despite cultural differences.

29 "Fulness" (*plērōma*, "full measure") insists that Paul would be there not only in presence, but in an overflow of blessing.

30 "I beseech you" (*parakaleō*) strongly implores the saints to strive together with him in prayer.

3. *The Cause for Prayer – Paul's greetings*
   16:1-27

Although there are some scholars and commentators who consider that ch.16 was not part of the original epistle, there are many who are persuaded otherwise. The various arguments for and against, which stem principally from manuscript differences, are set out in the many commentaries which have been written on the epistle to the Romans. Some of these views are briefly considered in the introduction to this work under the section "The integrity of the epistle".

Regarding the doxology at 16:25-27, which is found in some manuscripts at the end of ch.14 and in others at the end of ch.15, Wm Kelly states, "It is well-known that between chs.14 and 15 certain old editors inserted the doxology of 16:25-27. But there is no sufficient reason to disregard the weightiest witnesses of the ancient text, confirmed as it is by the internal evidence, which give the passage at the close of the epistle".

Concerning the subject matter of ch.16, views have been expressed that a list of greetings may mean something to certain people at the time of writing, but later such greetings are meaningless. The chapter, however, is not made up entirely of greetings, as the simple analysis given by Denney shows. He states that it consists of five distinct parts,

1. The recommendation of Phebe to the church (vv.1-2)
2. A series of greetings from Paul himself (vv.3-16)
3. A warning against false teachers (vv.17-20)
4. A series of greetings from companions of Paul (vv.21-23)
5. Doxology (vv.24-27)

If the view is held that ch.16 is not part of the original epistle, the question then arises, "What epistle did it conclude and to whom was Phebe commended?" If, as is held by many, and with good reason, this is the finest doxology that Paul ascribed in the NT, what epistle caused him to render such praise? Considered from another standpoint, what epistle takes precedence over the Romans as far as breadth or depth of truth is concerned? If ch.16 does not belong to the end of Romans, the alternatives are not convincing. It is more reasonable to accept the place that it has in the AV which is not without ample manuscript and internal evidence to support it.

v.1 "I commend unto you Phebe our sister, which is a servant of the church which is at Cenchrea:
v.2 That ye receive her in the Lord, as becometh saints, and that ye assist her in whatsoever business she hath need of you: for she hath been a succourer of many, and of myself also.
v.3 Greet Priscilla and Aquila my helpers in Christ Jesus:
v.4 Who have for my life laid down their own necks: unto whom not only I give thanks, but also all the churches of the Gentiles.
v.5 Likewise greet the church that is in their house. Salute my wellbeloved Epaenetus, who is the firstfruits of Achaia unto Christ.
v.6 Greet Mary, who bestowed much labour on us.
v.7 Salute Andronicus and Junia, my kinsmen, and my fellowprisoners, who are of note among the apostles, who also were in Christ before me.
v.8 Greet Amplias my beloved in the Lord.
v.9 Salute Urbane, our helper in Christ, and Stachys my beloved.
v.10 Salute Apelles approved in Christ. Salute them which are of Aristobulus' household.
v.11 Salute Herodion my kinsman. Greet them that be of the household of Narcissus, which are in the Lord.
v.12 Salute Tryphena and Tryphosa, who labour in the Lord. Salute the beloved Persis, which laboured much in the Lord.
v.13 Salute Rufus chosen in the Lord, and his mother and mine.
v.14 Salute Asyncritus, Phlegon, Hermas, Patrobas, Hermes, and the brethren which are with them.
v.15 Salute Philologus, and Julia, Nereus, and his sister, and Olympas, and all the saints which are with them.
v.16 Salute one another with an holy kiss. The churches of Christ salute you.
v.17 Now I beseech you, brethren, mark them which cause divisions and offences contrary to the doctrine which ye have learned; and avoid them.
v.18 For they that are such serve not our Lord Jesus Christ, but their own belly; and by good words and fair speeches deceive the hearts of the simple.
v.19 For your obedience is come abroad unto all men. I am glad therefore on your behalf: but yet I would have you wise unto that which is good, and simple concerning evil.
v.20 And the God of peace shall bruise Satan under your feet shortly. The grace of our Lord Jesus Christ be with you. Amen.
v.21 Timotheus my workfellow, and Lucius, and Jason, and Sosipater, my kinsmen, salute you.
v.22 I Tertius, who wrote this epistle, salute you in the Lord.
v.23 Gaius mine host, and of the whole church, saluteth you. Erastus the chamberlain of the city saluteth you, and Quartus a brother.
v.24 The grace of our Lord Jesus Christ be with you all. Amen.
v.25 Now to him that is of power to stablish you according to my gospel, and the preaching of Jesus Christ, according to the revelation of the mystery, which was kept secret since the world began,
v.26 But now is made manifest, and by the scriptures of the prophets, according to

> the commandment of the everlasting God, made known to all nations for the obedience of faith:
> v.27 To God only wise, be glory through Jesus Christ for ever. Amen."

1 Apart from what is recorded in two verses of scripture, nothing more is known about Phebe. What Paul has stated about her, however, has placed her among the great women of the Bible. To have one's name written into the word of God is a high honour in itself, but to be known also as a servant of the church and a succourer of many is praise indeed.

The word *sunistēmi*, chosen by Paul to commend Phebe has a worthy note about it. The apostle used it at 5:8, "But God commendeth his love toward us, in that, while we were yet sinners, Christ died for us". There is certainly no lack of worthiness in the commendation of God and it is equally certain that Paul's introduction of Phebe to the Romans represented her as a worthy sister in the Lord. It is, nevertheless, a letter of commendation. Not perhaps as formal as those mentioned in 2 Cor 3:1, but it was in that category. Such letters ought still to be part of church practice, as they commend the bearers and relieve the receivers of any anxiety as to who should share the freedom of assembly fellowship.

The sister is described as a servant (*diakonos*) of the church. This is the only occurrence in the NT where the word is used of a woman. There is nothing special about the word which would support the practice in ecclesiastical circles of creating the office of deaconess. Phebe was a servant of the church at Cenchrea. What form that service took is not revealed, other than the fact that she was a succourer of many. The word "succourer" has been thought to contain an idea of legal representation and it may be that Phebe was in such a position of prominence that would permit her to act for others. There is, however, a measure of conjecture about this and perhaps it is better to leave Phebe as a succourer of many and of Paul also.

2 The apostle now states the purpose of Phebe's commendation, "That ye receive her in the Lord". Associating the Lord with Phebe's reception means that He has to be taken into account also. The sister cannot be dismissed lightly or treated in an offhand fashion if the Lord's interest in her is made known. Not only so, but bringing in the Lord gives character to His servant, something the Romans doubtless would be swift to acknowledge.

Phebe was to be received "as becometh saints", or as the RV renders the phrase, "worthily of the saints". This can be understood of the worthy form of reception expected of the Romans, or of the worthiness of the reception Phebe deserved. The fact that it was to be "worthily of the saints" puts the highest standard on anything associated with the Lord's people. In effect, nothing is too good for them and only the best will do for them. So it is here, giving and receiving call for the highest response in Phebe's reception.

The charge laid upon the Romans is that they assist her in whatever business she had need of them. Morris suggest that the verb *paristēmi*, being intransitive, means "to stand by to help". The kind of business in which Phebe was engaged is not stated, but the Romans were charged to stand by her, to support her in whatever business she would pursue.

The character of Phebe is now stated. She had been a succourer of many. The word *prostatis* ("succourer") indicates that she was a person of some standing. She had been a protector of many, although how she did it is not stated. Nevertheless, the interests of others had been taken up by her, and even the apostle had benefited from her care. It was only right therefore that when Phebe needed assistance herself that it should be made available to her in good measure. This seems to be the obvious reason why Paul should speak up so strongly in her support. The opportunity was being given to the saints at Rome to pay back to this sister what others had not been able to do. If they did it "worthily of the saints" she would be handsomely rewarded.

3 The first of Paul's greetings is for Priscilla and Aquila, described here as "my helpers in Christ Jesus". In the vv. 3-15 there are 26 names and the mention of two believers who are not named. There are ten women mentioned and 16 men. The only two who can be identified with certainty are Priscilla and Aquila. Whether some of these believers were from Ephesus, as is held by some commentators, is not vital; the fact remains that they were all known to Paul and appreciated by him for various reasons. The list contains the names of Jews and Gentiles, the kind of men and women who formed the assemblies in apostolic times.

Priscilla and Aquila are a most intriguing couple. They are mentioned six times in the NT and always together. The AV names Priscilla first on four occasions and many have deduced from this that she was superior in some ways to her husband. Be that as it may, as a couple they were outstanding in their witness for the Lord. Like Paul, Aquila was a tentmaker, and it is possibly this fact that added something to their close association through life. The other five mentions of them are Acts 18:2,18,26; 1 Cor 16:19; 2 Tim 4:19. A study of these passages will yield ample reward for the time and labour expended.

Paul states here that Priscilla and Aquila were his helpers (*sunergous*) in Christ Jesus. The word *sunergos* signifies "a fellow-helper". The term is always used to describe those who worked together in the gospel. That this is so is clearly seen in the labours of Paul with this couple. How much they benefited from being so long in Paul's company at Ephesus is reflected in the help they were to Apollos. Although he was "mighty in the scriptures", they took him aside "and expounded unto him the way of God more perfectly (accurately)" (Acts 18:26).

4 Paul's expression of personal indebtedness to them is couched in figurative language. Colourful though it may seem, the action behind it can well be imagined. This couple had exposed themselves to danger on Paul's account. How and where are not recorded but since Paul was a marked man amongst his fellow-Jews, there must have been many occasions, apart from those recorded in the Scriptures, when he was sorely abused.

The time when Priscilla and Aquila stood by Paul must have been some years before. If all the churches gave thanks for Paul's deliverance, some time must have elapsed for the news of it to spread round the churches of the Gentiles. This no doubt refers to assemblies in regions of Gentile occupation. The believers in these churches were indebted to Priscilla and Aquila for what they had done for Paul, and like the apostle were grateful to them. There is an inference in this that the Gentile assemblies were dependent on Paul to a great extent for his ministry and the fact that he was delivered from danger was of great personal benefit to them. If they had lost him, the source of much spiritual help would have gone also.

5 There are two references to a church being in the house of Priscilla and Aquila, here and in 1 Cor 16:19. Since there is no record of a church having a special building until about the third century it is likely that the saints gathered in dwelling houses large enough to accommodate those in fellowship in a locality. There was a church in the house of Nymphas (Col 4:15) and there was also one in the house of Philemon (Philem 2). In apostolic times it was a fearless witness to the faith to link one's dwelling with the church of God. It is apparent that Priscilla and Aquila took that into account and considered the reproach worthwhile.

The well-beloved Epaenetus is not mentioned elsewhere in Scripture. The fact that he was the firstfruits of Paul's preaching in Achaia marks him out as special in Paul's sight. The designation "firstfruits in Achaia" seems to conflict with the statement of 1 Cor 16:15 that the house of Stephanas was the firstfruits in Achaia. Plummer considers that Epaenetus and Stephanas were converted at the same time and they were both therefore firstfruits. However, the RV, supported by good manuscript authority, gives "firstfruits of Asia" here, in which case there is no conflict between the two claims. Both bear witness to Paul's joy in recounting those who turned to Christ for salvation under his preaching.

6 Manuscripts differ regarding Mary's nationality. Some give the Jewish form and others the Latin. Whether Jewess or Gentile there is no means of linking her with any of the women in the Bible of the same name. She has, nevertheless, a wonderful commendation. The AV rendering is that she "bestowed much labour on us". The RV and other versions give "much labour on you". Assuming that "you" is the correct reading, the Romans would be very well aware of the fact that she worked hard for them and it must have been gratifying that the report of her labours had reached Paul and that he had made special mention of them. It is significant that much praise is given by the apostle to brethren and sisters who in the estimation of many would be classed as nondescript. This serves as a great encouragement to others who have no claim to fame or notoriety but are appreciated for what they do as humble servants of the Lord.

7 Andronicus and Junia were probably husband and wife. Many commentators (taking the second name as Junias) hold this view, although some consider they were both males. Paul's claims that they were kinsfolk, which may mean that they were fellow-Jews or relatives. Again, there is diversity of opinion on this point and it is impossible to settle it since there is no other reference to them in the Scriptures. The fact that Paul referred to them as his fellow-prisoners has led many to judge that they were both men, since it is not as likely that women were imprisoned. As there is no indication of when or where they were incarcerated, it does not follow automatically that they were imprisoned with Paul. It may mean that they shared the same fate for reasons similar to those which resulted in Paul's imprisonment. The fact that they paid such a price for testimony's sake is sufficient reason for Paul to pay tribute to them.

To be of note amongst the apostles does not mean that Andronicus and Junia were apostles. Many hold that they were, some going as far as to say that Junia, a woman, was an apostle of note also, or at least, an outstanding woman amongst the apostles. In the absence of corroborative evidence from the NT of women being in the apostolic band it is better to take the comment as it is in the verse. These two believers were of note amongst the apostles. They were highly esteemed by the apostles but for what reason is not stated.

Paul adds that they were in Christ before him. Since the apostle was converted within a year or two of Pentecost, this reference must put these two amongst the earliest believers. Perhaps they were saved at Pentecost, or they were amongst the great multitudes of men and women who were "added to the Lord" in Jerusalem when great signs and wonders were being done by Peter and the apostles (Acts 5:12-14).

8 There is no reference in the Scriptures to this man Ampliatus but according to historical records, the name occurs several times in connection with the imperial household at Rome. He was probably a slave, perhaps even a high-ranking slave, but over and above that he was in Paul's estimation, "my beloved in the Lord". There were thousands of slaves of every nationality in Rome and vast numbers of these were engaged in work in and around Caesar's palace. The identities of the majority were never known and since they were dispensable, that did not really matter much to Caesar. An amazing feature of Paul's list here is that out of the great multitude of unfortunates, he can select many by name and commend them for their labours for the Lord. Ampliatus comes into this category. To Paul he is "beloved in the Lord", no doubt having commended himself to the apostle at some stage, and in some way, demonstrating christian graces which were endearing.

9 Lightfoot on Philippians makes an interesting comment. He writes, "The name Urbanus ('Urbane' AV) is as common as Ampliatus. On an inscription of AD 115, Urbanus and Ampliatus occur next to each other in a list of imperial freedmen connected with the mint. The name 'Stachys' is comparatively rare. Yet at least one person with the name held an important office in the household close to the time when Paul wrote". Since, however, there is no further reference to these two men in the Scriptures, to identify them with historical records has a high degree of uncertainty about it.

From what Paul says about Urbanus, he seems to have been well-known as a fellow-worker (*sunergos*). The plural pronoun "our" suggests that the Romans knew him to be an active man amongst them in the Lord's work. He is not given the same commendation as Stachys who, like several others, seems to have endeared himself to the apostle.

10 It is significant that the apostle chooses another term when he considers Apelles. His greeting to him notes that he was approved in Christ. The word *dokimos* ("approved") has many shades of meaning attached to it. The verb form, *dokimazō* ("to put to the test", "to approve") almost always in the NT implies that the test is victoriously surmounted, the proved are also approved, the tried have stood the test. Being approved, the persons will be what they always have been. So it is that Apelles is approved. He has been tested in various ways, not to find out if there were shortcomings, but to prove what he really was, a genuine servant of the Lord. Vine makes the point that the phrase "in Christ" suggests that this approval had an essential association with his heavenly calling.

The name Aristobulus features in history as a grandson of Herod the Great. According to Lightfoot this man retired to Rome and ended his days quietly there. He was friendly with the emperor Claudius and it is thought that he transferred his slaves to him. Although they then belonged to the emperor they retained their former master's name and would be referred to as "the household of Aristobulus", even though they served in the imperial palace. In the absence of information in the Scriptures about Aristobulus and his household, what history has to say can only be considered as a possible explanation. What is gleaned from the historians, Josephus and others, is certainly interesting, but cannot be taken as the interpretation of the passage. What is of greater interest is that in this household there were those who were obviously believers and whose welfare, spiritual and otherwise, was the concern of the apostle to the Gentiles.

11 It may be that Herodion was a Jew of the house of Aristobulus. He was to Paul a kinsman, most likely a fellow-Jew and undoubtedly a believer. He was either a slave or a freedman, but sufficiently well-known to the apostle to deserve his greeting.

The household of Narcissus comes into the same category as the household of Aristobulus. Lightfoot states that there was a powerful freedman by the name of Narcissus whose wealth was proverbial, whose influence with Claudius was unbounded and who was immersed in the intrigues of his reign. He was put to death by Agrippina shortly after the accession of Nero, about three years before the epistle to the Romans was written. As was usual in such cases, his household would pass into the hands of the emperor, still retaining the name Narcissus. If this is the household to which Paul is referring, then there were believers amongst them and to them he sends his greetings. Since these people had been taken from their homelands, possibly never to return, it must have been a great encouragement to them to consider their blessings "in the Lord".

12 The three sisters mentioned in this verse have been the subject of many addresses and exhortations down the years. Tryphena and Tryphosa, probably two sisters in the flesh, even twins, have by the meaning of their names and the intensity of their labours provided much material to teachers and much encouragement to many who have been challenged by what Paul has noted concerning them. It seems their names mean "delicate" and "dainty" and when this is associated with the toil suggested in the word "labour" it does appear that Paul is engaging in a little irony. It is worthy of note that their toil was "in the Lord", and it is certain that whatever work was done in His name will earn its due reward.

The beloved Persis comes into the same category as Tryphena and Tryphosa. The present tense used with the two sisters indicates that their toil was going on. The use of the past tense with Persis would seem to indicate that her days of toiling were over. Perhaps she was old or sick, but regardless of that, she had earned Paul's commendation for she had laboured much in the Lord. Labouring in the Lord suggests that what these sisters did was unto Him and for His glory. Perhaps they were tireless in their support of the gospel and in work amongst the saints. What was done is not mentioned, but enough is said to indicate that doing the Lord's work was their main occupation, whatever else they did to maintain themselves and others connected with them.

13 Although Rufus was a fairly common slave name in apostolic times, the fact that there was a Rufus mentioned in Mark 15:21, makes it possible that the same person is in view. In Luke's account of events leading up to the crucifixion of the Lord, he records that the cross was laid on a man, Simon a Cyrenian. It is not an account of a man who offered to carry the cross, he was compelled to carry it, as Luke notes, "on him they laid the cross that he might bear it after Jesus".

Mark's account of the crucifixion scene states that the Roman soldiery compelled one, Simon a Cyrenian, to bear the cross: there follows what may be taken as a casual remark, "the father of Alexander and Rufus". From the way Mark inserts the reference, it seems that the relationship was so well-known he did not need to expand upon it. The conclusion may be drawn that being compelled to carry the cross had left an indelible impression upon Simon and his sons also.

The question arises, What about Simon's wife, the mother of Alexander and Rufus? Had she been won over? The possibilities are strong that the answer to the question is found in our verse, "Salute Rufus, chosen in the Lord, and his mother and mine". Much could be suggested from the phrase, "chosen in the Lord", although it most likely means a special choice for a special service. There is no conjecture required, however, for determining the mother's role – she was a mother to Paul, and for that care somewhere in the past he records his grateful acknowledgement.

14 There are five names listed in this verse. These believers are not mentioned elsewhere and so nothing is known about them. Some of the names were common to slaves and some to freedom. Either way it says much for Paul's appreciation of their standing as Christians that he should mention them by name regardless of their position in society. That there were brethren with them seems to indicate another house church. Even in apostolic times, Rome was a large city and believers might have been restricted by difficulties in travel to do much more than seek fellowship in particular localities. Their position, however, was known to Paul even though he had never been in Rome. This seems to suggest that he was kept informed of the situation by others who travelled freely in business. Roads were good in Roman times and merchants moved freely on them between cities. In this way Christians carried the gospel and Christianity spread rapidly. In the same way news from one church to another was carried freely also.

15 The mention of another five persons and all the saints that were with them suggests a christian group. This may have been another example of a church meeting in a house, although it may simply refer to believers in a locality. Much has been made of the meaning of the name Philologus, "a lover of the word", or "a lover of discourse". Whether the name given to him was in some sense prophetic is open to conjecture. Whether or not he was what his name suggests, the thought is interesting and certainly of spiritual value when applied in teaching. The fact, however, that Paul remembered names and the relationships of brethren and sisters and the saints associated with some of them proves the truth of what he wrote to the Corinthians, "that which cometh upon me daily, the care of all the churches" (2 Cor 11:28).

16 The holy kiss was a greeting between members of the same sex. It is mentioned in other places in the NT (see 1 Cor 16:20; 2 Cor 13:12; 1 Thess 5:26). The kiss was to be holy, a safeguard from abuse. The virtue of the kiss as a greeting indicates a warm sincere relationship. If it deteriorates into a formal action the greeting it is meant to convey becomes meaningless. The real test in apostolic times was the use of the holy kiss where there was a wide range of social differences. There could be a real strain between master and slave if the holy kiss was introduced. This situation of course was well appreciated by Paul, but no doubt he suggested it to break down barriers and bring believers to a common level when they were gathered together in assembly fellowship. His teaching elsewhere acknowledged the difference between masters and servants and so regulated the believers outside church gatherings, but inside all were alike, brethren and sisters before the Lord.

In the greeting, "all the churches of Christ salute you", Paul does not say which churches are included. His mixing with believers from many parts would certainly lay the basis for this greeting. Fellowship with saints would open up discussion and lead to greetings being exchanged and sent to the various assemblies scattered throughout the provinces.

The expression "churches of Christ" is not found elsewhere in the NT. Perhaps Paul wanted to stress that all the churches, regardless of their size, spiritual condition, or where they were, belonged to Christ and were all precious to Him. His interest in His church is cogently stated in Eph 5:25-27, "Christ also loved the church, and gave himself for it, That he might sanctify and cleanse it with the washing of water by the word, that he might present it to himself a glorious church, not having spot, or wrinkle, or any such thing".

17 There are some who think the warning of vv. 17-18 is an interpolation, since it seems to intrude abruptly into the context of greetings to the saints. Since, however, Paul had just referred to the churches of Christ and greetings sent from them, it is in keeping with his love for all the believers represented, to warn the Romans of any teachers who would cause divisions amongst them. The apostle therefore makes an appeal, "Now I beseech you brethren". It is not a command but a plea to the brethren to consider seriously what he was saying. There were troublemakers abroad and it was essential that they should be marked out for what they were, teachers of false doctrine. The word *skopeō* ("mark") means to keep a close watch. It is found in Phil 3:17, "Brethren, be followers together of me, and *mark* them which walk so as ye have us for an example". In that passage the marking leads to emulation and, being in a good sense, the exercise is highly commendable. If the marking here were to result in emulation, the outcome would be catastrophic.

Because of the definite article before "divisions and occasions of stumbling" it is thought that the propagators of error were fairly well-known. What is taught is not stated, but it was serious enough to be branded, "contrary to the doctrine". Even as Paul wrote to the Romans, the NT canon was not complete and little perhaps was in wide circulation. There was obviously a body of teaching and it is to this that Paul refers. The things that the saints had heard from him and from other apostles and from apostolic delegates were absorbed and passed on to others. Initially they learned from oral ministry but as time passed, what was made known in that way was committed to writing. It is significant, however, that Paul refers to the doctrine which they had learned.

The exhortation to mark, or turn away and keep away from false teachers seems harsh and many have looked upon Paul's advice in that way. Some have considered that a softer approach could perhaps win over false teachers and bring them back into line with the truth, but Paul makes no concessions of this nature. There are many issues at stake. Error can lead away the unwary. As Paul notes, those who advance false teaching cause divisions and are not concerned about the havoc that may result from their activities.

18 Although the purveyors of error seemed to be well-known, the apostle goes on to make his warning apply to all such. They are described in strong terms. They refuse to serve the Lord Christ. The word for service is *douleuō* ("to render bond-service"). They were slaves but they refuse to give bond-service to Christ; His authority is spurned. Paul is clear, they serve only their own appetites, meaning most likely that they were occupied with self-indulgence.

Despite their egotistical attitude, the false teachers were exceedingly plausible. They used "good words" (*chrēstologia*, occurring nowhere else in the NT). Vine states, "It simulates goodness". Morris, quoting Shedd, "It is the language of a good man hypocritically used by a bad man". These false teachers made fair speeches. They were plausible flatterers, who with fine style conveyed to their hearers that they were genuine and reasonable teachers.

Paul makes it clear that there were certain believers who were vulnerable. They are classed in the AV as "simple" (*akakos,* rendered in the RV as "innocent"). It means "without guile", or even "naive". They are the ones who need to be protected as their trusting nature leaves them open to corruption which comes with the teaching of false doctrine. They are not capable of making fine distinctions between what is right and what is wrong and they are therefore easy prey for the flatterers who make smooth and fair speeches. The surest way of combating error is to know the truth of the word of God, but the simple have limited learning capacities and require to be watched over carefully by those who exercise a care for the flock of God.

19 There seems to have been a readiness with the Romans to accept the gospel and its associated teachings. This appears to be what Paul is acknowledging in his reference to their obedience. The warning of the previous verses singled out the simple as being vulnerable to the doctrines of the false teachers. This may be the theme of this verse too, despite Paul's every confidence in the Romans. Until now he had no fears that they would be carried away with unsound teaching. Indeed the report of their obedience to the truth, as made known to them, had "come abroad"; it had reached out to all. This was an excellent testimony and one which gladdened Paul greatly. He makes that known, "I am glad therefore on your behalf", or as the RV renders the phrase, "I rejoice therefore over you".

Paul's desire for the Romans is twofold. He wants them to be wise unto that which is good and simple unto that which is evil. The word "simple" (*akeraios,* "unmixed", "unadulterated") is used of wine or milk not mixed with water, or of metal with no alloy. When used of people it carries the meaning of sincerity where motives are clean and pure. It occurs again in Matt 10:16, "harmless as doves", and in Phil 2:15 where it is rendered "harmless". There are three interesting words in Phil 2:15, "blameless", free from censure before men; "faultless"' free from censure before God; "harmless" free from censure before self. Morris concludes with a quotation which Hodge took from Grotius and calls it a neat summing up of what Paul is looking for, "too good to deceive, too wise to be deceived".

20 The assurance that the God of peace shall bruise Satan is obviously set against the effects of those who promote false teaching. They were messengers of Satan, doing his work of causing disharmony amongst the saints. The apostle recognised that the Judaisers were emissaries of Satan and he wrote to the Corinthians to warn them of the danger (2 Cor 11:13-15). However, in God's good time He will crush Satan, bringing him under the feet of the saints. It is a very fitting metaphor to bring in for the encouragement of those who were under trial and stress. Although the final crushing is prophetic, there is also a sense in which God gives the victory to His saints day by day as they resist the onslaughts of the evil one. It is probably victory in the present that Paul is advocating here. The word rendered "shortly" can mean "soon" or "quickly" and present triumph is not therefore ruled out.

The short prayer or benediction, "The grace of our Lord Jesus Christ be with you", may not indicate the end of the epistle at this point. It is probably a prayer for grace in view of the problems which the apostle has just considered. Perhaps it was a personal addition inserted here by Paul with his own hand. Normally this form of words is introduced at the beginning of Paul's epistles, ensuring those who will read them that the source of all grace is the Lord Jesus Christ and that grace is available to all who will call upon Him in sincerity for it. Here, however, the prayer is that the grace of the Lord Jesus Christ will be with the saints at Rome as an abiding consolation and encouragement.

21 Vine marks vv.21-27 as a postscript, consisting of salutations from the companions of the apostle at Corinth (vv.21-24), and the closing doxology (vv.25-27). In vv.3-15 the greetings were addressed to certain believers in Rome, brothers and sisters, but all very special in Paul's estimation. Now at the end of the epistle greetings are included from fellow-workers and friends who were with him at Corinth from where most probably the epistle was written.

Timothy is referred to a fellow-worker. In Paul's estimation there was none like him, as to the Philippians he wrote, "I have no man likeminded, who will naturally care for your state" (2:20). An expanded version of this verse might read, "I have no man of equal soul (*isopsuchon*) who will genuinely (*gnēsiōs*) care for your state (to the point of distraction)". The apostle's appreciation of his fellow-worker is well summed up in the same context, "But ye know the proof of him, that, as a son with the father, he hath served with me in the gospel" (2:22). Although not mentioned earlier in the epistle, Timothy joins with Paul and the others at the close and makes known his own personal interest in the Romans by sending greetings.

Paul introduces three brethren whom he calls, "my kinsmen" (see v.7). Robertson maintains they were his fellow-countrymen. However the name Lucius is Roman and Jason and Sosipater are Greek, which seems to militate against the view that they were Jews. Against this, however, the apostle's statement is clear, they were his kinsmen, his fellow-countrymen and there the relationship must be left. Three believers having these names are mentioned in the Acts (see 13:1, 17:5; 20:4). They may well be the brethren who were with Paul at Corinth, but since the names were fairly common, it is by no means certain that they were the men mentioned in Luke's account.

22 Here Paul allows his amanuensis to add his personal greeting. By doing so the name Tertius has been written indelibly into the word of God. The fact that there is such a personal note, "I Tertius who wrote this epistle" emphasises the genuineness of the communication. If it had been a forgery the personal touch would not have been added. The salutation "in the Lord" may be understood in several ways. It could mean that "he wrote in the Lord" as that is the order of the words in the original. If this is accepted, his intention was probably to convey to the Romans that his interest was not merely that of a scribe, but one who was conscious of the Lord's deep interest in what His servant Paul dictated. It may of course simply mean that the greeting was "in the Lord". He and those to whom the epistle was sent were in the same happy relationship "in the Lord" and by including the words character is added to the greeting.

The RV gives "I Tertius who write the epistle", substituting "write" for "wrote". Vine gives a lengthy explanation in support of this, in which he draws attention to the different perspective the Jews and the Greeks had compared with that of the English reader. Vine's conclusion is that the RV is correct in using the present tense as it indicates the time when the writer was actually penning his words and not some former occasion. This may seem a small point, but the revisers obviously attached enough importance to it to change what reads well to a word which seems out of place.

23 There are several believers in the NT who bear the name Gaius. There are three mentioned in the following passages: Acts 19:29; 20:4; 3 John 1. Since the name was a fairly common one in apostolic times, there is nothing about these men which would identify them with Paul's host. This Gaius is most likely to be the man Paul baptised at Corinth (1 Cor 1:14). It is almost certain that he is the same person called Titus Justus in Acts 18:7. This would mean that his full name was Gaius Titus Justus. Paul lodged with him in Corinth after he stayed with

Priscilla and Aquila. The fact that Paul can refer to him as "Gaius mine host" appears to confirm that the Corinthian believer is the same person who is now sending greetings to Rome. Probably the church met in his house. The reference suggests that he provided hospitality freely, in which case he must have been a man of substance.

Erastus held the responsible post of treasurer of the city. Clearly this exposed him to the scrutiny of others who did not share his faith. To live the christian life in these circumstances would not therefore be free from problems. It seems clear that this is the same Erastus that Paul sent with Timothy to Macedonia (Acts 19:22), and who stayed at Corinth (2 Tim 4:20). Paul's confidence in sending him with Timothy to Macedonia would indicate that he was a brother of some spiritual stature, who with Timothy could safely be trusted to cope with any aspect of the work which might arise. The fact that he sent greetings to Rome suggests that he was known there. This is not unusual, as travelling Christians in apostolic times were commonplace. They bore tidings as well as spreading the gospel as they travelled in business.

The mention of Quartus is intriguing. The only piece of information given about him is that he was a brother. That of course gives him a certain christian status but it does not link him with anyone in particular. He was obviously known to the Romans which accounts for the mention of his name in the Scriptures.

24 The RV, with most critical editors, rejects this verse as an interpolation. It is substantially the same as v.20 with the exception that the word "all" is included. If the verse is authentic it adds another note of encouragement for the Romans from Paul. His desire, indeed his plea, is that the abundant grace that is with the Lord Jesus Christ might be the portion of all.

25 This is the fourth doxology in the epistle. The others are to be found at 1:25; 9:5; 11:36. It is long and involved compared with the doxologies which are raised by Paul elsewhere. Its inclusion here has caused much concern amongst scholars. This is because some manuscripts place it at the end of ch.14 and others at the end of ch.15. Some manuscripts exclude the doxology altogether. This contributed to the many theories put forward as to whether ch.16 really forms part of the epistle to the Romans or was a separate letter addressed to Ephesus but included here. Apart from the many views expressed, as a fitting end to such an unfolding of the fundamentals of the gospel, it is well to consider it as part of the original letter and share with the apostle the praise that is due to God and to the Lord Jesus Christ for the wonders of the revelation made known to mankind.

The apostle lifts up his heart and acknowledges the measureless ability of God. He is able to establish the saints according to the gospel Paul preached. Paul calls it "my gospel", not to differentiate it from the gospel preached by other apostles and evangelists, but to express his personal confidence in what he preached. The many facets of the faith associated with the gospel have been set out in the epistle and all must be taken into account in understanding what Paul means by "my gospel". It may be that his mention of the preaching of Jesus Christ has reference to the contents of the gospel he preached. The preaching, or proclamation (*kērugma*) of Jesus Christ should be taken with "according to the revelation of the mystery". This means that the wisdom of man could never have devised a gospel that would deal with the issues covered by the gospel of God. It was entirely the product of the divine mind sent out for the obedience of faith.

The gospel was kept secret, or kept in silence by God throughout eternal ages. There was no announcement from God before the world was that the gospel would be proclaimed in time. Paul is not even thinking here of the silence of God in the dispensations of time leading up to the incarnation. He is thinking of the eternal God in eternal ages past who kept His silence, according to His own eternal purposes.

26 The mystery which was kept in the silence of God has now been revealed. It is now manifested (aorist tense). With the coming of Christ, the mystery is no longer kept secret; the gospel has been made known; the truth of it has been disclosed. The writings of the prophets in the OT gave ample hints that it was coming and that the Gentiles, indeed mankind worldwide, would be included in its scope. The declaration of it has the full authority of God; it goes out according to His commandment.

The eternal God had an eternal purpose enshrined in the mystery. The gospel was designed to be announced to all nations with a view to the obedience of faith. Here again, coming at the end of the epistle, the principle on which the gospel operates is stated. It is not of works. It is by faith and faith must be characterised by obedience. There must be submission to the terms and claims of the gospel. Apart from that there is no salvation.

27 Glory is now ascribed to God through Jesus Christ. The heart of the apostle is filled with gratitude and is lifted up with praise as he considers the wonders of all that he has enabled to pass on to the saints. His praise is addressed to "the only wise God". Some consider that this should read "To the only God, who alone is wise". There are other variations, but it is clear that Paul recognises one God and that it follows that this one God is the only wise God. All wisdom is with Him and therefore praise and glory should be addressed to Him as His rightful due for ever. Plummer's closing comment is, "To God only wise, that is, possessing original, infinite, eternal and unchangeable wisdom. This God is ever to be approached, whether in prayer or praise, in thanksgiving or supplication, through Jesus Christ".

Notes

1 Phebe's name means "shining". Vincent, quoting Renan states, "Phebe carried under the folds of her robe the whole future of Christian theology".

2 Vine notes that *prostatēs* ("succourer", "protectress") signified amongst Jews, a wealthy patron of a Jewish community. It appears that Phebe was a person who was active in various ways on behalf of others.

4 "Laid down" (*hupotithēmi*, "to place under", "to lay down the neck beneath the sword of the executioner") here means "risked". Whatever occasion it was, they took an extreme risk on Paul's behalf.

8 Amplias (RV Ampliatus, "large", or "enlarged") was "beloved" as at v.5. Barclay makes an interesting point that in the cemetery of Domatilla, which is the earliest of the christian catacombs there is a decorated tomb with the single name "Ampliatus" carved on it in bold and decorative lettering. Romans would have three names, but the single name indicates a slave and the elaborate tomb would suggest a slave of high rank. There is of course no means of knowing that Paul's Ampliatus is the same as the one in the cemetery of Domatilla.

9 Urbanus means "pleasant", "courteous". Barclay suggests that Apelles may be the Greek name that a Jew called Abel would take.

12 Tryphena means "dainty", "shining" whilst Tryphosa "delicate", "shining". Barclay suggests that the way Paul gives the names of these two sisters is like a complete contradiction in terms. Three times in the greetings he uses a certain Greek word for christian work and toil. It is the verb *kopiōn* ("to toil to the point of exhaustion", "to work to the stage of utter weariness"). He uses it of Mary (v.6), Tryphena and Tryphosa, and Persis. Barclay suggests that the names might mean "dainty" and "delicate" but both could work like trojans. Six of the nine women Paul greets in the passage are described as fellow-workers, or as those who have toiled in the Lord.

Robertson makes the point that Persis ("Persian") was not Paul's "beloved" but the "beloved" of the whole church.

13 Of Rufus ("red") the "chosen" one, Robertson comments, "Not the 'elect' but the 'select'". Morris states that all believers are chosen, but it seems that Paul is singling Rufus out, not placing him in the same category as all others. We should see him as a "choice" or "elite" believer.

14 There was a freedman of Augustus by the name Asyncritus ("incomparable"). Phegon means "burning". Hermes and Hermas took their names from the god Mercury. It was not uncommon for a slave to be so named. Patrobas means "paternal". These five are men but nothing is known about them in christian circles.

15 Julia ("soft-haired") was a common name for females in the imperial palace, probably because of Julius Caesar. Nereus means "a lamp". Vine suggests that Philologus and Julia were probably man and wife and Nereus and Olympas were their children. It appears to be a family and all the saints that were with them met in their house.

17 "Divisions" (*dichostasias*, "cleavages") occurs only here and Gal 5:20. Some consider that the marking and avoiding stops short of excommunication, but their company should be shunned entirely, presumably that they might be constrained to change their ways.

21 Timotheus ("honoured of God"), the well-tried and well-known associate of Paul was at time of writing possibly with Paul at Corinth.

For Lucius ("morning born", "of light") see Acts 13:1. Jason ("healing") could well be the Jason who hosted Paul. See Acts 17:5-9.

22 Tertius means "third".

23 Gaius ("lord"), clearly a man of some means, was the host (*xenos*, "a guest friend", "a host of strangers") of all the church.

25 "Stablish" (*stērizō* "to make stable") is idiomatic.